On the *Revival of the Religious Sciences* (*Iḥyāʾ ʿulūm al-dīn*)

"The *Iḥyāʾ ʿulūm al-dīn* is the most valuable and most beautiful of books."

—Ibn Khallikān (d. 681/1282)

"The *Iḥyāʾ ʿulūm al-dīn* is one of al-Ghazālī's best works."

—Aḥmad b. ʿAbd al-Ḥalīm (d. 728/1328)

"Any seeker of [felicity of] the hereafter cannot do without the *Iḥyāʾ ʿulūm al-dīn*"

—Tāj al-Dīn al-Subkī (d. 771/1370)

"The *Iḥyāʾ ʿulūm al-dīn* is a marvelous book containing a wide variety of Islamic sciences intermixed with many subtle accounts of Sufism and matters of the heart."

—Ibn Kathīr (d.774/1373)

"The *Iḥyāʾ ʿulūm al-dīn* is one of best and greatest book on admonition, it was said concerning it 'if all the books of Islam were lost except for the *Iḥyāʾ* it would suffice what was lost.'"

—Ḥājjī Khalīfa Kātib Čelebī (d. 1067/1657)

"The *Iḥyāʾ* [*ʿulūm al-dīn*] is one of [Imām al-Ghazālī's] most noble works, his most famous work, and by far his greatest work'"

—Muḥammad Murtaḍā l-Zabīdī (d. 1205/1791)

On Imām al-Ghazālī

"Al-Ghazālī is [like] a deep ocean [of knowledge]."

—Imām al-Ḥaramayn al-Juwaynī (d. 478/1085)

"Al-Ghazālī is the second [Imām] Shāfiʿī."

—Muḥammad b. Yaḥyā al-Janzī (d. 549/1154)

"Abū Ḥāmid al-Ghazālī, the Proof of Islam (Ḥujjat al-Islām) and the Muslims, the Imām of the imāms of religion, [is a man] whose like eyes have not seen in eloquence and elucidation, and speech and thought, and acumen and natural ability."

—ʿAbd al-Ghāfir b. Ismāʿīl al-Fārisī (d. 529/1134)

"[He was] the Proof of Islam and Muslims, Imām of the imāms of religious sciences, one of vast knowledge, the wonder of the ages, the author of many works, and [a man] of extreme intelligence and the best of the sincere."

—Imām al-Dhahabī (d. 748/1347)

"Al-Ghazālī is without doubt the most remarkable figure in all Islam."

—T.J. DeBoer

". . . A man who stands on a level with Augustine and Luther in religious insight and intellectual vigor."

—H.A.R. Gibb

"I have to some extent found, and I believe others can find, in the words and example of al-Ghazālī a true *iḥyāʾ* . . ."

—Richard J. McCarthy, S.J.

THE BOOK OF KNOWLEDGE

Kitāb al-ʿilm

Book 1 of

The Revival of the Religious Sciences

Iḥyāʾ ʿulūm al-dīn

The Forty Books of the Revival of the Religious Sciences (*Iḥyāʾ ʿulūm al-dīn*)

The Quarter of Worship

1 **The Book of Knowledge**
2 The Principles of the Creed
3 The Mysteries of Purification
4 The Mysteries of the Prayer
5 The Mysteries of Charity
6 The Mysteries of Fasting
7 The Mysteries of the Pilgrimage
8 The Etiquette of the Recitation of the Qurʾān
9 Invocations and Supplications
10 The Arrangement of the Litanies and the Exposition of the Night Vigil

The Quarter of Customs

11 The Proprieties of Eating
12 The Proprieties of Marriage
13 The Proprieties of Acquisition and Earning a Living
14 The Lawful and the Unlawful
15 The Proprieties of Friendship and Brotherhood
16 The Proprieties of Retreat
17 The Proprieties of Travel
18 The Proprieties of the Audition and Ecstasy
19 The Commanding of Right and the Forbidding of Wrong
20 The Proprieties of Living and the Prophetic Mannerisms

The Quarter of Perils

21 The Exposition of the Wonders of the Heart
22 Training the Soul, Refining the Character, and Treating the Ailments of the Heart
23 Overcoming the Two Desires
24 The Banes of the Tongue
25 The Banes of Anger, Malice, and Envy
26 The Censure of This World
27 The Censure of Greed and the Love of Wealth
28 The Censure of Fame and Hypocritical Ostentation
29 The Censure of Pride and Vanity
30 The Censure of Deceit

The Quarter of Deliverance

31 On Repentance
32 On Patience and Thankfulness
33 On Fear and Hope
34 On Poverty and Abstinence
35 On Unity and Trust
36 On Love, Longing, Intimacy, and Contentment
37 On Intention, Sincerity, and Truthfulness
38 On Vigilance and Accounting
39 On Contemplation
40 On the Remembrance of Death and the Hereafter

AL-GHAZĀLĪ

Kitāb al-ʿilm

THE BOOK OF KNOWLEDGE

Book 1 of the *Iḥyāʾ ʿulūm al-dīn*

THE REVIVAL OF THE RELIGIOUS SCIENCES

Translated *from the* Arabic
with an Introduction *and* Notes
by Kenneth Honerkamp
with a Foreword *by* Hamza Yusuf

Fons Vitae
2015

Revised version of the first published edition in 2015
and reprinted in 2024 by

Fons Vitae
49 Mockingbird Valley Drive
Louisville, KY 40207 USA

www.fonsvitae.com

The Fons Vitae Ghazali Series

Library of Congress Control Number: 2015957356

ISBN 978-1-94-1610-15-2

Cover art courtesy of National Library of Egypt, Cairo.
Qurʾānic frontispiece to part 19. Written and illuminated by ʿAbdallāh b. Muḥammad al-Ḥamadānī for Sultan Uljaytu 713/1313. Hamadan.

Printed in Canada

Contents

Imām Al-Ghazālī: The Proof of Islam

Hamza Yusuf Hanson

ALMOST A THOUSAND YEARS ago, in the city of Ṭūs in northern Iran, the pious wife of a simple wool carder gave birth to a boy they would name Muḥammad. At an early age, he was left an orphan. But before his father died, he placed Muḥammad, along with his brother Aḥmad, in the care of a devout and learned Muslim elder to ensure that his sons would receive an education in the religious sciences. The boys' father, a simple man with a great love for scholars, left a paltry sum of money with the guardian as recompense for the care of his sons. When the money ran out, the guardian wisely chose not to send the boys to an orphanage: instead, he placed them in a local school with an endowment that enabled poor students to be lodged, clothed, and fed while they studied. Such was the beginning of a life of learning for the two boys, who would both grow up to be world-renowned scholars and saints.

It was Muḥammad, though, who became the greatest and most celebrated scholar of his time. He radically elevated classical Islamic discourse in jurisprudence, theology, and spirituality, and firmly embedded Aristotelian logic and philosophical ethics into the Islamic tradition. Not only did he revive the religion of Islam, whose adherents had fallen into a state of confusion and crisis, earning him the honorific "Proof of Islam," but he also came to be recognized as one of the most influential intellectuals in human history. Imām al-Ghazālī's work shaped the discourse of Islamic scholars for centuries and, through Latin translations, even influenced the Christian scholastics of medieval Europe, such as St. Thomas Aquinas and arguably even some modern philosophers, such as Descartes and Hume.

The life of Abū Ḥāmid Muḥammad b. Muḥammad al-Ghazālī, who was born in 450/1058, is well known due to his autobiography and the writings of his peers who bore witness to the vast influence he wielded during his own life. Less well known and understood is that his contributions to the Islamic tradition are found more in the principles of jurisprudence and theology than they are in Sufism.

❁ ❁ ❁

After studying with Aḥmad al-Radhkānī in Ṭūs, Imām al-Ghazālī went to Jurjān, an Iranian city near the Caspian Sea, and studied with scholars there for three years. At the age of nineteen, he returned to Ṭūs and put to memory all he had learned in Jurjān. At twenty-two, he traveled to Nīshāpūr, then an administrative and intellectual center of the Saljūq dynasty of Central Asia, where he entered the Niẓāmiyya College and began studying with Imām al-Ḥaramayn Abū l-Maʿālī l-Juwaynī, arguably the greatest theoretical jurist and theologian of his age. Imām al-Juwaynī quickly recognized his student's gifts and took him under his wing. A philosopher of law, besides being a jurist and theologian in the Ashʿarī rational tradition, Imām al-Juwaynī perhaps had the greatest influence on young al-Ghazālī's thinking. In this meeting of scholarly minds, both the student and the teacher had the good fortune to benefit from the other's brilliance.

After Imām al-Juwaynī's death in 478/1085, Imām al-Ghazālī ventured on his own as a scholar and soon ascended to prominence in the Muslim world of his time. The public phase of his life began when he set out for the court of Niẓām al-Mūlk (d. 485/1092), the powerful and scholarly Saljūq minister of state who had founded the Niẓāmiyya colleges to be a beacon of orthodoxy amidst a sea of heresies and heterodoxies. Imām al-Ghazālī, who was tested by the court scholars and overwhelmed them with his knowledge and dialectical brilliance, greatly impressed Niẓām al-Mūlk, who recognized in him just the scholar he was looking for to unify his realm by fortifying orthodox faith and practice.

Not long after meeting the minister, Imām al-Ghazālī garnered the highly coveted position of professor of jurisprudence and theology at the renowned Niẓāmiyya of Baghdad, the flagship of a consortium of nine distinct but unified colleges that made up the most prestigious institution in the eastern Muslim world of that time. For Imām al-Ghazālī, who was barely thirty-three at the time, the position provided a platform for his prolific work as a writer, and he produced several tomes on legal theory, theology, ethics, logic, and law. His reputation spread far and wide, and he gained notoriety for his remarkable skills at debate, routing opponents with his penetrating intellect, vast erudition, and dazzling diction, all supported by a powerfully prodigious memory.

On the cusp of his fourth decade, however, his public approbation and adoration precipitated a profound spiritual midlife crisis for him. As he recounts in his brutally honest autobiography, *Deliverance from Error*, he knew then that he had to turn his gaze inward:

> I reflected on my intention in my public teaching, and I saw that it was not directed purely for God's sake but was instigated and motivated by my personal quest for fame and prestige. So I became certain that I was on the brink of a crumbling bank and already on the verge of falling into the Fire, unless I set about mending my ways.[1]

This introspection led him to the realization that he could no longer remain content merely with expositing rational and revealed truths that he had not personally experienced in his own heart. So he set out on a personal quest for realized truth.

❁ ❁ ❁

In 488/1095, Imām al-Ghazālī began the life of an itinerant seeker. Ostensibly setting out for hajj and preparing for death, as Muslims leaving for pilgrimage are wont to do, he settled all of his affairs, made sure his family was provided for, and took leave of his professorial duties at the Niẓāmiyya. He traveled to Damascus, became a sweeper at the Umayyad Mosque, and took up residence in a small muezzin's room that is still honored to this day as his retreat. He lived the life of an ascetic, later traveling to Jerusalem where he

---

1 Richard J. McCarthy, *Al-Ghazali: Deliverance from Error*, (Louisville, KY: Fons Vitae, n.d.), 78–79, with minor changes.

wrote his famous summation of creed. Probably in Damascus, he began writing his spiritual magnum opus, the *Iḥyāʾ ʿulūm al-dīn* (*Revival of the Religious Sciences*).

Imām al-Ghazālī understood well that Islam was facing a grave crisis. The Fāṭimid Caliphate in North Africa was politically active and had gained sovereignty in certain Muslim lands causing discord among Muslims. Meanwhile, scholars were largely engaged in pedantic finger-wagging and pursued specializations, and the academic elite did not engage with or educate the masses of Muslims: common people were susceptible to the worst forms of religious superstitions, and many occult sects were influencing thought. Furthermore, the Sufis had split into factions, and some had drifted far from normative Islam.

In the midst of such chaos and confusion, Imām al-Ghazālī knew that he had to chart a different course unfettered by conventional wisdom. He had absorbed the teaching of Imām al-Juwaynī and was markedly influenced by his intellectual freedom. Imām al-Ghazālī states that he heard Abū l-Maʿālī l-Juwaynī once say:

> I had read thousands of books; then I left the people of Islam with their religion and their manifest sciences in these books and embarked on the open sea, plunging into the literature that the people of Islam rejected. All this was in quest of truth. At an early age, I fled from the conformity of the opinions of others (*taqlīd*). But now I have returned from everything to the word of truth: hold to the religion of the old women. If the Truth does not grasp me by the grace of His justice so that I die in the religion of the old women and the result of my life is sealed at my departure with the purity of the people of Truth and the word of sincerity, "There is no deity but God," then alas for the Imām, al-Juwaynī.[2]

Imām al-Ghazālī adopted this disdain for blind conformity to the unrealized truth of others and spent much of his life refuting it in various works. In his autobiography he writes,

2 W. M. Watt, *A Muslim Intellectual: A Study of al-Ghazali* (Edinburgh: Edinburgh University Press, 1963), 23–24, with minor changes.

> The thirst for grasping the real meanings of things was indeed my wont and practice from my early years and in the prime of my life. It was an instinctive, natural disposition placed in my makeup by God, Most High, not something due to my own choosing and contriving. As a result, the fetters of servile conformism (*taqlīd*) fell away from me, and inherited beliefs lost their hold on me when I was still quite young, for I saw that the children of Christians always grew up embracing Christianity, and the children of Jews always grew up adhering to Judaism, and the children of Muslims always grew up following the religion of Islam. I also heard the tradition related from the Apostle of God—God's blessing and peace upon him—in which he said, "Every infant is born endowed with the *fiṭra*: then his parents make him a Jew or Christian or Magian." Consequently, I felt an inner urge to seek the true meaning of the original *fiṭra* and the true meaning of the beliefs arising through slavish aping of parents and teachers.[3]

The thirst for knowledge and his own philosophical bent led him to focus on logic and ethics, as well as on a deeper reflection and understanding that were all prerequisites to the study of the principles of jurisprudence (*uṣūl al-fiqh*).

In mastering the subject of ethics, he absorbed the work of the great moral ethicist and Qurʾānic exegete, al-Rāghib al-Iṣfahānī (d. fifth/eleventh century), and even memorized his book, *al-Dharīʿa*. But, like Ibn Sīnā (d. 428/1037) before him, Imām al-Ghazālī did not simply regurgitate the work of his teachers: he penned his own criticisms, additions, and modifications; he connected the works he read with other works, even across traditions and geographical boundaries. One of his earliest works was in virtue ethics, in which he took the Aristotelian tradition and revealed its congruence with Qurʾānic principles, making the Greek philosopher's work accept-

3 Richard J. McCarthy, *Al-Ghazali: Deliverance from Error* (Louisville, KY: Fons Vitae, n.d.), 54–55, with minor changes.

able to those who would otherwise dismiss its insights and benefits as merely "Hellenistic."

Aristotle argued that the soul is composed of three faculties—the rational, irascible, and concupiscent—and that each has a corresponding virtue: wisdom, courage, and temperance. The Greek philosopher concluded that when the rational faculty governed by wisdom regulates the irascible and concupiscent faculties of the soul and maintains them in virtuous moderation, the result is a fourth cardinal virtue, justice. Imām al-Ghazālī agreed with Aristotle's basic breakdown of the soul but developed Aristotle's understanding about justice arguing that, like Aristotle's approach, it is a cardinal virtue, but not due to the balance of the three faculties of the soul. Rather, it is a virtue as the result of a fourth faculty of the soul that Imām al-Ghazālī calls *ᶜadl*, which is the same word used for the virtue "justice" in Arabic, but here it means something more akin to "just balance." This fourth faculty acts as a governor or regulator over the other three faculties and has the corresponding virtue of justice. Imām al-Ghazālī understood that reason has to be governed by a balance that enables it to make wise decisions. We are creatures whose very physical uprightness reflects balance: balance is our very nature, and this internal sense of balance is what governs the faculty of reason to regulate through the virtue of wisdom the other two faculties of emotion and appetite. Imām al-Ghazālī saw balance as the most necessary of the faculties because it regulates and enables the others to fulfill their functions in maintaining a life of moderation in the three spheres of man. Hence, he called his ethical treatise, *Mīzān al-ᶜamal* (The balance of action). While this may appear to be a semantic and moot difference, the subtlety, when contemplated, is quite significant and reveals the Imām' s study of previous masters with an independent and ready mind able to challenge or modify the accepted opinions of the past.

Another key tool that Imām al-Ghazālī mastered and brought into the Islamic tradition is logic. His study of logic enabled him to realize its importance as a prerequisite for any intellectual endeavor because it was a preventive for errors in thought. It was also indispensable in performing the task of jurisprudence. He wrote at least six books on the subject, including a short textbook for jurists giving them the basics that he considered absolutely essential for anyone working in jurisprudence. In *al-Qisṭās al-Mustaqīm* (The upright scales), he argued that the Qurʾān uses logical proofs known as enthymemes to assert certain truths as axiomatic, thus revealing how the prophets themselves were highly skilled at syllogistic reasoning.

It was entirely due to Imām al-Ghazālī's groundbreaking work that logic became a *sine qua non* of Islamic education and a mainstay of the scholastic tradition. What many Muslims are unaware of today is that while Imām al-Ghazālī is most well known for his great work, the *Iḥyāʾ*, his greatest impact in the Islamic scholastic tradition is not in Sufism (*taṣawwuf*) but in his contribution to principles of jurisprudence (*uṣūl al-fiqh*).

A thousand years after he wrote them, Imām al-Ghazālī's four works on legal philosophy, culminating in his magnum opus, *al-Mustaṣfā*, are still considered esteemed sources, and the latter is arguably the most authoritative work on the subject ever penned. Complementing and completing the work of his teacher, Imām al-Juwaynī, Imām al-Ghazālī developed the *maqāṣidī* school of legal philosophy that later became the great schools of al-Qarāfī (d. 684/1285) and al-Shāṭibī (d. 790/1388). The *maqāṣidī* school takes the aims and objectives behind all rulings as a starting point and not the rulings themselves; as such, it is the "spirit-of-the-law" school. Imām al-Ghazālī brought to bear a radical notion in jurisprudence, which is a way to understand the intent and wisdom behind a ruling in order to determine, in any given circumstance, whether the ruling should be applied or not. He introduced the legal term *taḥqīq al-manāt*, which is strikingly similar to the Western moral concept of *epikeia*, which is that laws are created for purposes: hence, when a judge has a good legal reason not to apply the law, he implements the virtue of *epikeia*. (The principle of *taḥqīq al-manāt,* which can be translated as "ascertaining the effective cause," has a richer meaning than *epikeia*). Like *epikeia*, *taḥqīq al-manāt* both enables the jurist to decide when circumstances demand that the spirit of the law overrides the letter of law and also allows for personal discernment in areas of legal ambiguity. This approach to Islamic law echoes the Biblical principle, "the letter kills, and the spirit gives life." In other words, Imām al-Ghazālī understood that if the aims and objectives of the letter are not understood, they can be applied in unjust and ultimately soul-killing ways.

This fundamental change in approach did not—nor does it still—sit well with the literalists. It is the bane of every literal-minded zealot and explains the animus that literalist schools have always had for Imām al-Ghazālī. His transgression, in their eyes, is twofold: first, Imām al-Ghazālī introduced term logic, with its metaphysical implications astutely discerned and dismissed by Ibn Taymiyya (d. 729/1328), into Islamic jurisprudence and theology, thereby enabling a more creative and sophisticated tradition to develop at the hands of many scholars, including Fakhr al-Dīn al-Rāzī (d. 606/1210) and Saʿd al-Dīn al-Taftāzānī (d. 792/1390); and second, Imām al-Ghazālī revealed the subtleties of Islamic jurisprudence and rule-making with the requisite need for deep reflection and understanding in order to interpret and apply legal rulings intelligently.

In reality, Imām al-Ghazālī's earliest critics were not so troubled by *taṣawwuf* since most of them, including Ibn Taymiyya, were practitioners of some form of Sufism themselves. What galled Ibn Taymiyya most is the underlying metaphysics in which Imām al-Ghazālī anchors his theology and his profound reworking of Islam's legal philosophy toward a more rational and spirit-of-the-law approach. For Ibn Taymiyya, these were the true "dangers" of his thought, and he was undoubtedly Imām al-Ghazālī's leading critic. His devotees today display an odd and callous contempt for Imām al-Ghazālī, a man who has been known for a thousand years by the entire Sunni community as the "Proof of Islam."

What most drives the literalists' animus toward Imām al-Ghazālī is his Sufism. Attacks against his spirituality are parroted in countless modern works, yet, his own scholastic contemporaries largely considered his Sufism to be both derivative and normative. The *Iḥyāʾ* is mainly a reiteration and summation of the works of scholars who preceded him, such as al-Junayd (d. 298/910), al-Qushayrī (d. 465/1072), Abu Nuʿaym al-Iṣfahānī (d. 430/1038), al-Kalābādhī (d. 380/990 or 384/994), al-Hujwīrī (d. between 465/1072 and 469/1077), Abu Ṭālib al-Makkī (d. 386/998), and others. Nevertheless, Imām al-Ghazālī did make two profound contributions to the science of *taṣawwuf*. First, he elaborated on and significantly developed the work initiated by al-Ḥakīm al-Tirmidhī (d. between 318/936 and 320/938), who had explored the "secrets" behind the devotional practices of Islam. Imām al-Ghazālī did this by bringing the same *maqāṣidī* or "spirit-of-the-law" approach that he had brought to jurisprudence, whereby he explicated the entire religion using the lens of Sufism to reveal the inner meanings of the law. Unlike Sufi scholars who came before him and had argued that *taṣawwuf* was a third of Islam, as it was the science of *iḥsān*, Imām al-Ghazālī's unique contribution was to show that *taṣawwuf* is, in reality, the animating spirit of the entire corpus of Islam. He believed that without this animating force, religion was a dead thing. He critically referred to those scholars who failed to incorporate the practice of *taṣawwuf* in their Islam as "formalists" (*mutarasimūn*), people shackled by the trappings of Islam, which thus prevented them from undertaking the necessary journey to the core of faith and from realizing for themselves its truths.

Imām al-Ghazālī's second contribution was his reconstruction of the works of the past masters of *taṣawwuf* into a magisterial summation enveloped in a brilliant and unprecedented organizational structure, a type of intellectual architecture conducive to serious study of a transformative nature. This can be seen in the forty books of the *Iḥyā*ʾ which move the reader through a journey so well mapped out that, by the end of it, a thoughtful wayfarer has not only arrived at his desired destination but arrived completely transformed intellectually, spiritually, and psychologically.

Another type of criticism lodged against the Sufic works of Imām al-Ghazālī involves differences of opinion about practice and source validity: Ibn al-Jawzī (d. 597/1201) is, perhaps, the most prominent critic of this type. This criticism, which was somewhat misplaced, honed in on aspects of Imām al-Ghazālī's approach to asceticism and his reliance on weak and sometimes unsubstantiated *ḥadīth*s. Regarding the use of weak *ḥadīth*s, Imām al-Ghazālī himself acknowledged that he was not a scholar of *ḥadīth*, notwithstanding the fact that most scholars have permitted reliance on weak *ḥadīth*s for non-contentious matters, for example those relating to virtuous deeds. The fact that countless abridgments of his work as well as the many commentaries over the centuries have been penned is an affirmation of the high prestige in which Muslim scholars have held his work. And while the *Iḥyāʾ* was publicly burnt in Andalusia and Morocco upon its release due to some phrases considered highly controversial by the more literalist Mālikīs of Andalusia and North Africa, it fell to the redoubtable Mālikī jurist, Abū Bakr b. al-ʿArabī (d. 543/1148), to restore the stature of Imām al-Ghazālī among the Mālikī scholars. Ibn al-ʿArabī, considered among the greatest public intellectuals of Spain, was one of the last students that Imām al-Ghazālī agreed to teach. Ibn al-ʿArabī relates his experience with Imām al-Ghazālī more than once in his works. In one place, Ibn al-ʿArabī writes of meeting Imām al-Ghazālī at a retreat near the Niẓāmiyya College:

> He was completely inner-focused on the divine and had left the world behind him. When I entered into his presence, I said, "You are the lost thing I have been looking for all of my life. You are the Imām who will guide me." Our meeting was an epiphany of inward knowledge. I witnessed something from him that is ineffable. He was a man whom if you saw him, you saw a manifest spiritual state. If you knew him, you knew a vast ocean. Each time I questioned him, I was filled with inner joy at the response. I maintained visits at the retreat and placed myself upon his carpet. I benefitted from his seclusion and his spiritual activities. It was as if he relinquished any other occupations to be with me in order for me to realize my goal . . . .
>
> When that light arose upon me, dispelling what had previously enveloped me of darkness and gloom, I said, "This is what I have been seeking in truth! This, by the sacred trust of God, is the goal of every seeker, the destination of every wayfarer."[4]
>
> I read with him several of his books and heard from him the entire *Iḥyāʾ ʿUlūm al-Dīn*. I asked a question of one seeking to understand his creed and unveil his path so that I could

4 Saʿīd Aʿrāb, *Maʿ al-Qaḍī Abī Bakr bin al-ʿArabī* (Beirut: Dār al-Gharab al-Islāmī, 1987), 219–221.

> unravel the secrets of his symbolic language that he alludes to in his works that indicate complete understanding. So he began to answer as a wayfarer on a sound path would to a fellow seeker. He answered me orally as well as in his own hand.
>
> I discussed matters with Abū Ḥāmid when I first met him in Jerusalem in Jumāda al-Awwal, 490/1096. He had disciplined his soul with Sufic exercises for around five years prior to our meeting. He was completely engaged in that and had taken solitary retreat as his companion and rejected every group.[5]

Ibn al-ʿArabī is among the most influential and agreed upon scholars of Islam; hence the weight of his assessment of Imām al-Ghazālī is immense. Within a few decades of the *Iḥyāʾ* being burnt in Cordoba and in Fes, it became a major textbook of the Mālikīs and is taught to this day in the Qarawiyyin University in Morocco.

❁ ❁ ❁

The Qurʾān commands us to *Read, in the name of your Lord, who created: created man of clotted blood. Read, for your Lord is most generous, the One who taught the use of the pen, taught man what he did not know* [96:1–5]. The Prophet صَلَّىٱللَّهُعَلَيْهِوَسَلَّمَ said, "I was sent only as a teacher of knowledge."

Imām al-Ghazālī understood that knowledge is the starting point of any revival of the Islamic spirit, so he began his spiritual magnum opus, the *Iḥyāʾ*, with *The Book of Knowledge*. However, he redefined knowledge as something deeper than simply rote memorization. For him, knowledge had degrees and dimensions, as well as an existential import that demands realization in the heart of the agent of knowledge. Sound knowledge must penetrate a subject beyond the shell of understanding to the pith of experience. All of learning should be directed toward true knowledge—knowledge of God. In other words, for Imām al-Ghazālī, the quest for truth was ultimately a search for God. In redefining knowledge at the outset, the seeker is able to proceed on the path to self-realization set out

5 Saʿīd Aʿrāb, *Maʿ al-Qaḍī Abī Bakr bin al-ʿArabī*, 41–43.

by the *Iḥyāʾ*. Imām al-Ghazālī wanted nothing less than to revive the sciences of religion by restoring the centrality of knowledge.

His premise is that there are essentially two kinds of knowledge: practical knowledge (*muʿāmala*) and spiritual knowledge (*mukāshafa*); in the West, this is akin to the division between practical knowledge and speculative knowledge. He makes it clear that his book, the *Iḥyāʾ*, is solely about practical knowledge—knowledge that when acted upon will invariably lead to spiritual knowledge. Epistemologically, as is discernable from his other works, Imām al-Ghazālī was a realist and an essentialist, committed to the idea that the world is knowable and that communication among knowing agents is achievable. He was also committed to the truths of rational discourse—that deductive logic is possible and useful, that we can move from what is known universally to knowing what is unknown in its particularities. Conversely, he understood that the essence—or the universal—can be abstracted from the particular, so we can realize universal truths with certainty. At the same time, he acknowledged the limits of the intellect and its pitfalls.

Imām al-Ghazālī saw both revelation and reason as necessary to arrive at truth. He likens reason to sight and revelation to sunlight.

One of the most important sections in *The Book of Knowledge* identifies a fundamental problem of so-called scholars who mislead others with their pseudo-knowledge. Imām al-Ghazālī describes those afflicted with this pseudo-knowledge as "malicious scholars." About them he wrote,

> Among the grievous faults of the foul scholars is their overzealousness for the "truth." They hold their opponents in contempt and belittlement. This leads to false claims of equivalency and reciprocity. This excites in them incentives that compel them to advocate falsehood and further reinforces in them the desire to cling to the positions attributed to them. Had they brought forth more empathy, mercy, and sincerity in their private dealings rather than their zealous and belittling attacks, they would have succeeded. But upon realizing that stature is gained through devotees, and nothing increases one's followers like fanaticism, zeal, cursing, and *ad hominem* attacks, they took such means as their wont and

> tools and called it, "defending the religion and protecting Muslims." In reality, it is nothing more than causing others to perish and establishing heresies in their hearts . . . . Maybe the one hearing this will say, "People oppose what they don't know." Please, don't think that. You are dealing with an expert. So accept this advice from one who wasted a good deal of his life in the very thing he is describing. In fact, he was the best of the bunch, one-upping those who went before him in achieving such tools of disputation and exposition. Finally, God inspired him with discrimination and revealed his faults to him, enabling him to abandon such things and preoccupy himself with his own salvation.

This passage reflects the essential attributes of Imām al-Ghazālī's greatness: his profound authenticity, humility, and introspection, and his sincere desire for purity of heart, not just for himself, but for others as well. He undertook an arduous journey of self-knowledge, gleaned much from it, and wanted to share the fruit of his spiritual labors with others so that they too might set out on the well-trodden path of the prophets and their inheritors. He understood the spiritual journey and its concomitant experiences to be replicable, in today's language falsifiable, in each individual and hence the soundest and only truly scientific path that led to certainty. *The Book of Knowledge* is an abiding and timeless tome, as relevant today as it was a millennium ago. It echoes through the ages eternal truths and speaks to all of humanity.

❁ ❁ ❁

Imām al-Ghazālī recognized the two forces that were tearing apart the Muslim world in his day and that are, once again, rending it asunder in ours: revelation without reason, and reason without revelation. He established the balance in his own self and in the vast tradition he not only inherited but rekindled and further developed. Surprisingly, he never deviated from the orthodoxy he was steeped in, resisting the timeworn temptation of the genius to "choose for himself" (*heresia*). Among his many gifts was this ability to strike a balance between seemingly conflicting forces. He found the balance between retaining individuality and independent thought on the one hand and, on the other, the importance of maintaining the community in conformity with an orthodoxy that is, nonetheless, rooted in an individually realized knowledge. Like the prophets he so assiduously emulated, he went up against the mob and prevailed: his battle was for the essence of Islam, which he knew was balance, but balance with mercy at its core.

Imām al-Ghazālī saw salvation as largely universal and recognized that the mercy of God enveloped peoples of all faiths. He never waivered in his absolute adherence to the Qurʾān and the way of the Prophet, God's peace and blessings upon him, but understood both with a profundity that softened and transformed many of the ossified views of his time. He was not one who retreated or shied away from expressing his criticism of arrogant scholars in whom he saw his younger self, nor did he hesitate to speak bluntly about the Sufis of his time. Of them he wrote,

> The fourth and final group among humanity filled with delusion are the Sufis, and how great has delusion overwhelmed those of this age with the exception of the one protected by God. They are deluded in their dress, their talk, and their appearance. They mimic the sincere among the true Sufis in all these things.[6]

Imām al-Ghazālī was able to arrive at the quintessence of transmitted knowledge and realize for himself, through practice, the truths of experiential knowledge and then find a way of articulating the orthodoxy of both. In that sense, Imām al-Ghazālī is orthodoxy personified. He is the embodiment of normative Islam in all its sacred glory. In the millennium since his time, the world has witnessed the collapse of Muslim sovereignty and the colonization of Muslim lands, and there has been a tendency of late to assign blame for that decline. Some, especially Muslims committed to political Islam or others whose allegiance is to literalist Islam, have honed in on Imām al-Ghazālī and found in him their scapegoat.

6 al-Ghazālī, *Majmūʿa Rasāʾil al-imām al-Ghazālī*, prepared by Ibrahim Amin Muhammad, (Cairo: al-maktab al-Tawfikia, n.d.), 462.

The gripe of the political Islamists, who hold the natural sciences in highest esteem, is that Islam's decline is due to its neglect of these sciences, aided and abetted by Imām al-Ghazālī—the man who, in actuality, took the best of philosophy and integrated it almost imperceptibly into normative Sunni tradition. They believe that it was he who dealt a death knell to philosophy and, by extension, to natural science, then a branch of philosophy. They claim that his "singular focus" on the inner life of the Muslim etherealized the faith, causing Muslims to neglect worldly knowledge and lose their edge in science and technology. They would do well to examine his life and his work: they would find a man who called on Muslims to advance these areas, as he considered the material sciences to be a collective duty binding upon whatever sufficient number of Muslims was needed to acquire and promote them in accordance with society's needs.

As for the formalists and literalists, their bone of contention has been that Imām al-Ghazālī brought metaphysics and an inward focus to the outer forms of law and devotion. This common canard that is parroted by many popular Muslim writers, unbeknownst to them, was found first in the works of their orientalist forebears, who besmirched the Imām with these libelous claims. Despite recent research that has revealed the false premises of these attacks, many Muslims continue to spread such calumnies against the "Proof of Islam." The truth is that Imām al-Ghazālī was a practicing philosopher who single-handedly revived the religion, reaffirmed the centrality of knowledge in Islam, and reformed both the Sufis and the scholars by demonstrating the necessity of inward and outward harmony for the true purpose of Islam to be realized. He showed that while one could be a Sufi with sufficient but not great knowledge, one could not have truly great knowledge without being a Sufi.

It is Imām al-Ghazālī who synthesized the heart and the head of Islam, accommodating intellect and devotion within the same person without dissonance. He well understood that when a religion loses its metaphysical foundations, it loses its defenders, and in losing its defenders, it loses its intelligent devotees who no longer find answers for their doubts and troubling questions concerning faith and the world. So the religion, now defenseless against intellectual onslaught, has only simpletons and zealots who fill the void and whose only argument is blood. But blood is no argument, and while Islam now seems enveloped in a cloud of darkness, its light, though present behind the clouds, is only temporarily hidden. The clouds will invariably pass, and the truth will out. If the Imām is not seen, it is not due to his absence: he, like the religion itself, is tragically obscured in a veil of violence formed from the darkness of the days.

Imām Abū Ḥāmid al-Ghazālī is the mountain that is no longer seen through the smog of mental and emotional pollution arising from those "malicious scholars" he so accurately called out centuries ago, whose daily assaults on the towering intellectuals of the past unrelentingly issue forth from their impoverished platforms and pulpits in what passes for Islamic guidance in these troubled times. Even the buried bones of the great scholars of the past are no longer safe from these fanatics who blow up longstanding tombs with an impunity matched only by their stupidity and insolence. Such monsters stand in testimony to the prophesy that, "The end of time will not come until the latter part of my community curses the former part." But as long as the faithful have ears that hear and eyes that see, Imām al-Ghazālī will be heard and seen for what he truly is—the voice of revelation's reason.

Editor's Note

This translation of *Kitāb al-ʿilm*, book 1 of the *Iḥyāʾ ʿulūm al-dīn* of Ḥujjat al-Islam, Abū Ḥāmid al-Ghazālī, was made from the text of the published Arabic text of volume 1 (pp. 7–327) of the 900th anniversary edition of the *Iḥyāʾ ʿulūm al-dīn* by Dār al-Minhāj of Jedda (2011); the editors utilized additional manuscripts and early printed editons.

The blessings on prophets and others, as used by Imām al-Ghazālī, are represented by Arabic glyphs, as listed below.

Arabic	English	Usage
عَزَّ وَجَلَّ	Mighty and majestic is He	On mention of God
سُبْحَانَهُ وَتَعَالَىٰ	Exalted and Most High	On mention of God
عَلَيْهِمُ السَّلَامُ | عَلَيْهِ السَّلَامُ	Peace be upon him / them	On mention of one or more prophets
صَلَّى اللَّهُ عَلَيْهِ وَسَلَّمَ	May the blessings and peace of God be upon him	On mention of the Prophet
رَضِيَ اللَّهُ عَنْهُمْ | رَضِيَ اللَّهُ عَنْهُ	May God be pleased with him / them	On mention of one or more Companions of the Prophet
رَضِيَ اللَّهُ عَنْهَا	May God be pleased with her	On mention of a female companion of the Prophet

In addition, Arabic terms appear in italics, in accordance with the transliteration system of the *International Journal of Middle East Studies*. Common Era (CE) dates have been added.

This translation was reviewed against the Arabic on two separate occasions in 2013 and 2014 by James Pavlin, who also provided translations of the Arabic footnotes. Text in hard brackets has been added by the editors for clarification. References to Arabic works in the footnotes have been maintained where available, should the reader wish to consult the sources.

Biography of Imām al-Ghazālī

He is Abū Ḥāmid Muḥammad b. Muḥammad b. Muḥammad b. Aḥmad al-Ghazālī al-Ṭūsī; he was born in 450/1058 in the village of Ṭābarān near Ṭūs (in northeast Iran) and he died there, at the age of fifty-five, in 505/1111. Muḥammad's father died when he and his younger brother Aḥmad were still young; their father left a little money for their education in the care of a Sufi friend of limited means. When the money ran out, their caretaker suggested that they enroll in a *madrasa*. The *madrasa* system meant they had a stipend, room, and board. Al-Ghazālī studied *fiqh* in his hometown under a Sufi named Aḥmad al-Rādhakānī; he then traveled to Jurjān and studied under Ismāʿīl b. Masʿada al-Ismāʿīlī (d. 477/1084).

On his journey home his caravan was overtaken by highway robbers who took all of their possessions. Al-Ghazālī went to the leader of the bandits and demanded his notebooks. The leader asked, what are these notebooks? Al-Ghazālī answered: "This is the knowledge that I traveled far to acquire," the leader acquiesced to al-Ghazālī's demands after stating: "If you claim that it is knowledge that you have, how can we take it away from you?" This incident left a lasting impression on the young scholar. Thereafter, he returned to Ṭūs for three years, where he committed to memory all that he had learned thus far.

In 469/1077 he traveled to Nīshāpūr to study with the leading scholar of his time, Imām al-Ḥaramayn al-Juwaynī (d. 478/1085), at the Niẓāmiyya College; al-Ghazālī remained his student for approximately eight years, until al-Juwaynī died. Al-Ghazālī was one of his most illustrious students, and al-Juwaynī referred to him as "a deep ocean [of knowledge]." As one of al-Juwaynī star pupils, al-Ghazālī used to fill in as a substitute lecturer in his teacher's absence. He also tutored his fellow students in the subjects that al-Juwaynī taught at the Niẓāmiyya. Al-Ghazālī wrote his first book, on the founding principles of legal theory (*uṣūl al-fiqh*), while studying with al-Juwaynī.

Very little is known about al-Ghazālī's family, though some biographers mention that he married while in Nīshāpūr; others note that he had married in Ṭūs prior to leaving for Nīshāpūr. Some accounts state that he had five children, a son who died early and four daughters. Accounts also indicate that his mother lived to see her son rise to fame and fortune.

After the death of al-Juwaynī, al-Ghazālī went to the camp (*al-muʿaskar*) of the Saljūq *wazīr* Niẓām al-Mulk (d. 485/1192). He stayed at the camp, which was a gathering place for scholars, and quickly distinguished himself among their illustrious company. Niẓām al-Mulk recognized al-Ghazālī's genius and appointed him professor at the famed Niẓāmiyya College of Baghdad.

Al-Ghazālī left for Baghdad in 484/1091 and stayed there four years—it was a very exciting time to be in the heart of the Islamic empire. At the Niẓāmiyya College he had many students, by some estimates as many as three hundred. In terms of his scholarly output, this was also a prolific period in which he wrote *Maqāṣid al-falāsifa, Tahāfut al-falāsifa, al-Mustaẓhirī,* and other works.

Al-Ghazālī was well-connected politically and socially; we have evidence that he settled disputes related to the legitimacy of the rule of the ʿAbbāsid caliph, al-Mustaẓhir (r. 487–512/1094–1118) who assumed his role as the caliph when he was just fifteen years old, after the death of his father al-Muqtadī (d. 487/1094). Al-Ghazālī issued a *fatwā* of approval of the appointment of al-Mustaẓhir and was present at the oath-taking ceremony.

In Baghdad, al-Ghazālī underwent a spiritual crisis, during which he was overcome by fear of the punishment of the hellfire. He became convinced that he was destined for the hellfire if he did not change his ways; he feared that he had become too engrossed in worldly affairs, to the detriment of his spiritual being. He began to question his true intentions: was he writing and teaching to serve God, or because he enjoyed the fame and fortune that resulted from his lectures. He experienced much suffering, both inward and outward; one day as he stood before his students to present a lecture, he found himself unable to speak. The physicians were unable to diagnose any physical malady. Al-Ghazālī remained in Baghdad for a time, then left his teaching post for the pilgrimage. He left behind fortune, fame, and influence. He was beloved by his numerous students and had many admirers, including the sultan; he was also envied by many. The presumption is that he left in the manner he did—ostensibly to undertake the pilgrimage—because if he had made public his intentions to leave permanently, those around him would have tried to convince him to remain and the temptation might have been too strong to resist.

After leaving Baghdad, he changed direction and headed toward Damascus; according to his autobiography he disappeared from the intellectual scene for ten years. This does not mean that he did not teach, but that he did not want to return to public life and be paid for teaching. This ten-year period can be divided into two phases. First, he spent two years in the East—in greater Syria and on the pilgrimage. We have evidence that while on his return to Ṭūs he appeared at a Sufi lodge opposite the Niẓāmiyya College in Baghdad. He spent the second phase of the ten-year period (the remaining eight years) in Ṭūs, where he wrote the famed *Iḥyāʾ ʿulūm al-dīn*, a work that was inspired by the change in his outlook that resulted from his spiritual crisis.

When he arrived back in his hometown in 490/1097, he established a school and a Sufi lodge, in order to continue teaching and learning. In 499/1106, Niẓām al-Mulk's son, Fakhr al-Mulk, requested that al-Ghazālī accept a teaching position at his old school, the Niẓāmiyya of Nīshāpūr. He accepted and taught for a time, but left this position in 500/1106 after Fakhr al-Mulk was assassinated by Ismāʿīlīs. He then returned to Ṭūs and divided his time between teaching and worship. He died in 505/1111 and was buried in a cemetery near the citadel of Ṭābarān.

Eulogies in Verse

Because of him the lame walked briskly,
And the songless through him burst into melody.

On the death of Imām al-Ghazālī, Abū l-Muẓaffar Muḥammad al-Abiwardī said of his loss:

He is gone! and the greatest loss which ever afflicted me,
was that of a man who left no one like him among mankind.

Legacy and Contributions of al-Ghazālī

Al-Ghazālī's two hundred and seventy-three works span many disciplines and can be grouped under the following headings:

1. Jurisprudence and legal theory. Al-Ghazālī made foundational contributions to Shāfiʿī jurisprudence; his book *al-Wajīz* is major handbook that has been used in teaching institutions around the world; many commentaries have been written on it, most notably by Abū l-Qāsim ʿAbd al-Karīm al-Rāfiʿī (d. 623/1226). In legal theory, *al-Mustaṣfa min ʿilm al-uṣūl* is considered one of five foundational texts in the discipline.
2. Logic and philosophy. Al-Ghazālī introduced logic in Islamic terms that jurists could understand and utilize. His works on philosophy include the *Tahāfut al-falāsifa*, which has been studied far beyond the Muslim world and has been the subject of numerous commentaries, discussions, and refutations.
3. Theology, including works on heresiography in refutation of Bāṭinī doctrines. He also expounded on the theory of occasionalism.
4. Ethics and educational theory. The *Mīzān al-ʿamal* and other works such as the *Iḥyāʾ ʿulūm al-dīn* mention a great deal on education.
5. Spirituality and Sufism. His magnum opus, the *Iḥyāʾ ʿulūm al-dīn* is a pioneering work in the field of spirituality, in terms of its organization and its comprehensive scope.
6. Various fields. Al-Ghazālī also wrote shorter works in a variety of disciplines, including his autobiography (*al-Munqidh min al-ḍalāl*), works on Qurʾānic studies (*Jawāhir al-Qurʾān*), and political statecraft (*Naṣiḥat al-mūluk*).

Chronology of al-Ghazālī's Life

450/1058	Birth of al-Ghazālī at Ṭūs
c. 461/1069	Began studies at Ṭūs
c. 465/1073	Traveled to Jurjān to study
466–469/1074–1077	Studied at Ṭūs
469/1077	Went to Nīshāpūr to study with al-Jūwaynī
473/1080	al-Ghazālī composed his first book, *al-Mankhūl.*
477/1084	Death of al-Fāramdhī, one of al-Ghazālī's teachers.
478/1085	Death of al-Jūwaynī; al-Ghazālī left Nīshāpūr
1 Jumāda 484/ July 1091	Arrival in Baghdad
4 Ramaḍān 485/ 14 October 1092	Assassination of Niẓām-al-Mulk
484–487/1091–1094	Study of philosophy begins
Rabīʿ II 486/June 1093	Present at lectures in the Niẓāmiyya
Muḥarrām 487/February 1094	Present at the oath-taking of the new caliph, al-Mustaẓhir
487/1094	Finished *Maqāṣid al-falāsifa*
5 Muḥarrām 488/ 21 January 1095	Finished *Tahāfut al-falāsifa*
Rajab 488/ July 1095	Spiritual crisis
Dhū l-Qaʿda 488/ November 1095	Left Baghdad for Damascus
Dhū l-Qaʿda 489/ November – December 1096	Made pilgrimage and worked on the *Iḥyāʾ ʿulūm al-dīn*
Jumāda II 490/ May 1097	During a brief stop in Baghdad he taught from the *Iḥyāʾ ʿulūm al-dīn*
Rajab 490/June 1097	Abū Bakr b. al-ʿArabī saw him in Baghdad
Fall 490/1097	Leaves Baghdad for Khurasān

Dhū l-Ḥijja 490/ November 1097	Arrives in Khurasān, establishes *madrasa* in Ṭūs
Dhū l-Qaʿda 499/ July 1106	Returned to teaching in Nīshāpūr
500/1106	Wrote *al-Munqidh min al-ḍalāl*
500/1106	Returned to Ṭūs
28 Dhū l-Ḥijja 502/ 5 August 1109	Finished *al-Mustaṣfā*
Jumada I 505/December 1111	Finished *Iljām*
7 Jumada II 505/ 18 December 1111	Death of al-Ghazālī at Ṭūs

Translator's Preface

THE *BOOK OF KNOWLEDGE* is the first of the forty treatises or books that comprise Abū Ḥāmid al-Ghazālī's seminal work The *Revival of the Religious Sciences* (*Iḥyāʾ ʿulūm al-dīn*); it is by far the most extensive and detailed of these books, constituting about one-twelfth of the work itself. Its seven sections serve as a framework on which the remaining thirty-nine books are based. The *Book of Knowledge* however, unlike most of the remaining books of the *Iḥyāʾ ʿulūm al-dīn*, does not in itself include explicitly mystical or Sufic elements. Instead al-Ghazālī approaches his topic—knowledge—in the broader context of responding to the question of what constitutes valid knowledge, and focusing on the essentially ethical nature of knowledge that had been established during the early history of Islam. This was knowledge, the most basic characteristic of which was compliance with the textual sources of Islamic society, the Qurʾān, the custom and practices of the Prophet, or his *Sunna*, and the example of the righteous predecessors (*al-salaf al-ṣāliḥ*). This approach provides the epistemological principles that validate any pursuit of knowledge and the key to the direct and intimate knowledge of God; an essentially virtue-based ethical conduct that serves as a means of conforming to a vision of divine reality that constitutes the fabric of the spiritual life of the community as a whole. This affirmation of a normative mode of conduct based on conformity with the divine nature of reality, both inwardly and outwardly establishes a paradigm for valid knowledge while at the same time providing a degree of flexibility and inclusiveness that challenges certain preconceptions of many twenty-first century readers.

Al-Ghazālī's juxtaposition of epistemological principles in a semantic field defined by an ethical perspective was the greatest challenge the translation of this work presented. As residents of the 'Information Age,' we have been educated in a cultural matrix in which knowledge is nothing more than the data upon which our scientific-materialist world view is founded. Knowledge in this context constitutes the building blocks of our 'reality' while at the same time excluding the natural world as a context in which God becomes manifest in the multiple levels of human perception and interaction. Ernest Gellner understood this well when he wrote, "The price of real [sic] knowledge is that our identities, freedoms, norms, are no longer underwritten by our vision and comprehension of things. On the contrary we are doomed to suffer from a tension between cognition and identity."[7] When contrasted with the empiricist's view of what constitutes valid knowledge, al-Ghazālī's affirmation that the pursuit of knowledge is an inherently ethical undertaking that posits the existence of both blameworthy and praiseworthy elements seems at best a view from another time, outdated, archaic, and with no relevance to the times in which we find ourselves. Yet, Gellner himself argues that "Twentieth-century philosophy, has for some time accepted that epistemology is philosophy's current central task. . . "[8] I therefore came to perceive my task in this translation as one of bridging the essentially epistemological gap between the perception of valid knowledge as a construct based upon experience and valid knowledge as an ethical construct defined by faith and certitude. My translation has been undertaken in this light, keeping in mind at each and every moment that "translators are traitors" (*traductor traittore*), and so I have made every effort to remain steadfast to the thread of al-Ghazālī's discourse and to reflect the original text as reliably as possible.

I first became familiar with the text of The *Book of Knowledge* in Morocco in the early 1980s. Prior to this time, however, I had journeyed on the road of a seeker of knowledge (*ṭālib al-ᶜilm*), residing for a number of years in the rural traditional mosque-schools (*madrasa*) of Pakistan,[9] before eventually joining the ranks of the

7 Ernest Gellner, *Legitimation of Belief* (Cambridge: Cambridge University Press, 1957), 206.

8 Gellner, *Legitimation*, 207.

9 I spent the years between 1969 and 1979 in the North West Frontier Province (NWFP). At that time these institutions remained true to principles of the transmission of knowledge that al-Ghazālī speaks of in the present work, before the

students of the Qarawiyyin University of Fez, Morocco. It was this experience of over fifteen years in the company of students who "sat at the feet of their teachers," and devout scholars who, as mentors, exemplified a normative basis of conduct that reflected the highest aspirations, ideals and central value system of the majority, if not all participants of their faith tradition—Islam—that I came to realize the integral relationship between knowledge and ethical conduct that makes The *Book of Knowledge* the seminal text that it is.

This notion of virtue-based ethical conduct as the rationale behind Islamic society itself is not new. Tor Andrae has said, "The ethics of Islam consists of the observance of religious discipline."[10] Yet what actually constitutes "religious discipline" is an issue that continues to be addressed in both interfaith and intra-faith discourse today. Perhaps the most important facet of The *Book of Knowledge* can be grasped when the reader approaches its content not as information, but as a discourse that offers a response to that very question— "What constitutes religious discipline?" This perspective as the living element that imparts vitality and originality to this work has not been well represented in the previous translations of this work. I have attempted therefore to make my translation reflect the intimate discourse that was an integral facet of the teacher/student relationship in the Islamic sciences, asking the reader to keep in mind that Muslims of all walks of life were active participants in this educational or, in other words, transformational process of orientation and guidance that seeking knowledge comprised.

Al-Ghazālī's language in itself seldom presents any difficulty. His use of formal Arabic is masterly and intended for a scholarly audience, the majority of whom were his peers or colleagues in the pursuits of their various fields. Earlier translations tended to contextualize his language in an antiquated scholarly didactic that lost the intimate quality of his discourse with those he was directly addressing. In this they lost the sense of urgency and heartfelt counsel that characterizes the work and lends it the relevance so often lost in overly scholastic language that seldom reflects al-Ghazālī's

---

usurpation of many of these institutions by fundamentalists largely funded by oil revenues.

10 *In the Garden of Myrtles: Studies in Early Islamic Mysticism,* trans. Birgitta Sharpe (Albany: State University of New York Press, 1987).

actual discursive style or the discourse of his times. In The *Book of Knowledge* al-Ghazālī addresses those journeying upon the path of knowledge, and provides a personal response to those who, like himself, seek to negotiate the currents of the times without compromising themselves and their values, all the while integrating the essential ideals, values, and sensibilities provided by the Qurʾān and *sunna* into their individual and collective social identities.

The present translation is based on the text of the new edition of the *Iḥyāʾ ʿulūm al-dīn* in ten volumes, edited and annotated by Dār al-Minhāj[11] in Jedda. This edition is in commemoration of the 900th anniversary of the death of Imām al-Ghazālī. In punctuation and paragraph separation I tend to follow this edition for clarity's sake and in order to facilitate back-referencing for those with a knowledge of Arabic, who would like to compare my translation with the original text. In addition to the Dār al-Minhāj edition, I consulted the Būlāq first edition of 1269/1853 and the edition published by al-Ḥalabī, Cairo 1346/1927, with al-ʿIrāqī's *Kitāb al-Mughnī ʿan ḥaml al-asfār fī l-asfār fī takhrīj mā fī l-Iḥyāʾ min al-akhbār*. I also found Murtaḍā al-Zabīdī's *Itḥāf al-sādat al-muttaqīn bi-sharḥ Iḥyāʾ ʿulūm al-dīn* an invaluable aid in interpreting al-Ghazālī's more technical language and a key to unlocking a number of textual variants.

Other Books on al-Ghazālī and Previous Translations

A number of academic works have been written on Imām al-Ghazālī. Works on his times, life, and the major themes of his work are readily accessible in most libraries. Many of his works have been translated as well, including The *Revival of the Religious Sciences* (*Iḥyāʾ ʿulūm al-dīn*), of which this translation is the first book; yet to my knowledge a single authoritative translation of the complete work has not been done.[12]

It is usually the case that as a work is translated over time the translations improve and reflect the original text more reliably. Sometimes, however, works translated before the existence of

11 Abū Ḥāmid al-Ghazālī, *Iḥyāʾ ʿulūm al-dīn* (Jedda: Dār al-Minhāj, 1432/2011).

12 For a comprehensive overview of *Iḥyāʾ ʿulūm al-dīn* in a variety of formats and languages see www.ghazali.org/ rrs-ovr/.

high-quality bilingual dictionaries or before the introduction of computers become outdated and lack polish. Another issue is when translation is done into a language that is not the original tongue of the translator or that a translation may reflect the idioms and speech patterns of another era. Such was the case, for example, with English translations done in the Indian subcontinent in the years following independence. Moreover, it goes without saying that a knowledge of Arabic alone does not, necessarily, infuse a translation with an inner understanding that reflects the essential fabric of Islamic society and its social norms. All of the above issues in the previous translations of The *Book of Knowledge* have resulted in the need for a new translation.

Two prior editions of The *Book of Knowledge* exist. Nabih Amin Faris began his translation of The *Book of Knowledge*[13] in 1936 at the suggestion of Philip K. Hitti. Faris employed three texts and one manuscript including the text established by Murtaḍā l-Zabīdī in his *Itḥāf al-sādat al-muttaqīn*. The project was put on hold during the war and might have remained so had it not been for Sheikh Muhammad Ashraf of Lahore, Pakistan, who took an interest in the work and led to its eventual publication in 1962. A second translation of The *Book of Knowledge* was completed even earlier, in 1940, as a thesis submitted to the Faculty of the Kennedy School of Missions of the Hartford Seminary Foundation, by William Alexander McCall in partial fulfilment of the requirements for the degree of Doctor of Philosophy. The work begun in Hartford in 1939 was completed in 1940 after a period of residency in Syria.[14] I owe a debt of gratitude to both translators, as those who came before; yet both translations reflect linguistic conventions from the fields of philosophy and theology that contrast with the non-scholastic nature of Imām al-Ghazālī's prose and with his intimate discourse on the level of the heart. These works reflect an early stage in the translation of Islamic texts before "an infrastructure of conceptual

13 Abū Ḥāmid al-Ghazālī, *The Book of Knowledge*, trans. Nabih Amin Faris (Lahore: Sh. Muḥammad Ashraf, 1962).

14 William Alexander McCall, "'The Book of Knowledge,' Being a Translation, with Introduction and Notes of al-Ghazzālī's Book of the *'Iḥyā'*, *Kitāb al-ʿIlm*" (PhD thesis, Hartford Seminary, 1940).

understanding and English vocabulary"[15] found its way into the field, in particular through the works of William C. Chittick, Bruce Lawrence, and John Renard. I owe a particular debt of gratitude to John Renard for his masterful collection *Knowledge of God in Classical Sufism*,[16] which includes his excellent rendering of Chapter 31 of Abū Ṭālib al-Makkī's *Qūt al-qulūb*, on which Imām al-Ghazālī drew extensively in the composition of his *Book of Knowledge*. In this there is a certain poetic justice that the translator of al-Ghazālī's *Kitāb al-ʿilm* continues to find sustenance in the section on knowledge in the translation of Abū Ṭālib al-Makkī's *Qūt al-qulūb*.

What constitutes valid knowledge and its religious and socio-historical repercussions has become a vital area of discourse in multiple domains of academic and scholarly research today. Imām al-Ghazālī's *Book of Knowledge* offers a living example of the centrality this issue played in Islamic thought and its role in the ritual, cultural, and social fabric of Islamic society from the earliest times. The discourse of this work however extends beyond the realm of the scholar of Islam or of social-anthropology in the Islamic world. Anyone committed to the study of social psychology, as the science of the human soul, its states, and the manner in which they resonate in a given social milieu—in particular a scholarly one—will find this work to be of great interest.

Beyond academics, this work offers both the Arabic and the non-Arabic speaking Muslim community a treasure trove of the traditional wisdom teachings of Islam as they functioned in the discourse of the jurists and scholars of al-Ghazālī's times. The *Book of Knowledge* has been a hidden treasure for centuries. Now, guided by the light and selfless dedication of Gray Henry, Fons Vitae has assembled a team of individuals devoted to making the whole of the *Iḥyāʾ ʿulūm al-dīn* accessible to a larger than ever public in a well-produced English translation that provides those who give this

---

15 Arthur Buehler, *Revealed Grace: The Juristic Sufism of Ahmad Sirhindi (1564-1624)* (Louisville, KY: Fons Vitae, 2011). There is much to be gleaned from the translator's preface to A. Buehler's well-honed translations of some of the complete letters from Sirhindi's *Colllected Letters* concerning the art of translation.

16 John Renard, *Knowledge of God in Classical Sufism: Foundations of Islamic Mystical Theology* (ed. and trans.) (New York: Paulist Press, 2004), of particular interest here is his translation from pages 112–263.

book the time it merits the opportunity to expand their horizons. For this is a work whose multiple benefits surpass the bounds of any particular religious, intellectual, or academic orientation. As a professor at a large public university, I have always found a particular relevance in this work to my own station in life, and to this day I often open my copy to a random page and never cease to find inspiration and encouragement in Imām al-Ghazālī's gift to us across the centuries, the *Book of Knowledge.*

Acknowledgments

IN UNDERTAKING THIS TRANSLATION of The *Book of Knowledge*, I came to realize more and more the debt I owe an entire community of generous men and women, scholars and non-scholars that have sustained me throughout my years as a seeker of knowledge in Pakistan, Morocco, the United States, and France. I owe my gratitude first and foremost to my parents, who provided me with my first education and a home. Then in Kalam, in the Upper Swat Valley, an entire village took in and nourished in every manner a young man who was a total stranger from a foreign land. In this community there are individuals like the blacksmith in Sarkai, of the Malakand Agency, near Skhakout, who, whenever the boy collecting food offerings for the students in the mosque came to his door, would break his bread in half and send it with him to the mosque, even if on that day, there was only one bread for his family and himself. Or Sarkai Mulay Sahib, originally from Swat, who taught me grammar and conjugation, and who after forty years of teaching lost his voice, so that we had to listen intently to his elucidating remarks, while no less intently observing his every move, eager to emulate his example. Then there were those who, when beheld, reminded us of what we were truly seeking, the likes of Kabul Mulay Sahib, the imam of a small Mohmand village outside Mardan, or like Sidi Tuhamī al-ʿAṭṭār of Fes, Morocco. Each of these men was a walking book of knowledge, they have all informed the present translation in their own ways.

Within the domain of the academy, I owe so much to Dr. Alan Godlas, my friend and colleague at the University of Georgia, and Dr. Denis Gril of the University of Aix-en-Provence, France, my mentor in my doctoral studies, both of whom are mirrors of the spirit of Imām al-Ghazālī. I am grateful as well to His Majesty Muhammad VI of Morocco for the opportunities he has afforded me to pursue my academic interests in Morocco's rich spiritual heritage over the years through his generous invitations to attend the Hassaniyya Lectures of Ramadan in Rabat. To all of the above I dedicate this translation, for above all it has been this community, as individuals and in unison, scholars and non-scholars that have kept alive the essential values Imām al-Ghazālī so skillfully conveyed in The *Book of Knowledge*, and made them as relevant today as they were nine hundred years ago when, with his reed pen, he formed the final *mīm* of *salām*, the word with which he ends this treatise: *peace*.

Kenneth Honerkamp

بِسْمِ ٱللَّهِ ٱلرَّحْمَٰنِ ٱلرَّحِيمِ

The Revival of the Religious Sciences

Iḥyāʾ ʿulūm al-dīn

Author's Introduction

In the name of God, the Merciful, the Compassionate

FIRST, I PRAISE GOD abundantly and unceasingly even though the declaration of praise of the fervent is less than what is due to His majesty.

Second, I ask blessings and peace for His messenger, the leader of mankind, and on the rest of the messengers.

Third, I pray that He, who is exalted, [bring me] success in what I have resolved [to undertake, namely] the composition of a book on the *Iḥyāʾ ʿulūm al-dīn* [The Revival of the Religious Sciences].

Fourth, I hasten to enlighten you who are self-righteous and reject belief, and who go too far in your reproach and disapproval.

I am no longer obliged to remain silent because the responsibility to speak and to warn you has been imposed on me by your persistent blindness to the true state of the divine reality, and your insistence on fostering evil, stirring up opposition against anyone who, in order to conform to the dictates of knowledge, deviates from custom and the established practice of men. In doing this he fulfils God's prescriptions to purify the self and reform the heart, and thus redeems a life that has been dissipated in despair of remedy, and avoids the company of those who the Law Giver [Muḥammad] ﷺ described as "The person most severely chastised on the day of judgment will be the learned man whom God did not afford benefit from his knowledge."

By my life! There is no reason for your persistent disapproval except that malady which has become an epidemic among the multitudes. The malady [of ignorance] is not discerning the importance of the matter, the gravity of the problem, and the seriousness of the crisis. The next life is approaching, the present world is vanishing, death is imminent, the journey is far, provisions for the journey are scant, the dangers are great, and the road is blocked. The perceptive know that only knowledge and works devoted to God تَعَالَىٰ avail.

With neither guide nor companion, the journey on the road to the next life, with its many pitfalls, is difficult and tiring. The guides to the way are the learned who are the heirs of the prophets, but our age is void of them, and only the superficial remain, and Satan has mastery over most of them. All of them were so engrossed in their worldly fortunes that they came to see good as evil and evil as good, so that the science of religion disappeared and the light of guidance was extinguished all over the world. They made people imagine that there is no knowledge except the formal legal rulings of a government by which judges settle disputes when foolish people quarrel; or the ability to debate, which is displayed by the vainglorious in order to confuse and refute; or the elaborate and flowery language by which the preacher seeks to lure the common people. Apart from these three [types of knowledge] they could not find other ways to profit and [acquire] the riches of the world.

The knowledge of the next life according to which our predecessors walked and which God, in His book, called discernment, wisdom, knowledge, illumination, light, right guidance, and rectitude, has been quite forgotten. This is a calamity in religion and a grave crisis, [so] I considered it an important duty for me to compose this book in order to revive the religious sciences, to reveal the ways of the early imams, and to clarify the branches of knowledge the prophets and predecessors regarded as useful.

[Outline]

I have divided the work into four parts, or quarters, which are

1. The Quarter of Worship,
2. The Quarter of Customs,
3. The Quarter of Perils, and
4. The Quarter of Deliverance.

I have begun the work with the *Book of Knowledge* because it is of the highest importance to determine the knowledge that God عَزَّوَجَلَّ

has, through the Prophet ﷺ, ordered the elite to seek. For the Prophet of God ﷺ said, "To seek knowledge is a duty for every Muslim." In [the *Book of Knowledge*] I distinguish useful knowledge from that which is harmful; for he [Muḥammad ﷺ] said, "We seek refuge with God from any knowledge which does not benefit." [And also] to show the deviation of the present generation from the proper rule of conduct; they are deluded by the glimmer of a mirage and they are satisfied with the husk rather than the kernel of the religious sciences.

The Quarter of Worship comprises ten books:

1. The Book of Knowledge
2. The Principles of the Creed
3. The Mysteries of Purification
4. The Mysteries of the Prayer
5. The Mysteries of Charity
6. The Mysteries of Fasting
7. The Mysteries of the Pilgrimage
8. The Etiquette of the Recitation of the Qurʾān
9. Invocations and Supplications
10. The Arrangement of the Litanies and the Exposition of the Night Vigil

The Quarter of Customs also comprises ten books:

11. The Proprieties of Eating
12. The Proprieties of Marriage
13. The Proprieties of Acquisition and Earning a Living
14. The Lawful and the Unlawful
15. The Proprieties of Friendship and Brotherhood
16. The Proprieties of Retreat
17. The Proprieties of Travel
18. The Proprieties of the Audition and Ecstasy
19. The Commanding of Right and the Forbidding of Wrong
20. The Proprieties of Living and the Prophetic Mannerisms

The Quarter of Perils comprises ten books:

21. The Exposition of the Wonders of the Heart
22. Training the Soul, Refining the Character, and Treating the Ailments of the Heart

23. Overcoming the Two Desires
24. The Bane of the Tongue
25. The Censure of Anger, Malice, and Envy
26. The Censure of This World
27. The Censure of Greed and the Love of Wealth
28. The Censure of Fame and Hypocritical Ostentation
29. The Censure of Pride and Vanity
30. The Censure of Deceit

The Quarter of Deliverance also comprises ten books:

31. On Repentance
32. On Patience and Thankfulness
33. On Fear and Hope
34. On Poverty and Abstinence
35. On Unity and Trust
36. On Love, Longing, Intimacy, and Contentment
37. On Intention, Sincerity, and Truthfulness
38. On Vigilance and Accounting
39. On Contemplation
40. On the Remembrance of Death and the Hereafter

In the **Quarter of Worship**, I intend to mention some of the hidden elements of its etiquette, the subtleties of its rules, and the mysteries of its meanings. [These] are necessary for the scholar; without their knowledge no one [can be considered to be] versed in the science of the hereafter. Most of this is neglected in the art of jurisprudence.

In the **Quarter of Customs**, I intend to mention the rules of practical conduct current among people, their deep mysteries, intricate techniques, and the ways to be scrupulously pious. These are the rules of conduct that no religious person can do without.

In the **Quarter of Perils**, I intend to enumerate every blameworthy characteristic that the Qurʾān declared should be eliminated and from which the soul should be cleansed, and from what the heart should be purified. For each of these characteristics, I will give its definition, its true nature, the cause from which it originates, its inherent defects, the signs by which it is recognized, and the methods of treatment by which one can be saved from each one of them. [To all this], I add the evidentiary verses [of the Qurʾān] and traditions [of the Prophet Muḥammad ﷺ and the Companions رضي الله عنهم].

In the **Quarter of Deliverance**, I intend to enumerate every praiseworthy characteristic and desirable quality of those who are near God and of the righteous, [the qualities] by which a servant draws near the Lord of the worlds. For every quality I will give its definition, true nature, the means by which it is acquired, its fruit [from which benefit is received], the signs by which it is recognized, and its excellence for which it is desired. [I will outline all of this] along with evidentiary examples from [the fields of] law and reason.

[Previous Works on the Subject]

People have composed books concerning some of these ideas, but this book [the *Iḥyāʾ*] differs from them in five ways, by:

1. clarifying what they have obscured and elucidating what they have treated casually;
2. arranging what they scattered and putting in order what they separated;
3. abbreviating what they made lengthy and proving what they reported;
4. omitting what they have repeated; and
5. establishing the truth of certain obscure matters that are difficult to understand and which have not been presented in books at all.

For although all the scholars follow one course, there is no reason one should not proceed independently and bring to light something unknown, paying special attention to something his colleagues have forgotten. Or they are not heedless about calling attention to it, but they neglect to mention it in books. Or they do not overlook it, but something prevents them from exposing it [and making it clear].

So these are the special properties of this book, besides its inclusion of all these various kinds of knowledge.

[Arrangement of this Book]

Two things induced me to arrange this book in four parts. The first and fundamental motive is that this arrangement in establishing what is true and in making it understandable is, as it were, inevitable because the branch of knowledge by which one approaches the hereafter is divided into the knowledge of [proper] conduct and the knowledge of [spiritual] unveiling.

By the knowledge of [spiritual] unveiling I mean knowledge and only knowledge. By the science of [proper] conduct I mean knowledge as well as action in accordance with that knowledge. This work will deal only with the science of [proper] conduct, and not with [spiritual] unveiling, which one is not permitted to record in writing, although it is the ultimate aim of saints and the ultimate aim of the sincere. The science of [proper] conduct is merely a path that leads to unveiling and only through that path did the prophets of God communicate with the people and lead them to Him. Concerning [spiritual] unveiling, the prophets عَلَيْهِمُ ٱلسَّلَامُ spoke only figuratively and briefly through signs and symbols, because they realized the inability of people's mind to comprehend. Therefore since the scholars are heirs of the prophets, they cannot but follow in their footsteps and emulate their way.

[Outward and Inward Knowledge]

The knowledge of [proper] conduct is divided into (1) outward knowledge, by which I mean knowledge of the senses and (2) inward knowledge, by which I mean knowledge of the functions of the heart.

The physical members either perform acts of prescribed worship, or acts that are in accordance with custom, while the heart, because it is removed from the senses and belongs to the world of dominion, is subject to either praiseworthy or blameworthy [influences]. Therefore it is necessary to divide this branch of knowledge into two parts: outward and inward. The outward part, which is connected to the senses, is subdivided into acts of worship and acts that pertain to custom. The inward part, which is connected to the states of the heart and the characteristics of the soul, is subdivided into blameworthy states and praiseworthy states. So the total makes four divisions of the sciences of the practice of religion.

The second motive [for this division] is that I have noticed the sincere interest of students in jurisprudence, which has become popular among those who do not fear God تَعَالَىٰ but who seek to boast and exploit its influence and prestige in arguments. It [jurisprudence] is also divided into four quarters, and he who follows the style of one who is beloved becomes beloved.

So modeling the arrangement of this book after the books of jurisprudence is a clever way to win hearts over gradually. For the same [reason], someone who desires to have the authorities incline toward medicine composes it in the form of an astronomical chart set in tables and figures, which he calls the chart of health, in order for their interest in the study [of astronomy] to attract them to the study [of medicine]. Ingenuity in attracting hearts to the knowledge that is good for [one's] spiritual life is, however, more important than interesting them in medicine, which benefits only the physical body. The fruit of this branch of knowledge is the treatment of hearts and souls, through which one reaches a life that lasts forever. How inferior then is the medicine of the body, which is, by necessity, destined to decay before long.

Then let us ask God سُبْحَانَهُ for His success, for right guidance to the right course, for He is gracious and generous.

The Book of Knowledge

The first book of the Quarter of Worship and the opening book

of the *Revival of the Religious Sciences*

In the name of God, the Merciful, the Compassionate

The Book of Knowledge

It is composed of seven chapters.

Chapter 1: On the virtue of knowledge, education, and learning.

Chapter 2: On the elucidation of knowledge that is an individual obligation and [knowledge] that is a communal obligation; and the definition of jurisprudence and theology as [branches] of Islamic knowledge, and on the knowledge of the hereafter and this world.

Chapter 3: On what the folk consider to be the Islamic disciplines but are not, and the elucidation of the category of blameworthy knowledge and its scope.

Chapter 4: On the perils of disputation and the reasons people engage in dissension and dialectics.

Chapter 5: On the conduct incumbent on the teacher and student.

Chapter 6: On the perils of [the pursuit of] knowledge and scholars and the signs that differentiate between the worldly scholars and [those whose focus is on] the hereafter.

Chapter 7: On the intellect, its virtue and categories, and the reports related to it.

1

On the virtue of knowledge, education, learning, and evidence founded on transmission and reason.

The Virtue of Knowledge

Textual Evidence from the Qurʾān

GOD تَعَالَىٰ SAYS: *GOD WITNESSES that there is no deity except Him—and so do the angels and those of knowledge* [3:18]. Behold how God سُبْحَانَهُ وَتَعَالَىٰ begins [first] with Himself, second [with] His angels, and third with the people of knowledge. What a remarkable way to establish honor, virtue, loftiness, and rank. God تَعَالَىٰ also said: God *will raise those who have believed among you and those who were given knowledge, by degrees* [58:11].

Ibn ʿAbbās رَضِيَ ٱللَّهُ عَنْهُمَا said, "The scholars are superior to the believers by seven hundred levels; between each level is a journey of five hundred years."[1]

God عَزَّ وَجَلَّ said: *Say, "Are those who know equal to those who do not know?"* [39:9].

And He تَعَالَىٰ said: *From among His servants, only those who fear God are those who have knowledge* [35:28].

---

1 Abū Ṭālib al-Makkī, *Qūt al-qulūb*, 1:139.

And He تَعَالَىٰ said: *Say, God, and whoever has knowledge of the book, is sufficient as witness between me and you* [13:43].

And He تَعَالَىٰ said: *The one with knowledge from the book stated, "I will bring it to you"* [27:40]. This alludes to the fact that he accomplished this [task] through the efficacy of knowledge.

And [when] He عَزَّوَجَلَّ said: *But those who had been given knowledge said, "Woe to you! The reward of God is better"* [28:80] He made evident that the most essential nature of the hereafter is known through knowledge.

And He تَعَالَىٰ said: *And these examples We present to the people, but none will understand them except those of knowledge* [29:43].

And [God] تَعَالَىٰ said: *But if they had referred it back to the Messenger and to those of authority among them ...* [4:83]. He [Muḥammad] gave his judgment on current events in response to their inquiry and made their rank follow in the rank of the prophets by unveiling God's judgment.

And it has been said of His words تَعَالَىٰ: *O children of Adam, We have bestowed upon you clothing to conceal your private parts,* [clothing] means knowledge, *and as adornment*, means certainty; *but the clothing of piety*, meaning modesty, [*is superior*] [7:26].[2]

And He عَزَّوَجَلَّ said: *And We had certainly brought them a Book which We detailed with knowledge* [7:52].

And He تَعَالَىٰ said: *Then We will surely relate* [*their deeds*] *to them with knowledge* [7:7].

And He عَزَّوَجَلَّ said: *Rather, the Qurʾān is distinct verses* [*preserved*] *within the breasts of those who have been given knowledge* [29:49].

And He تَعَالَىٰ said: [*He*] *created mankind, and taught him eloquence* [55:3–4]. This He mentioned in the context of grace.

2 Abū Ṭālib al-Makkī, *Qūt al-qulūb*, 1:138.

The [Prophetic] Reports

THE MESSENGER صَلَّى ٱللَّٰهُ عَلَيْهِ وَسَلَّمَ OF GOD has said, "Whomever God wishes well, He gives discernment in matters of the religion, and inspires him with right guidance."[3]

And he صَلَّى ٱللَّٰهُ عَلَيْهِ وَسَلَّمَ said, "The scholars (*ʿulamāʾ*) are the heirs of the prophets."[4] It is well known that there is no degree above that of prophecy, nor nobility above the nobility of the heirs of that degree.

And he صَلَّى ٱللَّٰهُ عَلَيْهِ وَسَلَّمَ said, "All those who reside in the heavens and the earth ask forgiveness for the scholar."[5] What station could exceed the station of one for whom the angels of the heavens and the earth occupy themselves with asking forgiveness? He is preoccupied with himself; while they are preoccupied with asking for forgiveness for him.[6]

And he صَلَّى ٱللَّٰهُ عَلَيْهِ وَسَلَّمَ said, "Indeed wisdom increases the noble person in nobility and elevates the servant until he sits as though he were a king."[7] In this he pointed out its fruits in this worldly realm; though it is well known that the hereafter is more worthy and everlasting.

[The Messenger] صَلَّى ٱللَّٰهُ عَلَيْهِ وَسَلَّمَ of God also said, "There are two traits not to be found in a hypocrite: noble comportment and understanding of religion."[8] Do not, however, be in doubt concerning this *ḥadīth* on account of the hypocritical actions of some of this epoch's jurists; for [in the narration] he did not intend the term jurisprudence (*fiqh*) as you may suppose it to be. The explanation of the meaning of *fiqh* will soon follow, [let me say, however, that] the lowest degree of a jurist is to know that the hereafter is better

---

3 Al-Bukhārī, 71; Muslim, 1037; and the addition of, "and inspires him with right guidance" is in al-Ṭabarānī, *al-Muʿjam al-kabīr*, 19:340, and Abū Nuʿaym, *Ḥilya*, 4:107.

4 Abū Dāwūd, 3641; al-Tirmidhī, 2682; Ibn Māja, 223.

5 Abū Dāwūd, 3641; al-Tirmidhī, 2682; Ibn Māja, 223.

6 "Since a scholar is the cause for the attainment of knowledge by which souls are saved from all sorts of destruction, and since his effort is confined to that and the salvation of the worshipers is in his hands, and since reward is an element of his acts, everyone in the heavens and earth [should] strive to save him from the causes of destruction by seeking forgiveness for him." Al-Zabīdī, *Itḥāf*, 1:71.

7 Abū Nuʿaym, *Ḥilya*, 6:173; Quḍāʿī, *Musnad al-shihāb*, 979.

8 Al-Tirmidhī, 2684.

than this world, and this realization, if it is sincere and overwhelms all else, should absolve him of hypocrisy and ostentation.

And he ﷺ said, "The best of people is a believing scholar who benefits [others] when needed, and when not needed, [his knowledge] suffices him."[9]

And he ﷺ said, "Faith is without clothing; its dress is piety, its beauty is modesty, and its fruits are knowledge."[10]

And he ﷺ said, "The closest people to the degree of prophecy are the people of knowledge and those striving in the way of God. As for the learned, they provide guidance for the people in accordance with that which the prophets brought; while those striving in the way of God strive with their swords [to protect] that which the prophets brought."[11]

And he ﷺ said, "Surely, the demise of an entire tribe is easier [to bear] than the demise of a scholar."[12]

And he ﷺ said, "People are like deposits, like the deposits of gold and silver; the elect among them in [the time of] ignorance are the elect among them in Islam, if they comprehend it."[13]

And he ﷺ said, "The ink of the scholars and the blood of the martyrs will be weighed on the day of resurrection."[14]

---

9 Al-Bayhaqī, *Shuʿab al-īmān*, 1591, narrated by Abū l-Dardāʾ.

10 Ibn Abī Shayba, *Muṣannaf*, 36383, narrating from Wahb b. Munabbih; Ibn ʿAsākir, *Tārīkh Dimashq*, 63:389; Abū Ṭālib al-Makkī, *Qūt al-qulūb*, 1:138, "narrated by Ḥamza al-Khurāsānī from al-Thawrī, who relates the *ḥadīth* through ʿAbdallāh [back] to the Prophet ﷺ." Similarly it is found in al-Khaṭīb al-Baghdādī, *al-Faqīh wa-l-mutafaqqih*, 129–130.

11 Abū Ṭālib al-Makkī, *Qūt al-qulūb*, 1:139, "We have narrated this *ḥadīth* from ʿAbd al-Raḥmān b. Ghanam, from Muʿādh b. Jabal, who said, the Messenger ﷺ said '… This *ḥadīth* is also in al-Khaṭīb al-Baghdādī, *al-Faqīh wa-l-mutafaqqih* based upon the statement of Isḥāq b. ʿAbdallāh b. Abī Farwa.'"

12 Al-Bayhaqī, *Shuʿab al-īmān*, 1576; Ibn ʿAbd al-Barr, *Jāmiʿ bayān al-ʿilm wa-faḍlih*, 179; and Ibn ʿAsākir, *Tārīkh Dimashq*, 38:318.

13 Al-Bukhārī, 3353; Muslim, 2638.

14 Abū Nuʿaym, *Tārīkh Iṣbahān*, 2:178; Ibn ʿAbd al-Barr, *Jāmiʿ bayān al-ʿilm wa-faḍlih*, 153, from the *ḥadīth* of ʿAbdallāh b. ʿAmr and Abū l-Dardāʾ رضي الله عنهما. See al-Zabīdī, *Itḥāf*, 1:74.

And he said صَلَّىٱللَّهُعَلَيۡهِوَسَلَّمَ, "Whoever safeguards for my community forty *ḥadīth* from the *sunna* in order to transmit them [to others], I will be an intercessor for him and a witness on the day of judgment."[15]

And he صَلَّىٱللَّهُعَلَيۡهِوَسَلَّمَ said, "Whoever from my community transmits [lit. *ḥamila*, carries] forty *ḥadīth* will meet God عَزَّوَجَلَّ on the day of judgment as a scholarly jurist."[16]

And he صَلَّىٱللَّهُعَلَيۡهِوَسَلَّمَ said, "God تَعَالَىٰ will assuage the anxieties of anyone who has attained discernment in the religion of God عَزَّوَجَلَّ and send him sustenance from where he least expects it."[17]

And he صَلَّىٱللَّهُعَلَيۡهِوَسَلَّمَ said, "God عَزَّوَجَلَّ revealed to Abraham عَلَيۡهِٱلسَّلَامُ: "O Abraham, verily I am the All-Knowing, I love every knowing [one]."[18]

And he صَلَّىٱللَّهُعَلَيۡهِوَسَلَّمَ said, "The learned person is the one in whom God صَلَّىٱللَّهُعَلَيۡهِوَسَلَّمَ places His trust on the earth."[19]

And he صَلَّىٱللَّهُعَلَيۡهِوَسَلَّمَ said, "Among my community there are two classes of people: when they are sound, the people are sound, and when they are corrupt the people are corrupt; they are the rulers and the [people of] insight."[20]

And he صَلَّىٱللَّهُعَلَيۡهِوَسَلَّمَ said, "Should a day dawn on me in which I do not increase in the knowledge that brings me closer to God عَزَّوَجَلَّ, then I would not have been blessed by the rising of that day's sun."[21]

And he صَلَّىٱللَّهُعَلَيۡهِوَسَلَّمَ said, speaking of the excellence of knowledge over worship (*ʿibāda*) and martyrdom (*shahāda*), "The excellence of the scholar over a worshiper is like my excellence over the least of my Companions."[22] Look carefully how he has compared knowledge

---

15 Abū Nuʿaym, *Ḥilya*, 4:189; al-Bayhaqī, *Shuʿab al-īmān*, 1597; and Ibn ʿAbd al-Barr, *Jāmiʿ bayān al-ʿilm wa-faḍlih*, 205.

16 Ibn ʿAbd al-Barr, *Jāmiʿ bayān al-ʿilm wa-faḍlih*, 204.

17 Ibn ʿAbd al-Barr, *Jāmiʿ bayān al-ʿilm wa-faḍlih*, 216; al-Khaṭīb al-Baghdādī, *Tārīkh Baghdād*, 3:242.

18 Cited by Ibn ʿAbd al-Barr with a chain of narrators that is missing names from the beginning of the chain, *Jāmiʿ bayān al-ʿilm wa-faḍlih*, 236.

19 Ibn ʿAbd al-Barr, *Jāmiʿ bayān al-ʿilm wa-faḍlih*, 251. Testifying to the authenticity of this *ḥadīth* is the narration related by Quḍāʿī in his *Musnad*, 115, and Ibn ʿAsākir, *Tārīkh Dimashq*, 14:267, "The learned scholars are God's trustees among his creation."

20 Abū Nuʿaym, *Ḥilya*, 4:96; Ibn ʿAbd al-Barr, *Jāmiʿ bayān al-ʿilm wa-faḍlih*, 1108.

21 Abū Nuʿaym, *Ḥilya*, 8:188; Ibn ʿAbd al-Barr, *Jāmiʿ bayān al-ʿilm wa-faḍlih*, 318.

22 Al-Tirmidhī, 2685.

to the degree of prophecy and how he diminished the degree of worship performed without knowledge, though the worshiper is not without some knowledge of the regularly performed worship. Were it not for [this amount of knowledge], it would not be worship.

And he ﷺ said, "The excellence of the scholar over the worshiper is like the excellence of the [light of the] full moon over that of all the stars."[23]

And he ﷺ said, "Three [groups] will be granted intercession on the day of judgment: the prophets, the scholars, and the martyrs."[24] Therefore extol a rank that follows prophecy and surpasses martyrdom, with all that has come to us of the excellence of martyrdom.

And he ﷺ said, "God تَعَالَىٰ has not been worshiped by anything better than the understanding of religion. A single [person of] insight is more a threat to Satan than one thousand worshipers. Everything has support, and the support of this religion is insight (*fiqh*)."[25]

And he ﷺ said, "The most excellent [facet] of your religion is the simplest; the most excellent [facet] of your worship is insight."[26]

And he ﷺ said, "The believing scholar [with insight] exceeds the believing worshiper by seventy degrees."[27]

And he ﷺ said, "You are in a time in which [the people of] insight are many, orators are few, and those seeking [assistance] are few, and those giving [assistance] are many; acts [of devotion] are superior to [acquiring] knowledge. There will, however, come a time in which [the people of] insight [will be] few, and orators [will be] many, and there will be few who give [assistance] and many seeking it. At this time knowledge will be superior to acts [of devotion]."[28]

---

23 Abū Dāwūd, 3641; al-Tirmidhī, 2682; Ibn Māja, 223.

24 Ibn Māja, 4313.

25 Al-Ṭabarānī, *al-Muʿjam al-awsaṭ*, 6162; Abū Nuʿaym, *Ḥilya*, 2:192; al-Bayhaqī, *Shuʿab al-īmān*, 1583.

26 Ibn ʿAbd al-Barr, *Jāmiʿ bayān al-ʿilm wa-faḍlih*, 91, his wording; the first line is from Aḥmad b. Ḥanbal, *Musnad*, 3:479.

27 Ibn ʿAbd al-Barr, *Jāmiʿ bayān al-ʿilm wa-faḍlih*, 95, also narrated by Abū Yaʿlā, *Musnad*, 856, with additions.

28 Al-Ṭabarānī, *Musnad al-shāmiyīn*, 1225; Ibn ʿAbd al-Barr, *Jāmiʿ bayān al-ʿilm wa-faḍlih*, 103; Ibn ʿAsākir, *Tārīkh Dimashq*, 12:303.

And he ﷺ said, "Between the scholar and the worshiper (*ʿābid*) there are one hundred degrees; between each degree is the distance that a sleek stallion can gallop in seventy years."[29]

When it was said to him, "O Messenger of God! Which are the most worthy of acts?" he responded, "The knowledge of God عَزَّوَجَلَّ." Whereupon it was said, "We are asking about acts [of devotion]." So he ﷺ responded, "Knowledge of God ﷺ." Whereupon it was said, "We are asking about acts [of devotion] and you reply with knowledge." So he ﷺ said, "Verily, a minimum of acts [of devotion] will be of benefit if accompanied by knowledge; whereas great quantities of acts [of devotion] will be of no benefit if accompanied by ignorance."[30]

And he ﷺ said,

> God عَزَّوَجَلَّ will bring forth all [His] servants on the day of resurrection, and then He will raise up the scholars; whereupon He will say, "O company of scholars, the sole reason I entrusted My knowledge to you was so that knowledge of Me would be among you; I did not entrust My knowledge to you in order to chastise and punish you. Depart, for I have forgiven you."[31]

We ask God for the most excellent end.

The Traditions of the Companions and Others

ʿALĪ B. ABĪ ṬĀLIB رَضِيَ اللَّهُ عَنْهُ said to Kumayl, "O Kumayl, knowledge is superior to wealth. Knowledge protects you, whereas you must protect your wealth. Knowledge governs, while wealth is governed over. Wealth decreases with dispersal, while knowledge increases when distributed."[32]

---

29 Ibn ʿAbd al-Barr, *Jāmiʿ bayān al-ʿilm wa-faḍlih*, 129.

30 Ibn ʿAbd al-Barr, *Jāmiʿ bayān al-ʿilm wa-faḍlih*, 214.

31 Al-Bayhaqī, *al-Madkhal*, 567; Ibn ʿAbd al-Barr, *Jāmiʿ bayān al-ʿilm wa-faḍlih*, 232.

32 Al-Khaṭīb al-Baghdādī, *Tārīkh Baghdād*, 6:376; Abū Nuʿaym, *Ḥilya*, 1:79; Abū Ṭālib al-Makkī, *Qūt al-qulūb*, 1:134. His statement "wealth decreases with dispersal" does not negate his statement ﷺ "Charity does not decrease wealth." When wealth is given as charity and spent on other things, that portion is gone,

And he also said, "The scholar is superior to the one fasting, praying at night, or striving in God's cause. When a scholar dies a fissure opens in Islam that only a successor [of his degree] can close."[33]

And in verse he [ʿAlī] said, رَضِيَ ٱللَّهُ عَنْهُ,

Pride belongs only to the people of knowledge, as they are
The mentors, well guided, for those seeking the path

Each man's worth depends on what he knows best
While the ignorant for the people of knowledge are enemies

With knowledge gain victory and you will live forever
The people are dead and the people of knowledge are the living.

And Abū l-Aswad said, "There is nothing more exalted than knowledge; kings are rulers over the people, while the scholars are rulers over the kings."[34]

Ibn ʿAbbās رَضِيَ ٱللَّهُ عَنْهُمَا said, "Solomon the son of David عَلَيْهِمَا ٱلسَّلَامُ was given the option to choose between knowledge, and wealth and dominion, so he chose knowledge and was given wealth and dominion as well."[35]

Ibn al-Mubārak was asked, "Who are the people?" To which he responded, "The scholars." Then it was asked, "Who are the kings?" To which he replied, "The ascetics." Then it was put to him, "Who are the riffraff?" He said, "They are the ones who devour their religion."[36] He esteemed no one [more] among people than scholars, because the sole trait by which people are differentiated from all the animals is knowledge. A person is a person by virtue of that which ennobles him, not by the strength of his body, for a camel is more powerful than he is; nor is it by his awesome stature,

---

but it is replaced by other wealth. However, knowledge is like sharing fire. If one were to share knowledge, he would not lose any of it, rather, it would increase. Al-Zabīdī, *Itḥāf*, 1:86.

33 Abū Ṭālib al-Makkī, *Qūt al-qulūb*, 1:143; al-Khaṭīb al-Baghdādī, *al-Jāmiʿ li-akhlāq al-rāwī wa-ādāb al-sāmiʿ*, 350.

34 Ibn Qutayba, *ʿUyūn al-akhbār*, 2:121; Ibn ʿAbd al-Barr, *Jāmiʿ bayān al-ʿilm wa-faḍlih*, 311.

35 Ibn ʿAbd al-Barr, *al-Jāmiʿ bayān al-ʿilm wa-faḍlih* citing ʿAbdallāh b. al-Mubārak, 266.

36 Abū Nuʿaym, *Ḥilya*, 8:167; al-Khaṭīb al-Baghdādī, *Tārīkh Baghdād*, 7:201; Abū Ṭālib al-Makkī, *Qūt al-qulūb*, 1:153.

for the elephant is greater than he is; nor by his courage, for the lion is more courageous than he; nor by his appetite, for the ox has a greater stomach than he; nor is it due to the strength of his sexual desire, for the lowliest sparrow covers his mate more than he; rather he was created solely for the sake of knowledge."[37]

One of the wise said, "What a wonder, if I only comprehended! What has a person gained if knowledge has eluded him; and what has eluded him if he has gained knowledge?[38]

And he صَلَّى ٱللَّٰهُ عَلَيْهِ وَسَلَّمَ said, "Whoever has been given [i.e., memorized] the Qurʾān, but thinks that another has been given something more worthy than it has disparaged that which God تَعَالَىٰ has elevated."[39]

Fatḥ al-Mawṣilī رَحِمَهُ ٱللَّٰهُ asked, "Will not a sick person who is prevented from nourishment, water, and medicine die?" They said, "Indeed." He said, "The heart likewise, when it is prevented from attaining wisdom and knowledge for three days, dies."[40] He has certainly spoken the truth, for the heart lives and is nourished by knowledge and wisdom in the same manner that food nourishes the body. Whoever is bereft of knowledge has a heart that is sick, and its death is inevitable. However, he is not aware of this because love of the world, and his preoccupation with it overtakes his [good] sense. This is similar to how an overwhelming fear overtakes the immediate sense of pain, even though it [pain] has occurred. Then, when death relieves a person's worldly burdens, and he senses his own end, he will woefully lament his state to no avail. This is similar to the sense of the one who is saved from what he fears, and the one who has recovered from his drunkenness, regarding the injuries that afflicted him while [he was] in a state of drunkenness or fear. We seek protection with God on the day the veil is rent asunder. Indeed people are asleep, it is only when they die that they awaken [to their true state].

---

37 God تَعَالَىٰ says, *Indeed, the worst of living creatures in the sight of God are the deaf and dumb who do not use reason* [8:22]. These are the ignorant people who have not acquired true humanity by which the one possessing it is distinguished from the rest of the animals. Al-Zabīdī, *Itḥāf*, 1:89.

38 See also Ibn Qayyim al-Jawziyya, *Miftāḥ dār al-saʿāda*, 1:175.

39 Al-Bayhaqī, *Shuʿab al-īmān*, 2352; al-Khaṭīb al-Baghdādī, *Tārīkh Baghdād*, 9:396.

40 See also Ibn Qayyim al-Jawziyya, *Miftāḥ dār al-saʿāda*, 1:175; al-Shaʿrānī has cited this partially in his *Ṭabaqāt*, 1:80.

Ḥasan رضي الله عنه said, "The ink of the scholars will be weighed against the blood of the martyrs, wherein the ink of the scholars will prove weightier than the blood of the martyrs."[41]

And Ibn Masʿūd رضي الله عنه said, "Take care to seek knowledge now, before it vanishes. It vanishes with the demise of its transmitters. By Him in whose hand rests my soul, the men who died as martyrs for the sake of God would love that God send them back as scholars when they see the generosity shown to them. Indeed, no one is born a scholar; rather knowledge comes with learning."[42]

Ibn ʿAbbās رضي الله عنهما said, "Studying [to gain] knowledge during part of the night is more beloved to me than [remaining] awake in devotion [the entire night]."[43] Thus it has been reported from Abū Hurayra رضي الله عنه[44] and Aḥmad b. Ḥanbal رحمه الله.[45]

Ḥasan said, commenting on His تعالى words, *O Lord, bestow upon us bounties in this world and in the next* (2:201), "The bounty of this world is knowledge and worship, and in the hereafter, heaven."[46]

A wise man was asked, "What sort of things do you aspire to acquire?" To which he responded, "The things that, should your vessel sink, will swim with you." He meant knowledge. It was said that he intended by the sinking of the vessel the demise of the body at death.[47]

One of them [a wise man] said, "Whoever takes wisdom as [he would take in his hands] the reins of a bridle will be taken by

---

41 Reported by Abū Nuʿaym, *Tārīkh Iṣbahān*, 2:178, Ibn ʿAbd al-Barr, *Jāmiʿ bayān al-ʿilm wa-faḍlih*, 153, from the *ḥadīth* of ʿAbdallāh b. ʿAmr and Abū l-Dardāʾ رضي الله عنهما as attributed to the Prophet. It is also reported by al-Shīrāzī, *al-Alqāb*, from the *ḥadīth* of Anas as attributed to the Prophet. Perhaps Ḥasan heard it from Anas. Al-Zabīdī, *Itḥāf*, 1:90.

42 It is reported separately except for the middle section from "By Him in whose hand" to "generosity shown to them" in Aḥmad b. Ḥanbal, *Zuhd*, 899; al-Dārimī, *Sunan*, 144; Ibn ʿAbd al-Barr, *Jāmiʿ bayān al-ʿilm wa-faḍlih*, 1017.

43 ʿAbd al-Razzāq, *al-Muṣannaf*, 11:253.

44 Abū Nuʿaym, *Ḥilya*, 2:192.

45 Ibn ʿAbd al-Barr, *Jāmiʿ bayān al-ʿilm wa-faḍlih*, 108; Ibn Qayyim al-Jawziyya, *Miftāḥ dār al-saʿāda*, 1:174.

46 Al-Tirmidhī, 3488.

47 Ibn ʿAbd al-Barr, *Jāmiʿ bayān al-ʿilm wa-faḍlih*, 280.

the people as a guide. And whoever is known for wisdom will be regarded, in the eyes [of people], with reverence."[48]

Al-Shāfiʿī رَضِيَٱللَّهُعَنْهُ said, "The nobility of knowledge is such that, whoever it is attributed to, even in an insignificant amount, is joyful; and whoever it is withheld from, is distraught."[49]

ʿUmar رَضِيَٱللَّهُعَنْهُ said, "O people, seek knowledge assiduously! For God سُبْحَانَهُ possesses a mantle of love; whoever seeks even a single portion of knowledge, God عَزَّوَجَلَّ will bestow upon him His mantle. Thus if he commits a sin, he will still be regarded as in His good favor. If he commits the sin again, he will still be regarded as in His good favor. And if he commits the sin again, he will still be regarded as in His good favor. [It continues] thus, and He does not remove His mantle from him, even if he continues with that sin until he dies."[50]

Al-Aḥnaf رَضِيَٱللَّهُعَنْهُ said, "The scholars are almost like lords; the fate of every eminent rank, if not sustained by knowledge, will eventually be humiliation."[51]

Sālim b. Abī l-Jaʿd said, "My patron bought me for three hundred dirhams and freed me. I asked him what means of livelihood should I pursue? [Then] I occupied myself with the pursuit of knowledge. A year had not passed when the mayor of the city visited me, and I did not receive him."

Al-Zubayr b. Abī Bakr said, "My father wrote me from Iraq, 'Pursue knowledge! Should you become impoverished it will be wealth for you, and should you become wealthy it will be beauty.'"[52]

It was recounted thus in Luqmān's advice to his son, "O my son, frequent the learned and sit as closely to them as possible; for God سُبْحَانَهُ enlivens hearts with the light of wisdom as He brings the earth to life with rain from the sky."[53]

---

48 Ibn ʿAbd al-Barr, *Jāmiʿ bayān al-ʿilm wa-faḍlih*, 281.

49 Ibn ʿAbd al-Barr, *Jāmiʿ bayān al-ʿilm wa-faḍlih*, 295 without attribution; see al-Zabīdī, *Itḥāf*, 1:92, stating that it was related with a good chain of transmission.

50 Ibn ʿAbd al-Barr, *Jāmiʿ bayān al-ʿilm wa-faḍlih*, 300. Meaning, he could still petition Him for His favor, al-Zabīdī, *Itḥāf*, 1:92.

51 Al-Dīnūrī, *al-Majālasa wa-jawāhir al-ʿilm*, 324.

52 Al-Bayhaqī, *al-Madkhal ilā l-sunan al-kubrā*, 399.

53 Mālik b. Anas, *al-Muwaṭṭaʾ*, 2:1002; al-Bayhaqī, *al-Madkhal ilā l-sunan al-kubrā*, 445, attributed to ʿUbaydallāh b. ʿUmar رَضِيَٱللَّهُعَنْهُمَا.

One of them [a wise man] said, "When a scholar dies, the fish in the water and the birds in the air weep over him; his face will be missed, and mention of him will not be forgotten."[54]

Al-Zuhrī رَحِمَهُ ٱللَّهُ related, "Knowledge (*ʿilm*) is a masculine [term in Arabic], only noble people[55] hold it in great esteem."[56]

The Virtue of Learning

Verses [from the Qurʾān]

[In] His words تَعَالَىٰ: [*And it is not for the believers to go forth* [*to battle*] *all at once.*] *For there should separate from every division of them a group* [*remaining*] *to obtain understanding in religion* [9:122].

And in His words عَزَّوَجَلَّ: *So ask the people of the message* [who have knowledge] *if you do not know* [16:43; 21:7].

The [Prophetic] Reports

In his [the Prophet's] صَلَّىٰ ٱللَّهُ عَلَيْهِ وَسَلَّمَ words, "Whoever travels a path seeking knowledge; God will [guide him] to travel a path that leads to heaven."[57]

And he صَلَّىٰ ٱللَّهُ عَلَيْهِ وَسَلَّمَ said, "Verily the angels lower their wings [and cover] the seeker of knowledge out of pleasure for what he produces."[58]

And he صَلَّىٰ ٱللَّهُ عَلَيْهِ وَسَلَّمَ said, "Rising early in the morning and studying any portion of knowledge is superior to praying one hundred [prayer] cycles (*rakʿa*)."[59]

And he صَلَّىٰ ٱللَّهُ عَلَيْهِ وَسَلَّمَ said, "Any aspect of knowledge a man studies is better for him than the world and all it contains."[60]

---

54 See al-Zabīdī, *Itḥāf*, 1:93.

55 Literally, *dhukūr al-rijāl* (masculine men). Nobility is defined as those with honorable character traits such as bravery, generosity, compassionate kindness, and humility; here al-Zuhrī adds knowledge to these character traits.

56 Abū Nuʿaym, *Ḥilya*, 3:365; Ibn ʿAbd al-Barr, *Jāmiʿ bayān al-ʿilm wa-faḍlih*, 296.

57 Muslim, 2699.

58 Aḥmad b. Ḥanbal, *Musnad*, 4:239; al-Tirmidhī, 2682, for a complete version.

59 Ibn Māja, 219; Ibn ʿAbd al-Barr, *Jāmiʿ bayān al-ʿilm wa-faḍlih*, 114.

60 Cited by Ibn Ḥibbān, *Rawḍat al-ʿuqalāʾ*, 40, as being a saying of Ḥasan al-Baṣrī; Ibn ʿAbd al-Barr, *Jāmiʿ bayān al-ʿilm wa-faḍlih*, 255.

And he ﷺ said, "Seeking knowledge is an obligation on every Muslim."[61]

And he ﷺ said, "Seek knowledge even in China."[62]

And he ﷺ said, "Knowledge is similar to sealed storerooms, the keys to which are inquiry, so ask [and seek to know]; four [types of people] will be rewarded: the one who asks, the scholar [who responds], the one listening, and the one who loves all of them."[63]

And he ﷺ said, "It is not fitting for an ignorant person to remain silent about his ignorance, or for the scholar not to speak of his knowledge."[64]

In a *ḥadīth* [transmitted through] Abū Dharr رضي الله عنه, [the Prophet ﷺ said] "Attending a gathering in which there is knowledgeable discourse is superior to praying one thousand cycles [of prayer], or visiting one thousand sick [people], or attending one thousand funerals." It was then put to him, "O Messenger of God! Even [better than] the recitation of the Qurʾān?" To which he ﷺ responded, "Does the recitation of the Qurʾān render any benefit without knowledge?"[65]

And he ﷺ said, "Between one who dies while seeking knowledge in order to revive Islam and the prophets in heaven there is but one step."[66]

The Traditions [of the Companions and Others]

Ibn ʿAbbās رضي الله عنهما said, "I was humble as a seeker [of knowledge];

---

61 Ibn Māja, 224.

62 The implication in referring to China is distance—even if one must travel a great distance. Al-Bayhaqī, *al-Madkhal ilā l-sunan al-kubrā*, 324 and *Shuʿab al-īmān*, 1543. Ibn ʿAbd al-Barr, *Jāmiʿ bayān al-ʿilm wa-faḍlih*, 20.

63 Abū Nuʿaym, *Ḥilya*, 3:192.

64 Al-Ṭabarānī, *al-Muʿjam al-awsaṭ*, 5361.

65 Al-Ghazālī connects its narration to Abū Dharr, which points to the previous *ḥadīth*, stating "O Abū Dharr! Rising early in the morning and studying any aspect of knowledge..." The wording is in Abū Ṭālib al-Makkī, *Qūt al-qulūb*, 1:67, in which [Abū Ṭālib al-Makkī] said, "We narrate it from the *ḥadīth* of Abū Dharr..." See al-Zabīdī, *Itḥāf*, 1:99.

66 Al-Dārimī, *Sunan*, 366; Ibn ʿAbd al-Barr, *Jāmiʿ bayān al-ʿilm wa-faḍlih*, 219, from Ḥasan in *mursal* form, i.e., quoting directly from the Prophet without mentioning the Companion.

then I came to be regarded with honor and was sought after."[67]

Ibn Abī Mulīka رَحِمَهُ ٱللَّٰهُ thus spoke, "I have seen no one like Ibn ʿAbbās. When I see him, I see the most handsome man in appearance; when he speaks, he is the most eloquent man in speech; and when he expresses a judgment, he is the most knowledgeable."[68]

Ibn al-Mubārak رَحِمَهُ ٱللَّٰهُ said, "I marvel at how anyone who has not sought knowledge can prevail upon his soul to accomplish a single noble deed."[69]

One of them [a wise man] said, "I do not [ask for God's] mercy for anyone like [I ask for God's] mercy for two [types of] men; a man who seeks knowledge but has no comprehension, and a man who has comprehension, but does not seek knowledge."[70]

Abū l-Dardāʾ رَضِيَ ٱللَّٰهُ عَنْهُ said, "Studying an issue [of religious knowledge] is more beloved to me than spending the entire night in devotion."[71]

He said as well, "The scholar and the student are each partners in the good; while all other people are but rabble, there being no good in them."[72]

He said as well, "Be either a scholar, or a student, or one who listens; do not be a fourth [i.e., none of these], lest you perish."[73]

ʿAṭāʾ said, "A gathering held for the sake of remembrance (*dhikr*) atones for seventy gatherings held for the sake of entertainment."[74]

ʿUmar رَضِيَ ٱللَّٰهُ عَنْهُ said, "The death of a thousand worshipers [who spend] their nights in prayer and their days fasting is easier to endure than the death of a person [who is] intelligent and insightful in what God has permitted (*ḥalāl*) and forbidden (*ḥarām*)."[75]

Al-Shāfiʿī رَضِيَ ٱللَّٰهُ عَنْهُ said, "Seeking knowledge is superior to supererogatory devotions."[76]

---

67 Al-Dīnūrī, *al-Majālasa wa-jawāhir al-ʿilm*, 284.

68 Ibn ʿAbd Rabbihi, *al-ʿIqd al-farīd*, 4:8.

69 Ibn ʿAbd al-Barr, *Jāmiʿ bayān al-ʿilm wa-faḍlih*, 286; al-Dhahabī, *Siyar aʿlām al-nubalāʾ*, 8:398.

70 Ibn ʿAbd al-Barr, *Jāmiʿ bayān al-ʿilm wa-faḍlih*, 642 attributes this saying to al-Farrāʾ.

71 Al-Khaṭīb al-Baghdādī, *al-Faqīh wa-l-mutaffaqih*, 55.

72 Ibn Māja, 228; Ibn ʿAbd al-Barr, *Jāmiʿ bayān al-ʿilm wa-faḍlih*, 134.

73 Ibn ʿAbd al-Barr, *Jāmiʿ bayān al-ʿilm wa-faḍlih*, 142–144.

74 Abū Ṭālib al-Makkī, *Qūt al-qulūb*, 1:149.

75 Al-Haythamī, *Bughiyat al-bāḥith*, 2:813.

76 Abū Nuʿaym, *Ḥilya*, 9:119; al-Bayhaqī, *Manāqib al-Shāfiʿī*, 2:138.

Ibn ʿAbd al-Ḥakam رَحِمَهُ ٱللَّهُ said, "I was in the presence of Mālik, studying knowledge [with him] when the noon prayer came. So I gathered the books in order to pray [the supererogatory prayers], when he said to me, 'O you there! The thing you have risen to perform is not in any manner superior to that which you were already engrossed in, as long as your intention is sound.'"[77]

Abū l-Dardāʾ رَضِيَ ٱللَّهُ عَنْهُ said, "Anyone who believes that rising early in the morning with the intention of gaining knowledge is not striving [in the path of God] (*jihād*) is deficient in both opinion and reasoning."[78]

The Virtues of Teaching

Verses [from the Qurʾān]

His words عَزَّ وَجَلَّ, *and warn their people when they return to them* [*that they might be cautious*] [9:122], mean teaching and giving guidance.

His words تَعَالَىٰ, *when God took a covenant from those who were given the book, "You must make it clear to the people and not conceal it"* [3:187], is [an affirmation] of the obligation of teaching.

His words تَعَالَىٰ, *But indeed, a party of them conceal the truth while they know* [*it*] [2:146], is a prohibition against concealing [the truth]; just as He تَعَالَىٰ stated concerning testimony, *for whoever conceals it, his heart is indeed sinful* [2:283]. And the Prophet صَلَّى ٱللَّهُ عَلَيْهِ وَسَلَّمَ stated, "God only bestowed knowledge upon a scholar after taking the same covenant from him that He took from the prophets, that is, that they make it clear to the people and not conceal it.[79]

And He تَعَالَىٰ said, *Who is better in speech than one who invites* [*people*] *to God and does righteousness* [41:33].

And He تَعَالَىٰ said, *Invite to the way of your Lord with wisdom* [16:125].

And He تَعَالَىٰ said, *and teach them the Book and wisdom* [2:129].

---

77 Al-Khaṭīb al-Baghdādī, *Sharaf aṣḥāb al-ḥadīth*, 127; see al-Zabīdī, *Itḥāf*, 1:103.

78 I.e., rising in the morning to seek knowledge is a form of *jihād* and those who do not see this are deficient in opinion and reasoning. Ibn ʿAbd al-Barr, *Jāmiʿ bayān al-ʿilm wa-faḍlih*, 159.

79 Ibn ʿAdī, *al-Kāmil*, 2:287; Ibn ʿAsākir, *Tārīkh Dimashq*, 55:366.

The [Prophetic] Reports

ON SENDING MUʿĀDH رَضِيَ ٱللَّهُ عَنْهُ TO Yemen the Messenger صَلَّى ٱللَّهُ عَلَيْهِ وَسَلَّمَ of God said, "That God should guide a single man through you is better for you than [to possess] the entire world and all that is in it."[80]

The Messenger صَلَّى ٱللَّهُ عَلَيْهِ وَسَلَّمَ of God said, "Whoever acquires a single portion of knowledge in order to teach it to people will be given the recompense of seventy trustworthy [people]."[81]

Jesus عَلَيْهِ ٱلسَّلَامُ said, "Whoever studies, works, and teaches, is considered exalted in the kingdoms of the heavens."[82]

The Prophet صَلَّى ٱللَّهُ عَلَيْهِ وَسَلَّمَ said, "On the day of judgment God تَعَالَىٰ will call to the worshipers and those who strove [in the way of God], 'Enter heaven,' to which the scholars will reply, 'Due to our knowledge they worshiped and strove [in the way of God].'" Then God عَزَّ وَجَلَّ will say, "You are like some of my angels; intercede and your intercession will be accepted." "Then they will enter heaven."[83] This [exalted standing] is for those who transferred [their] knowledge by teaching, not for those who withheld knowledge [that is] necessary and did not transfer it [to others].

And he صَلَّى ٱللَّهُ عَلَيْهِ وَسَلَّمَ said, "God تَعَالَىٰ does not divest humanity of knowledge after He has bestowed it on them. Rather it disappears with the disappearance of the scholars; each time a scholar passes away, that which he had been granted of knowledge passes away with him until there are no scholars remaining. [At this time] the people take up with ignorant leaders, who, when questioned, give judgments without knowledge; they are misguided and they misguide [others]."[84]

80 Al-Bukhārī, 3701; Muslim, 2406, spoken to ʿAlī رَضِيَ ٱللَّهُ عَنْهُ; and Ibn al-Mubārak, *Zuhd*, 1375, with this wording.

81 Al-Ḥāfiẓ al-Mundharī, *al-Targhīb wa-l-tarhīb*, 1:126, has attributed this *ḥadīth* to al-Daylamī's *Musnad al-firdaws*. See al-Zabīdī, *Itḥāf*, 1:106.

82 I.e., the implication is that one learns and performs acts based on the knowledge he gained, and teaches others. Abū Nuʿaym, *Ḥilya*, 6:93; Ibn ʿAbd al-Barr, *Jāmiʿ bayān al-ʿilm wa-faḍlih*, 791, 1216.

83 According to al-ʿIrāqī this *ḥadīth* was narrated by al-Marhabī in *al-ʿIlm* citing the narration of Muḥammad b. al-Sāʾib from Abū Ṣāliḥ from Ibn ʿAbbās; see al-Zabīdī, *Itḥāf*, 1:107.

84 Al-Bukhārī, 100; Muslim, 2673.

And he ﷺ said, "Whoever comprehends knowledge and then hides it will be fitted with a bridle of fire on the day of resurrection."[85]

And he ﷺ said, "Truly an excellent offering! Truly an excellent gift! A wise word, heard and held onto tightly, then carried to your brother Muslim and taught to him, equals a year's devotions."[86]

And he ﷺ said, "The world is cursed, cursed is all that is in it, except the remembrance (*dhikr*) of God سُبۡحَانَهُ and that which is associated with it, or the teacher, or the student."[87]

And he ﷺ said, "Indeed, God, His angels, those who dwell in the heavens and the earth, even the ant in its hill and the fish in the ocean, all bless the one who teaches the people the path to beneficence."[88]

And he ﷺ said, "No Muslim can benefit his brother better than by passing on a kind statement that reaches him."[89]

And he ﷺ said, "A good word that a believer hears and acts on and teaches [to someone else] is better than a year of worship."[90]

The Messenger ﷺ of God went out one day and saw two gatherings. In one of them [people] were calling on God عَزَّوَجَلَّ and supplicating to Him; in the second [people] were teaching the people. Thus he said, "As for these [the first group], they are petitioning God; if He wishes He will give them [what they are asking for] and if He wishes He will not. As for these [the second group], they are teaching the people; and I was sent as a teacher." Then he turned to them and sat with them.[91]

And he ﷺ said, "The guidance and knowledge that God عَزَّوَجَلَّ has sent with me may be likened to heavy rain that reaches a parcel of land on which there was a fertile garden plot. When it receives water it sprouts forth herbs and grasses in great quantity. Then there was another arid plot that collected the water, and from it God brought benefit to the people; they drank from it, and irrigated

---

85 Abū Dāwūd, 3658; al-Tirmidhī, 2649; Ibn Māja, 261.

86 Al-Ṭabarānī, *al-Muʿjam al-kabīr*, 12:43.

87 Al-Tirmidhī, 2322; Ibn Māja, 4112.

88 Al-Tirmidhī, 2685.

89 Ibn ʿAbd al-Barr, *Jāmiʿ bayān al-ʿilm wa-faḍlih*, 202.

90 Ibn al-Mubārak, *Zuhd*, 1386; a similar *ḥadīth* was previously cited from al-Ṭabarānī.

91 Ibn Māja, 229.

and planted their fields. There was also a low lying arid parcel of land that neither held water nor gave forth pasturage."[92] The first he mentioned was an example of one who put his knowledge to good use; the second was an example of one who benefits others from his knowledge; and the third was one deprived of any benefit.[93]

And he صَلَّىٰ ٱللَّٰهُ عَلَيْهِ وَسَلَّمَ said, "When a human being dies all his works come to an end except three: knowledge that others benefited from..."[94]

And he صَلَّىٰ ٱللَّٰهُ عَلَيْهِ وَسَلَّمَ said, "One who guides toward goodness is as one who has performed it.[95]

And he صَلَّىٰ ٱللَّٰهُ عَلَيْهِ وَسَلَّمَ said, "Envy is permissible in only two instances: a person to whom God has given wisdom, he rules [with it] wisely and teaches it to people, and a person on whom God has bestowed wealth, from which he spends privately and openly."[96]

And he صَلَّىٰ ٱللَّٰهُ عَلَيْهِ وَسَلَّمَ said, "The mercy of God is on my successors." It was asked, "Who are your successors?" To which he responded, "Those who bring my *sunna* to life and teach it to God's servants."[97]

The Traditions [of the Companions and Others]

ʿUmar رَضِيَ ٱللَّٰهُ عَنْهُ said, "Whoever narrates a *ḥadīth* that someone acts on will be rewarded in the same manner as the one who acted on it."[98]

---

92 Al-Bukhārī, 79; Muslim, 2282.

93 The *ḥadīth* continues: "This is an example of one who has insight in religion of God and benefits from what God sent me with, knowledge and action. And the [second] is an example of one who will not raise his head [i.e., pay attention] and accept the guidance of God that I was sent with." Al-Bukhārī, 79.

94 Muslim, 1631. The *ḥadīth* continues: ". . . recurring charity, or knowledge that others benefited from, or a pious child who prays for him [for the deceased]."

95 Al-Tirmidhī, 2670. In Muslim, 1893, with a slightly different wording.

96 Al-Bukhārī, 73; Muslim, 816. The wording in Muslim is "a man upon whom God has bestowed great wealth, and he has the authority to disperse it for the sake of the truth."

97 Al-Ramhurmuzī, *al-Muḥaddith al-fāṣil bayna al-rāwī wa-l-wāʿī*, 1; Abū Nuʿaym, *Tārīkh Iṣbahān*, 1:111; and with this wording in Ibn ʿAbd al-Barr, *Jāmiʿ bayān al-ʿilm wa-faḍlih*, 220.

98 Al-Ḥākim al-Nīsābūrī, *al-Madkhal ilā l-ṣaḥīḥ*, 87; Ibn ʿAbd al-Barr, *Jāmiʿ bayān al-ʿilm wa-faḍlih*, 256, attributed to the Prophet.

And Ibn ʿAbbās رَضِيَ ٱللَّهُ عَنْهُمَا said, "Everything, even the fish in the ocean, asks forgiveness for the one who teaches people goodness."[99]

One of the scholars said, "The scholar is included among what is between God and His creation, so he should pay attention to how he is included [in that rank]."[100]

It was narrated that Sufyān al-Thawrī رَحِمَهُ ٱللَّهُ visited [the city] of ʿAsqalān and resided there for a time, and no one asked anything of him, so he said, "Hire me a conveyance so I can leave this city. This is a city in which knowledge is dying."[101] He only made that statement out of his sincere zeal for the virtue of teaching and to preserve his knowledge.[102]

ʿAṭāʾ رَضِيَ ٱللَّهُ عَنْهُ said, "I visited Saʿīd b. al-Musayyib and found him weeping, and I asked him, "What has caused you to weep?" He replied, "There is no one seeking [knowledge] about anything from me."[103]

A certain [scholar] said, "The scholars are [like] the lights of their time, each one is a luminary of his time from whom the people of his era are enlightened."[104]

Ḥasan رَحِمَهُ ٱللَّهُ said, "Were it not for the scholars, the people would have become like beasts." He meant that through their teaching [the scholars] they bring mankind from the boundary of brutishness to the boundary of humanity.

ʿIkrima [رَحِمَهُ ٱللَّهُ] said, "There is indeed a price for this knowledge." He was asked what it was; to which he responded, "That you bestow it on one well-suited to carry it and not lose it."[105]

Yaḥyā b. Muʿādh said, "The scholars are more compassionate to the community of Muḥammad صَلَّى ٱللَّهُ عَلَيْهِ وَسَلَّمَ than their own fathers and mothers." He was asked, "How is that?" To which he responded,

---

99 Literally, the one who teaches goodness to people, everything, even the fish in the ocean [ask] forgiveness for him. Al-Dārimī, *Sunan*, 355; Ibn ʿAbd al-Barr, *Jāmiʿ bayān al-ʿilm wa-faḍlih*, 180.

100 That is, the scholar is like a conduit for humanity to become closer to God, so he should be aware of the importance of this role and the obligations that it entails because he will be questioned about it. Al-Dārimī, *Sunan*, 139; Abū Nuʿaym, *Ḥilya*, 3:153, from Muḥammad b. al-Munkadir.

101 Ibn ʿAbd al-Barr, *Jāmiʿ bayān al-ʿilm wa-faḍlih*, 1046.

102 This implies that he must teach others in order to preserve his knowledge.

103 Ibn Abī Shayba, *al-Muṣannaf*, 26943 from ʿAṭāʾ from Saʿīd b. Jubayr.

104 Ibn Baṭṭa, *al-Ibāna*, 41.

105 Al-Ramhurmuzī, *al-Muḥaddith al-fāṣil*, 575.

"Because their fathers and mothers keep them safe from the fire of this world; while they keep them safe from the fire of the hereafter."[106]

It has been related, "The beginning of knowledge is silence, then attentive listening, then memorizing, then acting [on what one has learned], then transmitting one's knowledge [to others]."[107]

It has been related, "Teach your knowledge to whoever is ignorant of it; and learn from the knowledgeable; if you do this, you will learn what you were ignorant of and you will safeguard what you learned."[108]

Muʿādh b. Jabal [رَضِيَ ٱللَّهُ عَنْهُ] said, concerning [the excellence of] teaching and seeking knowledge, and I have seen it narrated directly from the Prophet, "Pursue knowledge, for pursuing it is reverence to God, seeking it is devotion, studying it with others is glorification, searching it out is striving in the path of God, teaching it to one who lacks knowledge is charity, bestowing it freely on those worthy of it brings proximity [to God]. [Knowledge] is an intimate companion in solitude, a friend in retreat, and a guide to religion; it heartens one in ease and difficulty; it is a vizier among noble companions and a close friend among strangers; it is a guiding light on the path to heaven. God elevates people [through knowledge], making them leaders, lords, and guides who are followed on the path of excellence; they are exemplars in goodness, their traces are followed closely and their comportment is closely noted; the angels seek out intimate friendship with them, and with their wings stroke them; every [creature] of the field or the desert seeks forgiveness for them, even the fish and the sea snakes of the oceans, the wild animals of dry land and its grazing beasts, [even] the heavens and its stars. All this because knowledge is the life of the heart [protecting it] from blindness, the light of eyesight [protecting it] from darkness, and the strength of the body [sustaining it] from weakness. The servant attains through it the stations of the upright and the loftiest degrees. Reflection on it equals fasting, and studying it with others equals devotion [i.e., superogatory prayers] through the night. Through it God عَزَّوَجَلَّ is

---

106 Al-Shaʿrānī, *Ṭabaqāt*, 1:80.

107 Abū Nuʿaym, *Ḥilya*, 6:362, and he reports something similar from Muḥammad al-Ḥārithī, 8:218.

108 Ibn ʿAbd al-Barr, *Jāmiʿ bayān al-ʿilm wa-faḍlih*, 647; Ibn ʿAsākir, *Tārīkh Dimashq*, 24:344, from al-Aḥnaf.

obeyed, by it He is worshiped, by it His unity is affirmed, by it He is lauded, and by it He is approached with piety. By it family ties are maintained, and by it the lawful and unlawful are known. Knowledge is the leader, and deeds his followers. Those who will be happy are inspired by it, and those who will be miserable are kept from it."[109]

We seek God's تَعَالَىٰ most excellent outcome for all deeds.

Rational Proofs

KNOW THAT THE GOAL of this chapter is [to gain] a realization (*maʿrifa*) of the virtue of knowledge and how precious it is. However, to the degree that one does not comprehend [the meaning of] virtue in itself or realize its essential function as a key attribute of knowledge or as one among its traits, there will be no means of understanding it. For certainly anyone who aspires to know whether Zayd [for example] is a wise man or not, while he does not comprehend the meaning of wisdom and its innate attributes, has strayed from the path.

Virtue (*faḍīla*) is derived from *faḍl*, which is something in excess or extra, that is, if two things both have a shared trait and one of them is distinguished with excess [i.e., more of that trait], it is said of it, "It is superior to it" and "it has superiority over it"; in whatever manner the excess may be a facet of the perfection of that thing. As it is said, "A horse is superior to a donkey," in the sense that it shares with it the ability to carry heavy burdens, whereas [the horse] exceeds it in strength, [it can] dart forward and wheel back, in its gallop, and its handsome appearance. Thus, were it to be determined that a donkey is distinguished by a higher market price, it could not be said that it is superior because that [price] would reflect an excess [valuation] concerning the body and a diminished [value] concerning the intrinsic traits. These [valuations] have nothing to do with the perfection of [the animals' traits]. Animals are sought

109 Abū Nuʿaym, *Ḥilya*, 1:238; Ibn ʿAbd al-Barr, *Jāmiʿ bayān al-ʿilm wa-faḍlih*, 268. In the *Ḥilya* it is reported as coming from Muʿādh b. Jabal and in the *Jāmiʿ* it is attributed to the Prophet.

after for their intrinsic traits and attributes not for the [strength] of their bodies.

If you have comprehended this point, it will not be hidden from you that knowledge is virtue, if you consider it in relation to all other characteristics; just as the horse possesses virtue, if you consider it in relation to all other animals. However, the strength of its gallop is virtue for the horse, but it is not virtue in an absolute sense. Knowledge is virtue in itself and in an absolute sense without attribution [of another quality to make it excellent], for it is an attribute of the perfection of God سُبْحَانَهُ by which He ennobles the angels and prophets. Even clever horses are better than the dull-witted. It [knowledge] is virtue in an absolute sense without attribution.

Know that a valuable object that is sought after can be classified as either that which is sought for other than itself, or that which is sought for itself, or that which is sought for other than itself and for itself as well. That which is sought for itself alone is of higher value and superior to that which is sought for [something] other than itself. Among those things sought for other than themselves are dirhams and dinars, for they are both metals without essential benefits. Had not God تَعَالَىٰ made them an easy means of fulfilling needs, they and pebbles would have similar value.

An example of that which is sought for its own sake is happiness in the hereafter and the delight of of gazing at the face of God تَعَالَىٰ.[110]

That which is sought for itself and for other than itself is similar to having a healthy body. For indeed the healthy leg, for example, is sought as a facet of the body that is free of pain, on the one hand, and that is able to walk, on the other, and that [helps people in] accomplishing [their] desires and necessities.

In this respect, when you look at knowledge, you should perceive it as a delight in and of itself and [as something to be] sought after for itself, and you should find it as a means to the abode of the hereafter

---

110 It is the loftiest and noblest of the types of blessings that God bestows and gives as a reward. It is what is intended by His تَعَالَىٰ statement, *And as for those who were [destined to be] prosperous, they will be in paradise...* [11:108]. That is pure good and unadulterated virtue. It consists of four elements: subsistence without perishing, power without weakness, knowledge without ignorance, and wealth without poverty. Al-Zabīdī, *Ithāf*, 1:125.

and its delights as well as a path to proximity with God تَعَالَىٰ, for there is no means of approaching Him but through it [knowledge].

The most exalted rank with regard to humanity is eternal bliss [in the hereafter], and the most excellent of things is that which serves as a means of attaining it. One will never attain it without knowledge and action. One will only attain the incumbent actions through the knowledge of how to complete them. The foundation of bliss in this world and the next is therefore knowledge; it is thus the most excellent deed of all.

How can this not be the case, when the virtue of anything is recognized through the nobility of its fruits. You have already understood that the fruit of knowledge is proximity to the Lord of the worlds, joining the realm of the angels, and being in lofty company; this is all in the hereafter.

As for the present world, there is reputation and dignity, the authority of [governance bestowed on] kings, and the inherent respect that resides in human nature, such that even the [most] stupid Turks and the [most] ill-mannered Arabs[111] find their natural dispositions compelled to recognize the dignity of their elders because of their distinction in the extent of their beneficial knowledge gained through [years of] experience. Even beasts naturally respect humankind, for they sense the distinguishing characteristics of humankind's perfection that surpasses theirs in degree.

This virtue of knowledge is absolute. However, the levels of knowledge differ, as will be explained, and their levels of virtue, without doubt, are ranked accordingly.

As for the excellence of teaching and learning [based on what has preceded], it is a manifest affair. For if knowledge is the best of undertakings, then acquiring it is a quest for that which is most excellent, and teaching it is a means to attaining [what is] most excellent.

---

111 During al-Ghazālī's time nomadic Turks and Arabs were commonly thought to have these character traits; this statement should not be interpreted as a reflection of his beliefs on race.

Elucidation

VERILY THE GOALS SOUGHT by mankind are comprised within [the domains of] religion and [this] world. There is no organization of religion without proper organization in [this] world. The world is the cultivated field of the hereafter and the means of reaching God عَزَّوَجَلَّ for the one who takes the world as a means and a temporary dwelling place and does not take it as a permanent abode and a homeland. The affairs of this world are arranged in an orderly manner only through the efforts of mankind. Their efforts, professions, and crafts can be collectively viewed as occurring within three classes of activity.

One of them relates to the basic activities of mankind, without which there would be no permanence in the world, and they comprise four categories of occupations: agriculture for nourishment, weaving for clothing, building for dwellings, and politics for cohesiveness and social order as well as to assure mutual cooperation for the sake of security and general social well-being.

The second category relates to what is needed for the preparation of the basic crafts and in service to them. For example, blacksmithing serves agriculture and a wide array of other crafts in the preparation of their tools. Also, the carding and spinning of wool and cotton serves weaving and provides the raw material for its craft.

The third category relates to activities that are associated with the final products of the basic activities and that enhances them, such as milling and bread making for agriculture, and bleaching and tailoring for weaving.

All [three elements cited] above, in relation to the order in this world, can be likened to the individual organs and members of the human being as they relate to the entirety of his person. These are also comprised of three categories: (1) the essentials, such as the heart, liver, and brain, (2) those that support them, such as the stomach, veins, arteries, sinews, and jugular veins, and (3) those that complete and perfect them, such as the nails, fingers, and eyebrows.

The noblest of all these human activities are the most fundamental; and the noblest of these fundamentals is the discipline of governance that assures social cohesiveness and mutual well-being. For this reason, this activity demands from the one who takes on its responsibilities a level of perfection that is not demanded for the other activities. And for this reason, the one who pursues that discipline, without doubt, will employ all the other crafts and disciplines.

The discipline of governance that assures the general well-being of the people and their guidance along the straight path of salvation in this world and the next is [made up of] four degrees.

The first and most exalted is the governance of the prophets عَلَيْهِمُ السَّلَامُ, whose governance extends over the entire population, the elite and the [common] folk, [and concerns] both [their] outward [deeds] and inward [thoughts].

The second is that of the caliphs, kings, and sultans. Their authority extends over the entirety as well, the elite and the [common] folk; however, [their authority is] for outward deeds, not inner thoughts.

The third is that of the scholars who know God عَزَّوَجَلَّ and His religion, those who are the heirs of the prophets. Their realm of governance extends over the inner thoughts and attitudes of the elite. The [common] people cannot comprehend them to the point of benefiting from them, and their authority does not extend to the compulsion and prohibition of the outward actions of the [common] folk.

The fourth is the [one] who admonishes. His authority is over the inner states and attitudes of the [common] folk.

The noblest of these four [disciplines] of governance, after that of the prophets, is disseminating knowledge, providing the admonition necessary to help the people to avert objectionable and blameworthy character traits and habits, and to guide [them] to praiseworthy character traits that [lead to] felicity; all of which constitute the aim of teaching.[112]

We stressed above that teaching is the noblest of disciplines and crafts because the nobility of a discipline or an occupation is recognizable through three traits: (1) by giving consideration to

---

112 It is a noble station. It is surpassed only by prophecy, messengership, and absolute veracity. The people associated with this station have combined the disciplines of law and Sufism [lit., veracity; *ḥaqīqa*]. The utility of knowledge relates to outward knowledge while the correction and guidance of souls belongs to the scholars of realization [i.e., Sufis] who influence the inward thoughts of their adherents. Al-Zabīdī, *Itḥāf*, 1:127.

the innate nature by which cognizance of the discipline is attained, such as the excellence of the rational sciences over that obtained by linguistics; this is so because wisdom is grasped by the intellect while language is grasped by hearing, and the intellect is more noble than hearing; (2) by considering the overall benefit provided, such as the superiority of agriculture over the goldsmith's craft; and (3) by giving consideration to the raw material of the particular occupation; the goldsmith's craft is superior to tanning, for example, because the material of one of them is gold and the material of the other is the hide of a dead animal.

It is therefore no secret that the Islamic disciplines—the understanding of the path [to] the hereafter—are apprehended only through the perfection of reason and the clarity of the acumen. The intellect is the noblest attribute a human being possesses, as we shall elucidate [in chapter 7], for through it he agrees to take on God's تَعَالَىٰ trust[113] and by it he achieves proximity to God سُبْحَانَهُ [in the hereafter].

Where the general benefit is concerned, no one doubts it [i.e., knowledge], for its benefit and fruit is eternal bliss in the hereafter.

As far as the nobility of material is concerned, how could it be hidden, when the teacher deals with the hearts and souls of humanity? The noblest creature on earth is the human being and the noblest aspect of the essential substance of a human being is the heart. The teacher is engaged in its perfection, enhancement, purification, and [with] bringing it into proximity with God عَزَّوَجَلَّ.

Thus, teaching knowledge is, from one point of view, an aspect of worship of God تَعَالَىٰ, and from another, it is an aspect of vicegerency [of people for] God تَعَالَىٰ. In fact it is the most exalted [kind of] vicegerency, because God تَعَالَىٰ has opened the heart of the scholar to the knowledge that is His most intimate attribute. Thus, the scholar is like the trusted keeper of His most precious treasures, even more, he is permitted to spend it on anyone in need.

What rank could be more exalted than that of being a servant who is an intermediary between his Lord سُبْحَانَهُ and His creatures in

113 This statement refers to the following verse: *Indeed, we offered the Trust to the heavens and the earth and the mountains, and they declined to bear it and feared it; but man [undertook to] bear it. Indeed, he was unjust and ignorant* [33:72].

drawing them closer to God and leading them to the heavenly abode.

May God, in His beneficence, make us among them;
and may the peace and blessings
of God be upon
every chosen
servant.

2

On praiseworthy knowledge and blameworthy knowledge, their categories and rulings, including an elucidation of what is compulsory for each individual and what is compulsory for the community as a whole, and the elucidation of the extent to which the fields of theology and jurisprudence are parts of the Islamic disciplines, and the excellence of the knowledge of the hereafter.

An Elucidation of Knowledge that is Compulsory for each Individual

THE MESSENGER ﷺ OF GOD SAID, "Seeking knowledge is an obligation for every Muslim."[1]

He ﷺ also said, "Seek knowledge even in China."[2]

People have differed about the knowledge that every Muslim is obliged to acquire; on this issue they have become divided into over twenty factions. We will not take the time to delve into all the details but rather will present the result, which is that each faction has made obligatory that knowledge in which they are engaged.

1 Ibn Māja, 224.

2 Abū Nuʿaym, *Ḥilya*, 3:192.

The theologians [say] it [the knowledge that is obligatory] is the knowledge of dialectical theology (*ʿilm al-kalām*); for through it one arrives at an understanding of the principle of [God's] unity and comes to know the essence of God سُبْحَانَهُ and His attributes.

The jurists [say] it is the knowledge of jurisprudence (*fiqh*); for through it you come to understand the acts of worship, the permitted and forbidden, and the conduct that is forbidden or permitted. They concerned themselves in these areas based on what most people needed, rather than on rare circumstances.

The exegetes of the Qurʾān and the narrators of *ḥadīth* [say] that it is the knowledge of the Book and the *sunna*; for through them one reaches all levels of knowledge.[3]

The Sufis [say] that the intent of it is this knowledge [of Sufism].[4] Thus some of them say, "It is the servant's knowledge of his own inward state and his station before God عَزَّوَجَلَّ."[5] Others have said, "It is the knowledge of sincerity, the defects of the souls, and the ability to distinguish the inspiration of an angel from the inspiration of a demon."[6] Others have said, "It is esoteric knowledge that is incumbent upon the elite among them [i.e., the scholars of that knowledge], they are the people of that [knowledge]."[7]

They have changed the general meaning [of obligatory for every Muslim] from its general sense.

Abū Ṭālib al-Makkī said, "The knowledge [that is obligatory] is knowledge of that which is comprised in the *ḥadīth* that speaks

---

3 These are two statements. The exegetes say it is the knowledge of the book of God, and the narrators of *ḥadīth* say it is the knowledge of the *sunna*.

4 That is, it is the knowledge of *taṣawwuf*. Then he explains their statements.

5 Abū Ṭālib al-Makkī, *Qūt al-qulūb*, 1:129, attributed this saying to Sahl al-Tustarī (203–283/818–896) and then cited all the sayings cited by Imām al-Ghazālī, some with attribution, and some without.

6 It is to distinguish between the idea of the spirit and the whispering of the soul, and between the certainty of knowledge and the cankerworms of the intellect (lit. trans. of *qawādiḥ al-ʿaql*). In this way, one can discern judgments. For these people, this is an obligation. This is the school of Mālik b. Dīnār, Farqad al-Sabakhī (?), ʿAbd al-Wāḥid b. Zayd, and their ascetic followers. Their teacher was Ḥasan al-Baṣrī, who spoke of these things and from whom knowledge of the heart [and its treatment] has been transmitted. Abū Ṭālib al-Makkī, *Qūt al-qulūb*, 1:129.

7 The wording of the narration in Abū Nuʿaym, *Ḥilya*, 6:95, is "acquire certainty." Certainty of knowledge is not incumbent except for the people of certainty. Al-Zabīdī, *Itḥāf*, 1:130.

of the foundations of Islam, which is his [i.e., the Messenger of God's] ﷺ saying, "Islam was built upon five foundations. . ."[8] Because these five are obligatory, the knowledge of the manner in which they are accomplished is obligatory, as is the extent of the obligation.

It is essential that the one seeking to grasp this be most certain and have no doubt about what we mention here. It is that knowledge, as we have presented it in the introduction of this book, can be divided into knowledge of one's conduct (*muʿāmalāt*) [with people and God] and knowledge of unveiling (*mukāshafa*) [of the unseen realm]; the sole objective intended [here, however] is knowledge of one's conduct [with people and God].[9]

The conduct that the adult servant of sound mind is responsible for is of three categories: creed, acts, and [acts] to abstain from.

Therefore, should a person of sound mind reach adulthood either by reaching puberty or attaining an age of maturity, then, for example, in the early morning, the first obligation incumbent on him is to learn the two statements of the testimony of faith (*shahāda*) and understand their meaning; this being, "There is no god but God and Muḥammad is His Messenger." It is not incumbent on him to ascertain the illumination of this for himself by means of insight, inquiry, or the scrutiny of proofs; rather, it is sufficient for him to affirm the truth of this and believe it decisively, with no feeling of doubt or anxiety for himself. This may be attained on the authority of custom and oral tradition alone, with neither investigation nor proofs, since the Messenger of God ﷺ was satisfied with the faith of the Bedouin through personal avowal of its truth and affirmation, without studying proofs.[10]

Upon accomplishing this he has fulfilled the obligation required of him at that time, as the knowledge that was obligatory on him

---

8 Al-Bukhārī, 8, Muslim, 16.

9 Knowledge of one's conduct with people and God, as the translation implies, comprises both the level of the heart and the physical body. On the level of the heart, it addresses inward conduct, while physically it addresses outward comportment, including the rites and rituals of Islam and one's conduct with people and God, which is of a more social nature. See al-Zabīdī, *Itḥāf*, 1:135.

10 See the *ḥadīth* of the conversion of Ḍamān b. Thaʿalba رضي الله عنه in al-Bukhārī, 63, and other narrations; also see al-Ghazālī, *al-Iqtiṣād*, 283.

at that moment was to learn and comprehend the two statements [of faith]. Beyond that there is nothing binding upon him at that moment; the proof being that should he die at that moment, he would have died obedient to God عَزَّوَجَلَّ, not disobedient. Any other obligations become incumbent only on the occurrence of contingent circumstances. They are not compulsory in the case of every individual; on the contrary one can conceive that they are not binding at all on some people.

These contingent circumstances include performing certain acts, abandoning others, or maintaining [the correct] creed.

As to performing certain acts, let us suppose that he [the person who reached maturity and learned the *shahāda*] lives past the early morning to the time of the noon prayer (*ẓuhr*). With the entrance of the time of the noon prayer it becomes obligatory on him to learn [about] ablutions and the manner of prayer (*ṣalāt*). Now, if he were in good health, and inasmuch as he would have waited until the passage of the sun from its meridian, he would not be capable of fully learning and performing [the prayer] in its time. Rather, the time would pass as he occupied himself with learning. It is therefore far-fetched to say, "We can assume his longevity, it is therefore obligatory on him to put learning before the time of the contingent act." One might say as well, "The obligatory nature of learning, which is a condition for a contingent act, comes after the obligation of the act itself; it is therefore not obligatory before the sun moves beyond its meridian." This process applies to the remaining prayers.

Then, should he live until the month of Ramaḍān, it would become obligatory for him to learn the manner of fasting; that is, he must know that it extends from early dawn until sunset, that making the intention to fast is obligatory, that abstaining from eating, drinking, and intercourse [is obligatory], and that this continues until the new moon [of Shawāl] is sighted.

Then, should he acquire wealth, or should he have had wealth upon attaining maturity, it would be obligatory for him to learn his obligations with regard to *zakāt*; although this would not become mandatory immediately. It would become mandatory a year from the time he had become a Muslim. If he only owned camels [for example], it would not be required of him to learn the guidelines for *zakāt* regarding sheep; and so on for all the other classifications [of *zakāt*].

Then, should the months of the pilgrimage arrive, he need not hasten to acquire knowledge of it. Since its accomplishment takes place over a period of time, there is no immediate need to [learn about it]. But it is incumbent upon the scholars of Islam to inform him that the pilgrimage is an individual obligation in Islam, with a flexible timeframe, upon everyone who possesses sufficient provisions and transportation [for the journey], if he owns property.[11] Then should he [the Muslim] in fact possess both [provisions and transportation] he [should] be determined to perform [the pilgrimage] immediately, and it becomes obligatory, when he makes the commitment, to learn the manner of making the pilgrimage. It is only obligatory, however, for him to learn the fundamental elements of the pilgrimage and its obligations, not its supererogatory elements. This is true because accomplishing them is supererogatory, thus learning them is also supererogatory; it is not a personal obligation.

With regard to the topic of the unlawfulness of neglecting [i.e., the requirement] to apprise people that the pilgrimage is obligatory whenever the individual is able to perform it, there are varying points of view that are more suitably discussed in the field of jurisprudence.

This step by step approach applies to acquiring knowledge of all the actions that are binding upon every Muslim (*farḍ ʿayn*).

As to the [acts] to abstain from, it is obligatory to acquire the knowledge thereof according to new events as they unfold. This varies as well, according to each individual's circumstances. Thus it is not obligatory upon someone who cannot speak to learn what is prohibited in speech, nor for the blind to learn what is unlawful to gaze at with one's eyes, nor for the Bedouin to learn [about] which houses it is unlawful[12] to reside in. All these prohibitions apply solely according to the dictates of changing conditions; so when

11 This means that beyond the necessary needs of the journey he also possesses a house and other basic necessities as well as the ability to support his family and himself for the duration of his journey. Al-Zabīdī, *Itḥāf*, 1:140.

12 In most manuscripts this appears as "unlawful"; in other manuscripts it appears as "lawful" (*mā yaḥillu*). Al-Ghazālī is making the point that just as blind men do not need to learn what one with sight must avert his gaze from, so the Bedouin, who

one is sure that such an obligation does not apply to him, it is not obligatory to acquire knowledge thereof.

For it is obligatory for him to be apprised of anything that may relate to him [in the domain of prohibited matters]. For example, if he were wearing silk clothing upon embracing Islam, or residing in an unlawfully obtained property, or gazing at a woman he could marry,[13] it is obligatory for him to be made aware of these [prohibitions]. But that which does not relate to his [present] circumstances, but which he may soon encounter, such as food and drink, then it is obligatory to learn of it. Hence, should he find himself in a land where drinking intoxicants and eating pork is the habit of the people, it is obligatory [for him] to learn this and to be made aware of it [i.e., the unlawful nature of their consumption]. He is required to learn about whatever he must know.

As for the creed and actions of the heart, knowledge of them is obligatory in accordance with [one's] thoughts. For example, should doubt arise in him concerning the meanings of the two testimonies of faith, it would be obligatory for him to learn that which permits him to efface all doubt. If he dies, however, having had no such thought, he would still have died in Islam according to the consensus [of the scholars], even though he had not learned that the word of God سُبۡحَانَهُ is pre-eternal, and He is perceivable, and He, most high, is not a locus for temporal attributes and events, as well as the other [issues] of creed.

However, these passing thoughts that make learning the articles of creed a necessity arise naturally and sometimes they arise from hearing other people in [his] land [speak of them].

Therefore, should he reside in a region in which innovation (*bidʿa*) has become pervasive and people openly discuss heretical ideas, it is appropriate that he be protected, upon reaching puberty, from these through instruction in the truth [where it applies in these matters]. For, if he submitted to false [doctrines] it would be obligatory to cleanse his heart of them. That is likely to be achieved only with difficulty; for example, if he were a Muslim merchant in

---

do not live in houses, do not need to learn the jurisprudence regarding houses (i.e., buying, renting, occupying abandoned properties, etc.).

13 Lit., not forbidden to marry (*maḥram*).

a region in which usury had become a pervasive practice, it would be obligatory for him to learn to protect himself from [transactions involving] usury.

This then is the truth about knowledge that is an individual obligation; meaning knowledge of how to perform an obligatory action. Whoever then knows the obligatory acts and the times in which they are incumbent has acquired the knowledge that is obligatory.

This also includes that which the Sufis have mentioned concerning [gaining] the insights necessary to differentiate thoughts from the enemy [Satan] from inspirations from angels; but this is only for those who have embarked upon it [the Sufi path]. But since people are, inclined, overwhelmingly, toward iniquity, pretension, and envy, it is therefore incumbent that they gain a working knowledge, to the degree necessary, from the [books in the] Quarter of Perils.[14] How could this not be incumbent upon a person when [the Messenger of God] صَلَّىٰ ٱللَّهُ عَلَيْهِ وَسَلَّمَ has said, "There are three destructive elements [in the human soul]: succumbing to avarice, following [one's] passions, and holding oneself in high esteem...."[15]

No human being is completely free of these traits. The remainder of the blameworthy conditions of the heart that we will mention, such as ostentatious pride and conceit and their sister traits, all derive from these three blameworthy [character] traits. Their elimination is an individual obligation that is impossible [to accomplish] without recognizing their boundaries, their causes, their symptoms, and their remedies. For whoever does not recognize evil will surely fall victim to it. The remedy [of any illness] is to counter its cause with its opposite; how would this be possible without a recognition of its cause and effect? The majority of that which we have called attention to in the Quarter of Perils is among the individual obligations, though they have been discarded by the majority of people who spend their time in that which is not beneficial [to them].

It is immediately obligatory to instruct him, if he has not converted from another faith, in the belief in heaven and the fire, and the day of gathering, and the resurrection; [he should be instructed] until

---

14 The Quarter of Perils, books 21 to 30.

15 Al-Ṭabarānī, *al-Muʿjam al-awsaṭ*, 5448; Abū Nuʿaym, *Ḥilya*, 2:343; and al-Bayhaqī, *Shuʿab al-īmān*, 731.

he reaches faith and can affirm the truth thereof, for this is how one completes the two statements of faith. For after affirming the truth of his [Muḥammad, صَلَّى ٱللَّٰهُ عَلَيْهِ وَسَلَّمَ] being a messenger [sent by God], it is obligatory to comprehend the message that he brought; which is, whoever obeys God and His messenger will be in paradise and whoever disobeys Him will abide in the fire.

When you have become aware of this step by step [process], you will know that this is the path of certainty in this matter and realize that each servant in the course of his states—day and night—will always be subject to the varying circumstances that affect his acts of worship and mutual conduct, each [of which] brings with it renewed obligations. It is thus necessary to ask about each singular incident as it befalls him, just as it is necessary to immediately learn and comprehend those events that he expects to occur in the near future.

Therefore it is clear that when he [Muḥammad, صَلَّى ٱللَّٰهُ عَلَيْهِ وَسَلَّمَ], used the term the knowledge (*al-ʿilm*), with the definite article (*al-*), in his statement "Seeking *the* knowledge is obligatory upon every Muslim,"[16] he meant the knowledge that must be applied practically and which is recognized as obligatory on every Muslim. The nature of the gradual process [of acquiring knowledge] at the time it becomes obligatory has been made clear. And God knows best.

An Elucidation of the Knowledge that is a Communal Obligation

KNOW THAT THE OBLIGATORY nature of an action is only distinguished from another action through the varying classifications of the disciplines. The disciplines that are associated with obligation that we are concerned with here are divided into those that are derived from the law and those that are not.

I intend by [those disciplines] "derived from the law" to be those communicated by the prophets عَلَيْهِمُ ٱلسَّلَامُ, not those derived from the intellect, such as mathematics, nor from experiment, such as medicine, nor from hearing, such as language.

16 Reported by Ibn Māja, 224.

The disciplines that are not derived from the law can be separated into [those that are] praiseworthy, [those that are] blameworthy, and those that are neutral.

As for the praiseworthy, such as [the disciplines of] medicine and mathematics, they are associated with worldly benefit, and that category is divided into those that become a communal obligation and those that are of great merit [to practice or learn] but are not an obligation.

Communal obligations include every form of knowledge that is indispensable to the establishment of the affairs of this world, [and include disciplines] such as medicine, which is necessary for the preservation of healthy bodies; and mathematics, which is necessary for [financial] transactions and the division of wealth in which wills and inheritance and other needs are involved. Should a region be without someone who practices these disciplines, the people of that region will fall into straightened circumstances; but should there be [at least] one individual established [in that discipline], it would suffice and the obligatory nature of [having someone knowledgeable in that discipline] would be lifted from the remainder of the community.

One should not be astonished by our saying, "Medicine and mathematics are among the obligations of the community." For the foundational crafts are also communal obligations, such as agriculture, the manufacture of cloth [and tailoring], and governance, even cupping. For were a region to be void of one who practices cupping, devastation would overtake its residents, and they would become anxious at being exposed to this devastation. For He who sent down the affliction sent down the remedy, provided instructions for its application, and provided the means to practice it. It is therefore forbidden to expose oneself to devastation by neglecting it.

With regard to what is considered virtuous though not obligatory, there is the meticulous study of the intricacies of mathematics, the niceties[17] of medicine, and other fields that can be dispensed with, however, any [field] can become beneficial with [one's] increased expertise in accordance with the need for it.

---

17 The word al-Ghazālī uses here is *ḥaqāʾiq*, usually translated as "realities." In this case, it means details beyond the essentials.

Concerning blameworthy [disciplines], there is the practice of magic and the making of talismans,[18] as well as legerdemain and deception.

Neutral practices include the knowledge of poetry that is free of caprice and the narration of oral histories of people and similar occupations.

With regard to the disciplines derived from the law, which is the aim of this explanation, they are all laudable pursuits, though at times confusion arises regarding what is thought to be the law but is actually reproachable. Therefore they [the disciplines] are also divided into praiseworthy and blameworthy.

As for those [disciplines] that are praiseworthy, they are the fundamentals, the branches (*furūʿ*), the preliminary [aspects] and the supplemental [branches of knowledge]. These are the four categories.

The first category is the fundamentals (*uṣūl*), which are four in number: The Book of God عَزَّوَجَلَّ, the *sunna* of His Messenger صَلَّىٱللَّهُعَلَيْهِوَسَلَّمَ, the general consensus of the community (*umma*), and the traditions of the Companions.

The consensus [of the community] is among the fundamental sources in that it indicates the *sunna*; it is thus a fundamental [aspect of] a secondary level. Likewise are the traditions of the Companions, for they also indicate the *sunna* because the Companions رَضِيَٱللَّهُعَنْهُمْ observed the inspiration and revelation [of the Qurʾān] and grasped through direct association the states which those who were not present could not perceive. Perhaps expression cannot encompass that which can be comprehended through direct association. From this aspect then, the scholars chose to follow their example and hold steadfast to their traditions, but that occurs under specific conditions and circumstances according to the followers [of these traditions]. The clarification of this is not, however, suitable for the topic under discussion.

The second category is the [subsidiary] branches [of knowledge], which comprise what has been deduced from the fundamental sources, not literally, but with meanings comprehended through

---

18 Talisman (*ṭilasm*, or *ṭillasm*, pl. *ṭilasmāt*) refers to what is secret and hidden, or knowledge of the formation of celestial forces and their manipulation through earthly objects.

reason; [when] comprehension is expanded [in this way] it provides a greater grasp of the stated term. For example, one can understand from his ﷺ statement, "Let not the judge pass judgment while he is angry";[19] that he should not pass judgment while retaining urine, or hungry, or in pain from an illness.

This category is comprised of two subcategories: one of them is involved with the public good in [this] world, and it is comprised of the pursuit of jurisprudence. Those who are accountable for it are the jurists, and they are the scholars of [this] world.

The second subcategory is involved with [acts] beneficial for the hereafter. It is the knowledge of the states of the heart and its inner attitudes—both the praiseworthy and blameworthy, and of all that is pleasing to God تَعَالَىٰ and all that is displeasing. The latter half of present work, the *Iḥyāʾ ʿulūm al-dīn* [The Revival of Religious Sciences], encompasses this category. This category also includes the knowledge that radiates from the heart to the limbs of the body in their worship and customs; this is what comprises the first half of this book.

The third category [that concerns] the preliminary aspects [of knowledge] provides the necessary tools [for understanding the essential disciplines], such as the discipline of [the Arabic] language and grammar. They are tools that facilitate the knowledge of the Book of God سُبْحَانَهُ and the *sunna* of the Messenger of God ﷺ. Language and grammar are not in and of themselves among the disciplines derived from the law, though the nature of the law necessitates delving into them, for this law was brought in the language of the Arabs, and every law comes through a language, thus the learning of that language becomes an essential tool.

Among the tools that serve the other disciplines are writing [and calligraphy], except that which is not absolutely necessary, as the Messenger ﷺ of God himself was unlettered. And though one might imagine [that some people have] the capability to memorize everything [they] have heard, and thus not need writing, generally this is not the case, because most people are unable [to memorize everything they have heard].

19 Al-Bukhārī, 7158, Muslim, 1717.

The fourth category is the supplementary disciplines, which refer to the knowledge of the Qurʾān. It is divided into that which directly relates to oral expression, such as the disciplines of the recitations and phonetics, and that which relate to meaning, such as Qurʾānic commentary, for meaning also relies on oral transmission, as language alone is inadequate as a source. Another aspect [of the Qurʾānic disciplines] concerns the judgments, such as understanding the verses that abrogate and [those] that are abrogated, those of a general and specific nature, textual and outward meaning, and finally the manner of employing certain verses to elucidate and explain others; and this is the discipline that is known as the principles of jurisprudence (*uṣūl al-fiqh*), which includes the *sunna* within its domain as well.

Where the supplementary [disciplines] engage the oral traditions from the Messenger of God and his Companions there is the discipline of the narrators of *ḥadīth*, their names, and the names and character traits of the Companions. Then there is the discipline of determining the rectitude of the narrators and their individual circumstances in order to differentiate the strong narrators from the weak;[20] and the knowledge of the dates of narrators in order to differentiate between *ḥadīth*s narrated without a Companion as a final narrator and [those narrated with] a complete chain of transmission (*musnad*); and it also includes anything related to these [disciplines].

These are the disciplines "derived from the law," and they are all praiseworthy pursuits; in fact they all fall under the category of knowledge that is a communal obligation.

Should you inquire, "Why have you included jurisprudence among the worldly pursuits and the jurists among the scholars of worldly pursuits?

Know that God عَزَّوَجَلَّ brought Adam عَلَيْهِ ٱلسَّلَامُ forth from the soil of the earth, and his descendants out of the essence of clay [Q. 23:12] and from a seminal fluid [Q. 86:6], then from the loins to the wombs, and from the womb to [this] world, then to the grave, then to judgment, and from there to heaven or the fire. This is their inception, their end, and the path they travel [in this world].

20 Here strength and weakness refer to the accuracy of the transmission of *ḥadīths*.

He created the world as provision for the journey to the future abode so that people can obtain from it suitable sustenance for their journey. Should they obtain it with justice, disputation [over sustenance] would cease and there would be no need of jurists. However, people [tend to] obtain it [i.e., sustenance] through desires that produce conflict. Thus the need arises for a ruler to govern them, and the ruler needs a law by which to govern.

The jurist therefore must be knowledgeable of the law of governance and the means of mediation between people when desires cause contention between them. The jurist must be the ruler's teacher and guide on the path of governance and control of the people, in order to set right their affairs in this world.

I swear, [this discipline, i.e., *fiqh*] is also related to religion, though it is not in and of itself [religion], rather it mediates worldly pursuits; for the world is the sown field of the hereafter, and religion is only perfected through the world. Worldly dominion and religion are twins. Religion is the principle, and the sultan is the protector; that which has no foundation will soon be razed, and that which lacks a protector is lost. There is no dominion of the worldly realm or regulation without legitimate authority,[21] and the means of regulating disputes is through jurisprudence.

And while governing people through legitimate authority is not an Islamic discipline of the first degree, it supports [those principles] without which religion cannot be practiced completely. Similarly, recognizing the methods of good governance [is necessary for religion]. Thus it is well known that the pilgrimage can only be completed by employing an armed escort to protect [the pilgrims] from the Bedouin along the pilgrimage path. However, the pilgrimage is one thing, while traveling the path to the pilgrimage is a second thing. Organizing the armed escort to allow the pilgrimage to be completed is a third thing, and the knowledge of the means of

---

21 God has shown mercy to Imām ʿAbdallāh b. al-Mubārak when he said in verse in his *Dīwān*, 66:

> God has removed all difficulty through the sultan
> From our religion, as a mercy from Him and pleasure.
>
> Were it not for the *imāms*, the paths would not be safe for us
> And the weak among us would be robbed by the strong among us.

armed defense, the use of ploys and intrigue, and [the applicable] conventions is a fourth. In summary, the practice of jurisprudence is the mastery of the various means of governance and safeguarding [the community] from harm.

A statement that is reported as a legitimate *ḥadīth* indicates that: "There are only three [types of people] who should give a legal opinion: a commander, one under orders, or one [who assumes] responsibility (*mutakallif*)."[22]

The commanders are the leaders, and they were [originally] those who gave rulings. Those under orders were their representatives, while the *mutakallif* is neither of these two. He takes upon himself that obligation though there is no need. The Companions رَضِيَ ٱللَّهُ عَنْهُمْ were wary of offering a ruling, to the point that each of them would direct [the questioner] to another Companion. They were not wary, however, when they were asked about knowledge pertaining to the Qurʾān or the path of the hereafter. In some of the narrations [of the aforementioned *ḥadīth*], in place of *mutakallif*, [the term] *murāʾī* [one seeking recognition] occurs;[23] for whoever assumes the grave responsibility of issuing legal opinions, while he has not been appointed [and thus he is not doing it] out of necessity, seeks only status and wealth.[24]

If one were to say, "This is correct if you are referring to judgments dealing with penalties, [reparation for] wounds, monetary compensation, and mediation of disputes; but it is not correct in reference to the Quarter of Worship (*rubʿ al-ʿibādāt*) that deals with fasting and the prayer or what is included in the Quarter of Customs (*rubʿ al-ʿādāt*) in the section on conduct that elucidates the lawful (*ḥalāl*) and the forbidden (*ḥarām*)."

---

22 This is in Abū Ṭālib al-Makkī, *Qūt al-qulūb*, 1:131, in which he states, "We have reported it in *musnad* form." Something similar is reported by Aḥmad b. Ḥanbal, *al-Musnad*, 6:22, and al-Ṭabarānī, *al-Muʿjam al-kabīr*, 18:76, which begins with "No one should explain traditions (or preach) except the commander..." And it has other paths of narration.

23 Ibn Māja, 3753, Abū Dāwūd, 3665; though the initial wording of the narrations of Aḥmad b. Ḥanbal and al-Ṭabarānī are similar.

24 That is, those who have been appointed and issue legal opinions because they are required to should do, but anyone else is seeking status and wealth.

Know that the jurist discusses three issues [that are] closely related to actions for the hereafter. These are Islam [itself], the prayer (*ṣalāt*), and the lawful and the forbidden. Therefore, if you ponder the ultimate aims of the jurist, you will know that he does not go beyond the boundaries of [this] world to [address] the hereafter. If you recognize this as it pertains to these three matters, it will become more apparent in other matters.

As for Islam, the jurist speaks of that which renders it sound and that which corrupts it, and of its conditions, he takes into account only the [affirmation of the] tongue. As for the heart, it is beyond the mandated authority of the jurist. For the Messenger of God صَلَّىٱللَّهُعَلَيۡهِوَسَلَّمَ withdrew it from [the mandate of] those who wield swords and govern when he stated, "Have you split open his heart?"[25] This refers to the one who killed a man who had pronounced the testimony of faith [just before his death], and gave the excuse that he had only spoken such out of fear of the sword. Thus, the jurist determines the soundness of one's Islam beneath the shadow of swords, knowing that the sword will not reveal doubtful matters to him or lift from his heart the curtains of ignorance and confusion. However, he is the advisor of the one who wields the sword, for the sword extends over his neck and the hand extends over his wealth. This utterance by the tongue protects his blood and wealth as long as he has a blood and wealth. That is in [this] world, and for this reason he [the Messenger of God صَلَّىٱللَّهُعَلَيۡهِوَسَلَّمَ] stated, "I have been commanded to wage war on people until they say, 'There is no god but God.' When they have said this, they have preserved their blood and wealth from me."[26] The result of that [testimony of faith] impacts blood and wealth [alone].

As for the hereafter, statements [of faith] will be of no benefit there; only the illumination, inner secrets, and sincerity of the heart will avail. And these are not aspects in the domain of jurisprudence. Should a jurist delve into them, it would be as if he delved into theology or medicine, which would both be beyond the scope of his discipline.

---

25 Al-Bukhārī, 4269; Muslim, 96, "he said this to" Usāma b. Zayd رَضِيَٱللَّهُعَنۡهُ.

26 Al-Bukhārī, 25; Muslim, 21; the wording is from Muslim.

As to the prayer (*ṣalāt*), the jurist rules on that which renders it sound when [the person] performing the formal ritual has conformed to the outward prerequisites, even though he may be oblivious throughout his entire prayer, from beginning to end, and [he may] be preoccupied with thinking about the finances of his affairs in the market, except at the time of the initial affirmation of "God is Great." This prayer will have no benefit in the hereafter in the same manner that a statement concerning Islam made only with the tongue carries no benefit. However, the jurist rules on the correct performance of the action, that is, if a person's performance of the prayer complies with the external requirements of the act. If it does, then he is protected from execution or corporal punishment. Whereas the reverence [before God] and the presence of the heart that constitutes the conduct that leads to the hereafter and renders outward acts beneficial is in no manner the domain of the jurist; and were he to delve into it, it would be outside his area of expertise.

As to the *zakāt*,[27] the jurist is concerned with that which clearly defines [the circumstances] in which a sultan can demand it [i.e., the payment of *zakāt*]. If one should refuse to pay it and the sultan seizes it by force, [the jurist] would judge that [the person's] liability was absolved.

It was related that the judge Abū Yūsuf used to endow his wealth to his wife at the end of the annual cycle when his *zakāt* was due and then request that she donate her wealth as a gift to him in order to avoid paying the *zakāt*. On hearing this, Abū Ḥanīfa رَحِمَهُ ٱللَّٰهُ said, "That is from his juridical judgment." [Imām al-Ghazālī writes] He spoke the truth, for that is part of worldly jurisprudence. However, its detriment in the hereafter is much greater than any misdeed; the likes of this knowledge is detrimental.

As for the permitted and the prohibited, [it is clear that] scrupulous abstinence from the prohibited is an aspect of religion. However, there are four degrees of abstinence.

The first [type of abstinence] is that which imposes a condition on the credibility of testimony. A person [who] lacks this abstinence [from the unlawful, i.e., he does things that are unlawful] would be

27 This is associated with the prayer, which makes it part of the second category (after Islam) that is indicated by the author رَحِمَهُ ٱللَّٰهُ.

excluded from giving testimony, obtaining a judgeship, or holding a position of authority; and it [this abstinence] constitutes guarding oneself against unlawful things that are outwardly evident.

The second type is the abstinence of the righteous. It is to preserve oneself from doubtful matters that may possibly be [lawful or unlawful]. He [the Messenger of God ﷺ] said, "Abandon that which provokes doubt in you for that which does not provoke doubt."[28] He said as well, "Sin slices into hearts."[29]

The third type is the abstinence of the pious; this is to forego what is undoubtedly lawful if one fears it could lead to the unlawful. He [the Messenger of God ﷺ] said, "No one is pious until he abstains from what is not objectionable out of fear of what is objectionable."[30] Examples of this would be to avoid talking about people's circumstances out of fear of being drawn into slander and to abstain from indulging desires out of fear of stirring up impulsive and reckless behavior that might tempt one to commit forbidden acts.[31]

The fourth type is the abstinence of the veracious. It is turning away from what is other than God ﷺ out of fear of being diverted for even one moment in life toward something that does not benefit [one] by drawing him nearer to God تَعَالَىٰ even though one knows and realizes that it does not lead to the prohibited.

All these degrees are beyond the scope of the jurist, except the first degree, which is abstention from anything that would invalidate one's legal testimony, ability to be a judge, or [anything

---

28 Al-Tirmidhī, 2518; al-Nisāʾī, *al-Sunan al-kubrā*, 5201.

29 Al-Ṭabarānī, *al-Muʿjam al-kabīr*, 9:149; al-Bayhaqī, *Shuʿab al-īmān*, 6892. This narration is traced back to ʿAbdallāh b. Masʿūd رَضِيَ ٱللَّهُ عَنْهُ. The Arabic term "*ḥawāzz*" (slices into) is the plural of "*ḥāzza*." To say "slices into hearts" (*ḥawāzz al-qulūb*) is to refer to those affairs that cut into and leave a mark on them. That is, they have an influence like the influence of cutting into a thing. Whenever acts of disobedience occur to them, then tranquility is lost to them. It is reported by Shimr (?) that the term is "*ḥawwāz*" which would mean that sin possesses hearts, controls them, and overwhelms them. It is also reported as "*ḥazzāz*" which is the intensive active participle of "*ḥazz*" (cutting). In a different edition of the *Iḥyāʾ* it has this spelling.

30 Al-Tirmidhī, 2451; Ibn Māja, 4215.

31 Recklessness (*al-baṭar*) is less severe than impulsiveness (*nashāṭ*) because it is a startled mindset that afflicts a person, turning the permissible bounty to evil, not establishing it in its rightful use, and diverting it from its true purpose. Al-Zabīdī, *Itḥāf*, 1:159.

that] undermines one's overall integrity. This being established, however, does not eliminate the sin in the hereafter. The Messenger of God ﷺ said to Wābiṣa, "Seek counsel from your heart, even though they counsel you, even though they counsel you, even though they counsel you."[32] The jurist does not speak of the predilections of hearts or the manner of dealing with them, rather he speaks only of that which undermines integrity.

Thus, the regard of the jurist is wholly oriented toward the worldly aspects of life that are the basis of the path to the hereafter. His speaking of sin, the attributes of the heart, or the tenets of the hereafter would enter his discourse as an intrusion in the same way any aspect of medicine, mathematics, astronomy, or theology would enter his discourse [as an intrusion]. It is similar to wisdom entering into the fields of grammar and poetry.

Sufyān al-Thawrī, an eminent scholar of exoteric knowledge (*ʿilm al-ẓāhir*), commented, "Seeking this [knowledge of *fiqh*] is not provision for the journey to the hereafter."[33] How could this be, while it is agreed upon that the eminence of knowledge is its performance. How could one suppose that it is the knowledge of oaths in matters of adultery, divorce by repudiation, forward buying in commercial dealings, rental agreements, or money changing and barter? Whoever learns these matters in order to attain proximity to God, most high, by practicing them is insane. Acts of obedience are those in which the heart and limbs act [in concert], and eminence is the knowledge of these acts.

If you were to ask: Why have you equated jurisprudence to medicine? Medicine relates to the worldly life, which is the well-being of the physical body, while *fiqh* relates to it as well as to the well-being of religion. This equivalence is contrary to the consensus of the Muslim community.

Know that [this] equivalence is not an inherent attribute; rather there is a difference between them, for jurisprudence is a more noble pursuit for three reasons.

---

32 Aḥmad b. Ḥanbal, *Musnad*, 4:228.

33 Abū Ṭālib al-Makkī, *Qūt al-qulūb*, 1:135; Ibn ʿAbd al-Barr, *Jāmiʿ bayān al-ʿilm wa-faḍlih*, 1956.

One is that jurisprudence is an Islamic discipline derived from the prophetic office, in contrast to medicine, which is not a part of the Islamic disciplines.

Second, absolutely no one who treads the path to the hereafter, whether sound or infirm,[34] can do without it; whereas only the infirm have need of [knowledge of] medicine, and they are a minority of people.

Third, jurisprudence functions in proximity to the knowledge of the path to the hereafter for it considers the physical components of actions whose origin and foundation lie in the attributes of the heart. Praiseworthy acts originate from praiseworthy attributes that assure salvation in the hereafter; while blameworthy acts originate from blameworthy attributes. The bond between the limbs and the heart is not secret.[35]

The origin of health and illness lies in the attributes of the bodily humors and their commingling, and these are among the attributes of the physical body, not of the heart. Therefore whenever jurisprudence is viewed in comparison to medicine, its superiority is apparent; likewise whenever the knowledge of the path of the hereafter is compared to jurisprudence, the superiority of the knowledge of the path of the hereafter is also apparent.

If you were to say: Set forth for me in detail what the knowledge of the path of the hereafter entails, and point out its basic features even though it may not be possible to delineate completely its specifics.

Know then that it entails two categories: (1) the knowledge of unveiling (*ʿilm al-mukāshafa*) and the knowledge of [practical] conduct (*ʿilm al-muʿāmalāt*).

The first category: The knowledge of unveiling is esoteric knowledge (*ʿilm al-bāṭin*). It is the culmination of all the fields of knowledge;[36] one of the gnostics (*ʿārifīn*) related, "I fear a bad ending

34 See al-Ghazālī, *al-Iqtiṣād*, 79.

35 This is the determining factor for every righteous or corrupt act. The Prophet ﷺ said, as reported in al-Bukhārī, 52, "Is there not in the body a lump of flesh, which, if sound, makes the whole body sound, and if corrupt, makes the whole body corrupt? And it is the heart."

36 This is the final concern of the gnostics; there is nothing beyond this concern that [is worthy] of consideration. Al-Zabīdī, *Itḥāf*, 1:162. The author رحمه الله has dedi-

(*sūʾa al-khātima*)[37] for whoever has no share of this knowledge. The smallest share of it is to affirm its veracity and consent to it for those who have a share in it."[38] Another related, "Whoever has two traits, innovation and ostentation, will not be endowed with this knowledge."[39] And it has been said, "Whoever is infatuated with this world or captivated by passion will realize nothing of it, though he may realize the knowledge of all other fields; the smallest penalty for whoever denies this [knowledge] is that he will be afforded no part of it."[40] Pertaining to this meaning it was recited:

Be content with he who conceals his slander from you
For in that sin abides its own chastisement[41]

It is the knowledge of the people of veracity and those brought near [to God]. Here I mean the knowledge of unveiling which is interpreted as a light that appears in the heart when it is cleansed and purified of blameworthy traits. Through that light, certain matters are unveiled. Previously, one used to hear the names for these matters, and then imagine vague meanings for them without clarity. Then at that moment they [the meanings] become clear, such that realization (*maʿrifa*) can be obtained of the essence of God سُبْحَانَهُ His eternal consummate attributes, His works, His wisdom in the creation of [this] world and the hereafter, and His preference for the hereafter over [this] world. A realization is also obtained of the meaning of prophecy and the prophet, [as well] as the meaning of revelation and the connotation of the terms angels and devils; the nature of Satan's enmity toward humankind, and how the angel [Gabriel] appeared to the prophets, and how revelation reached them; as well as the realization of the dominions of the heavens and earth, realization of the heart, and how the legions of the angels and satans

---

cated his book *al-Munqidh* to this point and its preponderance over every path and knowledge.

37 *Sūʾa al-khātima* means to die in a state of disbelief, having lost one's certainty in the face of the throes of death.

38 Abū Ṭālib al-Makkī, *Qūt al-qulūb*, 1:173.

39 Abū Ṭālib al-Makkī, *Qūt al-qulūb*, 1:173.

40 Abū Ṭālib al-Makkī, *Qūt al-qulūb*, 1:173. For this reason, al-Junayd رَحِمَهُ ٱللَّهُ said, "Faith (*īmān*) according to our knowledge is the small sovereignty (*al-wilāyat al-ṣughrā*)."

41 This verse is attributed to Ibn Nabāta al-Miṣrī in his *Dīwān*, 574.

clash therein, as well as the realization [of how] to differentiate the inspiration of an angel from the inspiration of Satan. [This light affords] knowledge of the hereafter; of paradise and the fire, the punishment in the grave, the traverse (*ṣirāṭ*),[42] the scales (*mīzān*), the calling to account (*ḥisāb*), and the meaning of the words of God تَعَالَىٰ : [*It will be said*], "*Read your record. Sufficient is yourself against you this day as accountant*" [17:14]; and what God most high meant in His words: *And indeed, the home of the Hereafter—that is the* [*eternal*] *life, if only they knew* [29:64]. [It will afford them as well] the meaning of encountering God عَزَّوَجَلَّ and beholding His noble countenance, the meaning of proximity to Him and residing in His presence, the meaning of obtaining happiness in the company of the highest assembly, and association with the angels and the prophets. [It will afford them as well] the meaning of the diverse degrees of the people of the gardens until they perceive one another there as one perceives the planets shining in the heavens; and beyond all this is that which would entail a lengthy explanation.

Thus, with regard to the meanings of these matters and having assented to their foundations, people are in different stations.

Some people perceive that all things related to that [listed above] are allegories. As to that which God has prepared for His righteous servants, eyes have not seen it, ears have not heard it, nor has it occurred to human minds. People know nothing [of the realities] of paradise but attributes and names.

Some people consider that a part of these matters are allegories and a part correspond to their essences as understood from their verbal expressions.

Likewise, others see that the highest degree of realization of God most high is realizing one's absolute inability to attain realization of Him.

Some make pretentious claims concerning the realization of God عَزَّوَجَلَّ.

Some say, "The limit of our realization of God عَزَّوَجَلَّ is where the common folk have halted in their beliefs: which is, that He exists, is omniscient, omnipotent, all-hearing, all-seeing, and speaks."

---

42 The traverse (*ṣirāṭ*) is a bridge suspended over the gulf over hell, sharper than a sword, and finer than a hair.

We mean by the knowledge of unveiling that the cover is raised until the evident truth in these matters manifests [itself] as clearly as if it were seen by the eye, leaving therein no doubt whatsoever. This is a potential within the essential nature of the human being, were not the mirror of the heart covered with layers of rust and the dross of impurities that accumulated from this worldly existence.

In particular, we intend by the knowledge of the path of the hereafter the means of polishing this mirror from the impurities that make up the veil [between us] and God most high and [prevent our] realization of His attributes and acts. Assuredly the purification and cleansing [of the heart] are attained by renouncing desires and following the examples of the prophets—may the blessings of God and His peace be upon them in all their states. Thus, commensurate with what is burnished from the heart and with its turning in the direction of the truth, [God's] realities will gleam in it. The only means to Him is with the application of spiritual discipline—the elucidation of which will follow in its proper place—and through knowledge and learning.[43]

This is not the knowledge written in books,[44] nor does one graced with something of it speak openly of it except with people similar to him, who are associated with him, through counsel or in secret.

This is the hidden knowledge that [the Messenger of God, ﷺ] intended by his words, "There is a knowledge with a hidden aspect, none know of it but the people of the realization of God most high; when they speak of it, those heedless of God عَزَّوَجَلَّ pay it no attention. So do not despise a scholar to whom God most high has given knowledge, for God عَزَّوَجَلَّ does not despise the one to whom He has given it [knowledge]."[45]

---

43 It is required of a master (*murshid*) to fulfill the reality in this statement, "It is necessary for a shaykh to show you their individual appearances (i.e., realities of the heart)." Al-Zabīdī, *Itḥāf,* 1:165.

44 This is the case because it is the knowledge of unveiled experiences which you grasp through witnessing, not from evidence and logical demonstration. It is also the case that what is written in books falls into the hands of deserving and undeserving people. If someone is not one of the people who have realized it, then he falls into tremendous confusion on which lie many levels of corruption. Al-Zabīdī, *Itḥāf,* 1:166.

45 This wording is in Abū Ṭālib al-Makkī, *Qūt al-qulūb,* 1:175, with a chain of narrators missing one or more narrators from the beginning of the chain (*muʿallaq*).

As for the second category [of the knowledge of the way to the hereafter], it is the knowledge of [practical] conduct and it comprises the knowledge of the states of the heart.

As for the praiseworthy states, they include patience, gratitude, fear and hope [in God], contentment [in God], abstinence, piety, sufficiency [in God], open-handedness, recognition of the grace of God most high in all states, excellence (*iḥsān*), thinking well [of people and God], good character, good mutual relationships, truthfulness, and sincerity. [It comprises as well] the realization of the realities behind these states, their limits, the causes by which they are obtained, their fruits and identifying signs, as well as the means of remedying weaknesses until they regain their strength, not ceasing until it returns, [and all of this is] included in the knowledge of the [way to the] hereafter.

As for blameworthy attributes [of the states of the heart], they include fear of poverty, discontent with [God's] decrees, spitefulness and resentment, envy, dishonesty, ambition to high station, love of praise, love of longevity to enjoy the mundane pleasures of this world, arrogance, ostentation, anger, conceit, enmity and hatred, acquisitiveness, avarice, passionate craving and vanity,[46] insolence [ingratitude] and discontent. [It comprises as well] being in awe of the wealthy and demeaning of the poor, pride and self-importance in wealth and ancestry, rivalry and boastfulness in wealth, knowledge, and position, haughtily rejecting [God's] right, and meddling in that which does not concern one. [It comprises as well] pomposity (*ṣalaf*),[47] affectation and currying favor, adulation, being too occupied with the faults in others to see one's own faults, a heart devoid of regret and humility, violent self-defense in the face of humiliation, weakness in the defense of [God's] right, and outwardly claiming brotherhood while holding secret enmity. [Among these traits as well are] feeling secure from the designs of God سُبْحَانَهُ from the loss of

---

Al-Ḥāfiẓ al-Mundhirī says in *al-Targhīb wa-l-tarhīb*, 1:135, that it is reported by al-Daylamī, *Musnad al-firdaws*, 802, and by al-Sulamī, *al-Arbaʿīn*, which is his work on Sufism.

46 *Badhkh* refers to the arrogance and overreaching of a person, in words and by exaggerated boasting.

47 *Ṣalaf* refers to praising and arrogantly claiming that a person has attributes that he/she does not have.

that which He had given, reliance on one's acts of obedience [rather than God's grace], plotting, treachery, and deceit, [excessive] hopes for longevity, rude harsh behavior, delight with worldly pleasure and grief over its loss, enjoying intimacy with creation and feeling alienation in separation from them, coarseness, heedlessness, zeal in worldly affairs, and a dearth of shame and compassion. These and their likes are among the attributes of the heart that are the sown fields of moral inequity and the seedbeds of illicit deeds; whereas, their opposites—the praiseworthy character traits—are the source of all obedience and proximity [to God].

Knowledge of the boundaries of these matters, their realities, causes, fruits, and influence are all aspects of the knowledge of the hereafter. According to the ruling of the scholars of the hereafter, [knowledge of these] is an individual obligation. Anyone who turns his back on these matters is doomed to perdition by the might of the King of kings in the hereafter, in the same manner that anyone who denies the outward obligations perishes by the sword of the sultans of [this] world according to the ruling of the jurists of [this] world. According to the jurists the individual obligation relates to [one's] well-being in [this] world, while [according to the scholars of the hereafter], this [the individual obligation] relates to [one's] well-being in the hereafter.

If one were to ask a jurist the meaning of one of these terms, even simply about sincerity for example, or trust [in God], or how to guard oneself against pretension, he would be at a loss [to respond], even though it is an individual obligation that if neglected means perdition in the hereafter. But were you to question him about allegations of adultery, divorce by repudiation, or [the permissibility of wagering] on racing and archery, he would set forth for you in minute detail volumes of explanations that would take ages and of which there is not the slightest need. And should there be a need, no region lacks someone to fulfill this duty and spare the jurist the burden and fatigue of his studies. Yes he ceases not to weary himself, day and night, memorizing and studying, all the while ignoring that which in itself is essential to religion. Should he then be consulted on this, he would reply, "I have occupied myself with it because it is the knowledge of religion and a communal obligation." [Thus he has] confused the matter for himself and for others with his pretexts.

The perceptive person knows that if his purpose is to fulfill the duty of a matter of communal obligation, he would give precedence to individual obligation over this; moreover he would give precedence to many [other] communal obligations. How many regions' only physician is a non-Muslim, whose testimony is not permissible even in matters that pertain to physicians regarding judgments in *fiqh*. Yet we see no one taking up [medicine], but [we see them] reviling one another over knowledge of jurisprudence, and in particular in contentious matters and polemics while the region is full of jurists who occupy themselves with rulings and respond to events as they unfold.[48]

I wish I knew how the jurists of religion could sanction this involvement in a communal obligation that others have already taken responsibility for, while [they] abandon that which no one has undertaken. Is there any other reason than that medicine does not facilitate access to being entrusted with [religious] endowments, issues of inheritance, and executive authority over the wealth of orphans; or to assume offices in the judiciary or government, and to gain advancement over one's peers as well as power to overcome one's enemies?

Woe to us! All trace of the knowledge of religion has been obliterated by the fraudulent behavior of the scholars of evil [intent]. God is our sole supporter! In Him we seek refuge that He may protect us from this deceitfulness that incurs the anger of the Merciful and the pleasure of Satan.

It used to be that the conscientious people among the scholars of outward [knowledge] recognized the excellence of the scholars of inward [knowledge] and masters of [the art of polishing] hearts.

Imām al-Shāfiʿī رَضِيَ ٱللَّهُ عَنْهُ would sit before Shaybān al-Rāʿī like a boy in a school and ask him how one should act in this situation and that. When it was said to him, "A scholar of your reputation

48 This was the case during al-Ghazālī's time—it was the opposite of what takes place now, when people tend to study the sciences rather than the humanities (including religion). The general concept remains the same: people study what leads to the highest income and greatest prestige, regardless of the needs of society as a whole.

questions this Bedouin?" he would reply, "This [man] has been given that which we have neglected (*aghfalnā*).[49]

Aḥmad b. Ḥanbal and Yaḥyā b. Muʿīn kept company with Maʿrūf al-Karkhī, who—in the knowledge of the outward—was not their peer; and they [learned from him by] asking questions.[50]

Why should this not be [the case]: when the Messenger of God ﷺ was asked, "What should we do if a matter comes to us that we have not found in the Qurʾān (*kitāb*) and *sunna*?" he said ﷺ, "Ask the righteous and [decide based on] the counsel among themselves."[51]

Thus it has been stated, "The scholars of outward knowledge are the adornment of the earth and the terrestrial realm, while the scholars of inner knowledge are the adornment of the heavens and the kingdoms.[52]

Junayd رَحِمَهُ ٱللَّٰهُ said,

> Sarī [al-Saqaṭī]—my teacher—asked me,
> "When you leave me with whom do you sit?"
> I said, "al-Muḥāsibī."
> To which he replied, "Yes, take from him his knowledge and exemplary conduct; dispense however with his hair splitting over matters of theology and his refutation of its theologians."
> Then when I departed I heard him saying, "May God make you a partisan of *ḥadīth* who is a Sufi, not a Sufi who is a partisan of *ḥadīth*."[53]

He pointed out that one who acquires *ḥadīth* and knowledge then takes the Sufi path will succeed; while one who takes the Sufi path before acquiring knowledge is gambling with his soul.

---

49 The Dār al-Minhāj edition has *ʿalimnā* (what we have learned) instead of *aghfalnā*, which appears in other editions. We believe *aghfalnā* makes more sense in this context.

50 Abū Ṭālib al-Makkī, *Qūt al-qulūb*, 1:158.

51 Abū Ṭālib al-Makkī, *Qūt al-qulūb*, 1:158. Ibn ʿAbd al-Barr, *Jāmiʿ bayān al-ʿilm wa-faḍlih*, 1612, narrates this as: "Assemble the devout servants of God from among the believers and let them take counsel between themselves, and do not take a decision based on one person's opinion (*raʾyi*)." Al-Khaṭīb al-Baghdādī reported something similar to this in *al-Faqīh wa-l-mutafaqqih*, 1153.

52 Abū Ṭālib al-Makkī, *Qūt al-qulūb*, 1:157.

53 Abū Ṭālib al-Makkī, *Qūt al-qulūb*, 1:158.

If you were to ask, "Why have you not listed theology and philosophy among the disciplines, and explained whether they are blameworthy or praiseworthy?"

Know that the sum of the beneficial proofs of theology (*ʿilm al-kalām*) are all to be found in the Qurʾān and the reports. Anything not found therein is either blameworthy disputation, which is among the innovations—as will be discussed below—or dissension associated with the contradictory claims of the parties as well as the verbose citing of statements, the majority of which are farcical and only instigate disdain in [one's] nature and scorn in [one's sense of] hearing.

A portion of [theological disputation] comprises that which is not related to religion, and the first generation [of Islam] was accustomed to this. In fact, total preoccupation with it [at the time of the first generation, was considered] an innovation. But today, judgments about it have changed since innovative doctrines that divert from conformity to the Qurʾān and *sunna* have appeared. A group has emerged that fabricates for itself deceptive doctrines and [this group] structures a well-crafted discourse for [these doctrines]. Thus, [theological disputation] that was considered illicit out of necessity has become permissible, even a communal obligation, [because] it is a measure that is used to confront the partisans of innovative doctrines should they attempt to promulgate their ideas. In the following chapter we shall discuss that in a limited context.

With regard to philosophy, in and of itself, it is not a discipline, rather it is comprised of four areas of inquiry.

One of them is geometry and mathematics, and as mentioned earlier, both are permissible. No one need be prevented from them except the one that you fear may transgress beyond them into blameworthy disciplines. The majority that practice [geometry and mathematics] go beyond them into innovation. Therefore, preventing the vulnerable from it is not for itself, rather it is comparable to keeping a child away from the river's edge out of fear that he may fall into the river, or as you would prevent a new convert to Islam from frequenting those who deny the faith out of fear for him, although frequenting them is not recommended even for those strong in their faith.

The second is logic. It is the investigation into [what constitutes] valid proofs and their conditions, and terms and their definitions. Both are elements of theology.

The third is metaphysics (*ilāhiyāt*). It is investigation into the essence and attributes of God سُبْحَانَهُ and it is equally an element of theology.

However, philosophers are not unique in this area of knowledge; rather they are unique in their doctrinal schools, some of which entail disbelief and some innovation. In the same manner, [the doctrine of] the rationalist theologians is not a discipline in and of itself; rather its partisans comprise a faction of theologians and people of rational inquiry and speculation who are unique in [having established] false doctrinal schools, just as philosophers have.

The fourth is [the field of the] natural [sciences], a portion of which contradicts the law and the true religion, thus it is ignorance and not even a discipline that occurs among the categories of the sciences; and a portion of it is the investigation of the characteristics of physical bodies, their intrinsic natures, and the manner in which they change and become transformed. This [category] resembles the point of view of physicians, except that a physician concentrates on the human body specifically from the point of view of sickness or health, while they [the natural scientists] scrutinize all physical entities inasmuch as they transform and move. Medicine, however, is superior to it, for there is a need for it, while there is no need for the [specific] branches of speculation among physical sciences.[54]

Thus, theology (*kalām*) became one of the vocations that are a communal obligation, [this was] in order to protect the hearts of the common folk from the delusional speculations of the partisans of innovation. That only occurred, however, as a result of the occurrence of innovation itself in the same manner that the need arose for people on the pilgrimage road to hire armed escorts because of the appearance of the inequity of the Bedouin and their highway robbery. For had the Bedouin renounced their hostilities [toward the pilgrims], hiring armed escorts would have ceased to be a prerequisite for the pilgrimage road. Similarly, had one of the

54 In al-Ghazālī's time pseudo-sciences such as alchemy and astrology were studied alongside the natural sciences.

partisans of innovation renounced his senseless ramblings, he would have had no need of any more [knowledge] than was already known in the time of the Companions رَضِيَ ٱللَّهُ عَنْهُمْ.

Therefore, let him who practices theological discourse know his own limitation where religion is concerned and [know] that his place in its respect is the place of an escort on the pilgrimage road; for were he to devote his attention exclusively to standing guard, he would not be among the collectivity of the pilgrims. If the theologian were to devote himself exclusively to polemics and argumentation, and not tread the path to the hereafter, nor busy himself with attending to his heart and its well-being, he would not be among the scholars of religion in any manner. The theologian possesses nothing of religion but the creed (*ʿaqīda*) that he shares with the entirety of the common folk; the creed [itself] is comprised of the outward practices of the heart and the tongue. He is differentiated from the common folk only in his practice of polemics and standing guard. As for the realization of God, His attributes and His works, and everything we have alluded to as being among the aspects of the knowledge of unveiling, it will not be attained through theology, rather, theology is most likely a veil and a hindrance from it. It is achieved only through devoted striving that God سُبْحَانَهُ has made the prelude to good guidance, as God تَعَالَىٰ spoke, *And those who strive for Us, We will surely guide them to Our ways. And indeed God is with those who do good* [29:69].

If you were to say, "You have reduced the role of the theologian to that of a guard of the creed of the common folk from the confusion of the innovators; similar to the role of the armed escorts that protect the pilgrims' goods from pillage by the Bedouin. And you have reduced the role of the jurist to the safeguarding of the law by which the governing authority is able to keep in check the iniquity that the unjust commit against one another. These two [roles] are lowly degrees of esteem in comparison to the Islamic disciplines; the scholars of this community that are renown for excellence are the jurists and the theologians, they are the preeminent of creation with God most high. So how can you demean their stature to these mean ranks in comparison to the high esteem of the Islamic disciplines?"

Know that anyone who recognizes the truth through people has become confounded in a maze of error. Know the truth, then you will recognize the people [of truth][55] if you are a traveler on the path of truth.

If you are satisfied with mere imitation (*taqlīd*) and speculation (*naẓar*) into the degrees of excellence well known among people, be sure not to ignore the Companions رَضِيَ ٱللَّهُ عَنْهُمْ and their lofty rank, for all those you have alluded to agree upon their preeminence and that there is no attaining to their summit in religion and no one could measure up to them. The preeminence was not due to [their mastery of] theology and jurisprudence; on the contrary, it was due to [their mastery of] the knowledge of the hereafter and traveling its path.

Abū Bakr رَضِيَ ٱللَّهُ عَنْهُ did not surpass the people [of his community] by an excessive amount of prayer, fasting, narrations, legal rulings, or discourse; but by a thing [or secret] that abided in his breast, as was born out by the master of humanity [i.e., the Messenger of God صَلَّى ٱللَّهُ عَلَيْهِ وَسَلَّمَ].[56]

So let your aspiration be in the seeking of that secret [or thing], for it is a priceless gemstone and well-guarded pearl; renounce everything that the majority of people hold in high esteem and venerate for various reasons and motives, whose elucidation would be too lengthy [for this section]. The Messenger of God صَلَّى ٱللَّهُ عَلَيْهِ وَسَلَّمَ passed away, leaving behind thousands of Companions رَضِيَ ٱللَّهُ عَنْهُمْ, all of whom were knowledgeable of God. The Messenger of God صَلَّى ٱللَّهُ عَلَيْهِ وَسَلَّمَ praised them all while there was no one among them who had mastered theological discourse, and only about ten from among them took upon themselves the task of making legal rulings.

Ibn ʿUmar رَضِيَ ٱللَّهُ عَنْهُمَا was one of them; when asked for a legal ruling he would respond to the inquirer, "Go to such and such a leader who has taken on the matters of the population and place it

55 Imām al-Ghazālī is citing the well-known saying of Imām ʿAlī [may God ennoble his face], who, when asked whether Ṭalḥa and al-Zubayr were mistaken [in their judgment] said, "O you, the affair is confounded in your mind, verily, one does not come to know the truth through men; know the truth and you will come to know its partisans (*ahl al-ḥaqq*)." Al-Zabīdī adds, "This means that an intelligent person, upon hearing a statement, looks into the statement itself; if it is true he accepts it whether the speaker himself is known to be truthful or not."

56 See al-Ḥakīm al-Tirmidhī, *Nawādir al-uṣūl*, 31.

around his neck."[57] He was here pointing out that rulings in judicial cases or judgments are the responsibilities of the government and ruling authority.

When ʿUmar رَضِيَ اللَّهُ عَنْهُ passed away, Ibn Masʿūd stated, "Nine-tenths of knowledge has perished." On which it was said to him, "Do you say this when the most illustrious of the Companions are still among us?" To which he responded, "I do not intend knowledge of rulings and opinions; I mean knowledge of God صَلَّى اللَّهُ عَلَيْهِ وَسَلَّمَ."[58]

Do you suppose that he intended the discipline of theology and dialectics? Why do you not strive to realize that knowledge of which nine-tenths perished with the passing of ʿUmar رَضِيَ اللَّهُ عَنْهُ? [ʿUmar] in fact was the one who closed the door on theology and dialectics and had Ṣabīgh beaten with a lash when he approached [ʿUmar] with a question about the [apparent] contradiction between two verses of the Book of God عَزَّوَجَلَّ and banished [Ṣabīgh] from [ʿUmar's] presence and ordered people to ostracize [Ṣabīgh].[59]

As for your statement, "The scholars of renown [of this community] are the jurists and the theologians."

Know that attaining preeminence with God most high is one thing, while attaining renown among the people is another thing. Abū Bakr رَضِيَ اللَّهُ عَنْهُ gained renown due to the caliphate; his preeminence was due to the secret that resided in his breast. ʿUmar رَضِيَ اللَّهُ عَنْهُ gained renown based upon his administration (*siyāsa*); his preeminence was due to his knowledge of God, of which nine-tenths perished when he passed away, to his commitment to drawing near to God most high in his governance, and to his justice and compassion for God's creatures; these are the imperceptible aspects in his innermost being. With regard to his outwardly visible attributes, it is conceivable that they could arise from one seeking rank, title, prestige, or from one desiring fame. Thus renown can be found in that which is destructive; while preeminence resides in the domain of inner secrets, perceptible to no one.

57 Abū Ṭālib al-Makkī, *Qūt al-qulūb*, 1:131.

58 Abū Ṭālib al-Makkī, *Qūt al-qulūb*, 1:139. Something similar has been reported by al-Ṭabarānī, *al-Muʿjam al-kabīr*, 9:163.

59 Ṣabīgh confronted people with obscure matters and questions about ambiguity in the Qurʾān. This narration is cited from al-Dārimī, *Sunan*, 146.

The jurists and the theologians are thus similar to the caliphs, the judges, and the scholars; they can be separated [into factions]. Among them are those who intend God in their knowledge, their rulings, and their defense of His path,[60] those who seek neither reputation nor esteem. These are the partisans of the good pleasure of God تَعَالَىٰ; their preeminence with God is because their works are founded on their knowledge and because they seek the countenance of God تَعَالَىٰ in their rulings and their opinions. All knowledge is action because it is an acquired effect, but not all action [comes] from knowledge.[61] A physician is able to increase in proximity to God most high through his knowledge, and thus he is recompensed for his knowledge inasmuch as he is doing it for the sake of God. Thus the sultan mediates between people for the sake of God. He stands in good pleasure and is rewarded before God صَلَّى ٱللَّهُ عَلَيْهِ وَسَلَّمَ, not in the sense that he has been entrusted with the knowledge of religion, but rather in the sense that he has taken responsibility for action through which he intends to draw near to God عَزَّوَجَلَّ with the knowledge he has.

The divisions of that which draws one near to God most high are three:

Knowledge in and of itself, which is the knowledge of unveiling.

Work in and of itself, which is comparable to the justice of the ruler, for example, and his [good] governance over the people.

A combination of knowledge and works, which is the knowledge of the path of the hereafter; those of this path are among the scholars and those who accomplish the worthy deeds.

Consider yourself: will you be, on the day of resurrection, among the company of those who accomplish worthy works solely for God most high or [will you be] among the scholars of God سُبْحَانَهُ, or in both companies, and thus play an active role in each. This is of much greater value for you than blind following merely to gain notoriety.[62] As has been said:

60 That is, the path of God عَزَّوَجَلَّ. Al-Zabīdī, *Itḥāf*, 1:190.

61 This is the case because certain actions are devoid of sincerity and intention. Thus they cannot be done out of real knowledge. Al-Zabīdī, *Itḥāf*, 1:190.

62 Al-Zabīdī, *Itḥāf*, 1:190, has *bi-mujarrad al-ishtihār* rather than *li-*.

Take that which you see and dispense with what you have only heard
In the sunrise there is that which renders you free of Saturn[63]

Therefore, let us relate something of the accounts of the lives of the early jurists, that you might know that those who presume to follow their methods have done them an injustice; and they [early jurists] will be their severest critics on the day of resurrection, for they sought knowledge only for the countenance of God. The examples of their states are a clear testimony to the indications of the scholars of the hereafter, an explanation of which will follow in [chapter 6:] On the Perils of [the Pursuit of] Knowledge, [subheading entitled] The traits of the scholars of the hereafter. They were not merely scholars of jurisprudence; on the contrary, they were diligently engaged in [seeking] knowledge of the heart and [learning] vigilance over it. They were prevented, however, from teaching and composing works on this [knowledge of the heart] by the same causes that prevented the Companions from composing works and teaching jurisprudence, even though they [the Companions] were independent jurists in the knowledge [of issuing] rulings. The obstacles and their causes are well known, there is no need to mention them [here].

So now we will cite something of the circumstances of the jurists of Islam, that you may learn from them that what we have mentioned [previously] is not criticism of them; on the contrary, it was a criticism of those who appear to take them as an example, [those who] presume to follow their paths while contradicting them in their knowledge and their exemplary conduct.

The jurists that constitute the leading figures in the study of jurisprudence and leadership of the community—I mean those with large followings in the schools of jurisprudence—are five: al-Shāfiʿī, Mālik, Abū Ḥanīfa, Aḥmad b. Ḥanbal, and Sufyān al-Thawrī رَحِمَهُمُ ٱللَّهُ.[64] Each of them was [1] a devoted servant [of God], [2] an ascetic, and [3] a scholar of the knowledge of the hereafter, as well as [4] a jurist, well-versed in the matters that concern the well-being of the community in this world, and [5] a seeker, through his knowledge of jurisprudence, of the countenance of God.

63 The verse is from al-Mutanabbī, al-ʿUkbarī, *Dīwān bi-sharḥ al-ʿUkbarī*, 3:81.

64 Al-Zabīdī, *Itḥāf*, 1:191.

Of all these five qualities, the contemporary jurists have followed them in but one: staunch commitment to and exaggeration in the study of the subordinate branches of jurisprudence. This is so because the other four qualities are only suitable for the hereafter, and this one quality suits [this] world and the hereafter—should one intend through it the hereafter. They have thus committed themselves to it for the sole reason that it suits this worldly context; then they claim in this [i.e., in their dedication to the study of jurisprudence] to be comparable to those *imāms*. But how far from the mark they are! Do not confuse angels with blacksmiths.

So allow us to cite something of their circumstances that will demonstrate these four qualities [of the scholars of the hereafter]; as for their mastery of jurisprudence, that is clear.

[Imāms of Jurisprudence]

Imām al-Shāfiʿī رَحِمَهُ ٱللَّهُ

THAT HE WAS A servant [of God] is manifest from the account that cites that he would divide the night into three parts: a third for the study of knowledge, a third for prayer, and a third for sleep.[65]

Al-Rabīʿ reported, "Al-Shāfiʿī رَحِمَهُ ٱللَّهُ would complete the recitation of the entire Qurʾān sixty times in the month of Ramaḍān; all of which was during prayer."[66] While al-Buwīṭī, one of his students, would complete the Qurʾān once a day.[67]

Al-Ḥusayn [b. ʿAlī b. Yazīd] al-Karābīsī narrated, "I spent several nights in the presence of al-Shāfiʿī رَحِمَهُ ٱللَّهُ; he would pray nearly one-third of the night; yet I did not see him recite more than fifty verses, or if he exceeded this, one hundred. Whenever he recited a verse conveying mercy he would ask God most high to bless him and all of the believers. Whenever he recited a verse conveying chastisement he would seek protection from it and would ask God for deliverance for himself and for all the believers. It was as though both hope and

65 Al-Bayhaqī, *Manāqib al-Shāfiʿī*, 2:157.

66 Al-Bayhaqī, *Manāqib al-Shāfiʿī*, 2:158.

67 Ibn ʿAsākir, *Tārīkh Dimashq*, 51:393.

fear were drawn together in him.[68] Behold how he limited himself to fifty verses—this indicates his deep penetration into the secrets of the Qurʾān and his reflection on them.

Al-Shāfiʿī رَحِمَهُ ٱللَّهُ said, "I have not satiated myself for sixteen years, for satiety weighs heavily on the body, hardens the heart, diminishes intelligence, induces sleep, and weakens one's capacity for devotions."[69] Carefully consider his sagacity in drawing attention to the hazards of satiety, then his steadfastness in devotion, since for its sake he abandoned it. The essence of devotion is lessening one's food.

Al-Shāfiʿī رَحِمَهُ ٱللَّهُ said, "I have never taken an oath in the name of God most high, neither truthfully nor deceitfully."[70] Behold his reverence and esteem for God most high, how this reveals his knowledge of God's sublimity سُبْحَانَهُ.

Al-Shāfiʿī رَحِمَهُ ٱللَّهُ was once questioned concerning a certain matter on which he remained silent. So it was said to him, "Are you not going to respond, may God bless you?" To which he responded, "Not until I know whether the merit resides in my silence or in the response [to your question]."[71] Consider [again] how carefully he guarded his tongue, for it is the body part that most intensely holds sway over the jurists and the most disobedient of [the body parts] in resisting control and subjugation. From this [narration] it is clear that he did not speak or remain silent except to obtain favor and seek reward.

Aḥmad b. Yaḥyā b. al-Wazīr related, "Al-Shāfiʿī رَحِمَهُ ٱللَّهُ left the candle market one day, and we followed him. When [we encountered] a man vilifying a scholar, al-Shāfiʿī looked at us and said, 'Safeguard your ears from hearing obscene language as you would safeguard your tongues from uttering it; for the listener is the cohort of the speaker. A shameless person looks for the vilest contents of his vessel [i.e., heart] and wants to pour it into yours. And were the speech of a shameless person to be warded off, the one who wards it off would be happy just as the one who spoke it would be miserable.'"[72]

68 Al-Bayhaqī, *Manāqib al-Shāfiʿī*, 2:158.

69 Ibn Abī Ḥātim, *Ādāb al-Shāfiʿī wa-manāqibihi*, 105.

70 Al-Bayhaqī, *Manāqib al-Shāfiʿī*, 2:164.

71 Ibn al-Ṣalāḥ, *Fatāwā*, 1:13.

72 Abū Nuʿaym, *Ḥilya*, 9:123.

Al-Shāfiʿī رَضِيَ ٱللَّهُ عَنْهُ said, "One wise man wrote to another, 'You have been given knowledge, so do not sully your knowledge with the darkness of sins, lest you remain in darkness on the day the people of knowledge stride in the light of their knowledge.'"[73]

As concerns his ascetic nature رَضِيَ ٱللَّهُ عَنْهُ, al-Shāfiʿī رَحِمَهُ ٱللَّهُ said, "He who claims that he has combined in his heart love of the world and love of its creator is indeed lying."[74]

Al-Ḥumaydī reported, "Al-Shāfiʿī رَحِمَهُ ٱللَّهُ departed for Yemen with some people of authority. [When he reached Mecca,] he distributed ten thousand dirhams. He pitched his tent in a place outside Mecca, and the people came to him [in great numbers]; he remained there until he had distributed all of it."[75]

[Then on another occasion,] upon leaving the public bath, he gave the attendant a great amount of money. He dropped his camel stick once, and a man raised it up to him, whereupon he rewarded him with fifty dinars.[76]

Al-Shāfiʿī's رَحِمَهُ ٱللَّهُ selfless generosity is so well known that attempting to recount it is of no avail. The essence of asceticism is selfless generosity; for anyone who loves something holds tight to it and is not willing to relinquish it. Only he in whose eyes this world is but a paltry thing relinquishes wealth, and that is the meaning of asceticism.

Proof of the extent of his asceticism and the rigor of his fear of God عَزَّ وَجَلَّ as well as his unremitting preoccupation with the hereafter [can be seen from] one occasion [when] Sufyān b. ʿUyayna narrated in his presence a *ḥadīth* that dealt with the tenderness [of the heart]. On hearing it, al-Shāfiʿī lost consciousness until it was said, "He has died." Someone said, "If he has died, the most eminent person of his epoch has died."[77]

Another [proof] is what was reported by ʿAbdallāh b. Muḥammad al-Balawī, who said, "I was sitting in the company of ʿUmar b. Nabāta reminiscing about the [sincere] servants and the ascetics when ʿUmar said to me, 'I have seen no one more conscientious nor more eloquent

73 Abū Nuʿaym, *Ḥilya*, 9:146.

74 See Ibn ʿAbd al-Barr, *al-Intiqāʾ fī faḍāʾil al-thalāthat al-aʾimmat al-fuqahāʾ*, 160.

75 Abū Nuʿaym, *Ḥilya*, 9:130; al-Bayhaqī, *Manāqib al-Shāfiʿī*, 2:220.

76 Al-Bayhaqī, *Manāqib al-Shāfiʿī*, 2:221.

77 Abū Nuʿaym, *Ḥilya*, 9:95; al-Bayhaqī, *Manāqib al-Shāfiʿī*, 2:175.

than Muḥammad b. Idrīs al-Shāfiʿī رَحِمَهُ ٱللَّهُ. [On one occasion] I went out with him and al-Ḥārith b. Labīd to al-Ṣafā—al-Ḥārith being a student of Ṣāliḥ al-Marrī—whereupon he [al-Ḥārith], who had a beautiful voice, began to recite the Qurʾān, he recited, *This is the day they shall not speak, nor will they be permitted to offer excuses* [77:35–36], and I saw that al-Shāfiʿī's رَحِمَهُ ٱللَّهُ color had changed and his hair stood on end and he shook violently and fell down in a faint. When he recovered he began to say, "I seek protection with You from the station of the liars and the rejection of the neglectful; O God, the hearts of the gnostics have humbled themselves to You, and in awe of You are those who long [for You]; my God! grant me Your beneficence, cover me with Your protecting veil and forgive my shortcomings by the munificence of Your countenance.'"

[Then al-Balawī] said, "We arose and departed. Upon arriving in Baghdad—while [al-Shāfiʿī] was in Iraq as well—I was sitting on the riverbank making my ablution for prayer when a man passed by and said, 'O young man, take good care in your ablutions and God will take good care of you, in this world and the hereafter.'

I looked up and beheld a man being followed by a large crowd of people, so I hastened to complete my ablution and took to following in his tracks, whereupon he noticed me and said, 'Are you in need of anything?'

[I replied] 'Yes, teach me something of that which God has taught you.'

He said to me, 'Know well that whoever is truthful with God [in his conduct] will be saved [from the fire of hell], and whoever fears for his religion will be secure from ruin, and whoever renounces [the pleasures of] this world, his eyes will know the coolness of beholding God's goodly recompense tomorrow. Shall I go on?'

I said, 'Of course.'

And he said, 'Whoever has mastered three traits has fulfilled [his] faith: one who commands the good and acts accordingly, one who forbids iniquity and acts accordingly, and one who keeps within the limits of God تَعَالَىٰ. "Shall I go on?'

And I replied, 'Of course.' He said, 'Be detached from this world and keen for the hereafter, be truthful to God تَعَالَىٰ in all your matters, and you will succeed with those who succeed.'

Whereupon, he passed on and I asked, 'Who is this [man]?' And they said, 'It is al-Shāfiʿī.'"[78]

Consider carefully how he fell down in a faint and then gave good counsel and [how these events] testify to his ascetic detachment and the severity of his fear [of God]. These degrees of fear and asceticism are only born of an intimate realization of God most high; for indeed, *From among His servants, only those who fear God are those who have knowledge* [35:28]. Al-Shafiʿi رَحِمَهُ ٱللَّهُ did not benefit from these [qualities] of fear and asceticism by possessing knowledge from the books on [the statutes of] 'forward buying' or 'renting and hiring,' or the other books of jurisprudence; on the contrary, [he benefited] from the knowledge of the hereafter that is founded upon the Qurʾān and the [prophetic] reports; for in them both are to be found the wisdom of the earlier and later generations.

As for his status as a scholar of the mysteries of the heart and the knowledge of the hereafter, you can recognize these [characteristics] from the wise sayings transmitted about him.

It was related that [when] he was asked what constitutes ostentation, he spontaneously replied, "Ostentation is a temptation that desire has fastened over the perception of the hearts of scholars. Thus they consider it through the evil choices of their souls, and it then makes their actions futile."[79]

Al-Shāfiʿī رَحِمَهُ ٱللَّهُ said, "Should you fear that self-esteem affects your acts, remember the good pleasure of Him you seek, and any blessing you aspire toward, and the chastisement you flee from, and any element of your well-being [that you] are thankful for, and any hardship you recollect; if you reflect upon one of these traits, your deeds of piety will appear paltry in your eyes."[80]

Look carefully at his mention of the reality of ostentation and the remedy for pride, while these are two of the greatest matters that imperil the heart.

Al-Shāfiʿī رَضِيَ ٱللَّهُ عَنْهُ said, "The knowledge of one who does not safeguard his own soul (*nafs*) will be of no benefit to him."[81]

---

78 Al-Bayhaqī, *Manāqib al-Shāfiʿī*, 2:176–177. Also see al-Zabīdī, *Itḥāf*, 1:196–197.

79 Ibn ʿAsākir, *Tārīkh Dimashq*, 51:334.

80 Ibn ʿAsākir, *Tārīkh Dimashq*, 51:413.

81 Al-Khaṭīb al-Baghdādī, *Tārīkh Baghdād*, 7:286.

And he رَحِمَهُ ٱللَّهُ said, "The inner thought (*sirr*) of one who obeys God most high through knowledge will benefit him."

And he رَضِيَ ٱللَّهُ عَنْهُ said, "There is no one who does not have someone who loves him and someone who hates him, this being the case be among those who obey God عَزَّوَجَلَّ."[82]

It is reported that ʿAbd al-Qāhir b. ʿAbd al-ʿAzīz, a conscientious and righteous man, used to ask al-Shāfiʿī رَضِيَ ٱللَّهُ عَنْهُ questions about conscientiousness, and al-Shāfiʿī رَحِمَهُ ٱللَّهُ accepted [these questions] from him because of [ʿAbd al-Qāhir's] conscientiousness. One day, he asked al-Shāfiʿī رَحِمَهُ ٱللَّهُ, "Which is preferable, patience, tribulation, or firm resolution?" Al-Shāfiʿī رَحِمَهُ ٱللَّهُ replied, "Being firmly established is the rank of the prophets, and no one is established before tribulation. When one is tested he is patient, and when he is patient he is firmly established. Do you not see how God most high tested Abraham عَلَيْهِ ٱلسَّلَامُ then established him firmly [in prophecy], and He tested Moses عَلَيْهِ ٱلسَّلَامُ then established him, and He tested Job عَلَيْهِ ٱلسَّلَامُ then firmly established him, and He tested Solomon عَلَيْهِ ٱلسَّلَامُ then established him and granted him dominion. The best of ranks is being firmly established, as God most high said, *And thus, We established Joseph in the land* [12:21]; and Job عَلَيْهِ ٱلسَّلَامُ, after being sorely tested, was firmly established in the land, as God تَعَالَىٰ states, *So We responded to him and removed what afflicted him of adversity. And We gave him* [*back*] *his family and the like thereof with them as a mercy from Us and a reminder for the worshipers* [*of God*] [21:84].

This discourse from al-Shāfiʿī رَضِيَ ٱللَّهُ عَنْهُ attests to his deep penetration into the mysteries of the Qurʾān and his discernment into the stations of the travelers to God عَزَّوَجَلَّ among the prophets and the saints; all of which constitutes the knowledge of the hereafter.

Al-Shāfiʿī رَحِمَهُ ٱللَّهُ was asked, "When might a man be considered to be a scholar (*ʿālim*)?" To which he responded, "When he has truly mastered one field of knowledge that he knows and then turns his attention to all other fields, to examine what has eluded him; then he will be a scholar." For it was asked of Galen, "You prescribe for one illness many medicines [that are] combinations of various elements." He replied, "The objective from them is one and the

---

82 Abū Nuʿaym, *Ḥilya*, 9:117.

same. The other compounds are used to lessen its individual effect; for one specific [medicine] could be deadly."

This and [other sayings] like it that are too numerous to count testify to his lofty rank in the realization (*maʿrifa*) of God most high and the knowledge of the hereafter.

Concerning his desire for the countenance of God most high through jurisprudence in particular and disputation concerning it, this is evident from that which he was related to have said, "I wished that people could benefit from this knowledge, and that nothing of it be attributed to me."[83]

Look how cognizant he was of the perils of knowledge and of pursuing a name by it, and how free his heart was from regarding anything of it, his sole intention in it being for the good grace of the countenance of God most high.

Al-Shāfiʿī رَضِيَ ٱللَّهُ عَنْهُ said, "I never contested a point with anyone and wanted them to be in error."[84]

And he said, "I have never spoken to anyone without wishing that God عَزَّ وَجَلَّ would grant him success, guidance, support, care, and protection. And I have never spoken with anyone while caring whether God clarified the truth through my words or his."[85]

He said as well, "Whenever I presented truth and evidence to someone, and he accepted it from me, it was only as a gift to him while I held firmly to affection for him. Whenever someone treated me with contempt for the truth and rejected evidence, it was only then that he was diminished in my eyes, and I dismissed him."[86]

These clear signs attest that he sought the countenance of God alone in the practice of jurisprudence and disputation. Regard carefully how people follow him in any one of these five traits, and then how they have deviated from him in them as well. For this reason Abū Thawr رَحِمَهُ ٱللَّهُ stated, "Neither I nor anyone else has ever seen the likes of al-Shāfiʿī رَحِمَهُ ٱللَّهُ."[87] Aḥmad b. Ḥanbal رَضِيَ ٱللَّهُ عَنْهُ said,

83 Abū Nuʿaym, *Ḥilya*, 9:118.

84 Al-Bayḥaqī, *al-Madkhal*, 172.

85 Abū Nuʿaym, *Ḥilya*, 9:118.

86 Abū Nuʿaym, *Ḥilya*, 9:117.

87 Al-Bayhaqī, *Manāqib al-Shāfiʿī*, 2:264.

"I have not performed one of the prayers for the last forty years without supplicating for al-Shāfiʿī رَحِمَهُ ٱللَّهُ."[88]

Give careful regard to the fair-mindedness of the supplicant [Ibn Ḥanbal] and to the lofty status of the object of the supplication. Then compare it to the peers and equals among the scholars in these times and the enmity and animosity between them, that you might recognize the shortcomings in their claims to follow in the footsteps of those scholars [like al-Shāfiʿī and Ibn Ḥanbal].

Ibn Ḥanbal's son, seeing his habit of making supplication for him [al-Shāfiʿī], asked his father, "What kind of man was al-Shāfiʿī that you make all this supplication for him?" Aḥmad said, "O my son, al-Shāfiʿī رَحِمَهُ ٱللَّهُ was like the sun for this world and well-being for people."

Therefore consider this, is there anyone who can succeed these two [i.e., al-Shāfiʿī and Ibn Ḥanbal]?[89]

Aḥmad also stated, "Everyone who lays his hand upon an ink bottle owes al-Shāfiʿī رَحِمَهُ ٱللَّهُ a great debt."[90]

Yaḥyā b. Saʿīd al-Qaṭṭān said, "I have not performed a single prayer for the last forty years without supplicating for al-Shāfiʿī. This is because of the knowledge God عَزَّوَجَلَّ granted him and how He made him amenable to the guidance it contained."[91]

Let us restrict ourselves to this brief account of his states, for they are virtually limitless. We have taken the majority of these citations on the virtues from the book composed by Shaykh Naṣr b. Ibrāhīm al-Maqdisī رَحِمَهُ ٱللَّهُ on the virtues of al-Shāfiʿī رَضِيَ ٱللَّهُ عَنْهُ.

88 Al-Bayhaqī, *Manāqib al-Shāfiʿī*, 2:254.
89 Al-Bayhaqī, *Manāqib al-Shāfiʿī*, 2:254.
90 Al-Bayhaqī, *Manāqib al-Shāfiʿī*, 2:255.
91 Al-Bayhaqī, *Manāqib al-Shāfiʿī*, 1:233–234.

Imām Mālik رَحِمَهُ ٱللَّهُ

HE WAS ALSO ADORNED by these five traits [of the scholar of the knowledge of the hereafter]. He was asked [for example], "What do you say, O Mālik, about seeking knowledge?" To which he responded, "[It is] a worthy pursuit; however, fix your gaze on that which is incumbent upon you from the time you arise until the time you retire for the night and remain steadfast therein."[92]

He رَحِمَهُ ٱللَّهُ held the Islamic disciplines (*ʿilm al-dīn*) in such high esteem that when he intended to narrate *ḥadīth* he would make his ablutions, then sit on the front edge of his low dais, comb out his beard and apply perfume, [then] settle into a sitting position, and with dignity and solemnity he would narrate *ḥadīth*. When asked about that, he responded, "Upholding the exaltedness of the *ḥadīth* of the Messenger of God صَلَّى ٱللَّهُ عَلَيْهِ وَسَلَّمَ is very dear to me."[93] He said as well, "Knowledge is light that God places wherever he wills, it is not [attested to by] great numbers of *ḥadīth* narrations."[94]

This reverence and solemnity point to the strength of his realization of the sublime nature of God most high.

His desire for the countenance of God most high, [which he sought] through knowledge [of the hereafter], is well attested to in his saying, "Dialectics in religion have no place."[95]

Al-Shāfiʿī's رَحِمَهُ ٱللَّهُ statement also demonstrates this, "I witnessed Mālik being questioned on forty-eight matters, he responded to thirty-two of them with, 'I do not know.'"[96]

Whoever seeks other than the countenance of God with his pursuit of knowledge will not permit himself to admit that he has no knowledge of a topic. This explains why al-Shāfiʿī رَضِيَ ٱللَّهُ عَنْهُ said, "When the scholars are mentioned, Mālik is the star that pierces

92 Abū Nuʿaym, *Ḥilya*, 6:319.

93 Abū Nuʿaym, *Ḥilya*, 6:318.

94 Abū Nuʿaym, *Ḥilya*, 6:319.

95 Al-Bayhaqī, *al-Madkhal*, 238.

96 Ibn ʿAbd al-Barr, *al-Tamhīd*, 1:73.

through the darkness, there is no one that I have benefited from more than Mālik."[97]

It has been narrated that Abū Jaʿfar al-Manṣūr forbade him [Mālik] from relating *ḥadīth* dealing with the topic of divorce pronounced under compulsion. Then he [al-Manṣūr] conspired to send someone to ask [Mālik] about just this matter. He thus narrated before a large assembly of people, "There is no divorce incumbent upon one who is compelled." Whereupon he [Mālik] was whipped [by the governor of Medina] but did not renounce the narration of *ḥadīth*."[98]

Mālik رَحِمَهُ ٱللَّهُ said, "A person who is truthful in his speech, not lying, will have the benefit of his mental faculties, and in later life he will not be afflicted with infirmity or feeble-mindedness.[99]

His asceticism toward the worldly life is clear from a report [that says]: al-Mahdī, the Amīr of the Faithful [the third ʿAbbāsid caliph], asked him one day whether he owned a house or not. To which he responded, "No, but I will relate to you that I heard Rabīʿa b. Abī ʿAbd al-Raḥmān say, 'A person's lineage is his house.'"[100]

[Hārūn] al-Rashīd [the fourth ʿAbbāsid caliph] asked him if he owned a house, to which he responded, "No." So he gave him three hundred thousand dinars and said, "Buy a house with it." He took it and did not spend any of it. Then when al-Rashīd decided to travel [from Hijaz to Iraq after completing the pilgrimage] he said to Mālik رَحِمَهُ ٱللَّهُ [who resided in Medina], "You should depart with us, for I propose imposing [the legal injunctions of] *al-Muwaṭṭaʾ* [Mālik's compilation of *ḥadīth*] on the population in the same manner in which ʿUthmān رَضِيَ ٱللَّهُ عَنْهُ imposed [i.e., standardized] the Qurʾān." Whereupon he responded, "As far as imposing *al-Muwaṭṭaʾ* on the people, there is no way to accomplish this because the Companions of the Messenger of God صَلَّى ٱللَّهُ عَلَيْهِ وَسَلَّمَ have scattered throughout the lands after [he died] and narrated [*ḥadīth*]. Every land has its [particular] knowledge [and scholarly tradition], and the Messenger of God صَلَّى ٱللَّهُ عَلَيْهِ وَسَلَّمَ related, 'The differing opinions of my community

97 Ibn ʿAbd al-Barr, *al-Tamhīd*, 1:74; Ibn Farḥūn, *al-Dībāj al-madhhab*, 1:63.

98 Abū Nuʿaym, *Ḥilya*, 6:312. The one who whipped him was the governor of Medina, Jaʿfar b. Sulaymān, and this was during the caliphate of Abū Jaʿfar al-Manṣūr.

99 Ibn ʿAbd al-Barr, *al-Tamhīd*, 1:70.

100 Ibn ʿAbd al-Barr, *al-Intiqāʾ fī faḍāʾil al-thalāthat al-aʾimmat al-fuqahāʾ*, 79.

are a mercy.'[101] As far as my leaving with you, there is no way to move forward on this, for the Messenger of God ﷺ stated, 'Medina is better for them, if they but knew it.'[102] He ﷺ also stated, 'Medina cleanses its impurities like the bellows of the blacksmith eliminate impurities from iron.'[103] Here are your dinars just as they were, take them if you like, or leave them."[104] Here Mālik meant, "You [intend to] oblige me to leave Medina on account of the munificence you have shown me, but I will not favor [this] world over the city of the Messenger of God ﷺ." Thus was the asceticism of Mālik in [relation to this] world.

When great wealth from all directions of the world came to him as a result of the widespread dispersal of his knowledge and his companions, he distributed it in worthy ways. His munificence attests to his asceticism in [relation to this] world and the little love he had for it. For asceticism is not solely an absence of wealth, on the contrary it is the emptying of the heart; Solomon عَلَيْهِ ٱلسَّلَامُ with all his dominion was among the ascetics.

[Mālik's] disdain for this world is well illustrated in the account related by al-Shāfiʿī رَحِمَهُ ٱللَّهُ, who said, "I saw at Mālik's door a string of fine mounts, steeds from Khurasan and mules from Egypt, the likes of which I had never beheld before. So I said to Mālik رَحِمَهُ ٱللَّهُ, 'How handsome they are!' He said, 'They are a gift from me to you, O Abū ʿAbdallāh.' To which I replied, 'Leave yourself one of them as a mount you might ride upon.' He replied, 'I would feel shame

---

101 Al-Bayhaqī, *al-Madkhal*, 152, with the wording, "The differing opinions among my companions are a mercy for you." Al-Nawawī, *Sharḥ ṣaḥīḥ muslim*, 11:91, states that "[Abū Sulaymān] al-Khaṭṭābī said that it has been reported from the Prophet ﷺ that he said, 'The differing opinions of my community are a mercy.'" ʿUmar had approved of this statement. These words refer to the origin of the narration being analyzed. He [al-Nawawī] said, "He [al-Khaṭṭābī] objected to the *ḥadīth* 'The differing opinions of my community are a mercy' because of two men [in the chain of narrators]. One of them is held in contempt based on his religion, and he is ʿAmr b. Baḥr al-Jāḥiẓ. The other is known to be foolish and morally depraved, and he is Isḥāq b. Ibrāhīm al-Mawṣūlī." See also al-Zabīdī, *Itḥāf*, 1:204–206.

102 Al-Bukhārī, 1875; Muslim, 1363.

103 Al-Bukhārī, 1871, 1883; Muslim, 1382, 1383.

104 Abū Nuʿaym, *Ḥilya*, 6:331. In this narration, al-Maʾmūn appears instead of al-Rashīd. The confirmation is correct, and God knows best.

before God عَزَّوَجَلَّ were I to tread the ground in which lies the Prophet of God صَلَّىٱللَّهُعَلَيْهِوَسَلَّمَ with the hoof of a beast of burden."[105]

Behold [Mālik's] munificence, he bestowed all of that at once [on al-Shāfiʿī] and [behold] his reverence for the very ground of Medina.

His aspiration for the countenance of God تَعَالَىٰ through knowledge [of the hereafter] and his disdain for [this] world is well attested to in this statement narrated from him, in which he said, "I entered upon Hārūn al-Rashīd, and he said to me, 'O Abū ʿAbdallāh, you must visit us [here in the palace] frequently so that our young people may hear [and learn] *al-Muwaṭṭaʾ* from you.'" Mālik continued by saying, "May God honor the Commander of the Faithful! This knowledge emerged from you [i.e., Quraysh] originally; if you hold it in high esteem, you will be held in esteem, and if you demean it, you will be demeaned." He said, "You have spoken the truth. Depart [all of you] for the mosque so that you can hear [and learn] with the people.""[106]

Imām Abū Ḥanīfa رَحِمَهُٱللَّهُ

He was also a [devout] servant of God, an ascetic, and a gnostic who held Him in awe, and sought the countenance of God most high with his knowledge.

As for being a devout servant [of God], this is recognized from Ibn al-Mubārak's narration, in which he said, "Abū Ḥanīfa رَحِمَهُٱللَّهُ was a man of noble character and devotion to prayer."[107]

Ḥammād b. Abī Sulaymān reported that he would spend his entire night in prayer.[108] It was related [concerning this matter] that he would [at first] spend half the night in devotion; then, one day, as he was passing down a thoroughfare [in Kufa] someone pointed him out, as he was walking along, and said to another, "This is the one who passes the entire night in devotion." From that moment he never ceased to spend all his nights in devotion; he said [of this], "I

105 See al-Qāḍī ʿIyāḍ, *Tartīb al-madārik*, 1:93.

106 Al-Bayhaqī, *al-Madkhal*, 686.

107 Al-Khaṭīb al-Baghdādī, *Tārīkh Baghdād*, 13:352. This is from a statement by Sufyān b. ʿUyayna. He reported also that he was called "the tent peg" (*al-watid*) because of the amount of his prayer.

108 Ibn ʿAbd al-Barr, *al-Intiqāʾ fī faḍāʾil al-thalāthat al-aʾimmat al-fuqahāʾ*, 194.

would feel shame before God سُبْحَانَهُ if I were described as worshiping Him in a way that did not apply to me."[109]

As for his asceticism [in relation to this world], al-Rabīʿ b. ʿĀṣim said, "Yazīd b. ʿUmar b. Hubayra [the governor of Kufa] dispatched me to bring Abū Ḥanīfa before him. He pressed him [Abū Ḥanīfa] to take charge of the treasury, [but] he declined and was given twenty lashes."[110] Behold how he fled from [appointment to] political position and patiently bore the chastisement [given him].

Al-Ḥakam b. Hishām al-Thaqafī said, "I spoke about Abū Ḥanīfa in Syria and said that he was the most trustworthy of all men. It occurred that the Sultan [Marwān] pressed him to take the position to oversee the keys of the treasury or be whipped. He chose their punishment over the punishment of God most high."[111]

It is related that Abū Ḥanīfa was mentioned in the presence of Ibn al-Mubārak, who said, "Are you mentioning a man to whom this world in its totality was offered and he fled from it?"[112]

Muḥammad b. Shujāʿ related, on the authority of one of his companions,[113] that it was said to Abū Ḥanīfa, "Abū Jaʿfar [al-Manṣūr]—the Commander of the Faithful—ordered that you be given ten thousand dirhams." Then he said, "Abū Ḥanīfa was not content [at hearing that]." So on the day on which [they] anticipated that the money would be brought, he [Abū Ḥanīfa] prayed the morning prayer and covered himself [from head to foot] with his robes and did not speak. The messenger Ḥasan b. Qaḥṭaba brought the money and entered his presence, but [still] he did not speak. One of those present said, "He only speaks to us one word at a time." They meant that this was his habit in speech. Then he [the messenger Ḥasan] said, "Place the money in this leather purse [and leave it] in the corner of the room." Some time after these events Abū Ḥanīfa made bequests of his household possessions, saying to his son, "When I die and you lay me to rest, take this purse and give it to Ḥasan b.

109 Al-Khaṭīb al-Baghdādī, *Tārīkh Baghdād*, 13:353.

110 Ibn ʿAbd al-Barr, *al-Intiqāʾ fī faḍāʾil al-thalāthat al-aʾimmat al-fuqahāʾ*, 255.

111 Ibn ʿAbd al-Barr, *al-Intiqāʾ fī faḍāʾil al-thalāthat al-aʾimmat al-fuqahāʾ*, 255.

112 Ibn ʿAbd al-Barr, *al-Intiqāʾ fī faḍāʾil al-thalāthat al-aʾimmat al-fuqahāʾ*, 321.

113 According to al-Zabīdī these companions were Ḥasan b. ʿAmāra Abū Muḥammad al-Kūfī who is counted among the authorities that al-Tirmidhī narrated *ḥadīth* from. Al-Zabīdī, *Itḥāf*, 1:211.

Qaḥṭaba and tell him, 'This is the trust you left with Abū Ḥanīfa.'" His son said, "I did that, and Ḥasan said, 'May God have mercy on your father, he was truly a man well-founded in his religion.'"[114]

It was reported that he was summoned to assume the authority of chief judge, to which he replied, "I am not suited for it." He was asked why, and he said, "If I were truthful, then verily I am not suited for it; and if I were a liar, then a liar is not suitable for judgeship."[115]

His knowledge of the affairs of the hereafter, the way of religion, and his intimate realization of God عَزَّوَجَلَّ is attested to by the rigor of his fear of God most high and his asceticism [in relation to this] world. Ibn Jurayj reported, "It has reached me that your man of Kufa, this al-Nuʿmān b. Thābit [Abū Ḥanīfa], is a man with an inexorable fear of God تَعَالَىٰ."[116]

Sharīk al-Nakhaʿī related, "Abū Ḥanīfa was a man of long silence, constant reflection, and little engagement in debate with people."[117]

This then is among the clearest of indicators of inner knowledge and occupation with the essential elements of religion; whoever has been given silence and ascetic [detachment], has been given knowledge in its totality.

These are but brief accounts of the conditions of the three *imāms*.

Imām Aḥmad Ibn Ḥanbal and Sufyān رَحِمَهُمَااللَّهُ

THOSE WHO FOLLOW THEM are fewer than the followers of these [three], and Sufyān has fewer followers than Aḥmad. However, their renown for conscientiousness and asceticism are well known. The entirety of this book is filled with accounts of their deeds and teachings, such that there is little need to elaborate on them now.

So now consider judiciously the lives and teachings of these *imāms*, and reflect deeply on these spiritual states, words, and works in [their] renunciation of [this] world and [their] single-minded commitment to God عَزَّوَجَلَّ. Is all of this merely the fruit of knowledge of the derived branches of jurisprudence; of [discourse on] forward

114 Ibn ʿAbd al-Barr, *al-Intiqāʾ fī faḍāʾil al-thalāthat al-aʾimmat al-fuqahāʾ*, 321.
115 Al-Khaṭīb al-Baghdādī, *Tārīkh Baghdād*, 13:329.
116 Ibn ʿAbd al-Barr, *al-Intiqāʾ fī faḍāʾil al-thalāthat al-aʾimmat al-fuqahāʾ*, 209.
117 Ibn ʿAbd al-Barr, *al-Intiqāʾ fī faḍāʾil al-thalāthat al-aʾimmat al-fuqahāʾ*, 201.

buying concerning commercial dealings, or rental agreements, or divorce by repudiation, or separation by oath, or oaths in matters of adultery; or is all of this the fruit of another [aspect of] knowledge, loftier and nobler than that?

Regard carefully those who claim to be following in the footsteps
of these [*imāms*]; have they been truthful
in their claims or not? And
God knows
best.

3

On what the common folk consider to be the laudable sciences, and what is not part of them; and the elucidation of the reason certain sciences are blameworthy and the elucidation of the changing names applied to the sciences, these being jurisprudence, knowledge, unity, admonition, and wisdom, and including the elucidation of the laudable aspects of the legal sciences as well as the blameworthy among them.

An Elucidation on the Reason Some Knowledge is Blameworthy

YOU MAY ASSERT, "KNOWLEDGE constitutes the cognition of a thing according to its inherent nature; this is among the attributes of God سُبْحَانَهُ. So how can any knowledge—being knowledge—be blameworthy?"

Know that knowledge in and of itself is not blameworthy; it only becomes blameworthy in relation to the rights of the servants, [and this is] for one of three reasons.

The first is that it causes harm in some manner or another, either to the one who pursues it or to a third party. This is similar to the manner in which the practice of sorcery and fashioning talismans—both being based on fact[1]—are held to be blameworthy; thus the Qurʾān testifies to it, and that it is a cause that could lead to the separation of a husband and a wife.[2]

The Messenger of God ﷺ [himself] fell victim to sorcery and became ill due to it, until Gabriel apprised him of it, and the object on which a spell was cast was removed from beneath a stone in the depths of a well.[3]

Sorcery is a pursuit that derives from the knowledge of the characteristics of subtle substances and reckonings calculated on the points on the horizon from which the stars rise. From these essential substances a shape in the form of the victim of the magic is conjured, and the rising points of the stars are carefully observed in relationship to it; in conjunction with that, words of obscenity and disbelief that oppose the law are uttered over it. By this means, one achieves the support and aid of satans, and there arises by all this—according to the customary decree executed by God تَعَالَىٰ—strange unnatural states in the person who is afflicted by sorcery.

Acquaintance with these procedures, inasmuch as it is only acquaintance, is not blameworthy, but they are suitable for nothing but harming the populace, and a means to evil ends is evil; this, then, is the rationale behind its being blameworthy. An even clearer example would be of someone who was tracking the footsteps of one of the saints in order to take his life, and he had sought shelter from him in a hidden place; now, if this wicked person inquired where he was [hiding], it would not be permissible to apprise him of it; rather, lying [about it] would be compulsory; [in spite of the fact that] revealing his location would be giving guidance and providing knowledge of a thing, it would a reprehensible act, for it would bring about harm.

1 That is, it confirms its existence, and it is not possible to deny it, even though there are different opinions about the nature of it. Here "fact" (*ḥaqq*) does not necessarily meant that which is the opposite of falsehood.

2 Reference Q. 2:102.

3 Al-Bukhārī, 3175; Muslim, 2189.

The second reason is that, in most cases, it is directly detrimental to the one engaging in it. This is similar to astronomy/astrology, which in itself is not essentially blameworthy, for it is comprised of two categories.

The first is [based on] precise measurement. The Qurʾān declares that the paths of the sun and the moon are precisely measured out, as God تَعَالَىٰ says: *The sun and the moon* [*move*] *by precise calculation* [55:5]; and as He, the most powerful of speakers, states as well, *and the moon—We have determined for it phases, until it returns,* [*appearing*] *like the old date stalk* [36:39].

The second delves into laws. Its goal is to infer the causes behind phenomenal events. This is similar to the physician's determination about the progress of a patient's illness by taking his pulse. It is [a science] based on an intimate comprehension of the effect of God's تَعَالَىٰ custom (*sunna*) and pattern in His creation. The law (*sharʿa*), however, is critical of it. The Messenger of God صَلَّىٱللَّهُعَلَيْهِوَسَلَّمَ said, "Should [God's] decree (*qadar*) be brought up, refrain from speech; and should the stars be brought up, refrain from speech, and should my Companions be brought up, refrain from speech."[4] He صَلَّىٱللَّهُعَلَيْهِوَسَلَّمَ affirmed as well, "I fear for my community after me [only] three [matters]: the injustice of the leaders, belief in the stars, and denying [the truth of God's] decree."[5] ʿUmar b. al-Khaṭṭāb رَضِيَٱللَّهُعَنْهُ stated, "Learn of the stars that which guides you by them on land and at sea, then refrain [from pursuing more knowledge of them]."[6]

Its pursuit has been prohibited based on the following three rationales:

One of them is that it is detrimental for most people; for if they were taught that phenomenal events occur as results associated with the movement of the stars, it would occur to them that the stars were the ultimate cause [behind the events] and that they were divine entities dictating [worldly affairs] because they are sublime heavenly substances. Awe of them would be magnified in hearts and a heart would remain turned toward them. They would perceive good and evil—as that which is hoped for or dreaded—deriving from them;

4 Al-Ṭabarānī, *al-Muʿjam al-kabīr*, 2:96; and Abū Nuʿaym, *Ḥilya*, 4:108.

5 Ibn ʿAbd al-Barr, *Jāmiʿ bayān al-ʿilm wa-faḍlih*, 1482.

6 Ibn Abī Shayba, *al-Muṣannaf*, 26162.

thus effacing the remembrance of God (*dhikr Allāh*) from the heart. A weak-minded person has his vision restricted to the intermediary causes [of events]; whereas the well-versed scholar is fully aware that the sun, moon, and stars all submit to the command of God سُبْحَانَهُ.

The example of the perception of the weak-minded [person's] conclusion that the light of the sun is due to the sun's rising is similar to the example of the ant—if it were given an intellect and found itself on a sheet of paper looking at the black ink as it traced words, it would believe that [words] arose from the pen; its perception does not extend to the awareness of the fingers, then from that to the hand, then from that to the motive behind he who sets the hand in motion, then from there to the capable intent of the scribe and from him to the creator of the hand, the ability [to write], and the intention. The perception of the majority of people is limited to the immediate causes [of events], they are disconnected from perception of the One who causes all causes. This is one rationale behind the prohibition of [pursuing] the field of astrology.

The second is that judgments derived from astrology are pure conjecture. Nothing is apprehended in specific cases, neither with certainty nor probability. Judgments based on it are judgments based on ignorance. Therefore condemnation of [astrology] is because it is considered ignorance, not knowledge.

According to what is said, astronomy was a miracle accorded to [the prophet] Idrīs عَلَيْهِ ٱلسَّلَامُ [by God],[7] when knowledge faded away and disappeared. Those events that accord with—and this only rarely—the accurate prediction of the astrologer are nothing but happenstance. For he may come to be apprised of certain [secondary] causes for which the [final] result is only realized through multiple conditions, the realities (*ḥaqāʾiq*) of which a human being has no means of understanding. If it should come to pass that God تَعَالَىٰ decrees the remaining causes, accuracy will result; and should He not decree [the causes], then he [the astrologer] will be inaccurate.

7 Based on the *ḥadīth* narrated in Muslim, 537: "One of the prophets used to draw a line (*khaṭṭā*), then whoever acted in agreement with it, that would occur." It was said that this was the Prophet Idrīs عَلَيْهِ ٱلسَّلَامُ and that the meaning of *khaṭṭ* is either astrology or geomancy (divination by means of figures or lines in the sand). See al-Zabīdī, *Itḥāf*, 1:224.

This case resembles the conjecture of a person that it will rain today whenever he sees clouds gathering and descending from the mountains, and in his mind he supposes it to be the case. However, the day may become hot and sunny and the clouds [may] dissipate, or it may occur otherwise, for clouds alone are not sufficient to bring rain, and the remaining causes are not to be comprehended. Likewise there is the conjecture of the mariner, reliant on his experience of the winds, that his ship will be out of harm's way [on its voyage]. Those winds [however] have subtle causes that he does not grasp; so at times his prediction is accurate and at times inaccurate. It is for this rationale that one [who is] strong [in his faith and conviction] forbids [the practice of] astrology.

The third [rationale behind forbidding astrology] is that there is no benefit in it. The least [that can be said] of its traits is that it is immersing oneself in superfluous matters that do not concern one and it is a waste of one's life—which is the most precious possession a human being has—without [accruing] benefit, which is the epitome of loss. The Messenger of God ﷺ passed by a man around whom people had gathered, and he asked, "What is this?" To which they responded, "A knowledgeable man." He asked, "Of what?" They said, "Of poetry and the family lines of the Arabs." To which he ﷺ responded, "Knowledge that does not benefit and ignorance that does no harm."[8] The Messenger of God عَلَيْهِ ٱلصَّلَاةُ وَٱلسَّلَامُ also said, "Knowledge is constituted in a precise verse (*āya muḥkama*), an established *sunna*, or a just obligatory act."[9]

Therefore, preoccupation in [the pursuit and practice of] astrology and that which resembles it is a hazardous undertaking and immersion in a sea of ignorance without any benefit whatsoever. Whatever has been decreed [by God] will be; there is no circumventing it. This is in contrast to the pursuit of medicine, for which there is a great need, and [in medicine] the majority of proofs are based on what is observable. It is in contrast as well to the interpretation of dreams,

8 Ibn ʿAbd al-Barr, *Jāmiʿ bayān al-ʿilm wa-faḍlih*, 1385.

9 Ibn ʿAbd al-Barr, *Jāmiʿ bayān al-ʿilm wa-faḍlih*, 1384; 1386, originally in Abū Dāwūd, 2885, and Ibn Māja, 54.

which, although it does comprise conjecture, delves into one part of the forty-six parts of prophecy[10] and there is no hazard in it.

The third reason [that knowledge may become blameworthy is that it is] immersion in a field in which the seeker is not firmly established. This is intrinsically blameworthy, similar to learning the minute details of a discipline before its evident essentials; or the hidden before the explicit; or like inquiry into the subtleties of divine reality, for it is the philosophers and theologians who strive for these without being firmly established in them; when in fact, only the prophets and the saints become established in this knowledge, in its entirety or certain of its branches. It is therefore obligatory to prevent people from inquiring into these matters and turn them to that which the law speaks of; for in that there is sufficiency for those who would be successful. How many individuals have become immersed in the sciences to their own detriment? Had he not immersed himself therein, his circumstances, where religion is concerned, would have been superior to where he finally ended up.

No one disagrees that knowledge may harm certain people, in the same manner that the meat of certain birds and varieties of fine sweets may harm a breast-feeding infant; in fact [in] many [cases] an individual's ignorance of certain matters benefits him.

It was related that a man complained to a physician of the infertility of his wife—that she did not bear children. The physician examined her pulse and told her, "You have no need of medication to conceive [a child], for you will die in forty days; your pulse has revealed it as such." The woman was terrified, and her life became bereft of all joy. She withdrew all her wealth, divided it [among her family], and made her last will and testament. She ceased eating and drinking until the time allotted her had passed, and she did not die. Her husband approached the physician and informed him that she had not died. The physician responded saying, "I know that, approach your wife now, and she will become pregnant." The husband said, "How can this be?" So he replied, "I recognized that she was overweight and her excess tissue had knotted itself around the opening of her womb, and I knew that she would only lose

10 Al-Bukhārī, 6983; Muslim, 2264. The *ḥadīth* reads: "The good vision of a righteous man is one forty-sixth of prophecy."

weight with the fear of death, so I frightened her in that manner so she would lose weight, thus removing the impediment to become pregnant."

This should awaken in you awareness of the harm inherent in certain subjects and bring you to understand the meaning of his ﷺ saying, "We seek protection from knowledge that brings no benefit."[11]

Consider this story carefully and do not delve into fields that the law has denounced and prohibited. Remain steadfast to the example set by the Companions رَضِيَ ٱللَّهُ عَنْهُم and constrain yourself to following the *sunna*, for well-being resides in abiding by good examples and peril abides in raising questions and acting independently. Do not boast much in your judgment of things, your intellectual gleanings, your reasoned proof, and your arguments; nor in your contention that, "I investigate things in order to recognize them according to their nature. What harm could befall me from pondering the sciences?" Its harm that comes to you is extensive. How many things have you striven to know, the very pursuit of which—should God not overtake you with His mercy—could bring harm to you and cause your downfall in the hereafter.

Know that in the same manner an astute, well-trained physician perceives the subtle qualities of treating the infirm, while someone having no knowledge thereof may consider it far-fetched. Yet, in like manner the prophets are the physicians of the heart, and the scholars are [the physicians] of the means of attaining [well-being in] the hereafter. Therefore, judge not their manners and customs against your own intellectual gleanings lest you perish. Not infrequently a person may experience discomfort in his finger, and based on his own judgment daub it [with ointment] until an astute, well-trained physician calls his attention to the fact that his treatment requires that he apply the ointment to the palm of his hand on the opposite side of his body, which he finds far-fetched in the extreme since he has no knowledge of the manner in which the nerves branch out from their origins and the manner in which they wind throughout the body. Likewise is the path to the hereafter.

---

11 Muslim, 2722.

There are secrets and subtle truths that the rational faculties have no means of encompassing or strength [to grasp] in the essentials of well-established customs of the law and their conduct, and in the creed on which people have founded their practices. Likewise in stones of a singular nature there are strange and marvelous properties that are unseen, even to those engaged in the profession [i.e., geologists], to the extent that no one is capable of discerning the reason that a magnet attracts iron.

The marvels and wonders comprised in the beliefs and actions, and their benefits, which render hearts lucid, pure, untainted, sanctified, and sound so they can ascend to God's تَعَالَىٰ proximity and partake of the gentle winds of His beneficence, are more numerous and far greater than that which are in medicinal substances and herbal remedies. In the same manner that the rational faculty is incapable of discerning the beneficial properties of medicinal substances, even given that experience can provide a means of acquiring knowledge of it, the rational faculty is incapable of discerning what benefits one in the hereafter, given that experience here [in this world] is not a means of reaching it. Experience would only be a means of reaching it if some of the dead were to return to us and apprise us of those beneficial, accepted deeds that bring us to a station of proximity to God تَعَالَىٰ, and of those [deeds] that distance us from Him, and also about the dictates of faith. There being no expectation of this, the benefits of the rational faculty [or intellect] should be sufficient to guide you to affirm the veracity of the Messenger صَلَّىٰ ٱللَّٰهُ عَلَيْهِ وَسَلَّمَ and bring or cause you to comprehend the ways leading to his good guidance.

Then after that, rein in the intellect from [influencing your] behavior and remain steadfast in following [the *sunna*], for nothing else will save you. For this very reason the Messenger of God صَلَّىٰ ٱللَّٰهُ عَلَيْهِ وَسَلَّمَ said, "In knowledge there is ignorance, and in speech self aggrandizement."[12] It is clear that knowledge is not ignorance, but it may provoke the mischief and harm provoked by ignorance.

---

12 Abū Dāwūd, 5012. The term *ʿayāl* in the *ḥadīth* means mentioning your honorable status to someone who has no interest in it and does not want to hear it. Al-Munāwī said in *al-Taysīr*, 1:345, "It is vexation. Thus the hearer is either knowledgeable and becomes bored, or he is ignorant and does not understand, and thus becomes wearied. It is derived from *ʿāl*, *al-ʿāla*, *yaʿīl*, *ʿayl*, and *ʿayāl*, for it is not

The Messenger of God ﷺ said, "A modicum of success [from God] is superior to a great deal of knowledge."[13] Jesus عَلَيْهِ ٱلسَّلَامُ was heard to say, "How many trees there are while not all of them bear fruit, and plentiful is fruit, yet not all is ripe, and how much knowledge there is and yet all is not beneficial."[14]

An Elucidation of the Names of the Disciplines that have been Altered

KNOW THAT THE ORIGIN of the confusion between the blameworthy disciplines and the legal [i.e., praiseworthy] disciplines was the distortion of the names of the praiseworthy [disciplines]. [These names] were changed and transformed—for corrupt reasons—to mean something other than the righteous predecessors and the first generation intended. The names [of these disciplines] are five: jurisprudence, knowledge, unity, admonition, and wisdom. These designations are all praiseworthy, and those to whom they are attributed are the masters of dignity in religion. But, in the present era, their meanings [i.e., what these five terms designate] have been transformed into [something] blameworthy. And hearts [i.e., people] have been reluctant to condemn them [i.e., the jurist, the scholar, etc.] because of the widespread practice of misusing these names.

---

known to which form it is related." In some manuscripts it is *ʿiyyan* (similar meaning) as in Abū Ṭālib al-Makkī, *Qūṭ al-qulūb*, 1:131.

13 Abū Ṭālib al-Makkī, *Qūṭ al-qulūb*, 1:131. He adds the statement "in another report" and mentions that the author follows it in this instance. Ibn ʿAsākir reported something similar in *Tārīkh Dimashq*, 60:348, with the wording, "A little divine guidance (*tawfīq*) is superior to extensive intellect."

14 Al-Khaṭīb al-Badhdādī, *Iqtiḍāʾ al-ʿilm al-ʿamal*, 67, with the wording, "Woe to you, O slaves to this world. What good comes from the wide light of the sun to a blind man who cannot see. Likewise, what good comes to a scholar from his extensive knowledge if he does not act according to it. How many fruit trees are there, but not all of them give benefit or could be eaten. How many scholars are there, yet none of you gain benefit from knowledge." It is transmitted with this wording by al-Zamakhsharī, *Rabīʿ al-abrār*, 4:123.

The First Term: Jurisprudence

The scholars have altered it by making it a specialized field of intellectual endeavor, rather than actually transforming or changing its meaning. They have particularized it to denote the knowledge of atypical branches of rulings, the scrutiny of the minutiae behind their reasoning process, and exaggerated debate over them, as well as the memorization of statements that are relevant to them. It is said of whoever scrutinizes them most deeply and involves himself the most in them that "He is the most knowledgeable of them in *fiqh*."

Yet, in the earliest times of this community the word *fiqh* was employed to denote the science of the path of the hereafter, the recognition of the minute evils of the souls or subtle afflictions of the souls, and those defects in one's actions that render them invalid, as well as [to denote] the overpowering insight into the base nature of this world, the intense perception of the precious gifts of the hereafter, and the heart overwhelmed by fear [of God].

This [meaning] is well demonstrated for you in God's تَعَالَىٰ statement: *Let them devote themselves to acquiring discernment in the religion* (yatafaqqahū), *so that they may warn their people when they return to them,* [*in order that they be on their guard*] [9:122]

[Clearly] that which comprises [this] admonition and warning is the [denotation] of *fiqh* [as discernment]; it is not the multifaceted opinions dealing with divorce, the freeing of slaves, oaths in matters of adultery, commercial dealings in which payment precedes delivery of merchandise, and rental agreements; for that there is neither admonition nor warning; on the contrary devoting oneself to such a pursuit, without cessation, only hardens the heart and divests it of apprehension [of God], just as we witness in these times among those devoted exclusively to it.

God تَعَالَىٰ states: *They have hearts with which they do not understand* [7:179]; and intends the meanings of faith not legal rulings.

I swear by my life that the two Arabic terms *fiqh* and *fahm* have but one meaning. In such we have used the terms in conventional usage both presently and in early times. God تَعَالَىٰ stated: *You* [*believers*] *are more fearful within their breasts than God. That is because they are a people who do not understand* [59:13]. Their lack of fear of God and exaggerated fear of men's domination [over them] is rendered [in this verse] as the result of their lack of discernment.

So look closely, [and ask yourself] whether that was the result of an absence of being well-versed in the varying views related to legal opinions, or of the absence of the disciplines we have mentioned [above].

The Messenger of God ﷺ said, "Scholars, the wise, people of discernment";[15] are nearer to the prophets because of their veracity.

Saʿd b. Ibrāhīm al-Zuhrī was asked, "Which of the people of Medina are the most discerning?" He responded, "The most pious of them,"[16] as though he were indicating the fruits of discernment (*fiqh*), for piety is the fruit of the discipline of inner discernment, not legal opinions or rulings.

The Messenger of God ﷺ said, "Shall I not apprise you of who is the true person of discernment?" To which they responded, "Certainly." So he said, "Whoever does not cause the people to lose hope of God's mercy, nor make them secure from God's plans, nor bring them to despair of God's beneficence [toward them], nor does he forsake the Qurʾān, turning from it for anything else."[17]

When Anas b. Mālik رَضِيَ ٱللَّهُ عَنْهُ related Muḥammad's ﷺ words, "That I should seat myself among a people mentioning God تَعَالَىٰ from early dawn until the sunrise is more beloved to me than the freeing of four slaves,"[18] he [Abū Ṭālib al-Makkī] said, "He looked at Yazīd al-Raqāshī and Ziyād al-Namīrī and said, "The gatherings for the mention of God تَعَالَىٰ were not like your gathering here; one of you relates an account of early times and delivers a sermon to his brethren and narrates *ḥadīth*—one after another; whereas we used to sit discussing belief, pondering [the meanings of] the Qurʾān, learning discernment in the science of the religion, and counting

15 Abū Nuʿaym, *Ḥilya*, 9:279; Ibn ʿAsākir, *Tārīkh Dimashq*, 41:200, with the variant, "*ʿulamāʾ ḥukamāʾ*; those who give them credence are near the station of the prophets."

16 Abū Ṭālib al-Makkī, *Qūt al-qulūb*, 1:137.

17 Ibn ʿAbd al-Barr, *Jāmiʿ bayān al-ʿilm wa-faḍlih*, 1510 attributed to the Prophet (and in al-Dārimī, *Sunan*, 305), and other collections stopping at ʿAlī b. Abū Ṭālib رَضِيَ ٱللَّهُ عَنْهُ.

18 Abū Dāwūd, 3667.

the graces that God had bestowed upon us."[19] He called pondering the meanings of the Qur'ān and counting God's graces attaining discernment.

He ﷺ said, "No devout servant of God can claim total discernment (*fiqh*) until he feels an aversion for all humankind for God's sake, and until he sees in the Qur'ān manifold levels [of comprehension]"; it has been narrated as well from Abū l-Dardāʾ ؓ that he said, concerning the [the Messenger's] words, "then let him look within himself and be more severe in his aversion."[20]

Farqad al-Sabakhī asked Ḥasan [al-Baṣrī] a question [dealing with knowledge] and he answered him. Then [al-Sabakhī] said, "The jurists differ with your opinion." To which Ḥasan responded, "May your mother be bereft of you, O Furayqid! Have you ever seen a jurist with your own eyes? A [true] jurist is a man of ascetic discipline toward this world, who is attracted to the hereafter, insightful in his religious practices, constant in the worship of his Lord, conscientious, who abstains from affairs of other Muslims [that do not concern him], has no intentions toward their wealth, and is a source of good guidance to the community."[21] He did not say in all that, "Well-versed in the varying views related to legal opinions."

I do not suggest that the term *fiqh* was not applied to legal opinions dealing with judgments related to the evident facets [of religious practice]; it was, but for the purpose of generality and comprehensiveness or for the purpose of sequential arrangement.[22] The term was mostly used [in relation to] knowledge of the hereafter. Only then, from this specific adaptation, did the confusion arise that drove people to devote themselves solely to its pursuit while shunning the knowledge of the hereafter and the judgments of the heart. In the propensity to devote themselves to jurisprudence they found an ally in human nature itself. The knowledge of the inner states is complex and its application difficult; and it is virtually impossible to attain political position, judgeships, rank, and wealth

---

19 Abū Ṭālib al-Makkī, *Qūt al-qulūb*, 1:150.
20 Ibn ʿAbd al-Barr, *Jāmiʿ bayān al-ʿilm wa-faḍlih*, 1515, 1516, both as attributed to the Prophet and stopping at Abū l-Dardāʾ ؓ, the *waqf* is sound in this instance.
21 Abū Ṭālib al-Makkī, *Qūt al-qulūb*, 1:153.
22 Here al-Ghazālī makes the field of legal rulings secondary to the sciences of the hereafter. Al-Zabīdī, *Itḥāf*, 1:235.

through it. Satan therein found a means of beautifying the pursuit of jurisprudence for the hearts of people by means of this specific adaptation of the term *fiqh*; that itself is a laudable term from the perspective of its religious usage.

The Second Term: Knowledge (*ʿilm*)

[The term] had been applied to the knowledge of God تَعَالَىٰ, His signs and acts among His servants and creation; so much so that when ʿUmar رَضِيَ ٱللَّٰهُ عَنْهُ died, Ibn Masʿūd رَضِيَ ٱللَّٰهُ عَنْهُ said, "Nine-tenths of knowledge has died"; he employed the definite article and then interpreted his words to mean "knowledge of God," as mentioned earlier.

They [contemporary scholars] have also particularized it [knowledge] such that they use it for the one who occupies himself in exaggerated debate with his adversaries over the minutiae of *fiqh* rulings and their like. It is then stated, "He is truly a man of knowledge" or "He is a stallion of knowledge." Those who do not engage in these practices, nor occupy themselves therein, are numbered among the generality of poorly prepared scholars, and are not counted among the ranks of the people of knowledge. This is also an aspect of particularization, in spite of the fact that the majority of narrations that have characterized the excellence of knowledge and knowledgeable persons refer to those knowledgeable of God عَزَّوَجَلَّ, His laws, acts, and attributes.

The term [knowledge] has now come to be applied to anyone who does not comprehend anything of the disciplines of the law other than the formal refutation over differing legal opinions.[23] Yet because of this he is counted among the stallions of the scholars in spite of his ignorance of the interpretation of the Qurʾān, the [transmitted] reports, the schools of jurisprudence, and their like. This [particular definition of knowledge] has been the reason behind the ruin of many seekers of knowledge.

23 That is, one who only understands formal refutation and differing legal opinions.

The Third Term: Unity (*tawḥīd*)

Today this term has come to mean theology (*kalām*), knowledge of the means of debate (*mujādala*), an encompassing grasp of the means to refute an opponent, the ability to speak affectedly by employing detailed questions and specious arguments, and the invention of binding assumptions [based upon reason], such that some factions have labeled themselves the people of justice and unity.[24] The dialectical theologians are called the scholars of unity, despite the fact that during the first era [of this community] nothing that is particular to this field of inquiry was known. On the contrary, there was rigorous censorship on anyone who opened the door of debate and disputation. The Qurʾān contains clear proofs that all minds can readily accept on first hearing them, and this is well known to everyone.

Knowledge of the Qurʾān was knowledge, in its entirety. The term *tawḥīd* was, for them, an expression of a different subject that the majority of the dialectical theologians did not comprehend; and if they comprehended it, it was not evident in their comportment. They saw that all affairs are from God عَزَّوَجَلَّ by way of a vision that turns one's attention away from [secondary] causes and intermediary means. Thus one perceives neither good nor evil originating from any source but God عَزَّوَجَلَّ. This is a noble station, one whose fruit is absolute trust (*tawakkul*) in God, as we shall elucidate in the *Kitāb al-tawḥīd wa-tawakkul* [Book 35, *On Unity and Trust*].

Among the fruits [of this knowledge] is that one ceases complaining about others [for one's misfortunes], ceases feeling anger toward them, and feels satisfaction and acceptance of God's تَعَالَىٰ decrees.

One of its fruits is reflected in Abū Bakr al-Ṣiddīq's رَضِيَ اللَّهُ عَنْهُ statement when he was asked if he wanted a doctor when he had fallen ill. He responded, "The doctor caused my illness."[25]

Another statement was attributed to Abū Bakr, when he had fallen ill and was asked, "What did the doctor say about your illness?"

24 *Ahl al-ʿadl wa-l-tawḥīd*, they are better known as the Muʿtazilī faction.

25 This statement has been attributed to more than one of the Companions. The majority of narrations originate from ʿAbdallāh b. Masʿūd رَضِيَ اللَّهُ عَنْهُ, as is the case in al-Bayhaqī's narration in *Shuʿab al-īmān*, 2267; see al-Zabīdī, *Itḥāf*, 1:237.

He said, "He said to me, 'Verily, I accomplish all that I intend.'"[26] Other examples will follow in *Kitāb al-tawḥīd wa-tawakkul* [Book 35, *On Unity and Trust*].

Unity (*tawḥīd*) is a precious jewel that is enclosed in two outer husks, one [is] more distant from the heart of the matter than the other. People have specified the name itself [*tawḥīd*] for the outer layer and busied themselves with protecting it while neglecting the essential core altogether.

The first husk [of these two coverings] is to say with your tongue, "There is no god but God" (*lā ilāha illa-Llāh*). This is termed the attestation of unity, [it] contradicts the doctrine of the trinity that the Christians attest to; but this [attestation] may originate from a hypocrite whose outward conduct contradicts his inward state.

The second husk is that there is not within the heart the least contradiction or denial of understanding this attestation; on the contrary, the exterior of the heart envelops its conviction and affirms its veracity. This is the doctrine of unity among the generality of the people. The dialectical theologians—as previously stated—are the guardians of this husk; [they guard it] from the confusion of theological innovators.

The third [facet] is the heart of the matter. It is seeing that everything that may arise is from God تَعَالَىٰ ; [one sees] with a perception that severs one's regard from all intermediaries. And that one worships Him such that his worship is solely for Him; he worships none other than He. Obeying desire (*hawā*) is excluded from this unity; for whoever obeys his desire has taken his own desires as his object of worship. God تَعَالَىٰ says, *Have you seen he who has taken as his god his* [*own*] *desire* [*hawā*]? [45:23]. The Messenger صَلَّىٰ ٱللَّٰهُ عَلَيْهِ وَسَلَّمَ said, "In the sight of God تَعَالَىٰ the most loathsome god worshiped on the face of the earth is desire (*hawā*)."[27]

In reality, whoever thinks deeply knows that the worshiper of carved images is not worshiping the image, he is worshiping his passionate desire while his soul leans toward the religious practices of his forefathers. Thus he obeys that inclination; and the inclination

26 Abū Nuʿaym, *Ḥilya*, 1:34.

27 Ibn Abī ʿĀṣim, *al-Sunna*, 3; al-Ṭabarānī, *al-Muʿjam al-kabīr*, 8:103, with a similar narration.

of the soul toward habitual behavior is one of the meanings that the term *hawā* conveys.

This attestation of unity excludes both bitterness toward others and inclining toward them. For how can anyone who sees everything originating in God عَزَّوَجَلَّ experience bitterness toward other than He? This was the station [of faith] that the term *tawḥīd* conveyed, and it is among the stations of those who affirm God's truth.

Notice what it has been turned into, and with which husk people have been satisfied. And notice how this became a means of preserving boastfulness and vainglory in that which is praiseworthy in name, but has become totally emptied of the meaning that true praise merits.

This is similar to the impoverishment of one who rises early, and faces the direction of Mecca (*qibla*), and says, *I have turned my face toward He who created the heavens and the earth, inclining toward truth* [6:79]. It is the first lie with which he opens each day to God while the face of his heart is not turned toward God عَزَّوَجَلَّ exclusively; for if he intended by "face" the outward face only, he directed himself solely toward the shrine of the Kaʿba [in Mecca], and this only directs him [away] from all other directions. The Kaʿba is not the direction to the One who created the heavens and the earth unless the one turning toward it is turning to Him [God], who is exalted above having directions and realms limit Him.

If, however, he intended the face of the heart—which is the status the servant seeks—how can his speech be taken as truthful while his heart wavers between his desires and worldly wants, [it is] distracted and connives to accrue wealth, position, and multiple opportunities [in all these things], and is turned totally toward them? So when has he turned his face in the direction of the One who created the heavens and the earth?

These words are a summation of the reality of unity. The one who attests to unity is one who perceives naught but the One (*al-wāḥid*), the Absolute Truth (*al-Ḥaqq*). He directs his face only to Him, and he exemplifies God's تَعَالَىٰ words, *Say, "God* [*revealed it*]*." Then leave them in their* [*empty*] *discourse, amusing themselves* [6:91]. The intended meaning here is not the utterance of the tongue; the tongue is but an interpreter, truthful at times, lying at others.

The locality for the vision of God تَعَالَىٰ only [comes] from where the interpretation arises, and that is the heart, the repository of unity and its source.

The Fourth Term: Remembrance and Admonition

God تَعَالَىٰ has declared, *remind [them]! for indeed remembrance* (dhikrā) *benefits the believers* [51:55].

Many reports have been related that praise the gatherings held for remembrance. Such is the saying of the Messenger ﷺ, "When you pass by the gardens of heaven, gaze therein." He was asked, "What are the gardens of heaven?" To which he responded, "Gatherings for remembrance."[28]

In a *ḥadīth* [he said], "God possesses angels traveling through the sky—other than the angels that watch humankind—when they see a gathering for remembrance they call one another, saying, 'Hasten to your heart's desire!' They thus descend upon them, and cover them [with their wings], and listen.' Will you not then...remember God and admonish your own souls."[29]

This has been distorted in our day to the point that you see most of those engaged in admonition [of the people] resorting to stories, poetry, ecstatic outbursts, and outrageous utterances.

As for stories, they are an innovation in religion, and predecessors have passed on the prohibition of frequenting storytellers. They have said, "That did not exist in the times of the Messenger of God ﷺ, nor in the times of Abū Bakr and ʿUmar رَضِيَ ٱللَّهُ عَنْهُمَا, it was only in the *fitna* [period of discord or tribulation] that storytellers appeared.[30]

28 Al-Tirmidhī, 3510.

29 Al-Bukhārī, 6407; Muslim, 2689 with something similar.

30 Ibn Māja, 3754; Aḥmad b. Ḥanbal, *Musnad*, 3:449: "The first storyteller was Tamīm al-Dārī رَحِمَهُ ٱللَّهُ. He asked permission of ʿUmar b. al-Khaṭṭāb رَضِيَ ٱللَّهُ عَنْهُ to relate stories while standing, and ʿUmar permitted him that. Blameworthy storytelling began with the discord that arose between the Muslims after the murder of ʿUthmān b. ʿAffān رَضِيَ ٱللَّهُ عَنْهُ.

It was narrated that Ibn ʿUmar رضي الله عنهما walked out of the mosque, saying, "I only walked out on account of the storyteller; if it had not been for him I would not have left."[31]

Ḍamra related, "I said to Sufyān al-Thawrī, 'Shall we turn our faces toward the storyteller?' He responded, 'Turn your backs to innovations in the religion.'"[32]

Ibn ʿAwn narrated, "I came upon Ibn Sīrīn, and he asked, 'What news has passed today?' So I said, "The amir has forbidden storytellers to relate their tales."[33]

Al-Aʿmash entered the [congregational] mosque of Basra and saw a storyteller relating a tale in which he said, "Al-Aʿmash narrated to us. . ." So he strode into the gathering and began to pluck out the hair from under his armpit, to which the storyteller shouted out, "O Shaykh, have you no shame?!" So he [al-Aʿmash] said, "Why? I am practicing the *sunna*, and you are lying! I am al-Aʿmash, and I have never narrated a story to you."[34]

Aḥmad b. Ḥanbal said, "The greatest liars are the storytellers and aggressive mendicants."[35]

ʿAlī رضي الله عنه expelled the storytellers from the [congregational] mosque of Basra; but on hearing Ḥasan al-Baṣrī he allowed him to stay.[36] For in his discourse he spoke of the knowledge of the hereafter, warned of approaching death, called attention to the faults of the soul, the flawed actions, and satanic promptings and how to protect oneself from them. He also admonished people to remember God's graces and blessings, and kept in mind the servant's shortcomings in expressing gratitude. He also spoke of the insignificance of the worldly life and its defects, meagerness, and brevity, and of the magnitude of the hereafter and its terrors.

This is the praiseworthy admonition prescribed by the law that was encouraged in the *ḥadīth* of Abū Dharr رضي الله عنه, wherein he stated, "Attending a gathering of remembrance is superior to praying a thousand prayer cycles (*rakʿa*); attending a gathering of

---

31 Abū Ṭālib al-Makkī, *Qūṭ al-qulūb*, 1:151.
32 Abū Ṭālib al-Makkī, *Qūṭ al-qulūb*, 1:151.
33 Abū Ṭālib al-Makkī, *Qūṭ al-qulūb*, 1:151.
34 Abū Ṭālib al-Makkī, *Qūṭ al-qulūb*, 1:151.
35 Abū Ṭālib al-Makkī, *Qūṭ al-qulūb*, 1:151.
36 Abū Ṭālib al-Makkī, *Qūṭ al-qulūb*, 1:148.

knowledgeable discourse is superior to visiting a thousand people who are ill; attending a gathering of knowledgeable discourse is superior to attending a thousand funerals." Whereupon it was asked, "O Messenger of God صَلَّى ٱللَّٰهُ عَلَيْهِ وَسَلَّمَ! And [a gathering for] reciting the Qur'ān?" He responded, "Is there any benefit in the recitation of the Qur'ān without knowledge?"[37]

Ibn ʿAṭā' رَحِمَهُ ٱللَّٰهُ said, "A single gathering of remembrance atones for seventy gatherings of heedless distraction."[38]

The people who rhetorically embellished their speech have taken these *ḥadīths* as a proof of their own purity [in their gatherings]. They have joined the term 'admonition' to their outlandish fables, all the while forgetting the praiseworthy path of real remembrance (*dhikr*). They occupy themselves with tales that only lead to differences of opinion, addendums, and deletions, [they have] clearly departed from the stories that occur in the Qur'ān itself and [even] add to them. Indeed there are stories that benefit those who listen to them; yet therein is that which is harmful even if it is accurate. Whoever opens that door for himself confounds truth with lies and that which is beneficial with that which is harmful; for this reason it was banned. This is why Aḥmad b. Ḥanbal said, "How needy the people are of a veracious storyteller."[39]

If [for example] the story dealt with the tales of the prophets عَلَيْهِمُ ٱلسَّلَامُ as they relate to the affairs of their religions, and the storyteller was well versed in sound narration, I see no objection.

But beware of falsehood and tales about matters that lead [naive minds] to errors of negligence or concessions that common people have limited understanding of and [are unable] to grasp. Their states [are] as exceptional errors that require acts of expiation and [are only] rectifiable by worthy deeds that will overcome them. The people [in these cases] may take refuge with that in his concessions and errors of negligence and prepare an excuse for himself therein. He argues that such and such was related by some of the authoritative elders and notables; and since all of us are susceptible to disobedience, there should be no surprise if I disobey God, for those who are of

37 Abū Ṭālib al-Makkī, *Qūt al-qulūb*, 1:149; also see Ibn Ḥajar al-ʿAsqalānī, *Lisān al-mīzān*, 1:495, and al-Zabīdī, *Itḥāf*, 1:99.

38 Abū Ṭālib al-Makkī, *Qūt al-qulūb*, 1:149.

39 Abū Ṭālib al-Makkī, *Qūt al-qulūb*, 1:151.

loftier station than I have disobeyed Him. This only emboldens him before God, and he knows naught of it.

So after he safeguards himself from these two perils of storytelling, there is no harm in it. From there let the worthy storyteller return to that which the Qurʾān deals with and choose narrations from the sound books of reports.

There are those who seek to justify the fabrication of stories that motivate obedience, supposing that their intention here is to call the people to God (*al-Ḥaqq*). This is a satanic delusion, for veracity is always an alternative to falsehood. What God صَلَّىٰٱللَّهُعَلَيْهِوَسَلَّمَ and His Messenger صَلَّىٰٱللَّهُعَلَيْهِوَسَلَّمَ have mentioned do not need [people to] fabricate admonition. How could this fabrication not be criticized when even the use of rhyming prose is frowned upon, and considered affectation.

Saʿd b. Abī Waqqāṣ رَضِيَٱللَّهُعَنْهُ told his son ʿUmar, who came to him with a request in which he used rhyming prose, "This is what causes my dislike of you, so I will never grant your request until you repent."[40]

The Prophet صَلَّىٰٱللَّهُعَلَيْهِوَسَلَّمَ told ʿAbdallāh b. Rawāḥa that rhymed prose between three words was *sajaʿ*, [saying], "Take heed of rhyming prose, O Ibn Rawāḥa."[41] Rhyming prose was considered prohibited if it exceeded two words. For this reason when a man, speaking of the blood-money of an unborn child said, "How should we pay the blood-money of one who has neither drunk nor eaten, neither shouted nor cried out, such a person goes without blood-money." To which the Prophet صَلَّىٰٱللَّهُعَلَيْهِوَسَلَّمَ responded, "[You used] rhyming prose like the rhyming prose of the Bedouin?"[42]

As for poetry, using it often in admonition is blameworthy. God تَعَالَىٰ said, *And the poets—[only] the deviators follow them; Do you not see that in every valley they roam?* [26:224–225]. He تَعَالَىٰ said as well, *And We did not give [Prophet Muḥammad] knowledge of poetry, nor is it befitting for him* [36:69].

The majority of the poetry employed by those who admonish the people is related to depictions of passionate love and the beauty of

---

40 Abū Ṭālib al-Makkī, *Qūṭ al-qulūb*, 1:168.

41 Abū Ṭālib al-Makkī, *Qūṭ al-qulūb*, 1:169; Abū Yaʿlā also relates something similar, 4475, from a saying of ʿĀʾisha رَضِيَٱللَّهُعَنْهَا.

42 Muslim, 1282.

the beloved and the bliss of union and the pain of separation. This sort of gathering is only frequented by the crude commoners whose inner states are replete with carnal appetites, and whose hearts are incessantly attracted by gazing at attractive shapes and forms. Poetry only moves in their hearts [the base apects] that resided therein; so [as they listen] the fires of carnal desire are lit in their hearts, they scream and cry out and go into ecstatic states. The majority of that, or the totality of it, all goes back to varying degrees of immorality. It is therefore only fitting [in such circumstances] to use poetry that contains good counsel and wise sayings as illustration and to put people at ease. And the Messenger ﷺ said, "Surely in some poetry there is wisdom."[43]

Should the gathering include a group of the elect whose hearts are immersed in the love of God تَعَالَىٰ, and there is no one else with them in attendance, then for those there is no harm in poetry whose outward meaning alludes to people. For indeed one attending a gathering of a Sufi audition allows everything he hears to alight upon the state that has overwhelmed his heart. The clear elucidation of this will come in the *Kitāb al-samāʿ* [Book 18, *The Proprieties of the Audition and Ecstasy*].

This is why al-Junayd رَحِمَهُ ٱللَّهُ spoke with a small gathering of about ten—if there were more he would cease speaking—and attendees never exceeded twenty.[44]

A gathering of people presented themselves at the door of Ibn Sālim, and it was said, "Speak, your companions are present." He responded, saying, "These are not my companions, they are the companions of my teaching circle." He meant, "My companions are the elect."[45]

As for ecstatic outbursts,[46] I intend here two categories of speech that some of the Sufis have innovated.

43 Al-Bukhārī, 6145.

44 Abū Ṭālib al-Makkī, *Qūṭ al-qulūb*, 1:155.

45 Abū Ṭālib al-Makkī, *Qūṭ al-qulūb*, 1:155; Ibn Sālim was the master of Abū Ṭālib al-Makkī.

46 According to the people of realization (*ahl al-ḥaqīqa*), these are statements expressed by the tongue that are connected to pretentious claims. The people of the path (*ahl al-ṭarīqa*) are not pleased when someone expresses them, even if they are true statements. See al-Zabīdī, *Itḥāf*, 1:250.

One of them involves making excessive, exaggerated claims of passionate love for God تعالى and union [with Him] that renders one unfettered from the outward practices of the religion, such that one group of people claims to have become one with God, to have [experienced] unveiling, and have witnessed God with their own eyes, and addressed Him in the fashion of speech. They say, "We were told such and such, and we said such and such." They claim in this an affinity with al-Ḥusayn b. Manṣūr al-Ḥallāj, who was crucified for voicing words of this type. In attesting to their point of view, they cite his words, "I am the Truth" (*ana al-Ḥaqq*); it has also been related that Abū Yazīd al-Bisṭāmī said, "Glory be to me, glory be to me."

This category of speech is exceedingly harmful for the [common] people, to the point that a party of farmers deserted their pursuit of cultivation and expressed claims similar to these. This kind of speech appeals to human nature, for it contains the suspension of actions all the while sanctifying the soul by attaining spiritual stations and states. The ignorant cannot restrain themselves from making these sorts of pretentious claims for themselves, or from seizing upon these confused exaggerated statements. Then whenever they are criticized for them, they are entirely able to say, "This critique is founded upon knowledge and dialectic and knowledge is a veil, and dialectic is the work of the soul; while this discourse [of ours] only appears from the inner dimensions of the soul, unveiled by the light of the Truth (*al-Ḥaqq*)."[47]

---

47 Al-Quṭb al-Qasṭalānī says in his book *Iqtiḍāʾ al-fāḍil bi-iqtiḍāʾ al-ʿāqil*: "As for their statement that knowledge is the veil of God, even though seeking it is an aspect of the greatest veil, it is a word of truth by which is intended falsehood. There is an attribute of deficiency by which someone who is devoid of perfection can be embellished. The people of the path mention that only about others who are described as having obtained the knowledge of the law and realization with which they are distinguished according to the people of this affair. Thus, they have been given access to the Unseen based on a witnessing granted them according to their level of redemption. They are through God with God, turning away from consideration of their own attributes. Whoever is in such a state is distracted in his state from any vision concerning knowledge. As for the one who is deprived of external and internal knowledge, he deserves to know what he needs concerning the path which he seeks. If he refuses and becomes arrogant, he is then far distant from attaining the way of happiness." See al-Zabīdī, *Itḥāf*, 1:251.

The sparks of this and its like have flown throughout the land, and its harm to the [common] people has been immense. Executing them is legally better than saving ten people.

With regard to Abū Yazīd al-Bisṭāmī رَحِمَهُ ٱللَّهُ, that which has been related from him is not well testified to—even if it had been heard from him—he was most likely recounting from God عَزَّوَجَلَّ words he was repeating to himself; it is as if he heard and then spoke, *Indeed, I am God. There is no deity except Me, so worship Me* [Q. 20:14]. It is only fitting that that should be understood from him as in the guise of a story.[48]

The second variety of ecstatic utterances involves words that are not understood whatsoever. They have clear literal meaning, but contain dreadful interpretations and are of no consequence.

This is for two reasons: they are either not comprehensible to whoever spoke them, because they arise from a mental lapse or confused imagination that results from his limited capacity to comprehend the speech he heard; this is generally the case.

Or, it may be comprehensible to him, yet he has no capacity to communicate their meaning and intention in words that reflect his understanding of them because of his limited practice in intellectual discourse and his complete lack of education and [inability] to express meanings in appropriate words.

There is no benefit from this variety of utterance. It only confuses hearts, overwhelms minds, and perplexes intellects; or [these utterances] are taken to mean things that were never intended and each person is allowed to understand them based upon his own desire and nature.

He صَلَّىٱللَّهُعَلَيْهِوَسَلَّمَ stated, "When one of you addresses a people with speech they do not understand, it is a cause for tribulation among them."[49]

48 See al-Ghazālī, *Mishkāt al-anwār*, 41; al-Ghazālī, *Maqṣad al-asnā*, 127, in which the author explains these utterances in another fashion.

49 Muslim narrated a *ḥadīth* similar to this in the introduction to his *Ṣaḥīḥ*, 1:11, narrating from Ibn Masʿūd; al-ʿAqīlī, *al-Ḍuʿafāʾ*, 3:937.

He ﷺ said as well, "Speak to people in a manner they recognize, avoid what they will deny; do you want them to believe God and His Messenger lie?"[50]

If this is the case when the speaker understands but does not convey it [clearly] to the mind of the listener, [then imagine the situation] if the speaker himself does not understand. In the case in which the speaker understands and the one hearing does not, it is not permitted to mention it.

Jesus عَلَيْهِ ٱلسَّلَامُ stated, "Do not entrust wisdom to those who do not merit it, lest you do it an injustice, and do not withhold it from those who merit it lest you do them an injustice; be as a skilled physician who places the appropriate medicine in the place of the illness."[51] And in another wording, "Whoever entrusts wisdom to those who do not deserve it shows his own ignorance; whoever withholds wisdom from those who merit it has been unjust. Indeed, wisdom has its right as do those who merit it; give to each their rights."[52]

With regard to outrageous utterances, what was mentioned above about ecstatic utterances applies here as well. However, [they are] characterized by another aspect, which is the distortion of the terms of the law, [these terms are distorted] from their apparent meanings to esoteric issues from which no benefit can come, [with] any form of comprehension. [An example of this] is the Bāṭinīya and their allegorical interpretations.

This too is unlawful, and its harm immense. When terms are distorted from their requisite outward meanings without the safeguarding of the tradition that has been transmitted from the master of the law [the Prophet Muḥammad] ﷺ, and without even a minute rational proof to justify it, then people can no longer rely on or trust these terms.

The benefits afforded by their meanings from God's سُبْحَانَهُ وَتَعَالَىٰ speech and the speech of the Messenger ﷺ fall by the wayside, and [one] cannot rely on the meanings that originate from it that

50 Al-Bukharī, 127, narrating from ʿAlī b. Abī Ṭālib رَضِيَ ٱللَّهُ عَنْهُ; al-Ṭabarānī attributes it to the Prophet in *al-Muʿjam al-awsaṭ*, 8192; al-Bayhaqī has something similar in *Shuʿab al-īmān*, 1231.

51 Ibn ʿAsākir, *Tārīkh Dimashq*, 68:63, as part of a long narration.

52 Abū Ṭālib al-Makkī, *Qūṭ al-qulūb*, 1:156; there is something similar in Ibn ʿAbd al-Barr, *Jāmiʿ bayān al-ʿilm wa-faḍlih*, 703, 704.

lead to understanding. Esotericism or esoteric interpretation has no exactitude, rather these [practices] are vulnerable to a range of speculative thought and any number of points of view may arise [from them].

This is another aspect of the innovation prevalent in our times and its immense harm. Its partisans intend [in this] the enigmatic and unfamiliar, for souls are drawn to the unfamiliar and delight in it.

In this manner the Bāṭinīya ["esotericists"] have demolished the entire body of the law through [their] interpretation of its literal terms and then by applying [their interpretation] according to their own opinion. We have related much of their methodology in the book [entitled] *al-Mustaẓhirī*, written in refutation of the Bāṭinīya.[53]

An example of the interpretive style of the people of outrageous utterances as ascribed to some of them is in the interpretation of God's تَعَالَ speech, *Go to Pharaoh, indeed he has transgressed* [20:24]. He [the Bāṭinī] pointed to his heart and said, "This is the intended meaning of Pharaoh, it [is the heart] that has transgressed all bounds over humanity."

And in God's تَعَالَ statement [to Moses], *Throw down your staff* [28:31]. [They say] it means, "you should cast down everything one leans on and depends on other than God عَزَّوَجَلَّ."

And of the saying of the Messenger صَلَّى ٱللَّهُ عَلَيْهِ وَسَلَّمَ, "Partake of the pre-dawn meal before fasting (*suḥūr*) for in *suḥūr* there is blessing."[54] [They say] in this he is asking forgiveness in the pre-dawn hours.

There are many such examples. It has reached the point that they have distorted the Qurʾān from beginning to end from its literal meaning and from the elucidations transmitted from Ibn ʿAbbās رَضِيَ ٱللَّهُ عَنْهُ and the rest of the scholars of this community.

The false nature of some of these interpretations is clear beyond a doubt. For example, there is the replacement of Pharaoh with the heart. Pharaoh was a physical personality, whose existence and the imprecation of Moses against him have been handed down to us

---

53 See al-Ghazālī, *al-Mustaẓhirī*, the full title of this work is: *Faḍāʾiḥ al-Bāṭiniyya wa-Faḍāʾil al-Mustaẓhiriyya* [The infamies of the Bāṭinīya (esotericists) and the virtues of the exotericists] partially translated by Richard J. McCarthy in *Al-Ghazali: Deliverance from Error*, 151–244. The best published Arabic edition is the one prepared by Muḥammad ʿAlī l-Quṭb.

54 Al-Bukhārī, 1923: Muslim, 1095.

in succession by reliable sources. This is similar to Abū Jahl and Abū Lahab and others among the disbelievers. They do not belong to the species of demons and angels that cannot be perceived such that an interpretation of the terms is required.

Likewise it [is clearly a distortion] to ascribe the meaning of "asking forgiveness" to the pre-dawn meal in Ramaḍān. For the Messenger ﷺ used to take his sustenance and say, "Take the pre-dawn meal"[55] and "Hasten to the blessed nourishment."[56]

The falsehood of these issues is ascertained through authoritative transmission and sense perception, and some are known through common opinion. That applies to affairs that are not related to sense perception. All of that is unlawful and wayward, and it is a corruption of religion for the people [of the community]. Nothing of it has been handed down from the Companions nor from the Followers, nor from Ḥasan al-Baṣrī, in spite of his dedication to invite and admonish the people.

The only apparent meaning of the Messenger's ﷺ words, "Let the dwelling place of one who interprets the Qurʾān according to his particular opinion be in hellfire,"[57] is to this type [of interpretation], which is that his [i.e., the one using his own opinion] objective and sole opinion is to confirm and verify an issue [according to his perspective]. Thus he drags the testimony of the Qurʾān down to it and applies it without any philological, linguistic, or traditionally transmitted proof of its application in this manner.

Let it not be understood from this that one must not interpret the Qurʾān employing rational extrapolation and reflection; for there are verses for which there have been transmitted from the Companions and Qurʾān commentators five, six, and [even] seven meanings, and it was known that all of them could not have been heard from the Messenger ﷺ. They are contradictory and cannot all be accepted. The extrapolation of such cases is ascertained through capable comprehension and long reflection. This is why the

---

55 It is recounted in al-Bukhārī that the Messenger ﷺ partook of the pre-dawn meal with Zayd b. Thābit رضي الله عنه, 576.

56 Abū Dāwūd, 2163; al-Nisāʾī, 4:145; and in Aḥmad b. Ḥanbal, *Musnad*, 4:126, it is worded as *al-ghadāʾ* (breakfast or lunch) instead of *al-ghidhāʾ* (nourishment) as in Abū Dāwūd and al-Nisāʾī.

57 Al-Tirmidhī, 2951.

Messenger صلى الله عليه وسلم said of Ibn ʿAbbās رضي الله عنهما, "O God, give him insightful understanding in religion and teach him interpretation."[58]

And whoever, among the people of outrageous utterances, deems licit the likes of these interpretations, knowing that they in no manner reflect the philological sense of the terms and supposing [all the while] that his intention is to call people to the truth, is identical to one who deems licit inventing and fabricating [*ḥadīth*] of the Messenger of God صلى الله عليه وسلم. [Similarly,] what he perceives as necessarily true is not what the law has given voice to; he is like the one who fabricates a *ḥadīth* for every matter he considers just and worthy, [and claims it is] from the Messenger of God صلى الله عليه وسلم. That is inequity and malevolence and [he] renders himself accountable to the well-known forewarning from his صلى الله عليه وسلم saying, "Whoever intentionally lies about me has prepared for himself a seat in hellfire."[59] Indeed the malice [behind this] interpretation of these terms is even more overwhelming and tremendous; for it invalidates confidence in the terms [of the law] themselves and cuts one off from benefit and comprehension of the Qurʾān in its totality!

Now you know how Satan turned those who call people [to religion] from the praiseworthy knowledge to the blameworthy. It is all due to the confusion sown by reprehensible scholars who distort the [meanings inherent in] the names. If you were to follow those [scholars] and rely on the well-known terms [we are discussing] without regard to the manner in which it was understood among the first generation, you would be like one who sought noble status by following a person who is called a wise man (*ḥakīm*). When in fact in the present era the name *ḥakīm* is used to denote [indiscriminately] a physician, poet, or an astrologer. This is the result of neglecting the [issue of] the distortion of terms.

The Fifth Term: Wisdom (*ḥikma*)

The name *ḥakīm* [wise man] has come to unconditionally denote physicians, poets, astrologers, even one who rolls dice [and tells the

58 Al-Bukhārī, 143 without "teach him interpretation"; the complete narration is in Aḥmad b. Ḥanbal's *Musnad*, 1:266.

59 Al-Bukhārī, 110; Muslim, 3.

fortunes] of peasants squatting on sides of the roads.[60]

Yet wisdom has been praised by God عَزَّوَجَلَّ, who stated, *whoever has been given wisdom has certainly been given much good* [2:269].

The Messenger of God صَلَّىٱللَّهُعَلَيْهِوَسَلَّمَ said, "A single word a man learns of wisdom is superior for him than the [this] world and all that it comprises."[61]

Look carefully at what wisdom used to denote and how it has been distorted, and liken it to the remaining terms [discussed here]. Beware of the deceptions of the malicious scholars of religion, for their malice is a greater threat to the religion than that of the satans [themselves]; through their mediation Satan finds a means of extracting the religion from the very hearts of humankind. For this reason, when the Messenger of God صَلَّىٱللَّهُعَلَيْهِوَسَلَّمَ was asked about the worst of humankind, he refused to respond and simply said, "O God, forgiveness." When those present persisted, he stated, "They are the reprehensible scholars."[62]

[By now] you have come to distinguish laudable knowledge from blameworthy knowledge, and [you understand] the cause for the confusion. The choice is now yours: either look at yourself and take as your exemplars the predecessors or descend by the rope of deception and take after those who came after them. Every field of scholarly inquiry that the predecessors found fulfillment in has been effaced; and most of the fields that people today so eagerly devote themselves to are innovation in religion and modern novelties. How correct was the Messenger of God صَلَّىٱللَّهُعَلَيْهِوَسَلَّمَ when he stated, "Islam began as a stranger and it will return as a stranger just as it began, blessedness is for the strangers." It was asked of him, "Who are the strangers?" To which he responded, "Those who restore that which the people have corrupted of my *sunna*; and those who bring back to life my *sunna* which the people have destroyed."[63]

---

60 The term used for peasants is *akuff al-sawādiyya*, lit. black palms. In *Itḥāf*, 1:263, there is an explanation that it relates to farmers whose hands are dirtied from working with the soil.

61 See al-Zabīdī, *Itḥāf*, 1:263, for a discussion of this *ḥadīth*.

62 Narrated in similar fashion by al-Dārimī, *Sunan*, 382.

63 Muslim, 146; the complete narration is in al-Tirmidhī, 2630.

In another narration [he ﷺ said], "They are the ones who grasp tightly to that which you follow today."[64] In another *ḥadīth* [he ﷺ said], "The strangers are a few righteous people in the midst of a multitude, there are more who loathe them than those who love them."[65]

Those fields of scholarly pursuit have become strange inasmuch as one who discusses them is looked at with aversion and loathing. Thus al-Thawrī رَحِمَهُ ٱللَّهُ declared, "When you see a scholar who has many friends, know well that he is mixing falsehood with truth."[66] If he spoke with veracity, they would loathe him.

An Elucidation of the Praiseworthy Elements in the Praiseworthy Disciplines

KNOW WELL THAT KNOWLEDGE, from this point of view comprises three categories.

One category is blameworthy in both small and large amounts.

One category is praiseworthy in both small and large amounts; with increase it becomes better and more meritorious.

One category is praiseworthy to the point of sufficiency; however, one who exceeds this limit or delves into its minutiae is not praiseworthy.

An example of this is the states of the physical body. Some states are praiseworthy, a little or a great deal, like health and beauty; others are blameworthy, a little or a great deal, like unattractiveness and malicious character; others are praiseworthy in moderation, like expending one's wealth, for wastefulness is not praiseworthy while it is an expenditure, and like courage, for rash actions in battle are not praiseworthy, although they are a part of courage. Knowledge is similar to this.

The blameworthy category—in both small and large amounts—is that in which there is no benefit, neither in religion nor in the

64 Abū Ṭālib al-Makkī, *Qūṭ al-qulūb*, 1:143; Ibn Waḍāḥ reported something similar in *al-Bidaʿ*, 72.

65 Aḥmad b. Ḥanbal reports something similar, *Musnad*, 2:177.

66 On this point, see Abū Ṭālib al-Makkī, *Qūṭ al-qulūb*, 1:143.

worldly life, or its harm overcomes its benefit, like knowledge of sorcery, talismans, and astrology; certain aspects of [these] have no benefit whatsoever. [So] devoting one's lifetime, which is a human being's most precious possession, to it is wasteful; and squandering precious possessions is blameworthy.

Another aspect [of blameworthy knowledge] is that in which the harmful aspects of it outweigh what one supposes one may attain through it, for example, acquiring some worldly desire which is, in comparison to the harm incurred by it, inconsequential.

With regard to the category that is praiseworthy to the farthest extent of its fields of inquiry, [this category] is knowledge of God تَعَالَىٰ His attributes, His acts, and His manner in overseeing His creation, and His wisdom in basing the degrees of the hereafter on the degrees of this world. This is knowledge to be sought in and for itself and by means which lead to felicity in the hereafter. Spending one's allotted time and striving for it [this knowledge] to the utmost limits of one's strength still falls short of the mark of [what one is] obligated [to do]. It is an ocean whose depths are beyond comprehension. Those striving for it can only hover on its shores and shallow edges according to what has been facilitated for them. No one has waded into its utmost limits but the prophets, the saints, and those well-founded in knowledge; all in accordance to their varying degrees, and to the extent of their strengths and the differences of God's تَعَالَىٰ destined decrees for each of them.

This is the undisclosed knowledge [of God] that is not set down in books. In its early stages [one's] awareness of it is reinforced by learning and study and by witnessing the states of the scholars of the hereafter, whose signs and attributes will soon be disclosed [in this chapter].

In the later stages it is reinforced by spiritual striving and devotional practices, by cleansing the heart and emptying it of worldly attachments, and by following the examples of God's prophets and friends. Let it be made clear, however, that everyone striving toward his end, [will attain it] according to God's decree not according to one's efforts. Spiritual striving, however, cannot be dispensed with, and applying oneself assiduously is the key to good guidance; there is no [other] key to it besides [this].

With regard to the disciplines that are praiseworthy only to a precise extent, these are the disciplines we discussed in [relation to] communal obligations. For every discipline there is a minimal position, a moderate position, and an extensive examination beyond the moderate that continues to the end of one's life.

Be one of two men, devote [yourself] to yourself or devote yourself to others after freeing yourself from [your own] occupations. Beware however that you not devote yourself to the well-being of others before the well-being of yourself. Now, if you are occupied with yourself, devote yourself to nothing but attaining the knowledge that is obligatory for you, as your circumstance dictates, and to that which relates to the outward acts of learning the prayer, ablutions, and fasting.

The only truly important point that everyone disregards is the knowledge of the attributes of the heart, those that are praised and those that are condemned; for no human being is without blameworthy attributes, such as greed, envy, pretentious behavior, pride, arrogance, and other such character traits, all of which are among the traits that devastate [the heart]. Ignoring them to occupy oneself with outward practices is like applying a topical ointment to skin afflicted with sores and abscesses and attaching little importance to drawing out the diseased substance infecting the body with cupping and purging.

Those who have become preoccupied with marginal aspects of the religious sciences[67] delineate [in their discourse] the outward religious practices in the [same] manner that roadside physicians[68] prescribe topical ointments for diseased skin. While the scholars of the hereafter indicate [in their discourses] the importance of cleansing the heart and expunging the source of malice by rendering its soil infertile and uprooting its weeds, all this is in the heart. The majority [of people], in this respect, flee in fear toward outward acts and away from the cleansing of hearts because of the apparent ease of bodily acts and the difficulty perceived [in treating] the acts of

67 They are those who are content with the outer shell rather than the inner essence. They look to external matters without examining inner secrets. Al-Zabīdī, *Itḥāf*, 1:269.

68 They sit by the road and dispense medicine to people, taking advantage of their ignorance. Al-Zabīdī, *Itḥāf*, 1:269.

the heart. In like manner a person turns to topical ointments out of fear of drinking very bitter medicines. They continue applying the ointments, untiringly, even as the infection increases and the diseases multiply.

If you are one in quest of the hereafter, a seeker of salvation fleeing eternal devastation, then busy yourself with attaining the knowledge of the imperfections of the heart and their remedies, and follow the course of action we have set out in the Quarter of Perils (*Rubᶜ al-muhlikāt*).

That [course of action] will undoubtedly sweep you along to praiseworthy stations mentioned in the Quarter of Deliverance (*Rubᶜ al-munjiyyāt*), for when the heart is emptied of the blameworthy, it becomes filled with the praiseworthy. When the earth is cleared of weeds, varieties of green crops and sweet smelling herbs sprout abundantly. If the heart has not been emptied of its flaws do not occupy yourself with communal obligations,[69] particularly if some people in the community have established them. A man who destroys himself seeking the well-being of others lacks intelligence. What could be more foolhardy than a man whose clothing [is infested by] serpents and scorpions intent on killing him, while he [himself] searches for a fly-swatter to fend off the flies from others who do nothing for him. They cannot even save him from the trial he is experiencing from those serpents and scorpions [that are] so intent upon [killing] him.

If you have emptied your soul [of blameworthy traits] and cleansed it, and you have become capable of renouncing sin outwardly and inwardly, such that [this] has become your practice and habitual custom—and how far are you from that?—then occupy yourself with communal obligations, taking care to observe the gradual steps therein.

Begin with the Book of God تعالى, then the *sunna* of His Messenger صلى الله عليه وسلم, then with knowledge of Qurʾān interpretation and all the sciences of the Qurʾān; including the science of abrogating and abrogation, the separated verses and [those] connected in recitation, and the verses established in accepted meaning and

69 That is, if the heart is not emptied of that, then do not busy yourself with communal obligations at all. See al-Zabīdī, *Itḥāf*, 1:269.

those of a figurative nature. And likewise pursue the study of the *sunna* in gradual steps.

Then occupy yourself with the branches of knowledge, which is knowledge of the schools of jurisprudence without polemics, then the principles of jurisprudence (*uṣūl al-fiqh*), and so on to the remainder of the sciences as long as you live and time permits.

Do not immerse yourself, however, in one field of inquiry, seeking to grasp it in its entirety, [for] knowledge is vast and life is short. These sciences are instruments and introductions, they are not to be sought for their own sake, rather for the sake of other [sciences]. With regard to what is sought for other than itself, it is necessary that one not forget the main goal and become distracted from it.

Limit yourself to the widely studied aspects of the knowledge of language, to the point that you understand the language of the Arabs and can speak it. Only occupy yourself with obscure vocabulary terms as they appear in the Qurʾān and *ḥadīth*, forsake profound study therein.

Only concern yourself with grammar to the point it relates to the Qurʾān and *sunna*. Every branch of knowledge has a minimum, a median, and an all-encompassing purview. Here we will indicate them in the field of *ḥadīth*, Qurʾān interpretation, jurisprudence, and dialectical theology, that you may compare them with other areas of inquiry.

The minimum purview of Qurʾān interpretation constitutes twice the proportion of the Qurʾān itself, similar to the work of ʿAlī l-Wāḥidī l-Nīsābūrī,[70] *al-Wajīz*; the median purview constitutes three times the proportion of the Qurʾān itself, similar to al-Nīsābūrī's *al-Wasīṭ*; beyond these limits is an all-encompassing purview that there is no need to pursue, as there is no accomplishing this even [if one works at it] to the end of one's life.

With regard to *ḥadīth*, the minimum purview is acquiring the essentials of the two *Ṣaḥīḥ*s (*ṣaḥīḥayn*) by comparing and correcting a copy [for yourself] from a scholar knowledgeable in the science of *ḥadīth* texts.

As for learning the names of narrators of *ḥadīth* by heart, you have been relieved of this task by those who came before you and

70 ʿAlī l-Wāḥidī l-Nīsābūrī—see al-Zabīdī, *Itḥāf*, 1:272.

took it on in your stead; all that is left for you is to rely on their books. It is not obligatory for you to memorize the *ḥadīth* texts of the two *Ṣaḥīḥ*s, rather acquire enough familiarity with these works to be able to find what you need when you need it.

With regard to the median purview, you may add to the two *Ṣaḥīḥ*s those *ḥadīth* not included in them that are narrated in the other sound collections of *ḥadīth*.[71]

With regard to an all-encompassing purview, what lies beyond that is to accumulate everything transmitted, whether weak, strong, sound or dubious accompanied with the myriad chains of transmissions and knowledge of the circumstances of the transmitters, their names, and qualities.

As for jurisprudence, a minimum purview would include that comprised in *Mukhtaṣar al-Muznī*,[72] رَحِمَهُ ٱللَّٰهُ and which we organized into *Khulāṣat al-mukhtaṣar*.[73] The median purview in jurisprudence constitutes three times the proportion of its like, proportionate to that which we put forward in *al-Wasīṭ min al-madhhab*. An all-encompassing purview would constitute that which we have set forth in *al-Basīṭ*, including everything beyond that among the lengthy works of jurisprudence.

With regard to dialectical theology (*kalām*), its purpose is the preservation of the essential creeds of faith transmitted by the people of the *sunna* (*ahl al-sunna*) among the righteous predecessors, and nothing else. Anything beyond that is seeking to unveil the divine realities of matters [beyond our common comprehension] in a manner not suited to it.

The purpose of preserving the *sunna* is achievable from the level of the minimum purview with a summary text on essential creed (*muʿtaqad mukhtaṣar*) similar to that which we have provided in *Kitāb qawāʿid al-ʿaqāʾid*, which constitutes part of the present work [Book 2, *The Principles of the Creed* of the *Iḥyāʾ ʿulūm al-dīn*]. The median purview in *kalām* would reach one hundred pages, which is the extent of that which we have delineated in *Kitāb al-Iqtiṣād fī*

71 The four sound collections are al-Nisāʾī, *Sunan al-ṣughrā*; Abū Dāwūd, *Sunan Abū Dāwūd*; al-Tirmidhī, *Jāmiʿ al-Tirmidhī*; Ibn Māja, *Sunan Ibn Māja*.

72 Al-Zabīdī, *Itḥāf*, 1:273.

73 The complete title is al-Ghazālī, *Khulāṣat al-mukhtaṣar wa-naqāwat al-muʿtaṣar*, published by Dār al-Minhāj, all praise be to God تَعَالَىٰ.

l-iʿtiqād.[74] This becomes necessary for contesting an innovator in matters of doctrine and challenging his innovation with that which renders it futile and eliminates it from the hearts of the common people; though this is only worthwhile with the common people [if accomplished] before their own partisanship has become ingrained in them.

With regard to the theological innovator who has learned polemics—even if only a minimum, using *kalām* with him is rarely of any use. For should you overcome him in debate, he will not abandon his particular school. He will blame his own shortcomings and imagine that there is a response [among his doctrinal allies] that he is unable to produce, and that due to your strength of argumentation you have confounded him.

In the case where the common person has been turned [away] from the truth by means of polemics, the possibility remains that they may be set straight using similar means before their fanaticism for heretical tendencies has become ingrained in them. If, however, their fanaticism becomes ingrained, their case is hopeless; as fanaticism is a major means by which doctrinal matters become ingrained in [the hearts and minds of] people. This is another of the perils of reprehensible scholars, for they do their utmost to promote partisanship for the truth [of their views], and they regard those who differ with them with ridicule and contempt. This in turn produces in them [those who differ] adversarial and confrontational predilections. Their motivations become devoted to overcoming their adversaries using spurious argumentation themselves and their aim is strengthened to hold fast to the theological leanings that they ascribe to. If, on the other hand, they come forward from a position of benevolence, compassion, and good counsel in private—not in a display of partisanship and contempt—they succeed in their goals.

But, as recognition and prestige are only attained by winning followers, and there is no better means of enticing followers than fanatical zeal, cursing, and maligning one's adversaries, they have taken partisanship as their habit and procedural methodology, calling it "protection of the faith" and "defense of the Muslim community."

---

74 *Al-Ghazālī's Moderation in Belief*, trans. Yaqub.

In reality it only leads to the destruction of the people and the firm establishment of theological innovation in the souls.

As for the study of differing opinions[75] that have arisen in these latter times and that have been the origin of written opinions, books, and argumentative discourse, the predecessors were not familiar with such things. Beware, lest you fall in with them, and avoid them as you would avoid a deadly poison, for it is a disease for which there is no cure. This is what has [made] the jurists—all of them—turn to strive for recognition and boasting (*mubāhā*); a clear exposition of the havoc and dangers that I shall soon detail for you.

Someone who says, "People are adversaries of that of which they are ignorant." Do not suppose this to be the case! For you have encountered here a person [i.e., al-Ghazālī] knowledgeable in these matters. Accept this advice from a man who wasted many years of his life on these issues and surpassed those who had come before him in composing books, exacting inquiry, [engaging in] polemics, and elucidating scholarly matters; only [after all that] did God inspire in him His good reasoning (*rushd*) and make clear to him his error, whereupon he abandoned these matters and occupied himself with (perfecting) the inner facets of his own being.

Do not be deceived by one who tells you, "Legal opinions are the pillars of the law, and the reasons for it are only known through the branch of divergent opinions." For, in fact, the subtle reasoning of the various schools are dealt with in the school [i.e., in the literature of the school itself], and anything beyond this is contention that the forerunners of this community and the Companions did not know. In fact they were more knowledgeable of the reasoning behind legal opinion than anyone else. Moreover it is not beneficial [even] in the science of the schools of jurisprudence themselves, and it is deleterious and it corrupts the natural discernment of jurisprudence. Whoever witnesses for himself the intuition of the *muftī* when his natural discernment is correct in a matter of jurisprudence, [knows] that it is impossible for him to accommodate the conditions of polemical debate in most affairs. Whoever has had his disposition habituated to the conventions of polemical debate has also had

75 These are the issues that occur among the different schools of jurisprudence. See al-Zabīdī, *Itḥāf*, 1:275.

his mind made compliant to the criterion of polemical debate. He then becomes fearful of complying with the natural discernment of jurisprudence. For indeed, those who occupy themselves with [polemical debate] are [really] occupied in attaining fame and rank [among their peers]. They attempt to justify themselves in this by saying that they are inquiring into the subtle reasoning of their respective schools. Yet, it may come to pass that [the one engaged in polemical debate] dies, having never turned his attention to the true knowledge of the schools of jurisprudence.

So be safe from the demons of the *jinn* and safeguard yourself from the demons among humankind; for they have given every respite to the demons of the *jinn* from the task of temptation and leading astray [God's pious servants].

In sum, the most satisfied state of mind for the sagacious is to deem yourself alone in the universe with God, in front of you is death, the day of judgment, reckoning, heaven, and the fire; ponder deeply on what will serve you best in that which is before you and abandon all else. Peace (*wa-l-salām*).

A venerable elder saw a scholar in a dream and asked him, "What resulted from those sciences that you used to dispute and debate over?" [To which he] opened his hands, palms up, and blew on them and said, "Blown away and dispersed like dust in the wind, I only found benefit in two prayer cycles in the depths of the night that were cleansed for me of all pretension."[76]

In a *ḥadīth* [there is a saying]: "A people only become lost after they had guidance when they become disputatious." Then he recited: *They did not present the comparison except for* [*mere*] *argument. But,* [*in fact*], *they are a people prone to dispute* [43:58].[77]

In another *ḥadīth* on the meaning of God's تعالى statement: *As for those in whose hearts is deviation* [*from truth*], *they will follow that of it which is unspecific, seeking discord and seeking an interpretation* [*suitable to them*]. *And no one knows its* [*true*] *interpretation except God* [3:7]. They are the people of contentious disputation that God تعالى intended in his speech, *Beware of them* [63:4].[78]

76 Abū Ṭālib al-Makkī, *Qūṭ al-qulūb*, 1:132; Abū Nuʿaym, *Ḥilya*, 10:257.

77 Al-Tirmidhī, 3253; Ibn Māja, 48.

78 Al-Bukharī, 4547; Muslim, 2665 as attributed to the Prophet, "When you see the people who follow the allegorical sense of the revelation… [know] that those are

One of the predecessors said, "There will appear at the end of time a people for whom the door of pious action will be closed, and the door of contentious disputation will be opened."[79]

In one of the reports [it is related]: "You dwell in a time when you are inspired to undertake pious acts; [however] there will soon come a people who will be inspired to contentious disputation."[80]

In a well-known report [it is narrated], "The most detestable of people to God تَعَالَىٰ is the most vehement in pressing his point in an argument."[81] While in another [it is stated], "Every people that has been given the knowledge of logical disputation has been prevented from the path of pious actions."[82]

And God
knows
best.

---

the ones God meant, 'beware of them.'"

79 Abū Ṭālib al-Makkī, *Qūṭ al-qulūb*, 1:138.

80 Abū Ṭālib al-Makkī, *Qūṭ al-qulūb*, 1:138. It is similar to what al-Awzāʿī said in al-Khaṭīb al-Baghdādī, *Iqtiḍāʾ al-ʿilm al-ʿamal*, 122: "When God intends evil for a people, he opens for them the way of disputation and prohibits them the way of good deeds."

81 Al-Bukharī, 2457; Muslim, 2668.

82 Abū Ṭālib al-Makkī, *Qūṭ al-qulūb*, 1:138 said, "Al-Ḥakam b. ʿUyayna narrated from ʿAbd al-Raḥmān b. Abī Layla, who said that the Messenger of God صَلَّىٱللَّهُعَلَيْهِوَسَلَّمَ said, "No people … (the rest of the *ḥadīth*)."

4

On the reason people turn their attention to the knowledge of variant opinions and a detailed elucidation of the perils of polemics and disputation, including the conditions incumbent for its permissibility.

[Knowledge of Variant Opinions and the Perils of Disputation]

KNOW THAT THE RESPONSIBILITIES of caliphate, after God's Messenger ﷺ, were assumed by the rightly-guided caliphs, who were themselves the foremost among those knowledgeable of God [in their times]; [they were] people of insight [who comprehended] His laws. They independently issued rulings in judiciary contexts; they sought the opinions of other jurists only in circumstances that required consultation and that rarely. Scholars thus immersed themselves in acquiring the knowledge of the hereafter and devoted themselves solely to it. They deferred to one another when rulings were sought that pertained to the statutes regarding people's affairs, all the while devoting the totality of their efforts to

God, as has been recorded in the narratives dealing with their lives.[1]

When the responsibilities of the caliphate, after them, were assumed by people who did not merit it, who had no independent knowledge of rulings or decrees, they were forced to seek support from jurists, to seek their companionship in all circumstances, and to seek their rulings as the course of events necessitated.

There remained, however, among the Followers of the Companions those who kept to the original standards of the community, persevered in the pure religion, and emulated the example of the scholars among the predecessors. When sought after [by the rulers], they fled and turned away, making it necessary for the caliphs to insist [under duress] that they assume posts in the judiciary and offices of state.

The people of those eras saw the high standing afforded to the scholars and the devotion shown them by the leaders and the rulers, this, despite their aversion of them. Thus they extended themselves to seek knowledge and acquire high standing and recognition from the ruling elite. They devoted themselves to acquiring knowledge related to legal opinions and offered themselves to the ruling elite, grew conversant with them and sought positions of authority and gifts. Some of them were unsuccessful in this and others succeeded, but even the successful were humbled by [having] to request [their] sustenance and afflicted by the lost dignity. The jurists—after being sought after—became the seekers; and—after their preeminence and lofty status for avoiding the rulers and princes—they became humiliated by turning toward them; except those that God accorded His good grace in every era among the scholars of His religion.

In those times [scholars] were mainly interested in acquiring the knowledge of rulings and judicial matters because of the severe need of them in the districts and areas under the sovereign authority of the state.

Then, after them there appeared notables and princes who had heard the statements of people learned in the tenets of theological

---

1 As narrated in al-Dārimī, *Sunan*, 137: ʿAbd al-Raḥmān b. Abī Layla reported, "In this mosque I have encountered one hundred and twenty of the Helpers (Anṣār), every one of them who narrated a *ḥadīth* wished that his brother had spared him this, and any one of them that was asked an opinion wished that his brother had spared him that opinion."

doctrines, and they became disposed toward hearing [these] proofs. Their propensity for this expressed itself in a desire for disputation and debate in the area of dialectical theology. So people devoted themselves to acquiring knowledge of theology and produced many works on the subject, systematizing therein accepted pathways of debating techniques and deriving the arts of refutation in scholarly discourse. They alleged that their intention was to defend God's religion, safeguard the *sunna* of the Messenger of God ﷺ, and defeat innovators of religious doctrine; [they did this] just as those before them alleged that their goal in the preoccupation with rulings was the religion itself. They took upon themselves the responsibilities of providing a legal foundation for the Muslim community. All of this [they alleged] they did out of compassion for God's people and a desire to offer good counsel to them.

Then, after that, there appeared among the notables those who took exception to delving into scholastic theology and opening the door of disputation. [They took exception] because opening that door had caused blatant fanaticism and the spread of bitter hostilities that gave rise to the spilling of blood and devastation throughout the land. They became disposed toward polemical debate on matters of jurisprudence [instead], and the elucidation of the preferable status of the schools of al-Shāfiʿī and Abū Ḥanīfa رَضِيَ ٱللَّٰهُ عَنْهُ in particular. Thus the people abandoned dialectical theology and the arts of knowledge and swarmed around the divergent views of al-Shāfiʿī and Abū Ḥanīfa عَلَيْهِ ٱلسَّلَامُ specifically. They placed less importance on the divergent views of Mālik, Sufyān al-Thawrī, Aḥmad, and others رَحِمَهُمُ ٱللَّٰهُ. They alleged that their goal was to derive the fine points of the law, establish the foundational tenets of the schools, and facilitate the [understanding of] principles behind legal rulings; [in pursuit of this goal] they increased the output of written works on these and derivative topics, and they systematized the categories of disputation techniques and literary works. They are as devoted to it today[2] as they were in the past. We have no idea what God will bring to pass in the eras that come after us.

This [reason] by itself is the cause for the singular devotion [we see today] to disputations and divergent opinons, there is none other.

2 That is, until the time of the author, which was 498 AH. Al-Zabīdī, *Itḥāf*, 1:282.

If the elite of this world had had a propensity for debating divergent opinions with any other *imām*, or for any other science, the people would have followed their propensity. [In this] they would not have passed in silence over the pretext that they were preoccupied with knowledge of the religion and [said] that their only aim in this was gaining proximity to the lord of the worlds.

An Elucidation of the Duplicity Involved in Comparing these Disputations with the Deliberations of the Companions and the Mutual Consultations of the Predecessors

Know that those scholars [discussed earlier] brought the people around to that [point of view] by asserting that, "Our goal in polemical discourse is inquiry into the truth of a matter in order to render it clear and evident, for truth is worth seeking." [They also assert that] "Mutual support when regarding knowledge and sharing ideas is beneficial and effective. That was the custom of the Companions رَضِيَ ٱللَّهُ عَنْهُمْ in their mutual consultations. For example, take their consultation over the inheritance of the grandfather and brothers, and the penalty for drinking wine, and whether the leader of the community was liable to a fine should he err, as was reported about the miscarriage of the woman who feared ʿUmar رَضِيَ ٱللَّهُ عَنْهُ, and on the questions of inheritance and other matters. The decisions handed down from al-Shāfiʿī, Aḥmad, Muḥammad b. al-Ḥasan, Mālik, Abū Yūsuf, and others among the scholars رَحِمَهُمُ ٱللَّهُ of this community are similar to these [issues]. May God تَعَالَىٰ have mercy on them all."

My comments here are to inform you of the duplicity of this claim; [I mean] that affording mutual support in seeking the truth of a matter is an aspect of the religion. Yet, to be valid, this point of view must meet eight incumbent conditions and indicators.

The First Condition: A person cannot busy [himself] with a matter that is part of the communal obligations if he [has not first] attended to his personal obligations.

Whoever has a pending personal obligation but engages in a communal obligation, and maintains that his aim is accessing the truth of a matter, is a liar. His example is like someone who abandons the prayer and goes into business purchasing clothing and becomes involved in the weaving trade, and says, "My intention in this is to cover the bodies of those who perform the prayer naked for they cannot find clothing."

This example [of people with no clothing to pray in] may in fact occur, and as an event it is even possible [although rare]. In like manner the jurist may suppose that the occurrence of the exceptional events that are the subject of inquiry concerning divergent opinions are possible; yet those engaged in polemic argumentation [often] ignore more essential matters that are personal obligations upon which there is general agreement.

[For example] whoever is faced with the repayment of a debt at a given time, and then immediately establishes and enters into the sanctity of the prayer—which is the most evident means of proximity to God تَعَالَىٰ —has disobeyed his Lord. It does not suffice for a person to be considered obedient because his acts fall into the category of acts of obedience if he pays no attention to the precise moment, incumbent conditions, and order of occurrence.

The Second Condition: He should not deem a communal obligation more important than polemic disputation.

If a man perceives a matter of greater imperative [at a given moment] and acts upon something else [of lesser importance], he has disobeyed [God] in his act. He is similar to a person who sees a group of people, whom other people have ignored, dying of thirst and while he is capable of reviving them by providing them with water to drink, he instead commits himself to learn blood-letting, maintaining that it is a communal obligation because, should the region become bereft of it, people would perish. Then when told that there is in fact in the region a group of people knowledgeable in blood-letting that suffice the region's needs, he responds, "This does not exclude this pursuit from being a communal obligation."

The situation of one who does this [leaves blood-letting] while neglecting to occupy himself with the actual calamity of the thirsty group of Muslims is similar to the situation of one who is occupied with polemic discourse in a region in which many communal obligations have been neglected, [to the point that] there is no one to undertake them.

As for the issuing of rulings, it has been undertaken by a group of scholars, [while at the same time] there is no region that is without any number of neglected communal obligations to which the jurists give no regard. The most noteworthy is the practice of medicine. In most regions, there are no Muslim physicians whose sworn testimony is permissible for those cases in which the word of a physician is necessary according to the law. Yet there is not one among the jurists who want to take up [medicine instead of jurisprudence].

The same circumstances apply to commanding good (*amr bi-l-maʿrūf*) and forbidding evil (*nahy ʿan al-munkar*), which are among the communal obligations. It is likely that during a session of debate on the fine points of jurisprudence, a participant in the debate will see silk being worn or used as carpeting. Yet he remains silent and continues to debate an issue that would never, in the course of events, occur, and should it occur, there is already an assemblage of jurists [in the region] to deal with it. Then he claims [in all this] that he wishes to attain proximity to God تَعَالَىٰ by means of engagement in [what he sees as] a communal obligation.

Anas رَضِيَ ٱللَّهُ عَنْهُ reported that it was said, "O Messenger of God, when will commanding good and forbidding evil be abandoned?" To which he صَلَّى ٱللَّهُ عَلَيْهِ وَسَلَّمَ responded, "When flattery appears among your best, and lewdness among your wicked ones, dominion over the affairs of men will pass to your youth, and the pursuit of jurisprudence will fall to the basest among you."[3]

The Third Condition: The scholar participating in the debate should be capable of independent judgment.

He [the scholar] should offer rulings based on his own opinion, not that of the school of al-Shāfiʿī or Abū Ḥanīfa or others; such that, should the position of the school of Abū Ḥanīfa appear valid to him he would discard that which accorded with the school of al-Shāfiʿī and issue his ruling according to what appeared valid to him; this is [what] the Companions رَضِيَ ٱللَّهُ عَنْهُمْ and the leaders of the community used to do.

3 Ibn Māja, 4015. The meaning of "flattery" (*idhān*) here is leniency (*mulāyana*) in speech. It is derived from *mudāhana*, which is the removal of sound advice. The term *idhān* is used by Abū Nuʿaym, *Ḥilya*, 5:185 and Ibn ʿAbd al-Barr, *Jāmiʿ bayān al-ʿilm wa-faḍlih*, 1048.

With regard to a person who has not reached the rank of independent judgment—which is the case of everyone today—he can only offer an opinion on a matter demanded of him by passing on the view of the founder of his school. For, even if he perceived the weakness of [a particular position of] his school it would not be permissible to forsake [his school]. What benefit does he derive from debate when the views of his school are already known and he has no opinion based on any other [school]?

And in those instances that are problematic to him he has to admit that, "The founder of the school most likely has a response, but I am not independently qualified to offer my opinion where a foundational tenet of the law is concerned."

Were his discussion about matters in which there are two opinions or statements from his [school's] founder, then that would be a more similar situation; for here he would most likely offer an opinion based on one of them and benefit from the discourse by inclining toward one of the two sides of the matter. However, one never sees polemic discourse taking place in this manner; more likely an issue that has two points of view or two divergent statements [from the founder of the school] is passed over completely and an issue that has long been settled is sought after.

The Fourth Condition: One should only engage in polemic discourse that addresses an actual event or one very likely to occur.

The Companions رَضِيَ ٱللَّهُ عَنْهُمْ only consulted one another about events that had recently occurred or those whose occurrence would most likely arise, as in the case of inheritance law. Yet, you will not see the scholars of disputation or disputants giving their attention to critiquing issues about which there is a real need of legal opinions; rather they seek out issues over which drums are beaten[4] in which to maximize opportunity for dialectic, whatever the matter [being argued]. They may even abandon altogether questions that occur often, saying, "This is an issue that was passed down from the oral

4 This is a metaphor for issues that are well-known, that people gather around. The drum also indicates that these issues have partisans and may give rise to rivalry and inter-communal strife; during this period the partisans of Imām al-Shāfiʿī and Imām Abū Ḥanīfa often gathered and debated. Al-Zabīdī, *Itḥāf*, 1:288.

tradition[5] [and was then recorded in books], or this is among the obscure issues[6] [of the school] and is not among those over which drums are beaten."

How strange that they seek the truth [in a particular matter], and then they ignore a point at issue because its origin is from the oral tradition, while access to the veracity of an issue is through the oral narrations themselves; or [they ignore it] because it is not a point that incites turmoil.

Let us elaborate no more on this; the aim in realizing the truth of a matter is brevity in speech and reaching the goal promptly, not drawn-out expositions.

The Fifth Condition: That disputation in seclusion is more beloved and significant to the scholar involved than holding it in a well-attended assembly in the presence of notables and sultans.

Seclusion is more conducive to purposeful thought, and more appropriate for clarity of mind, insight, and the recognition of the truth in a matter. Whereas in attending an assembly, instincts arise that stimulate affectation and pretense and compel each of the two participants to covet victory for himself over his opponent, whether he is on the side of the truth or falsehood. You know [very well] that their desire for well-attended assemblies and congregations is not solely for the sake of God. It often happens that one of them stays alone with another, remaining silent for a long period of time, not addressing him. He may suggest a subject to him, but he does not respond; then, should a person of importance appear,[7] or a congregation be assembled, not a single arrow from his bow of artifices will be unused until he [in the end, without doubt] is the most proficient in speaking (*kalām*).

---

5 "So and so has related this from an elderly scholar, and it was set down by so and so in such and such a book." Al-Zabīdī, *Itḥāf*, 1:288.

6 According to al-Zabīdī: *Zawāyā* are "matters that are only discussed in private." He takes the word to indicate a Sufi lodge and adds the familiar saying, "You have no idea how many hidden things there are in the *zawāyā* (*wa-mā darū kam fī l-zawāyā min khabāya*)."

7 The Arabic term *maqdam* is a verbal noun that means the arrival of a person of authority, and thus the gathering is to meet the prominent person. Al-Zabīdī, *Itḥāf*, 1:289.

The Sixth Condition: In seeking the truth of a matter he should be like a person searching for a lost animal.

He [should] make no distinction whether the stray is found by himself or by someone assisting him; he should regard his companion [in polemic discourse] as a collaborator not as an adversary. He thanks him when he apprises him of error and makes the truth of a matter clear to him. This is similar to the case of his taking one path in search of his lost animal and his companion directs his attention to the lost animal along another path; in this [case] he would thank him, not criticize him, he would be content with him and honor him.

This was the manner of consultation of the Companions رضي الله عنهم; such that when a woman refuted ʿUmar رضي الله عنه and directed his attention to the truth of a matter while he was delivering his sermon in a large congregation of people, he responded, "A woman has hit the mark, while a man has missed."[8]

A man asked ʿAlī رضي الله عنه a question, to which he responded. Then the man said, "This is not the case, O Commander of the Faithful, in fact it is such and such." He responded, "You are right and I am wrong; above every possessor of knowledge is one [more] knowing."[9]

Ibn Masʿūd rectified an error made by Abū Mūsā l-Ashʿarī رضي الله عنه, and Abū Mūsā said, "Do not ask [me] anything while this learned man is in your presence."[10] That occurred when Abū Mūsā was asked about the circumstances of a man who was killed while fighting in the way of God, to which he responded, "He is in paradise." He [Abū Mūsā] was the governor of Kufa at the time. Ibn Masʿūd said, "Repeat your question for the governor, he may not have understood." So he repeated [the question], and he [Abū Mūsā] repeated his answer. Then Ibn Masʿūd said, "I say, if he were killed and had reached the truth of the matter [that is, his intention was valid], he is in paradise." Whereupon Abū Mūsa responded, "It is as he has said."[11]

Such is the equity of one who seeks the truth. But were one to mention similar instances at the present time to the least knowledgeable

---

8 Al-Sakhāwī, *al-Maqāṣid al-ḥasana*, 320.

9 Ibn ʿAbd al-Barr, *Jāmiʿ bayān al-ʿilm wa-faḍlih*, 865. Allusion is to 12:76: *over every possessor of knowledge is one* [*more*] *knowing.*

10 Mālik, *al-Muwaṭṭaʾ*, 2:607.

11 Abū Ṭālib al-Makkī, *Qūt al-qulūb*, 1:148.

jurist he would reject it and consider it far-fetched, saying, "There was no need to say, 'had reached the truth of the matter,' for that is a well-recognized fact for everyone."[12]

Look carefully at the disputants in your own times. How dark one's face becomes should the truth of the matter be made clear by the tongue of his adversary. How humiliated he is by it, and how he strives his utmost to refute [the other's] accomplishment, and how he criticizes—as long as he lives—anyone who silences him with his arguments. Then he shamelessly compares himself to the Companions رَضِيَ اللَّهُ عَنْهُمْ in their collaborative quest for the truth [in matters of religion].

The Seventh Condition: He should not prevent his associate[13] in a polemic dispute from shifting from one proof in favor of another or from one category of proof to another.

This was the manner in which the predecessors conducted their disputations. And he should eliminate all the innovative subtleties of dialectics from his discourse. How can he say, "The mention of this point is not incumbent upon me" [or] "This contradicts your former statement; it is therefore not to be accepted from you." For certainly making one's way back to the truth of a matter always contradicts the fallacious nature of an argument and its acceptance is obligatory.

[These days] you see that all the scholarly gatherings are taken up with defending [points of view] or arguing [against them]. It has reached a point that one participant making a point draws an analogy between a principle [of the law] and a primary cause [behind the law] that he believes applies to the case being argued. Whereupon it is said to him: "What is your proof that the ruling that bears upon this foundational principle is subject to this primary cause?" To which he responds, "This is as it appears to me, if a better clearer point of view appears to you, state it that I might reflect upon it." Whereupon his opponent persists and says, "There are implications

---

12 The condition cited by Ibn Masʿūd رَضِيَ اللَّهُ عَنْهُ is understood from the saying of the Messenger of God صَلَّى اللَّهُ عَلَيْهِ وَسَلَّمَ as narrated in al-Bukhārī: "Whoever wages war in order that the word of God be most elevated. . . is in paradise." See al-Zabīdī, *Itḥāf*, 1:290.

13 His associate in seeking the truth of the matter under disputation is in fact his opponent in the debate.

here beyond those you have cited, I am well aware of them, but will not cite them; for I am not obligated to mention them." The scholar making the original point then states, "It is incumbent upon you to bring forth any claim you have on this point." His opponent continues to insist that there is nothing incumbent upon him, and so the scholarly gatherings for disputation go on and on in this manner of cross-examination and its like.

All the while this poor fellow is unaware that his statement, "I am well aware of them, but will not cite them" is a lie against the law. For if he does not grasp the implication of a point in the argument, but claims to in order to overcome his adversary, then he is an iniquitous liar who has disobeyed God سُبۡحَانَهُۥ وَتَعَالَىٰ and [he is] liable to His wrath for claiming cognizance while being devoid of it. If, on the other hand, he is truthful, then he has deviated from the path of righteousness by concealing knowledge he has of a matter of the law, that his brother Muslim has asked about so that he can comprehend it and give it careful consideration; if it [his opinion on the law] is firm, then he [his brother Muslim] would revert to it. If it is weak then he would render him aware of the weakness of the argument and bring him out of the darkness of ignorance into the light of knowledge.

There is no disagreement that it is a binding obligation to reveal what is known of the knowledge of the religion after being asked about it. His saying, "It is not incumbent upon me" means that, according to the conventions of dialectics that we have innovated out of the desire and yearning for artifice and wrestling with words, "it is not incumbent upon me." Otherwise, it is incumbent [upon him] according to the law; for in refusing to speak, he is either a liar [about knowing it] or someone who is corrupt.

Give careful consideration to the deliberations of the Companions and the mutual consultations of the predecessors رَضِيَ ٱللَّهُ عَنۡهُمۡ. Have you ever heard anything that resembles this sort of conduct? Was anyone ever prevented from shifting from one proof in favor of another, or from changing from analogical proofs (*qiyās*) to traditions (*āthār*), or from citing a report (*khabar*) to citing a Qurʾānic verse?

In fact all their disputations were conducted in this manner; they would speak of everything that came to them as it came, all the while reflecting therein.

The Eighth Condition: One should only engage in disputation if he expects to benefit from it from someone who is immersed in knowledge.

For the most part scholars of our times avoid disputation with the illustrious and notables, [out of] fear that the truth of matters will appear on their tongues; they prefer to debate those beneath themselves, hoping to spread falsehood among them [for they lack the ability to refute their deceptions].

Beyond these conditions there are many fine points, but these eight incumbent conditions will guide you rightly to those who engage in dispute for God and those who do so under another pretext.

In conclusion, know that anyone who is not contesting Satan, who has overrun his heart and is his worst enemy, who never ceases to tempt him to his own demise, has then engaged in disputation with someone else in matters that a person of independent judgment has already been rewarded for finding the truth of the matter, or are sharing in the reward for [finding it]. He has become the laughingstock of Satan and is an example for the sincere at heart. This is why Satan rejoices in his misfortune after having plunged him into the dark world of perils that we will enumerate and elucidate in detail. We ask God for His utmost support and success.

An Elucidation of the Perils of Disputation and the Destruction of Morals that Results from it

Know and realize in yourself that a gathering of scholarly disputation organized with the aim of overcoming and silencing [an opponent] with irrefutable arguments, where high station and distinction are put on display in the presence of people, and where pride, vainglory, and rivalry are employed to curry the favor of the populace, [that this gateway] is the origin of all blameworthy character traits in God's view and all praiseworthy character traits in the eyes of His enemy, Iblīs. The relationship of these traits to the blameworthy inner qualities such as arrogance, self-importance, envy, rivalry, self-justification, and love of status and more, is [like] the relationship of drinking wine to the blameworthy outer traits of fornication, calumny, murder, and theft.

It is as if a person, given the choice between drinking and all the other reprehensible deeds, deems drinking insignificant, and thus takes it up; whereupon that [choice] leads him to commit the other sins out of his drunkenness.[14] The case of one overcome by the love of silencing an adversary with irrefutable proofs and triumphing in argumentation and seeking high rank and exaltation is similar, for his love of these traits leads him to conceal the malignant traits of his soul and arouses in him all the [other] reprehensible character traits. The proofs delineating the blameworthy nature of these character traits based on traditions and Qurʾānic verses will come in the Quarter of Perils of the present work. But let us now point out a comprehensive assemblage of those traits aroused by engagement in disputation.

Among them is envy: The Messenger of God ﷺ stated, "Envy eats away worthy deeds like fire eats away wood."[15]

No participant in disputation is ever devoid of envy; for sometimes he overcomes [his opponent], while at others [times] he is overcome; at times his discourse is praised, at other [times] the discourse of others is praised. As long as he remains in this world, there will always be a scholar of note known for the extent of his knowledge and perception [into matters of the law]—or at least he imagines that he exceeds him in scholarly discourse and acuity. He will, without a doubt, envy him and desire that whatever blessings have been bestowed upon [his opponent] be taken away and for the faces and hearts of the populace be turned away from [his opponent] toward himself.

Envy is indeed a burning fire, whoever is afflicted by it is already in an unending state of painful torment in this world and, no doubt, the torment of the abode of the hereafter is more severe and overwhelming. For this reason Ibn ʿAbbās رَضِيَ اللَّهُ عَنْهُمَا stated, "Acquire

---

14 Such as fornication, killing, and other acts. Thus, drunkenness is called the mother of corrupt behavior, as in al-Nisāʾī, 8:315.

15 Abū Dāwūd, 4903; Ibn Māja, 4210.

knowledge wherever you find it, but do not accept the sayings of the jurists about each other, for they are as jealous as goats in a pen."[16]

Among them is arrogance and exalting oneself over people: The Messenger of God ﷺ stated, "Whoever acts with arrogance, God will bring low; and whoever is humble, God will raise up."[17]

The Messenger of God ﷺ also stated, relating from God تَعَالَىٰ, "Magnificence is my loincloth and majesty is my cloak; whoever contests with me in them I will break."[18]

No participant in disputation is ever devoid of arrogance over his contemporaries and colleagues or from proclaiming that he has capabilities beyond what he has. It reaches the point that they actually fight over a place [of honor] in a gathering and vie with one another therein over elevated or reduced status [in seating] and proximity to the cushion of the presiding scholar or distance from it, as well as precedence in entering when the streets are narrow.

A deceitful dimwitted fraud among them might even make the excuse that [by his arrogance] he is only trying to preserve the pre-eminence of knowledge and that a believer is forbidden from debasing himself. He interprets the term humility, that God سُبْحَانَهُ and all the prophets held as a laudable quality, as signifying baseness, and the term arrogance, which is detested by God, as signifying eminence of the religion. He distorts these terms and thereby misguides the populace; just as it was done with the terms wisdom and knowledge and others.

Among [the negative traits] is spite: It is rarely the case that a participant in disputation is ever devoid of it; The Messenger of God ﷺ stated, "A [true] believer is not spiteful."[19]

The profusion of narrative traditions critical of spite is known to all. You will not see a participant in disputation that is capable of disguising the spite he feels toward the person who nods in

---

16 Ibn ʿAbd al-Barr, *Jāmiʿ bayān al-ʿilm wa-faḍlih*, 2125.

17 Ibn Māja, 4176, reports something similar; see al-Zabīdī, *Itḥāf*, 1:295, for a detailed account of this *ḥadīth*.

18 Muslim, 2620; Abū Dāwūd, 4090, and the wording is his.

19 Al-Nisāʾī, 6:11, narrated: "Faith and envy (*ḥasad*) cannot reside together in the heart of a believing servant." His statement "reside together. . ." (*yajtamiʿān*) is based on linguistic usage or an ellision, for the wording of the author is "A [true] believer is not spiteful." See al-ʿAjlūnī, *Kashf al-khafāʾ*, 2:293.

agreement to [a point made in] the discourse of his opponent, and he will even pause in mid-speech, and not listen carefully, and this forces him—when he realizes what he has done—to conceal his spite and embellish it in actuality. The purpose of his restraint is to secrete [his own] hypocrisy, but inevitably, in most cases, it makes its way to the surface.

How could anyone ever be devoid of this [malicious quality] when it is unimaginable that all the listeners [at a gathering] could concur on the validity [of every proof] of his discourse, and extol his every circumstance concerning his allegation and his clear pronouncement? Moreover, if even the lowliest cause were to come from his opponent, and that [lowliest cause] produce the slightest consideration for his speech, spite would be implanted in his chest that would take the length of his lifetime to weed out.

Among them is calumny, [which] God تعالى likened it to consuming the flesh of a corpse [49:12]. Those participating in disputation continue to zealously consume dead flesh; for he never ceases to recount [the points of] his opponents discourse and to criticize him. The best that he can be mindful of [in this] is to relate truthfully what he recounts of him and not lie in retelling the account; for inevitably he will recount that which reveals the deficiency of his [opponent's] discourse, his weakness, and lack of distinction. This is calumny; as for lying, it is slander.

In like manner he [i.e., the disputant] is incapable of holding his tongue from impugning the good repute of a person who shifts from [listening to] his discourse and turns to listen to his opponent; this reaches a point that he accuses him of ignorance, foolhardiness, a lack of understanding and stupidity.

Among them is self-justification: God تعالى stated: *Do not justify yourselves; He is most knowledgeable of the God wary*" [53:32].

A sage was asked, "What is repugnant veracity?" He responded, "A man's praise for himself."

A participant in a disputation is never devoid of the propensity to praise himself, his ability to overwhelm [his opponents], and his pre-eminence among his contemporaries. Nor does he cease praising himself by stating [when challenged by an opponent asking for a particular proof], "I am not among those from whom examples of this sort are hidden," or [he says during his discourse] "I am well versed in the branches of the Islamic sciences, I have independent authority in the fundamental principles of jurisprudence, and I am singularly gifted with a good memory of *ḥadīth*." There is much more by which he praises himself, sometimes as a boast and other times in order to promote his discourse. It is well known, however, that boasting and promoting oneself are both blameworthy qualities, whether from the point of view of the law or the rational faculty.

Among them is spying and pursuing the failings of people: God ﷻ stated: *Spy not on one another* [49:12]

A scholar engaged in disputation is never devoid of looking into the errors of his peers and pursuing the weak points of his adversaries. It has reached the point that when he is apprised of the arrival of a disputant in his region, he looks for someone well-informed of [this man's] circumstances and seeks to expose—by questioning—anything offensive about him, and amasses for himself a resource to be used to degrade and shame him should the need arise. He even seeks to uncover details of his youth and any physical defects [he may have]; for he may stumble upon an inadvertent error or a defect such as infections of the scalp or other imperfections. Then, if he senses even a minute threat from [his opponent], he would allude to it [quietly], if he restrains himself; and those present would deem this appropriate on his part and consider it a refined means of intimate discourse. Nothing would prevent him from completely exposing him with derision and insolence, if he were an insolent braggart, as has been recounted about a group of renowned scholars of polemic discourse who were considered among the stallions of the discipline.

Among them is experiencing joy over the misfortune of others and displeasure at their good fortune.

Anyone who does not desire [the same good] for his brother Muslim that he desires for himself is far from the comportment of a [true] believer. Everyone vying to outdo another through a display of personal pride and prominence will inevitably experience joy at that which engenders grief in his peers and colleagues who are vying with him for prominence. The feeling of mutual loathing between them is like that between competing wives of the same husband. Just as one of them sees her companion from a distance, and then has muscle spasms and turns pale, so you will see the one engaged in disputation [react] when he sees another. He glowers and loses concentration as though he has seen a demonic jinn or a ferocious lion.

Where is the familiarity and peaceful atmosphere that was the custom during the gatherings of the eminent scholars of the religion; and where is the mutual brotherhood and support and their sharing during good times and bad that has been transmitted to us, such that al-Shāfiʿī said, "Knowledge among the people of reason and preeminence is a bond of kinship."

I have no idea how a group of people who claim to be following his school of jurisprudence has turned the pursuit of knowledge into the absolute enmity that exists between them. Can it be imagined that any sociability can prevail while in quest of triumph and vainglory?

But oh! How far from the mark! How far from the mark! It is sufficient to apprise you of the malice of a thing that it obliges you to assume the character traits of hypocrites, and separates you from the character traits of the believers and the righteous.

Among them is hypocrisy. There is no need to cite the testimonies [from the Qurʾān and *ḥadīth*] as to its reprehensible nature as a character trait. Yet, [disputants] are compelled [by the very nature of disputation] to employ it. For they regularly encounter their adversaries in the company of their friends and supporters in circumstances in which there is no way to avoid affable speech, displaying warm feelings, and showing esteem for their status and circumstances. All the while, that addressee, the addressed, and everyone who hears that from them knows that it is lying, duplicity, hypocrisy, and corrupt behavior. They display mutual love and respect in speech, while detesting one another in their hearts. We seek protection from God—the magnificent—from such conduct. For the Messenger of God ﷺ stated: "A people who have learned knowledge and abandoned its application, who manifest mutual love and esteem in speech while detesting one another in their hearts, and sever ties of kinship, God has cursed them for that; He will make them deaf and blind [to the truth]." Narrated by al-Ḥassan.[20] The present state of affairs testifies to that [most clearly].

Among them is disdain and averting the truth [of a matter] with the intention of contesting it.

This has reached the point that the most detested thing to a scholar engaged in disputation is for the truth [of a matter] to be made apparent on the tongue of his opponent; [even then]—regardless of the manner [in which] it became apparent—he is ready to roll up his sleeves and employ his utmost strength to oppose and contest it. In its rebuttal he will employ the utmost of his skills of deception, cunning, and false pretext. With time this contesting of the truth [of matters] become second nature in him; every word of discourse he hears [of his opponent] he instinctively contests, until it overwhelms his heart, and even where evidence drawn from the Qurʾān and the narrative tradition of law are concerned, he contests them one against the other.

Aggressive disputation—even in the face of falsehood—has been warned against; the Messenger of God ﷺ even counseled in favor of ceasing to contest a matter in which the truth is employed to oppose falsehood. The Messenger of God ﷺ stated, "Whoever ceases disputing a matter in which he is in the wrong, God will build him a residence in the meadows of heaven; and whoever ceases disputing a matter in which he is in the right, God will build a residence in the highest heaven."[21]

God تعالى has equated a man who invents a lie against God with a man who denies the truth of a matter; He تعالى has stated, *and who wrongs themselves more than one who invents a lie against God, or denies the truth* [*of a matter*] *when it reaches him* [29:68]; and He تعالى stated, *Who wrongs themselves more than one who utters a lie against God, and denies the truth when it comes to them* [39:32].

Among [the character traits] are ostentation and currying the favor of the populace, and making every effort to win over their hearts and gain their attention.

20 Al-Ṭabarānī, *al-Muʿjam al-kabīr*, 6:263; Abū Nuʿaym, *Ḥilya*, 3:109; Ibn ʿAsākir, *Tārīkh Dimashq*, 13:100; narrating from a similar tradition, from the *ḥadīth* of Salmān رضي الله عنه attributed to the Messenger of God ﷺ.

21 Al-Tirmidhī, 1993; Ibn Māja, 51.

Ostentation is an incurable disease that gives rise to the greatest of major sins—as will be explained presently in *Kitāb al-riyāʾ* [Book 28, *The Censure of Fame and Ostentation*]; and the sole purpose of one engaged in disputation is to appear before the populace and gain their acclaim.

These ten character traits comprise the origins of the innate nature of all the reprehensible character traits, besides those [traits] that arise among those people among them who have no grip on themselves, such as disputes that lead to hitting, slapping, the tearing of clothing, grasping beards, cursing parents, reviling teachers, and the outright slanderous defamation of character. Thus those people [with these character traits] are not to be counted among the reputable scholars; however, the scholars of rank and those among them in full possession of their rational faculties in particular are never free of these ten traits.

Yes, some of them are safe [from these traits] among themselves, but only in the company of someone of a clearly lesser rank than himself or someone clearly above him, or who is far from his region and from influencing in any manner his ability to gain his livelihood; otherwise not one of them is devoid of these traits with their peers and those who compare with them in rank.

Then, from each of these ten traits ten more traits, just as base, branch out. We will not cite them at length nor expound on them one by one. Examples of them include disdain for others; unrestrained anger; hatred; ambitious desire; love of seeking wealth and high station as a means to triumph [over opponents]; boastfulness; disrespect for others; hubris; exalting and patronizing the wealthy and powerful; and accepting gifts from their ill-gotten wealth; adorning oneself through the possession of horses, means of transport, and clothing of questionable nature [according to the law]; regarding the populace with contempt through arrogance and conceit; obsession with what does not concern one; excess speech; the purging of fear and reverence from the heart and its being overwhelmed by heedlessness. It reaches a point that a man among them prays, oblivious in his prayer to which [of the five prayers] he prayed, what he recited in his prayer, and who he is conversing with. He feels no awe [of God] in his heart, having spent his entire life pursuing subjects that will serve him in disputation, like eloquent speech, rhyming prose, and memorizing rare examples from the traditions, and countless other examples, although all these matters are of no benefit in the abode of the hereafter.

Scholars of disputation differ from one another according to their ranks [of age and experience], and these ranks are numerous. None of even the most illustrious among them in piety and the most gifted in intellect is ever devoid of the sum and substance of these base traits; their chief goal, however, is concealing them and striving against the base urges of the soul.

Know that these base traits are also inseparable from the person engaged in admonition and spiritual counsel if his intention is currying favor with the populace, establishing status, and attaining wealth and distinction. Likewise they are inseparable from anyone engaged in the pursuit of the tenets of knowledge of a school of jurisprudence and rulings, if he is seeking a legal position or responsibility over endowments, or advancement over his peers.

In sum, these traits are inherent in anyone who seeks knowledge for other than the recompense of the abode of the hereafter. Knowledge does not disregard or ignore the scholar, rather it brings him to eternal death and destruction, or it brings him to eternal life [in the abode of the hereafter]. Thus the Messenger of God ﷺ stated, "The person most severely chastised on the day of judgment will be the learned man whom God did not afford benefit from his knowledge."[22]

So even though it did not benefit him, it caused him harm. If only he had been spared it altogether. O, what a lamentable state of affairs! What a lamentable state of affairs. The peril of knowledge is huge, he who pursues it is seeking a means to the everlasting kingdom and perpetual bliss; his portion is either dominion or destruction. He is like one seeking political might and authority in this world; if the aim is not in accord with the acquisition of vast wealth, he does not hope for a safe haven among the outcasts,[23] on the contrary, there will be no escaping a life of utter humiliation.

22 Al-Ṭabarānī, *al-Muʿjam al-ṣaqhīr*, 1:182; Quḍāʿī, *Musnad al-shihāb*, 1122; and al-Bayhaqī, *Shuʿab al-īmān*, 1642.

23 The Arabic term *ardhal* refers to those people who live a life secure from tumult because no one pays attention to them. Al-Zabīdī, *Itḥāf*, 1:303.

If you state, "In permitting disputation there is a benefit, which is to awaken a desire in the populace to pursue the knowledge [of religion]; for if there had been no love of authority, the sciences would have fallen into ruin and been effaced from the earth."

[I would reply], "You have spoken truthfully in what you have mentioned from one perspective, but there is still no real benefit. For were it not for the promise of a ball and bats and playing with sparrows, young children would have no desire to enter school, but that does not demonstrate that these are praiseworthy pursuits." [Then, your statement], "If there had been no love of authority, then knowledge would have fallen into ruin," does not demonstrate that one who seeks authority is saved. Rather, he is among those about whom the Messenger of God ﷺ stated, "Verily, God will strengthen this religion with a people who have no redeeming character traits whatsoever."[24] And he ﷺ said as well, "Verily, God will strengthen this religion with an iniquitous man."[25]

The one seeking authority is in [evident] ruin and perdition, yet through him the circumstances of others may be rectified and enhanced, on the condition that he summons them to abandon this world. This is the case of anyone whose outward circumstances are similar to the circumstances of the scholars among the predecessors, while he conceals [from others] his intention to achieve power and influence. He is like a candle that burns itself to give light to others; the well-being of others is his own ruin.[26]

Should he summon [people] to seek this world, he is as the example of a burning fire that consumes itself and everything it comes into contact with.

The scholars are of three varieties:

(1) He who destroys himself and others; they speak openly of seeking the goods of this worldly domain and are dedicated to their acquisition.

---

24 Al-Nisāʾī, 8833.

25 Al-Bukhārī, 3062; Muslim, 111.

26 Al-Ṭabarānī reported, *al-Muʿjam al-kabīr*, 2:166, as attributed to the Prophet, "The example of the scholar who teaches people to be good but forgets about it for himself is like a lamp that lights the way for people and then burns itself out."

(2) He who strives to benefit himself and others; they are those who summon [people] to God تَعَالَىٰ, who have renounced the world, outwardly and inwardly.
(3) He who destroys himself while aiding others; he summons [people] to the abode of the hereafter, having rejected the goods of this worldly life outwardly, while his inward intention is to gain favor with the populace and establish preeminence [over them].

Consider carefully which variety you are and how you have busied yourself in preparation. Do not imagine that God تَعَالَىٰ accepts any knowledge or action that was not accomplished sincerely for His countenance alone. You will soon be apprised in the *Kitāb al-riyāʾ* [Book 28, *The Censure of Fame and Ostentation*], in fact in the entire *Rubʿ al-muhlikāt* [Quarter of Perils] of that which frees you of any doubts on this subject, God تَعَالَىٰ willing.

5

On the Comportment Incumbent upon the Student and the Teacher

WITH REGARD TO THE student, his incumbent conduct and responsibilities are numerous; their varying aspects may be categorized under ten headings:

The first responsibility of the student is to give precedence to purifying his soul from reprehensible character traits and blameworthy qualities.

Seeking knowledge is the worship of the heart, the prayer of the innermost mystery, and inward intimacy with God تَعَالَىٰ. Just as the prayer—that is a responsibility of the outward bodily limbs—is only valid when performed in a state of outward purity from the secretions or impurities, likewise inward devotion and nurturing the heart with knowledge is only valid when it is purified of offensive character traits and noxious qualities.

The Messenger of God صَلَّى ٱللَّهُ عَلَيْهِ وَسَلَّمَ said, "The religion was founded upon cleanliness."[1] It is thus inwardly and outwardly.

God تَعَالَىٰ stated, *Indeed those who associate partners* (mushrikūn) *with God are unclean* [9:28]; [thus he] called the intellect's attention to [the fact that] purity and impurity are not limited to exterior

1 Narrated by al-Rāfiʿī, *al-Tadwīn fī akhbār Qazwīn*, 1:176, with the wording, "Verily God built Islam upon cleanliness," and by al-Tirmidhī, 2799, "Verily God is pure, he loves purity, one who is clean loves cleanliness."

circumstances and discerned by the senses [alone]. One who associates partners with God may have clean clothing and a washed body, yet his essence is impure, meaning his inward being is polluted with noxious substances.

The term "impurity" is an expression for substances which one avoids and seeks to distance oneself from. The term "noxious substances" are inward qualities that are more imperative to avoid; for though they are certainly impure in a given circumstance, they become destructive with the passage of time. For this reason the Messenger of God ﷺ stated, "Angels do not enter a house in which there is a dog."[2] The heart is a house, it is a place to which the angels descend, where their traces abide, and a dwelling in which they find repose; reprehensible character traits, like uncontrolled anger, carnal desire, rancor, envy, arrogant pride, conceit, and their like are barking dogs; how would angels enter therein while it was overrun with dogs? God تَعَالَىٰ only casts the light of knowledge into the heart by means of the angels. [God تَعَالَىٰ states,] *It is not God's wont to speak [directly] to a human being, unless by inspiration or from behind a veil, or by the sending of a messenger* [42:51]. Verily it is the angels who are responsible for imparting the mercy of knowledge that is sent to the heart. They are hallowed, untainted, and devoid of blameworthy qualities; they take note only of the pure and good, and they make their abodes, with the treasures of God's mercy that they possess, only in the hearts of the virtuous and pure.[3]

---

2 Al-Bukhārī, 3225; Muslim, 2106.

3 Al-Ghazālī also said, "If you ask, 'how could a disbeliever come to believe, or a sinner come to be obedient, or a misguided person come to guidance, given that the demons do not leave the heart of a disbeliever, sinner, or misguided person because the blameworthy qualities are dispersed in him? Thus the various kinds of good qualities which are only received from God عَزَّوَجَلَّ by the mediation of angels could never enter a place that possesses the condition just mentioned. If the angels cannot enter, then he cannot obtain the good qualities which they bring, thus they will not reach him. Based on that, every disbeliever is obliged to remain in that condition. If someone is not created as a protected believer, there is no way for him to reach faith, based on this understanding.' The answer is thus: For the demons, there are times of forgetfulness, and for the blameworthy qualities, there are times of remission. Likewise, for the angels, there are times of absence, and for the many good qualities, there are times of laxity. Thus when an angel finds an empty heart, even for a brief moment, he settles in there. He shows it the good that he has. If he encounters acceptance from it, and when it confronts him with

I am not saying, "The intended meaning of the word 'house' is the 'heart,'" or "That of 'dog' is 'uncontrolled anger' and 'blamable qualities'"; rather I say, "It is to call attention to this meaning." For there is a distinction between actually changing the outward [literal meaning of things] to the inward [meanings] and between calling attention to the inward [aspect of things] by citing the outward, all the while confirming the literal meaning of the words themselves. The Bāṭinīya[4] have been differentiated [and declared unorthodox] on this subtle point. For this [path of ours] is the path of reflection, which is the well-traveled road of the learned and the upright. This is so because the meaning of reflection is to take into account what has been said to someone else, and not limit it to that [i.e., their particular circumstances]. It is as when an intelligent person sees another's misfortune and thus there is a lesson in it for him to reflect on, to attain awareness that he too is liable to encounter misfortunes, and [then further] that the mundane world is always in a state of flux [and cannot be counted on]. His lessons are drawn from [the experiences] of someone else. Then they are applied to himself, and from there he recognizes the essential nature of the world. This is praiseworthy reflection.

So reflect on the house, which is a human edifice, in relation to the heart, which is a house among the edifices of God تَعَالَىٰ, and on the dog—reproached for his quality, not his form, that being his predatory and unclean [nature] in relation to the essential quality of the dog, that being the ferociousness of a predatory animal.

Know that the heart, teeming with uncontrolled anger, and an avid desire to possess worldly goods and fight over them like dogs, with a craving to tear asunder the esteem and reputations of people,

---

expectation and longing, he transfers to it what he has to fill it. If, however, he encounters annoyance from it, and he hears from it the armies of demons [diabolical armies] calling for help and bringing frenzied qualities as aid, then he departs from him and abandons him." See al-Ghazālī, *al-Imlāʾ*, 23.

4 The Bāṭiniyya were a school of Islamic thought that was known for interpreting religious texts exclusively on the basis of hidden rather than literal meanings. Imām al-Ghazālī was a severe critic of the Bāṭiniyya and composed several works responding to their points of view, which he believed were a rejection of the literal meanings of the Qurʾān and *sunna* and opened the door to misinterpretation and controversy on the one hand and perplexity among the commonality of believers on the other.

is a dog in essential meaning but in the form of a heart. The light of inner vision discerns the meanings, not the form. In this world, however, forms tend to prevail over meanings and the meanings are concealed [and resonate] within them, whereas in the abode of the hereafter forms will reflect meanings and meanings shall prevail. On the day of resurrection, each individual will be raised up in the form of their inner essence; a person who ripped the good reputations of people to pieces will be raised as a vicious dog, one avid to acquire their belongings as a ravenous wolf, one arrogant over them in the form of a leopard, and one seeking authority over the populace as a lion.

Traditions have been passed down to that effect, and the reflective faculty of the people of outward and inner vision have witnessed these things,[5] and witnessed various evidence in dreams; for those who are sleeping, once they have distanced themselves from the realm of the senses, draw near to that realm [of the hereafter], for sleep is the brother of death, so they may see in their sleep creatures bearing these qualities as we have mentioned them here.[6]

If you were to ask: "How many students with reprehensible character have gained knowledge?"

How you have missed the mark! How far you are from [understanding the nature of] the true knowledge that will be of benefit in the abode of the hereafter, and that will ensure salvation.

---

5 The disposition of the author liberally promotes, through the subtleties indicated by the texts, the evidence of understanding and perception. He رحمه الله has said, "There is no denying that when knowledge and the totality of rational investigation indicate it, enlightened hearts will not reject it, and no aspect of the pillars of the law oppose it. Thus it is not debatable, and there is no concern for the condemnation of the ignorant or the aversion of the blind follower (*muqallid*). Thus much of what comes in the law is associated with causation. Therefore, the people of reflection see the means of transferring it (a term) from its cause to what is in its meaning and using it as an allegory from the perspective of soundness in transferring it to it (the new meaning). If this were not so, then the Prophet would not have said, "Perhaps the full attainment of awareness is first with the one who hears (something). Then he conveys the understanding to someone who is more insightful than him." See al-Ghazālī, *al-Imlāʿ*, 23.

6 From his statement "witnessing various evidence" to his statement "we have mentioned them here" is an addition from another edition. There is confirmation of the relation of this sentence to the rest of the paragraph in al-Ghazālī, "*Kīmiyāʾ al-saʿāda*," 136–137. God knows best.

For the very beginning of that knowledge is his awareness that disobedience is a destructive deadly poison. Have you ever seen anyone take poison knowing it was deadly?

What you hear from those adopting the outward forms are narrations they have picked up, then repeated once on their tongues and another time in their hearts; this has nothing to do with knowledge at all. Ibn Masʿūd رَضِيَ اللَّهُ عَنْهُ said, "Knowledge is not a question of the quantity of narrations [one cites], it is light cast into the heart."[7]

Another among them said, "Verily, knowledge is experiencing the awe of God's presence;[8] as in the words of God تَعَالَىٰ, *From among His servants, only those who fear God are those who have knowledge* [35:28].[9]

It is as though [this verse] is an allusion to the most particular of the fruits of knowledge, for this reason one of those who had attained true knowledge of God said, "The meaning of their words, 'We pursued knowledge for other than God, but knowledge refused to be for other than God alone'[10] is that knowledge refused and rejected us and did not reveal its true character to us; all we gained access to was its formal discourse and its words."

If you say: I have seen a faction of truly learned jurists who have achieved excellence in both the subsidiary branches and foundational principles [of the law] who are counted among the stallions of their field, yet their character traits are blameworthy, they have not cleansed themselves thereof.

Let it be said [in response], "If you were cognizant of the degrees into which knowledge is categorized, and you knew the [true] value of the knowledge of the abode of the hereafter, it would be clear to you that the knowledge that they have occupied themselves with is of little value with regard to [true] knowledge; its true value is what is

---

7 Narrated by Aḥmad b. Ḥanbal, *al-Zuhd*, 867; it also has, "but knowledge is experiencing the awe of God in His presence (*khashiya*)."

8 Narrated by Aḥmad b. Ḥanbal, *al-Zuhd*, 867; it also has, "but knowledge is apprehension of God (*khashiya*)."

9 This is the same as mentioned above from ʿAbdallāh b. Masʿūd رَضِيَ اللَّهُ عَنْهُ. It is reported, Abū Nuʿaym, *Ḥilya*, 1:131. See also al-Suyūṭī, *al-Durr al-Manthūr*, 7:20.

10 This statement is from Sufyān al-Thawrī, as al-Ghazālī states in *al-ʿUzla* [*The Proprieties of Retreat*, book 16 of the *Iḥyāʾ ʿulūm al-dīn*].

applied in actions accomplished for God تَعَالَىٰ alone, [and then] when it is undertaken with the intention of drawing close to God تَعَالَىٰ."

An allusion to this has already been given, and a more extensive clearer exposition of this will soon be given to you, God تَعَالَىٰ willing [in chapter 6].

The second responsibility of the student is to diminish his ties with mundane occupations and distance himself from family and homeland.

Ties and relationships are things that preoccupy one and distract him from his goal. *God has not created for a man two hearts in his breast* [33:4]. Whenever one's attention is divided it falls short of discerning the subtle realities of things, for this reason it is said, "Knowledge will not grant you a portion of itself until you give yourself entirely to it; however, if you give yourself entirely to it, you are still in peril of its granting you a portion."[11]

When dispersed over a number of diverse subjects, attention is like a brook whose waters have been distributed [over a diverse area], the earth absorbs some of it and some of it evaporates in the air, and then there is nothing left of it that can be channeled [in one stream] and reach the cultivated area.

The third responsibility of the student is that he not conduct himself in an arrogant manner toward knowledge, nor dominate the teacher. On the contrary, he should place the reins of every aspect of his affair in his teacher's hands completely; submit to his good counsel in the manner that an illiterate patient would put himself in the hands of a compassionate well-versed physician.

It is incumbent on him to show humility toward his teacher and seek (God's) good pleasure and distinction in his service. Al-Shaʿbī related, "Zayd b. Thābit performed the funeral prayer and his mule was brought to him so he could mount it. Ibn ʿAbbās رَضِيَ ٱللَّهُ عَنْهُمَا came and held his stirrup, whereupon Zayd spoke, saying, "Leave it be, O cousin of the Messenger of God." So Ibn ʿAbbās رَضِيَ ٱللَّهُ عَنْهُمَا said, "This is how we were told to treat scholars and the venerable." Zayd b.

11 Al-Khaṭīb al-Baghdādī, *al-faqīh wa-l-mutafaqqih*, 864; al-Khaṭīb al-Baghdādī, *al-Jāmiʿ lī-akhlāq al-rāwī wa-ādāb al-sāmiʿ*, 1570.

Thābit kissed his hand and said, "This is how we were told to treat the people of our Prophet Muḥammad's ﷺ household."[12]

The Messenger of God ﷺ stated, "Flattery is not among the character traits of the believer, except in the case of seeking knowledge."[13]

It is therefore not befitting the student to act arrogantly with the teacher. Among the indications of his arrogance toward the teacher is his disdain from accepting instruction that did not originate from the notable and famous [among the scholars]. This is pure folly, for knowledge is the means of redemption and salvation [in the abode of the hereafter]. A person fleeing from a savage lion attempting to devour him draws no distinction between whether the person guiding him to a means of flight is famous or unknown. The ferocity of the lions of hellfire for those ignorant of God تعالى is greater than the ferocity of any lion.

Wisdom is the lost object of the believer; he seizes it whenever he has the opportunity, he adorns with a necklace of gratitude whoever leads him to it. For this it was spoken:

> Knowledge is at war with the young and arrogant
> Just as a flood is at war with the high ground[14]

Knowledge is thus only attained with humility and by humbly lending one's ear. God تعالى stated, *Verily in that is a reminder to one possessed of a heart, or who lends an ear, earnestly witnessing* [*the truth*] [50:37]. One being "possessed of a heart" [refers to someone] naturally disposed to the pursuit of knowledge who has the intellectual capacity, but the capacity to understand does not suffice him until he "humbly lends an ear" and witnesses earnestly, with presence of heart. He receives everything that is cast before him by listening attentively, with humility, gratitude, joy, and gracious acceptance.

So let the student be for his teacher like a gentle fertile land that has received ample rainfall. All parts of the land have absorbed it,

---

12 Ibn ʿAbd al-Barr, *Jāmiʿ bayān al-ʿilm wa-faḍlih*, 832 with a complete narration originating from al-Ṭabarānī, *al-Muʿjam al-kabīr*, 5:107; and al-Ḥākim al-Nīsābūrī, *al-Mustadrak*, 3:423.

13 Ibn ʿAbd al-Barr, *Jāmiʿ bayān al-ʿilm wa-faḍlih*, 859; al-Khaṭīb al-Baghdādī, *al-Jāmiʿ li akhlāq al-rāwī wa-ādāb al-sāmiʿ*, 1473.

14 See al-ʿUkbarī, *al-Tibyān*, 63; and al-Ḥabashī, *Nashr ṭayy al-taʿrīf*, 245.

and the land has yielded in its totality and accepted it. He takes as his own whatever manner of learning his teacher alludes to and leaves his own opinion behind; for the error of his teacher is more beneficial to him than his being accurate himself. This is because experience renders one conscious of fine points that would be unbelievable if [only] heard, even though their benefit is boundless. How often will a physician treat a patient suffering from a fever with warmth in order to increase his strength so that he can bear the trauma of the actual treatment; anyone who has no experience of this would find it hard to believe.

God تَعَالَىٰ has called attention [to the nature of this aspect of the teacher/student relationship] in the story of Moses and al-Khiḍr عَلَيْهِمَاٱلسَّلَامُ. When al-Khiḍr said [after Moses asked to accompany him and learn from him], *You are incapable of having patience with me; how could you be patient with something of which you lack a thorough understanding* [18:67–68]. Whereupon he imposed on Moses the conditions of silence and compliance, saying, *If then you would follow me, ask me of nothing until I myself have given you an account thereof* [18:70]. Then Moses lost patience and persisted in questioning him [on the events he witnessed] until that became the reason for their parting ways.

In sum, judge every student who persists in holding to his own opinions and preferences beyond the teacher's preferences [for him] a failure and a lost cause.

If you say, "Questioning is a thing decreed [by the religion]; has not God تَعَالَىٰ stated, *Ask the possessors of God's remembrance* (ahl al-dhikr) *if you know not* [16:43; 21:7].'"

Know that the issue is as you have stated it. However, [it pertains only to] asking about those matters that the teacher has permitted questioning about; it is a blameworthy attribute to ask questions about that which you have not yet attained the degree [of knowledge] to comprehend; this is why al-Khiḍr prevented Moses عَلَيْهِٱلسَّلَامُ from questioning [him]. This means, desist from asking questions before their time. The teacher is most knowledgeable of those matters that are relevant to your state, and of the times to make them known [to you]. The [proper] times of questioning are not reached until the time of the disclosure is reached, in each of its ascending degrees.

ʿAlī رَضِيَ اللَّهُ عَنْهُ stated,

> Among the rights of the scholar among you are that you do not question him in excess, nor press him for the response; do not insist on a response should he delay to respond, and do not grab his clothing when he gets up [in a gathering]. Do not divulge any secrets to him, nor ever disparage anyone in his presence; do not look into any lapses on his part, and should he falter, accept his excuse. It is incumbent upon you to honor and to hold him in high esteem for the sake of God تَعَالَىٰ, as long as he stands firm in God's commandments. Do not sit in front of him, and should he require assistance, be the first of your people to rise to his service.[15]

The fourth responsibility is for anyone who immerses himself in the pursuit of knowledge to be wary—in the beginning—of lending an ear to discussions dealing with divergent opinions among the people; whether he is pursuing the fields of knowledge of this world or the knowledge of the abode of the hereafter.

Paying attention to that [divergent opinions] bewilders his reason or the student's reason and perplexes his mind; it diminishes his judgment and causes him to despair of ever attaining comprehension and awareness. He should first master the one praised path that is pleasing to his teacher, then lend an ear to the varying schools and obscure matters of jurisprudence.

The student should be wary of his teacher, however, if he [the teacher] is not capable of independently giving preference to one point of view [over others] but instead tends to pass on [to the student] the opinions of the other schools and views already stated therein; for [in this] he is more liable to mislead than guide aright. The blind are not fit to guide and lead the blind; and anyone in this state has gone beyond [blindness] to the impaired vision of bewilderment and the wilderness of ignorance.

Prohibiting the student in the beginning of his path from [delving into] obscure matters of jurisprudence is similar to prohibiting a recent convert to Islam from association with disbelievers; likewise authorizing a scholar well-grounded [in jurisprudence] to inquire

15 Al-Khaṭīb al-Baghdādī, *al-Faqīh wa-l-mutafaqqih*, 856, has a similar narration.

into matters of divergent opinion is similar to encouraging a warrior [well versed in the arts of war] to assault the enemy [on the battlefield]. For the same reason the ill-prepared person is prohibited from attacking the ranks of the unbelieving enemy although the courageous are encouraged therein.

Being heedless of these fine points of divergence, some ill-prepared scholars suppose that following the example of scholars of repute on uncomplicated matters of law is allowable; they do not comprehend that the role of the scholars of repute differs from that of the less prepared scholars. This is why it was said, "Whoever saw me in the beginning became trustworthy [in behavior], and whoever saw me at the end [of my quest] became a heretic;"[16] for at the end of the quest for knowledge actions turn inward and the members of the physical body become still except to perform the obligatory acts. It may appear to anyone looking [at him] that he is idle, lethargic, and neglectful. How you have missed the mark! How you have missed the mark! That is the station of the heart immersed in the reality of witnessing and presence, permanently resolute in the remembrance that is the best of all practices.

Comparing the ill-prepared scholar with the scholar of repute based on what one can see of his outward state is a mistake similar to the reasoning of someone who puts a small amount of impurity into the water contained in a receptacle [used for ablutions]; he explains that should double this amount of impurity be tossed into the sea, the sea being larger than the water receptacle, [it would not be tainted for ablutions] so that which is permissible with the sea is even more permissible with the receptacle. This poor person does not realize that in its overwhelming power the sea is able to transform an impure substance into water; for it transforms an essentially impure substance by its overpowering influence until it takes on its own attribute [which is pure and able to purify]; a small amount of an impure substance will overwhelm the receptacle and transform the water therein to its attributes [i.e., it will become impure and not able to purify].

In similar fashion things were made permissible for the Messenger of God ﷺ that were not permissible for others;

16 Al-Ghazālī, *Mīzān al-ʿamal*, 347.

for example it was permissible for him to have nine wives.[17] For he was able to treat his wives with a degree of justice and equality that surpassed [what] others could do even though his wives were many; as for others, they were incapable of being equitable at all times. Furthermore, the Prophet's wives were harmful for him and drew him into disobedience to God تَعَالَىٰ, [in order] to seek their goodwill. Whoever compares angels to blacksmiths will never flourish.

The fifth responsibility is for the student in pursuit of the sciences to not leave a single aspect of the study of the praiseworthy sciences or any branch of them without giving them careful consideration, in order to apprise himself of its significance and purpose.

Then, if he is blessed with a long life, he can seek to delve deeply into it, otherwise, he should [first] occupy himself with the most essential areas among them and acquire a comprehensive view therein, and study the remainder peripherally;[18] for the sciences complement and are interrelated to one another.

The immediate benefit to the student [of pursuing a broad range of subjects] is that he rids himself of antipathy toward one area of study due to his ignorance of it; for people are enemies of that which they are ignorant of. God تَعَالَىٰ states, *If they do not find good guidance through it, they will say, "This is a made-up tale drawn from ancient legend"* [46:11].

And a poet said,

Whoever's mouth has the bitter taste of illness
Will find even sweet water bitter to his taste[19]

The sciences are of varying gradations. Some carry the servant along on his path to God تَعَالَىٰ, others support his quest in one way or another; they also have well-ordered stages arranged according to proximity and distance from the objective and they have guardians who uphold their integrity, like those who man the fortresses and frontier outposts [of a realm]. Everyone has his own standing, and

---

17 As narrated in al-Bukhārī, 268. The expression "nine wives" is from the transmission of Saʿīd from Qatāda from Anas. Likewise, he has the expression "eleven wives."

18 See al-Zabīdī, *Itḥāf*, 1:321.

19 This is from al-Mutanabbī, al-ʿUkbārī, *al-Tibyān fī Sharḥ al-Dīwān*, 3:228.

if he is seeking the countenance of God alone, his recompense—according to his rank—will be in the abode of the hereafter.

The sixth responsibility [of the student] and the judicious path is to pursue in each field the best it has to offer since a lifetime generally does not allow one to pursue the totality of the sciences. In some cases one must be satisfied with a fragrance alone while concentrating all his strength on knowledge that is achievable without difficulty, in order to realize the most noble of the sciences, the knowledge of the abode of the hereafter. Here I mean the two categories of knowledge, the science of conduct and science of unveiling, for the object of the science of conduct is unveiling, and the object of the science of unveiling is the realization of God عَزَّوَجَلَّ.

I do not mean by these two sciences the conviction that common people seize on as something inherited or as something snatched up in an impromptu manner; nor the path of meticulous theology and dialectics [as used] in defense of one's views against the subterfuges of opponents, as is the object of the theologian. Rather, I intend here the knowledge that is an aspect of certainty, that is the fruit of the light that God تَعَالَىٰ casts into the heart of a servant whose inner state is cleansed of offensive character traits and noxious qualities through [spiritual] striving until he attains the degree of faith of Abū Bakr رَضِيَ اللَّهُ عَنْهُ, that would exceed the entirety of creation if it were weighed against it; as testified to by the leader of humankind صَلَّى اللَّهُ عَلَيْهِ وَسَلَّمَ.[20] I in no manner imagine that what the common [person] believes and that which has been systemized by theologians, who surpass the general believer [in their degree of faith] only because of their fabrication of discourse, and because they have named this fabrication "theology" [is the same]. ʿUmar, ʿUthmān, ʿAlī, and all the Companions رَضِيَ اللَّهُ عَنْهُمْ would not have comprehended [that theology]. And so it is that Abū Bakr رَضِيَ اللَّهُ عَنْهُ surpassed them, [because of] the inner thought that resided in his chest.

It is astonishing that anyone can hear the likes of these statements from the master/conveyor of the law صَلَّى اللَّهُ عَلَيْهِ وَسَلَّمَ and then take lightly what he has heard, and follow his own inclination and suppose it is the irrational idle sayings of the Sufis.

20 Attributed to the Prophet صَلَّى اللَّهُ عَلَيْهِ وَسَلَّمَ by Ibn ʿAdī, *al-Kāmil*, 4:201; and al-Bayhaqī, *Shuʿab al-īmān*, 35, reports it from ʿUmar.

One must act with deliberation in such instances, for in similar circumstances you may lose all your capital assets; so seek diligently that secret that is beyond the wares of the jurists and theologians. For only your diligence in ardent striving will lead you rightly to it.

To summarize, [know that] the most noble and the true goal of all the sciences is the realization of God عَزَّوَجَلَّ. It is an ocean, the ultimate depths of which is beyond comprehension; the highest degree attainable by any human being [where it is concerned] is the degree of the prophets, then the saints, and then those who follow in their footsteps.

It has been narrated that [in a miniature] two sages from among the sages of ancient times were depicted in a mosque; in the hand of one of them was a parchment on which it was written, "If you attain excellence in all things, do not suppose you have attained excellence in anything until you realize God تَعَالَىٰ and know that He is the Cause of all causes, and brings all things into being." While in the hand of the other [was written], "Before I came to know God سُبْحَانَهُ I would drink and still be thirsty; then when I knew Him, my thirst was quenched without drinking."

The seventh responsibility [of the student] is not to delve into all the various fields of knowledge at once; rather one should pay attention to the order [of things], beginning with what is foremost importance then the next in importance [and so on]; and not delve into a field of study until one has sufficiently mastered the preceding field.

This is because the sciences are arranged in necessary order; some are pathways to others. The successful [seeker of knowledge] pays attention to that order and its ascendant grades. God تَعَالَىٰ states, *Those to whom we brought the Book read it as it should be read, they are the ones that believe in it* [2:121]; meaning, they do not pass beyond an area of study until they are well grounded in it theoretically and practically.

So let [the student's] intention toward every area of knowledge [that he undertakes] be to liberate himself from it in order to attain the next ascendant level. It is not fitting that the student pass judgment on a particular field of knowledge because of the occurrence of differences between its partisans, nor because of an error committed by one of them or various individuals among them; nor because of their noncompliance with the obligation to put the knowledge into action. You will see a faction of scholars that has foregone regarding rational and juridical arguments on the pretext that its partisans would have acknowledged and stated them if this pursuit were founded on systematized principles. This doubt [concerning these two areas of study] was cleared up in our book *Miʿyār al-ʿilm*.[21] Then you see [another] faction believing [that] the practice of medicine is futile, because of an error they witnessed a doctor make.

One faction believed in the veracity of astronomy because of the correct prediction of one person; and another faction believed in its futility because of a mistaken prediction from one person. This is all erroneous; a thing should be understood in and of itself, not everyone has mastered each of the sciences, for this reason ʿAlī رَضِيَ ٱللَّهُ عَنْهُ said, "Do not attempt to access knowledge of the Truth through men, come to know the Truth and you will know its partisans."

The eighth responsibility [of the student] is to understand the manner in which the noble nature of the sciences is ascertained; in this I intend two things: (1) one is the noble nature of the fruit [itself]; and (2) the second is the reliability of the proof and its soundness.

An example of that is [the difference between] the religious sciences and the science of medicine; the fruit of one of them is eternal life, and the fruit of the other is the ephemeral life [of the body]; thus the science of religion is by nature more noble. And similar [from the point of view of the second facet] are the science of mathematics and astrology; for indeed mathematics is nobler because of the reliability of its proofs and their efficacy.

If one were to compare mathematics to medicine, medicine would be nobler, given its fruit while mathematics would be nobler given its proofs. However, attention to the fruit is foremost, for this reason medicine is of a more noble nature even though it mainly depends on conjecture.

By this it should be evident that the most noble of the sciences is the [pursuit of] the knowledge of God عَزَّوَجَلَّ, His angels, His books, His messengers, and knowledge of the path that renders

21 See Ghazālī, *Miʿyār al-ʿilm*.

these sciences accessible. And take care lest you covet anything else, or aspire to anything beside it.

The ninth responsibility [of the student] is for the intention of the student at each moment to be the enhancement of his inner state and its adornment with the virtues of excellent character; and in the imminent future it should be proximity to God سُبْحَانَهُ and ascension to the heavenly hosts with the angels and those brought near [to God's presence].

He should seek neither positions of power, nor wealth, nor stature, nor contention with people of low standing, nor [should he] boast among his peers. One whose goal is [proximity to God] will seek—without a doubt—the closest [science] to his goal, which is the science of the abode of the hereafter. Given this, it is inappropriate for him to regard any of the sciences with disdain; in this I include the science of rulings, grammar, and the science of [Arabic] language, as they all apply to the Qur'ān and *sunna*; as well as the other areas of study we have included among the preparatory and complementary branches of knowledge, the pursuit of which is a communal obligation.

Let no one understand from our hyperbolic praise of the science of the abode of the hereafter any disdain of these [other] sciences. For those [scholars] who take on the responsibility for these fields are similar to those men who man the fortresses and those who reside and serve therein, and those warriors striving in the way of God. Among them are those who engage in combat, and those who lend support to others, and those who distribute water or protect and look after their mounts; not one of them will go unrewarded as long as their intention is that the word of God تَعَالَىٰ be raised to its utmost; not the acquisition of spoils of war. The case of the scholars is similar. God تَعَالَىٰ states, *God will exalt by many degrees those of you who have attained faith, and* [*above all*] *such as have been vouchsafed* [*true*] *knowledge* [58:11]. And He states, *They have differing degrees* [*from one another*] *in the sight of God* [3:163].

Preminence is a relative matter. Our low opinion of moneychangers when compared to kings is not indicative of low station when they [i.e., the moneychangers] are compared to street sweepers. Do not imagine that anything that descends beneath the most elevated of ranks is an ignoble rank; rather the foremost rank is for the prophets, then the saints, then the scholars firm in knowledge, then the righteous ones according to their varying degrees.

To summarize, [know that] anyone who accomplishes even an atom's weight of good shall see it; and anyone who commits an atom's weight of iniquity will see it. Whoever seeks God تَعَالَىٰ through the pursuit of knowledge—whatever knowledge it may be—He will without doubt benefit him and raise him in rank.

The tenth responsibility is for the student to understand the relationship of the sciences to the goal being sought.

In the same manner that one favors the lofty and nearby to that which is distant, and that which is of most concern to that which is not, where the meaning of concern is that which is of concern to you, then that which is of most concern is that which remains eternal and everlasting and nothing [truly] concerns you more than your state in this lower realm or the abode of the hereafter; and since it is not possible to join the pleasures of this abode with the blessings of the abode of the hereafter—as the Qurʾān made clear—and as testified to by enlightened insight seen as distinctly as with one's own eyes. As one realizes this, this world becomes a stage on the journey, the body a mount [for the journey], and actions become the strivings made toward the goal. There is no goal other than the encounter with God عَزَّوَجَلَّ, for that [encounter] comprises all the divine munificence; even though few in this world appreciate its worth.

The sciences, in respect to the eternal joy of the encounter with God تَعَالَىٰ and the sight of His noble countenance—I intend [here] that which the prophets sought and understood the nature of, not that which the commoners and the theologians quickly presume—comprise three ranks. These you will understand through a comparative example.

[The example] is that of a slave whose freedom and right to own property are dependent on completing the pilgrimage to Mecca. He has been told, "If you complete the pilgrimage and complete [all its requisite rites], you will have gained both freedom and the right to own property; whereas if you undertake the road to the pilgrimage and make the preparations for it but are thwarted along the way by unavoidable obstacles, you will only gain your freedom from the wretchedness of slavery, not the enjoyment of the right to own property." In this he has three classes of action to occupy himself with.

The first is to prepare the requisite means [to make the journey] by acquiring a she camel, and cobbling together a water-bag, accumulating provisions and transport.

The second is to journey and depart from his homeland and set his face toward the Kaʿba, stage by stage.

The third is to take part in the requisite rites of the pilgrimage, one rite after another.

Then, after completing all the requisites and removing the *iḥrām* coverings of the pilgrimage rites and [making] the farewell circumambulation, he has earned the right to present himself for his freedom and the right to own property [promised him]. In every station [he reaches] there are stages, from the initial preparation of provisions for the journey to the end [of that stage], from beginning the journey across the uninhabited desert to his final destination, and from the initial obligatory rites of the pilgrimage to their completion. The proximity of one who has begun the rites of the pilgrimage to felicity is not the same as the proximity to it of one who has nearly accumulated the required provisions and transport, nor is it the same as the proximity of one who has commenced his journey; though he is nearer to it [than he who has not yet departed].

The sciences are also comprised of three categories:

One category is similar to the accumulation of provisions, transport, and buying a female camel: this is the science of medicine and jurisprudence and that which is associated with the well-being of the physical body in the physical world.

Another category [of the sciences] is similar to traveling across uninhabited wasteland and crossing empty tracks: this is the purification of the inward state of reprehensible character traits; and scaling those lofty heights is traveling the path that even the foremost and those who came after them were unable to surmount, save those accorded divine provision. Attaining this knowledge is like attaining knowledge of the directions to a road through the desert and its stages of journeying. Yet, just as this knowledge of the stages of the journey and the paths through the empty wasteland provides no benefit without actual travel, in like manner the knowledge of what constitutes worthy character traits provides no benefit without actually rectifying [oneself]; however undergoing education without the requisite knowledge is impossible.

The third category [of the sciences] is similar to the pilgrimage itself and its obligatory rites: this is knowledge of God تَعَالَىٰ, His attributes, His angels, His acts, and the entirety of that which we confirmed in our discussion concerning the science of unveiling.

At this point the journeyer has succeeded and attained true bliss. This success is achievable for every journeyer on the path, as long as his objective is the true goal, which is [eternal] well-being.

Attainment of [such] bliss, however, is solely for those who have a realization of God تَعَالَىٰ; they are those brought near, blessed with rest and satisfaction and a garden of delights in nearness to God.

As for those who come short of this apex of excellence, theirs is success and [eternal] well-being; as God تَعَالَىٰ states, *Then, if he be of those brought near; there shall be for him rest and satisfaction, and a garden of delights. And if he be of the companions of the right hand; then, "Peace be upon you," from the companions of the right hand* [56:88–91].

Whoever does not turn toward the goal, or respond to it; or who responds for his own self-interest, with no intention of exemplary conduct or servanthood, rather for personal gain in this world, is among the companions of the left hand and those lost on the path, "For him, boiling water will be the welcome and burning in fire."

Know that this is the truth of certainty for scholars firm in knowledge; I mean to say that they have understood this by way of the inner perception, which is sounder and more manifest than visual perception. In this they have exceeded the bounds of uncritical imitation of what one has heard [from figures of authority]. Their situation is that of one who has been informed of a fact and affirms its truth, then he perceives it for himself and realizes its truth inwardly. The situation of others is that of one who accepts the truth of what one has heard with trust and good faith, but has not been favored with inward vision and personal perception.

True bliss is a result of the science of unveiling, and the science of unveiling is the fruit of the science of conduct that comprises journeying on the path of the abode of the hereafter and traversing the ascendant tracks of the [science of the] attributes. The path of effacing reprehensible character traits is the result of the science of attributes, and the knowledge of the path of cultivating inner conduct and how to travel the path, which are all aspects resulting from the knowledge of physical well-being and maintaining a health regimen. Physical well-being is dependent upon collective activity, common interests, and mutual needs, by which clothing, food, and shelter may be achieved. The organization of all this is entrusted to the governing authority, while the legal statutes dealing with managing the citizens according to equitable good governance is incumbent upon the scholar of the law.

As for the means of assuring the physical well-being of the body, these are in the hands of the physician. The one who said, "There are two sciences: the science of the physical body and the science of religions,"[22] has indicated that it is jurisprudence. He meant by this the science of the outward aspects of the law, not the precious jewels of the inner sciences.

If you ask, "Why have you likened the study of jurisprudence and medicine [in your example] to preparation of provisions and transport animals?"

Know well that the entity that is striving toward God تَعَالَىٰ to realize proximity is the heart, not the physical body; nor do I intend by the heart that perceivable flesh [in the chest], rather it is a hidden mystery of God's تَعَالَىٰ intimate secrets, that not apprehended by the senses, and a subtle entity of His subtleties; at times expressed by the term spirit and at times by the term tranquil soul; in the terminology of the law, it is referred to as the heart. The heart is the mount—which is the primary means of making the journey to that innermost mystery—and by its mediation the entire physical body becomes a means of transport and an instrument of that subtle entity.

The removal of the covering of that innermost mystery is an aspect of the science of unveiling; it is a topic one speaks sparingly of, [in fact] it is not permissible to even speak of it; the extent of what it is persmissable to say is, "[The heart] is a precious jewel and an exquisite pearl of a loftier nature than these bodies that are

---

22 This statement was attributed to Imām al-Shāfiʿī رَضِيَ اللَّهُ عَنْهُ, Abū Nuʿaym, *Ḥilya*, 9:142.

perceptible to the eye, it is an aspect of divinity, as God تَعَالَىٰ states, *They ask you of the spirit; say* [*to them*] *the spirit is the concern of my Lord* [17:85]."

Every created being is related to God تَعَالَىٰ. However, its [a heart's] relationship is of a loftier nature than that of any of the physical members of the body; the entirety of creation and dominion is God's alone, and dominion is superior to creation. This precious subtle entity, the bearer of God's تَعَالَىٰ trust[23] that preceded from the realm of command—it is because of this lofty rank that the [creation] of the heavens, the earths, and the mountains all refused to bear and were in trepidation of it.[24]

Do not comprehend from this exposition its existence in pre-eternity, for anyone voicing pre-eternity of the spirits is a self-deceiving fool who does not understand what he is giving expression to.[25]

Let us restrain [ourselves] from the elucidation of this science, as it exceeds that topic in which we are presently involved.

This subtle entity is striving toward the intimate proximity to the Lord, for it is among the affairs of the Lord; from Him is its origin and to Him is its return. As for the physical body, it is its mount that it rides upon and its means by which it strives [toward its destination]. The physical body on the path of God تَعَالَىٰ is like the mount for the physical body on its way to the pilgrimage, and like the water skin that is necessary for the body to make its journey.

Each of the sciences whose aim is the well-being of the physical body is thus a facet of the general well-being of the means of traveling the path; there is no doubt that the science of medicine is one aspect of this, for it is necessary for maintaining bodily health. For even someone living in isolation would be in need of it; whereas in the case of jurisprudence, were a person to live in complete isolation, it is imaginable that he could dispense with it. Human beings, however, have been created in a manner that renders subsisting in total isolation impossible. And since they cannot independently secure their nourishment by tilling the soil, planting, [baking]

23 A reference to Qurʾān 33:72.

24 This is an allusion to Qurʾān 33:72.

25 This refers to philosophers and anyone who follows them. See al-Zabīdī, *Itḥāf*, 1:332.

bread, cooking; and providing themselves with clothing and shelter, as well as making all the implements necessary to accomplish all these pursuits, humankind is obliged to intermingle and mutually accommodate the necessities of others.

As humankind interacts with one another, their desires are aroused and they vie with one another for the objects they desire, [then] fall into conflict and warfare. They perish, externally, on account of their wars, just as they perish internally, on account of [the four] opposing bodily humors. Medicine preserves the balance of the opposing bodily humors inwardly and good governance and justice assures and maintains balance in outward conflicts. Medicine is the science of assuring equilibrium among the bodily humors; while jurisprudence is the science of assuring the equilibrium of the human condition with its interpersonal relations and individual conduct; all of which preserves and protects the physical body that is the means of traveling [God's تَعَالَىٰ path].

Anyone who devotes himself solely to the science of jurisprudence or medicine, if they do not strive to overcome their soul, or seek to assure the inner well-being of their heart, is similar to a person who purchases a she camel, her fodder, the skin for a water vessel and cobbles it together and then does not set out to cross the barren wastes on the pilgrimage route. A person who occupies himself during his entire life with the detailed terminology that is used in legal disputation is like a person who has occupied his life in the detailed means by which the cording used to cobble the water skins for the pilgrimage can be made sound.

The relationship of these people [devoted to jurisprudence] to the actual traveler on the path to perfect his heart's circumstances or one who achieves something of the science of unveiling, is like the relationship of those people [engrossed in preparation] to the actual travelers on the road of the pilgrimage or those engaged in its requisite rites.

So first give careful thought to this, and accept free advice from one who undertook and only arrived at it, for the most part, after expending great effort and boldly breaking [away] from the general public—the commonality among them and the elite—by divesting [myself] of their imitation based upon vain caprice and passion.

This should suffice, with regard to the role of the student.

An Elucidation of the Functions of the Guide and the Teacher

KNOW THAT IN REGARD to the knowledge that every human being has acquired, there are four stages, similar to the stages of the acquisition of wealth. For the possessor of wealth, there is the state of acquisition, in which he earns it. Then he accumulates it and becomes one who is self-reliant, who need not ask others, whereupon he becomes one who reaps the benefits of wealth by spending it on himself. The last stage is that of distributing wealth to others, whereupon he becomes a generous well-intentioned benefactor. This is the loftiest stage.

Knowledge is acquired in a way similar to wealth; it has a stage [when one is] striving after it and acquiring [it], a stage of accumulation and self-reliance, a stage of reflection, which entails contemplation of that which one has acquired, and [during which one] takes satisfaction in it, then a stage of enlightening others, which is the loftiest of ranks.

One who has acquired knowledge, and acted upon it, and imparted it to others is praised in the heavenly domains as a person of great worth; he is like the sun that sheds light on others, being thus a light unto itself, or he is similar to fragrant musk that imbues others with its fragrance, while being fragrant unto itself.

On the other hand, whoever imparts knowledge to others but implements nothing of it is like an notebook, that provides benefit to others but is devoid of knowledge itself, or a whetstone that sharpens other things but cuts nothing, or a needle that clothes others but remains unclothed itself, or it is similar to the wick of a lamp that illumes for others while consuming itself in its own flame; as the poet [al-ʿAbbās b. al-Aḥnāf] said:

I became as though I were the wick of a lamp, ignited
Giving light for people, burning in its own flame[26]

26 Al-ʿAbbās, *Dīwān al-ʿAbbās b. al-Aḥnāf*, 221.

In whatever manner one is engaged in instruction, he has taken on a momentous task of grave consequence; so let him guard well his conduct and the role incumbent upon him.

The first function [of the teacher] is benevolence toward his students, [he should behave] in such a manner that he treats them like his sons.

The Messenger of God ﷺ stated, "I am for all of you as a father to his son."[27] He meant redeeming them from the fire of the abode of the hereafter, which is of greater imperative than the parents redeeming their child from the fire of this world.

For that reason the teacher's responsibility is more grave than that of parents; for though the father is the primary cause of the child's present existence and his ephemeral life, the teacher is the primary cause behind his immortal life. Were it not for the teacher, the student would eventually divert that which his father had rendered unto him into everlasting annihilation; whereas from the teacher he derives the benefit of everlasting life in the abode of the hereafter. I mean the teacher of the sciences of the hereafter, or the sciences of this world whose purpose is the abode of the hereafter, not this ephemeral world. For learning with the intention of this world only, is devastation and devastating. We seek the protection of God from such as that.

Just as it is the responsibility of the sons of a father to love and support one another mutually in attaining all their goals, the responsibility of the students of a single teacher are mutual love and affection, which is only possible if their shared goal is the hereafter. If their shared goal were this world there would be naught but envy and loathing.

The scholars and the youths of the hereafter are all journeying to God تَعَالَىٰ, traveling to Him on the path from this world, whose years and months are stages of the path. The companionship shared on the path between travelers to the cities and towns [of this world] is the basis for mutual love and affection [between them]; so what would [you imagine about] the journey to the most exalted paradise and shared companionship [on that journey] to be?

27 Abū Dāwūd, 8; al-Nisāʾī, 1:38; Ibn Māja, 313.

There is no limit to the bliss of the hereafter, so there is no discord between the youths of the hereafter; but there is no such extensive pleasures of this world, thus it is never devoid of the distress of competition.

Those who incline to seek positions of authority through the pursuit of the sciences are departing from the requisite conduct of God's تَعَالَىٰ dictate, *Indeed the believers are all brothers* [49:10]. Rather, they are conducting themselves in accordance with His تَعَالَىٰ words, *The arrogant on that day will be enemies of one another, all of them except the righteous* [43:67].

The second function [of the teacher] is to follow the example of the master/conveyor of the law—may the peace and blessings of God be upon him.

He should therefore seek no remuneration for the of dissemination knowledge, nor intend in it any recompense or gratitude; rather, he should teach for the countenance of God تَعَالَىٰ seeking [only] proximity to Him. He should perceive no indebtedness to him on the part of those he teaches; although indebtedness is a necessary obligation on their part; rather he should perceive excellence as being theirs, for they have made the goal of their hearts the intimate proximity to God تَعَالَىٰ by sowing knowledge therein. This is similar to the person who lends you a parcel of land to plant therein and harvest its fruits for yourself, your benefits from it are greater than those of the parcel's proprietor; how could you presume that [the student] should be indebted to you, when your recompense, in God's eyes, for the instruction you impart is greater than the recompense of the student. Had it not been for the student you would have not achieved this recompense [at all].

So seek compensation from God تَعَالَىٰ alone, as God تَعَالَىٰ states, *O my people, I seek no riches from you for this* [*message*]*: my reward rests with none but God* تَعَالَىٰ [11:29]. For riches and all that this world comprises are there to serve the physical body, and the physical body is there to convey the soul and its trusted mount. Knowledge renders service, for by it the soul attains a noble stature. So whoever uses knowledge to gain riches is like someone who wipes the soles of his shoes upon his face[28] in order to clean them, making that to which service is rendered into the servant and the servant into that to which service is rendered; which is an inversion of the intuitive reason.[29] Such a person is like the person standing among the ranks of the offenders [of God's laws] on the day of judgment, his head lowered in shame before his Lord.[30]

From the most general point of view however, distinction and merit belong to the teacher.

[Nevertheless] regard carefully how the affair of the religion has ended up in the hands of a people who claim that their sole goal in pursuing the sciences of jurisprudence and theology and in teaching these two and other sciences is seeking to draw near to God تعالى . But then they expend wealth and [use their] standing, endure a variety of humiliations in the service of the sultans in order to keep remunerations flowing freely; and if they forsake these services, they would be forsaken and no one would look to them.

Furthermore [these people] expect the student to sustain the teacher at every turn of fate, to come to the aid of [the teacher's] supporters and treat his enemies with animosity, and be like a donkey for all his requirements, be subservient before him, and fulfill his requests; then, should [the student] fall short in his [perceived] obligation to his teacher, he will rise up against him and be the worst of his enemies.

It is contemptible for any teacher to content himself with such circumstances and find pleasure in it; and he should say: "My sole goal in teaching is the dissemination of knowledge, seeking [in this] God's تعالى intimate proximity and the defense of His religion."

Mark well all the indications, that you might recognize the degrees of subtle deceptions.

The third function [of the teacher] is to not hold back anything from the guidance he provides his student.

---

28 According to al-Zabīdī the majority of manuscripts employ the wording *maḥāsinihi*; in some he found (*bi-wajhihi*), upon his face; to which he added, "The meaning of good qualities (*maḥāsinihi*) returns essentially to this meaning [face]." Al-Zabīdī, *Itḥāf*, 1:338.

29 *Wa-dhālika huwa al-intikās ʿalā ummi al-raʾs.*

30 This is an allusion to Qurʾān, 32:12.

This means that [the teacher] should prevent [the student] from advancing to a level of knowledge that he is not prepared for, or undertaking the subtle points of a science before having mastered its fundamentals. Here let the teacher call his attention to the fact that the true goal of the pursuit of knowledge is intimate proximity to God تَعَالَىٰ, and not positions of authority, prestige or competition; and let him disparage, as far as possible, [the existence of] these traits in his student; for the damage the corrupt scholar causes is greater than the benefit he may render [to others].

Should he come to know through his own insight that his student is pursuing knowledge solely for [the benefits of] this world, he should look carefully at the subjects he is pursuing. If it is the science of disagreement in jurisprudence, or dialectics in theology, or the rulings in disputes and judgments, he should dissuade him from those pursuits, for they are not among the sciences of the abode of the hereafter nor among the sciences of which it has been said, "We have pursued knowledge for other than the sake of God, but knowledge [itself] refused to be for other than God." Indeed the sciences [intended in this statement] are Qurʾānic exegesis and the science of *ḥadīth*, and that which the first generation occupied themselves with, those that deal with the knowledge of the abode of the hereafter, and the science of inner conduct and the training of the soul. However, if the student pursues these sciences intending the benefits of this world, there is no objection to allowing him to carry on in this, for he is simply preparing himself in hopes of providing admonition and gaining followers. At one time or another in this pursuit he may awaken; as therein are sciences capable of instilling the heart with pious fear of God تَعَالَىٰ, that denigrate the present world and venerate the hereafter. Those sciences may turn him to rectitude toward the hereafter until he takes the good counsel that he exhorts others with, and the love of esteem and prestige become like the grain scattered around a snare with which to trap a bird. This is God's تَعَالَىٰ manner with His servants; He created desire so that by its means creatures would continue to leave offspring, He also created the love of reputation as a means of reviving the sciences. One can expect these sciences to fulfill the same role.

With regard to [the student who] devotes [himself] to the study of outright disagreement, disputation in theology, and familiarity with arcane subfields, and abandons the other sciences, these [sciences that he studies] engender nothing in their devotee save hardness of heart, unawareness of God تَعَالَىٰ and tenacity in waywardness, and striving for authority. This is [true] except in a person whom God تَعَالَىٰ has visited with His mercy or has diversified his preoccupation with these pursuits with other sciences of the religion. There is no better proof of this than experience and eyewitness accounts.

Regard well, ponder, and contemplate, that you may perceive the reality of what concerns both individual servants and entire regions. God تَعَالَىٰ [alone] provides support.

Sufyān al-Thawrī رَضِيَ ٱللَّهُ عَنْهُ was seen in a state of sorrow, so someone asked, "What is wrong with you?" To which he responded, "We have become shopkeepers for the sons of this low world, one of them devotes himself to us until he has acquired knowledge then becomes an administrator of the state, a judge, or a treasurer of state funds."[31]

The fourth function [of the teacher]—and among the most subtle of the art of teaching—is deterring the student from reprehensible conduct by way of intimation to whatever extent possible.

This should not be explicit criticism, and [should be] by way of clemency not condemnation. For explicit criticism of reprehensible conduct rips aside the veil of reverence, it unleashes a response of arrogant self-defense and only provokes an increased desire to persevere [in error]. The Messenger of God صَلَّىٰ ٱللَّهُ عَلَيْهِ وَسَلَّمَ—and he is the guide of every teacher—stated, "If people were forbidden from crumbling dried camel droppings between their fingers, they would crumble them, saying, 'We have only been forbidden this because there is something to it.'"[32]

---

31 Abū Ṭālib al-Makkī, *Qūt al-qulūb*, 1:133.

32 Al-Zabīdī, *Itḥāf*, 1:341, cites al-ʿIrāqī, "I have only found this *ḥadīth* narrated by al-Ḥassan not linked to a Companion (*mursal*) and it is weak. It was narrated by Ibn Shāhīn." I have found a text in the handwriting of al-Dāwūdī with this wording from Ibn Shāhīn, "Were people forbidden from crumbling thorns between their fingers, they would say there is incense in it." There is a similar meaning from the *ḥadīth* of Abū Juḥayfa, "Were you forbidden to come to the mountain of Ḥajūn (in Mecca), then you would come to it."

The story of Adam and Eve عَلَيْهِمَاٱلسَّلَامُ and that which they were forbidden may draw your attention to this [function of the art of teaching]. I only cite this story that you might reflect upon it as an example, not that you might spend the night retelling it.

Correcting behavior by intimation also leads virtuous souls and bright minds to deduce its meanings. Thus, one benefits from the joy of comprehending its meaning by further yearning for knowledge of it. One then knows that this is not beyond the capacity of his intelligence.

The fifth function for the one responsible for certain sciences is not to criticize or disparage other fields of learning to his student.

For example, the habit of the teacher of the sciences related to the study of language is to habitually disparage jurisprudence, and the teacher of jurisprudence customarily denigrates the study of *ḥadīth* and Qurʾān commentary, [holding that they are] transmissions pure and simple, merely handed down oral accounts, and nothing but a pastime of old women, in which intellectual discernment has no use. Also, the teacher of theology deters others from the pursuit of jurisprudence by saying, "That is but a secondary branch [of knowledge], and discourse on women's issues. What value is there in that in comparison to [discussing] the attributes of the All Merciful?"

These are the blameworthy attributes of teachers to be avoided; in fact, anyone with a mastery of only one field should provide for the student the means of accessing other fields; and should he have a mastery of multiple fields of knowledge, it is incumbent upon him to direct [the student] step by step [through the sciences] as he advances from one stage to another.

The sixth function [of the teacher] is to confine the student [to the material that is] at the level of his comprehension.

He therefore does not convey to [the student] that which his intellect has no means of accessing or that which would overcome it and create in him an aversion to its pursuit. In this the teacher is following the example of leader of mankind [the Prophet Muḥammad] صَلَّىٱللَّهُعَلَيْهِوَسَلَّمَ when he stated, "We—the company of the prophets—have been commanded to rank people according to the stations due them, and to speak to them in accordance to their intellects."[33] Then later [the teacher] can reveal the matter fully to [the student] when he knows [the student] has reached intellectual maturity.

The Messenger of God صَلَّى ٱللَّهُ عَلَيْهِ وَسَلَّمَ related, "No one speaks to a people on a matter that their intellects cannot grasp without that causing trial and tribulation among some of them."[34]

ʿAlī رَضِيَ ٱللَّهُ عَنْهُ pointed to his chest [saying], "Verily there is extensive knowledge here, if only I could find those to bear its burden."[35]

He رَضِيَ ٱللَّهُ عَنْهُ spoke truly in this, for the hearts of the upright are the graves of the mysteries. It is therefore inappropriate for the scholar to disclose everything he knows to everyone. This is true when the student is capable of understanding him, yet incapable of benefiting from it. What then, of the case when he is incapable of understanding?

[It is related that] Jesus عَلَيْهِ ٱلسَّلَامُ said, "Do not hang precious stones around the necks of swine, for surely wisdom is more precious than jewels, and whoever has an aversion to wisdom is worse than swine."[36]

Thus it has been said, "Measure everyone according to the standard of his intellect, and weigh him in the scales of his comprehension so that you may secure him from harm [on the one hand] and that he benefit from you [on the other], lest animosity be aroused due to differing standards."[37]

A scholar was asked a question [one day] and he did not respond. The one asking said, "Have not you heard that the Messenger of

---

33 These are in fact two *ḥadīth*s: "We rank people according to the stations due them" is narrated by Abū Dāwūd, 4842, as attributed to the Prophet; and "We—the company of the prophets—likewise have been commanded to speak to them in accordance with their reason," was narrated by al-ʿAqīlī, *al-Ḍuʿafāʾ*, 4:1534. The meaning here is similar to the meaning of the *ḥadīth* narrated in al-Bukhārī, 127, as transmitted from ʿAlī b. Abī Ṭālib رَضِيَ ٱللَّهُ عَنْهُ, "Speak to people according to that which they can understand."

34 Al-ʿAqīlī, *al-Ḍuʿafāʾ*, 3:937, from ʿAbdallāh b. ʿAbbās رَضِيَ ٱللَّهُ عَنْهُمَا; Muslim in his introduction to *Ṣaḥīḥ*, 1:11, which is transmitted from ʿAbdallāh b. Masʿūd رَضِيَ ٱللَّهُ عَنْهُ.

35 Narrated by al-Khaṭīb al-Baghdādī, *Tārīkh Baghdād*, 6:376; Abū Ṭālib al-Makkī, *Qūt al-qulūb*, 1:134.

36 Narrated by Abū Ṭālib al-Makkī, *Qūt al-qulūb*, 1:156, see also Ibn ʿAsākir, *Tārīkh Dimashq*, 68:63.

37 Abū Ṭālib al-Makkī, *Qūt al-qulūb*, 1:156. Its origin is from the statement of Yaḥyā b. Muʿādh, "Feed each person from his own stream, and pour out for him according to his cup."

God ﷺ stated, 'Whoever conceals beneficial knowledge will arrive on the day of resurrection bridled with a bridle of fire?'[38] To which he responded, 'Leave the bridle and be off with you, if someone who would benefit came along and I concealed it, then bridle me.'"[39]

God تعالى said, *And do not give the weak minded your property* [4:5]; this is a word of warning that protecting knowledge from those who corrupt and degrade it is a priority. Imparting knowledge to the unworthy is not less an injustice than holding it back from those worthy to receive it. As was said in a poem [by al-Imām al-Shāfiʿī]:[40]

Shall I scatter my pearls before herders of sheep?
That they be hidden away by shepherds?

For they enter each night ignorant of their true worth
So I am not at the point where I garland beasts with them

Should God the Gracious (*al-Laṭīf*) in His beneficence be good to me
And I meet by chance those worthy of knowledge and wisdom

I would spread forth benefits and benefit from friendship personally
And if not [it would remain] put away and hidden with me

For whoever grants knowledge to the ignorant wastes it
And whoever forbids [it to] those worthy has committed an injustice

The seventh function [of the teacher] is to teach the poorly prepared student the clear and evident aspects [of the sciences] that befit him, and not mention to him that beyond this there are minutiae that he is keeping hidden from him.

For that [information] would weaken his resolve toward [mastering] the basics and bewilder his heart; it would make him imagine that his teacher is acting in a miserly fashion toward him. For everyone imagines himself capable of acquiring the entirety of the minutiae of every science. There is not a single soul who is not

38 Ibn Māja, 265.

39 Al-Rāghib al-Iṣfahānī, *al-Dharīʿa ilā makārim al-sharīʿa*, 181.

40 Al-Shāfiʿī, *Dīwān*, 128–129.

content with God سُبْحَانَهُ for the flawless intellect he has been given; [while in fact] the greatest fools among them and those of the feeblest intellect are the ones most pleased with their flawless intellects.

This should make it clear that anyone among the commoners who lives within the limits of the law, and in whose soul the doctrinal creeds transmitted by the predecessors are vouchsafed, and who does not ascribe human attributes to God, nor hold allegorical interpretations [of Qurʾānic verses], and is of exemplary comportment and whose rational faculties cannot be expected to bear more than that, should not be confounded in his belief [by exposing him to the polemics of scholarly debate on such topics]. In fact, how much better to leave him to the practice of his livelihood, for if the allegorical interpretations of the outward meanings [of the Qurʾān] were presented to him, his understanding of the creed would disintegrate around him, and he would not easily accommodate the code of the educated elite; and by doing this, the barrier between him and disobedience would be lifted, and he would become a vicious demon, destroying himself and others.

In fact, [as a general principle] it is unacceptable [to delve deeply with the commoners into the complex realities of the sciences; rather, one should limit himself to educating them in the [fundamentals] of worship, in the duties of the profession they practice, and fill their hearts with longing for paradise and trepidation of hellfire, as evidenced by the Qurʾānic discourse. Do not arouse in them doubt, for doubt at times affixes itself to the heart, and it becomes difficult to free [the heart] from it, so [the heart] loses hope and perishes.

From the most general point of view, it is unacceptable to open the door of inquiry and discourse to the commoners; for this would only impede for them the practices of their professions by which humanity is sustained and by which the perseverance of the educated elite is assured.

The eighth function [of the teacher] is to apply his knowledge.

Otherwise, his deeds belie his words. For knowledge is grasped by inner perception while works are grasped [outwardly] by eyesight; those who have eyes are numerous, so one's works that contradict one's knowledge preclude guidance. Verily, people ridicule and reproach anyone who avails himself of a thing and then says,

"Do not avail yourselves of this, for it is deadly poison." Such only increases their aspiration for it, and they say, "If this were not the sweetest and most delicious of all things, he would not have kept it to himself [in this fashion]."

An example of the guiding teacher in relation to the seeking student is like the example of the engraved stamp on damp clay, or a wooden peg and its shadow; how could the stamp leave an impression on the clay if it were not engraved, and how could the shadow be upright and straight while the peg is crooked? Thus it is stated [by a poet]:

> Do not forbid certain behavior and then commit it
> The shame upon you for doing such would be great[41]

God تَعَالَىٰ states, *Do you order righteousness of the people and forget yourselves* [2:44]?

For this reason, the burden the scholar bears [to shun] disobedience is of greater consequence than the burden of an uneducated person. For his inequities will lead multitudes astray, for they take him as their example. [As the Messenger of God صَلَّىٰ ٱللَّٰهُ عَلَيْهِ وَسَلَّمَ stated,] "If someone initiates an evil practice, he will bear its burden and the burden of whoever practices it."[42]

For this reason ʿAlī رَضِيَ ٱللَّٰهُ عَنْهُ stated, "Two men have broken my back. A shameless scholar, and devout fool; the uneducated servant deceives people with his pious behavior, while the shameless scholar drives them away [from piety and religion] by his reprehensible conduct.[43] And God تَعَالَىٰ knows best.

41 Abū l-Aswad al-Duʾalī, *Dīwān*, 404. See also Ibn Ḥijja al-Ḥamawī, *Khizānat al-adab*, 8:564.

42 Muslim, 1017.

43 Abū Ṭālib al-Makkī, *Qūt al-qulūb*, 1:140.

6

The Perils of [the Pursuit of] Knowledge

An Elucidation of the Traits of the Scholars of the Hereafter and of the Reprehensible Scholars

WE DISCUSSED PREVIOUSLY WHAT has been reported about the merits [of the pursuit of] knowledge and the scholars [who are seeking the hereafter]. In numerous traditions dealing with reprehensible scholars there are severe warnings making it evident that they will be the most severely chastised of the creation on the day of resurrection. It is of tremendous importance to realize the traits that separate the scholars of this world from the scholars of the hereafter. We intend by the scholars of the world those reprehensible scholars whose goal in the pursuit of knowledge is to revel in [the joys of] this world, and gain esteem and high positions in the eyes of its inhabitants.

The Messenger of God صَلَّى ٱللَّهُ عَلَيْهِ وَسَلَّمَ stated, "The most severely chastised of people on the day of resurrection will be a scholar upon whom God bestowed no benefit from his knowledge."[1]

1 Al-Ṭabarānī, *al-Muʿjam al-ṣaghīr*, 1:182; Quḍāʿī, *Musnad al-shihāb*, 1122; al-Bayhaqī, *Shuʿab al-īmān*, 1642.

It was also narrated that he ﷺ related, "No one is [truly] knowledgeable until he acts in accordance with his knowledge."[2]

The Messenger of God ﷺ stated as well, "There are two kinds of knowledge: knowledge of the tongue, that is God's تَعَالَىٰ proof against the sons of Adam, and knowledge of the heart, this is beneficial knowledge."[3]

He ﷺ stated as well, "At the end of days there will be ignorant servants and scholars who are utter reprobates."[4]

He ﷺ also stated, "Do not pursue knowledge in order to employ it to boast among the scholars, nor to dispute the foolhardy, nor to curry the favor of the populace; whoever acts in such a manner is destined for the fire."[5]

He ﷺ also stated, "Whoever conceals knowledge that he has acquired, God will bridle him with a bit made of fire."[6]

He ﷺ stated as well, "There is something that I fear for you more than the Antichrist." It was asked, "What is that?" Then he responded, "Leaders that lead [others] astray."[7]

He ﷺ stated on another occasion, "Whoever increases in knowledge but does not increase in guidance, only increases in distance from God تَعَالَىٰ."[8]

Jesus عَلَيْهِ ٱلسَّلَامُ asked, "How long will you mark out the path for wayfarers who travel through the night while you reside with the bewildered."[9]

This and other reports validate the grave consequences entailed in the pursuit of knowledge; and affirm that the scholar is liable

---

2 Narrated by al-Khaṭīb al-Baghdādī, *Iqtiḍāʾ al-ʿilm al-ʿamal*, 17. It is reported from Abū l-Dardāʾ رَضِيَ ٱللَّهُ عَنْهُ with the wording, "There is no association of knowledge to a scholar until he is acting according to it." Al-Zabīdī said that al-ʿIrāqī mentioned, "I did not find it attributed to the Prophet."

3 Narrated by al-Khaṭīb al-Baghdādī, *Tārīkh Baghdād*, 5:107–108; Ibn ʿAbd al-Barr, *Jāmiʿ bayān al-ʿilm wa-faḍlih*, 1151.

4 Narrated by al-Ḥākim al-Nīsābūrī, *al-Mustadrak*, 4:315 and Abū Nuʿaym, *Ḥilya*, 2:331.

5 Ibn Māja, 259.

6 Ibn Māja, 265.

7 Aḥmad b. Ḥanbal, *Musnad*, 5:145.

8 Al-Daylamī, *Musnad al-firdaws*, 5887, according to al-Zabīdī narrating from al-ʿIrāqī, "This *ḥadīth* is generally considered to be a saying of Ḥasan al-Baṣrī." Al-Zabīdī, *Itḥāf*, 1:351.

9 Narrated by al-Khaṭīb al-Baghdādī, *Iqtiḍāʾ al-ʿilm al-ʿamal*, 60.

for either eternal damnation or eternal bliss; and that by pursuing knowledge—should he not attain eternal bliss—he will be forbidden any state wherein well-being lies.

The Traditions [from the Companions]

ʿUmar رَضِيَ اللَّهُ عَنْهُ stated, "I fear most for this community a hypocritical scholar." To which they said, 'How can a hypocrite be a scholar?' He responded, "Learned of tongue, ignorant of heart and deeds."[10]

Ḥasan said, "Be not one of those who accumulate the knowledge of the scholars, the wise sayings of the sages and [then] advance in the manner of acting like a fool."[11]

A man said to Abū Hurayra, "I wish to acquire knowledge but I fear I shall squander it." He responded, "In your abandoning [the pursuit of] knowledge you have already wasted it."[12]

Ibrāhīm b. ʿUyayna[13] was asked, "Of all the people, whose regret will be most lengthy?" He responded, "In this temporal world, he who shows kindness to someone who shows no gratitude; after death it is the negligent scholar."

Al-Khalīl b. Aḥmad declared, "Men are of four types: a man who knows and knows that he knows, he is a scholar, so follow him; a man who knows yet does not know that he knows, he is asleep, wake him; a man who does not know and knows he does not know, he is seeking correct guidance, so teach him; and a man who does not know and does not know he does not know, such a person is ignorant, shun him."[14]

Sufyān al-Thawrī رَحِمَهُ اللَّهُ said, "Knowledge calls to action, if a person responds to it affirmatively [it is retained]; if not, knowledge takes flight."[15]

---

10 It is reported by al-Ḍiyāʾ, *al-Aḥādīth al-mukhtāra*, 236, but it is originally from Aḥmad b. Ḥanbal, *Musnad*, 1:22.

11 Ibn ʿAbd al-Barr, *Jāmiʿ bayān al-ʿilm wa-faḍlih*, 1262.

12 Narrated by Ibn ʿAsākir, *Tārīkh Dimashq*, 67:367; and in al-Jāḥiẓ, *al-Bayān wa-l-tibyīn*, 1:257, narrating from Abū Hurayra al-Naḥwī.

13 "Ibrāhīm b. ʿUtba, one of the ascetics." Al-Zabīdī, *Ithāf*, 1:352.

14 Ibn ʿAbd al-Barr, *Jāmiʿ bayān al-ʿilm wa-faḍlih*, 1538.

15 Narrated by al-Khaṭīb al-Baghdādī, *Iqtiḍāʾ al-ʿilm al-ʿamal*, 41.

Ibn al-Mubārak رَحِمَهُ ٱللَّهُ related that, "As long as a man strives for knowledge he is a knowledgeable man; should he come to believe that he has acquired knowledge, he has become an ignorant man."[16]

Fuḍayl b. ʿIyāḍ رَحِمَهُ ٱللَّهُ said, "I feel compassion for three people: a man [who had been held] in high esteem brought low, a wealthy man impoverished, and a scholar made sport of by the world."[17]

Ḥasan [al-Baṣrī] said, "The chastisement of the scholars is the death of the heart, the death of the heart is striving to obtain this world through the deeds of the hereafter."[18]

In this regard a poet said:[19]

Astonished I was by one who barters good guidance for waywardness
Yet one who barters religion for this world is more astonishing

More astonishing than either is he who barters his own religion
For someone else's worldly life, this indeed of all is most astounding

God's Messenger صَلَّى ٱللَّهُ عَلَيْهِ وَسَلَّمَ stated, "Indeed the scholar will be severely chastised, the residents of the fire will circle him in amazement at the severity of his punishment." By this he meant the corrupt scholar.

Usāma b. Zayd reported, "I heard the Messenger of God صَلَّى ٱللَّهُ عَلَيْهِ وَسَلَّمَ say,

> 'The scholar will be brought forward on the day of resurrection and cast into the fire, his intestines will spill forth, and he will circle them as a donkey treads around the millstone. Those abiding in the fire will encircle him, and ask,
>
> 'Why are you here in such a state?' and he will respond,

---

16 It is reported by Ibn Qutayba without attribution, *ʿUyūn al-akhbār*, 2:118.

17 Al-Bayhaqī, *al-Madkhal ilā l-sunan al-kubrā*, 576, which has narrations attributing it to the Prophet.

18 Al-Bayhaqī, *Shuʿab al-īmān*, 1696; Ibn al-Mubārak, *al-Zuhd*, 1514.

19 This poem is attributed to Mālik b. Dīnār (d. c. 131/748), a Basran who engaged in public exhortation (*wāʿiẓ*), was a storyteller, and an ascetic who frequented Ḥasan al-Baṣrī. Al-Zamakhsharī, *Rabīʿ al-abrār*, 4:185; Ibn Khallikān, *Wafayāt al-aʿyān*, 6:170; al-Damīrī, *Ḥayāt al-ḥayawān*, 1:422; and al-Yūsī, *Zahr al-akam*, 1:288.

> 'I used to enjoin [others] to undertake good works and I accomplished nothing myself; and [I used to] forbid wickedness while I was wicked myself.'"[20]

The punishment for the disobedience of the scholar in particular is doubled because he disobeys despite his knowledge, for that reason God عَزَّوَجَلَّ states, *Indeed, the hypocrites will be in the lowest depths of the fire* [4:145]; this is because they renounced knowledge after receiving it.

[In the Qurʾān,] God portrays the Jews as being more mischievous than the Christians, even though they have not appointed for God سُبْحَانَهُ a son, nor have they said, "He is the third of three"; instead they denied [the Prophet and Islam] despite their comprehension [of these matters]. As God تَعَالَىٰ says, *Those to whom We gave the scripture know him as they know their own sons.* [2:146]. He تَعَالَىٰ states as well, *but [then] when there came to them that which they recognized, they disbelieved in it; so the curse of God will be upon the disbelievers* [2:89].

And God تَعَالَىٰ says in the tale of Balʿām b. Bāʿūrāʾ, *And recite to them, [O Muḥammad], the news of him to whom we gave [knowledge of] Our signs, but he detached himself from them...* until He تَعَالَىٰ states, *So his example is like that of the dog: if you chase him, he pants, or if you leave him, he [still] pants* [7:175–176]. The same is [true] for the corrupt scholar, for Balʿām was given the Book of God تَعَالَىٰ yet he inclined toward his desires until he was likened to a dog; meaning, whether wisdom was bestowed on him or not, his sole disposition was toward his base passions.

According to Jesus عَلَيْهِ ٱلسَّلَامُ, "The similitude of the reprehensible scholars is as a boulder that has fallen into the mouth of a river; it neither absorbs the water, nor allows the water to reach the crops being irrigated by it; or [it is] as the conduit from a privy, outwardly [it is] white-washed, inwardly [it is] malodorous; or [it is] similar to a tomb, outwardly [it is] well-built and cared for, inwardly [it is] full of the bones of the dead."[21]

All these reports and traditions make it abundantly clear that the scholar who comports himself as do the sons of this world is of a

---

20 Al-Bukhārī, 3267; Muslim, 2989.

21 Abū Ṭālib al-Makkī, *Qūt al-qulūb*, 1:141.

lesser rank and liable to more severe chastisement [in the hereafter] than the ignorant; and that those who prosper and will be brought near to God [in the hereafter] are the scholars of the hereafter. There are clear traits that render them recognizable.

[The Traits of the Scholars of the Hereafter]

Among these traits are that they do not seek worldly gain through their knowledge. For the minimal degree any scholar may understand is that he has come to realize the paltriness of this world, its squalid murkiness and ephemeral nature; and [that he has come to realize] the great consequence and eternity of the hereafter; with the pureness of bliss therein and the resplendence of its kingdom. He knows as well that the two are opposites, they oppose one another like the two wives of a husband; when you satisfy one of them you annoy the other. Or similar to the two pans of a balance scale, however one is weighed down the other be lighter, or like the East and the West, however you approach one of them you only distance yourself from the other; or like two drinking bowls, one full the other empty, when you pour the contents of one into the other until it becomes full, you empty out the other.

For whoever has not come to realize the paltriness of this world, its squalid murkiness, and the way its pleasure is mixed with pain, wherein anything of goodness eventually passes away, [he] lacks even minimal insight. For surely one's own eyes and life experience bring one to realize that [very fact]; how can one be among the scholars and have no intelligence?

Whoever has no knowledge of the enormous consequence of the matter of the hereafter and its perpetuity is a disbeliever and despoiled of faith; how could such a one of no faith be among the scholars?

Whoever has no knowledge of the contradiction between this world and the hereafter, or [does not know] that reconciling the two is but hoping for the impossible, is ignorant of the laws of all the prophets; even more, he is a disbeliever of the entirety of the Qurʾān from its beginning to its end; how could such a one be counted among the ranks of the scholars?

Whoever has come to know all this, and then prefers not the hereafter over this world is a captive of Satan; he is one whose own desire has caused him to perish, and his misery has overcome him. How could anyone of such standing be counted among the assembly of the scholars?

Among the traditions of David عَلَيْهِ السَّلَامُ is a story relating that God تَعَالَىٰ said, "The least I do to a scholar that prefers his capricious passions over love of Myself is to forbid him the bliss of intimate conversation with Me; O David, do not ask any scholar intoxicated with the world about Me, for he will only be a hindrance to you from the path of My love. Such are the highwaymen among My servants; O David, should you see one seeking Me, be a servant to him; O David, whoever returns to Me one who has fled [from Me] I will decree for him the rank of a sagacious scholar, and whoever I decree [the rank of] a wise scholar, I will never chastise [in hell]."[22]

This is why Ḥasan رَضِيَ ٱللَّهُ عَنْهُ stated, "The penalty meted out to the scholars is death of the heart, and the death of the heart causes one to seek this world by means of actions intended for the hereafter."[23]

For this reason as well Yaḥyā b. Muʿādh al-Rāzī remarked, "Verily the brilliance of knowledge and wisdom depart when worldly gain is sought through them."[24]

Saʿīd b. al-Musayyab رَحِمَهُ ٱللَّهُ said, "Should you see a scholar associating with the princes [know that] he is a thief."[25]

ʿUmar رَضِيَ ٱللَّهُ عَنْهُ said, "When you see a scholar enamored with this world be wary of him where your religion is concerned, for every lover is engrossed in that which he loves."[26]

Mālik b. Dīnār رَحِمَهُ ٱللَّهُ related, "I read in some of the books of time gone by that God تَعَالَىٰ says, 'The minimum that I mete out to

---

22 Abū Ṭālib al-Makkī, *Qūt al-qulūb*, 1:141; Aḥmad b. Ḥanbal narrated the final part of this report in *Kitāb al-zuhd*, 977.

23 Ibn ʿAbd al-Barr, *Jāmiʿ bayān al-ʿilm wa-faḍlih*, 1165.

24 Ibn Abī l-Dunyā, *Dhamm al-dunyā*, 476, ascribed to "one of the sages of old."

25 Narrated by Ibn al-Ṭuyūrī, *al-Ṭuyūrīyāt*, 690, by way of Saʿīd b. al-Musayyab from ʿUmar b. al-Khaṭṭāb رَضِيَ ٱللَّهُ عَنْهُ.

26 Ibn ʿAbd al-Barr, *Jāmiʿ bayān al-ʿilm wa-faḍlih*, 1174, from a similar statement of Jaʿfar b. Muḥammad

the scholar, should he be enamored with this world, is that I eliminate from his heart the sweet bliss of intimate discourse with Me.'"[27]

A man wrote to one of his brothers [in the religion], "Knowledge has been granted you, so do not extinguish the light of your knowledge with the obscurity of sin, and thus be left in the darkness on the day the people of knowledge hasten onward in the light of their knowledge."[28]

Yaḥyā b. Muʿādh al-Rāzī رَحِمَهُ ٱللَّٰهُ used to tell the scholars of this world, "O you to whom knowledge is reputed; your palaces are like those of the caesars, your dwellings are like those of the Persian nobility, your clothing is like that of Ṭāhir b. al-Ḥusayn,[29] your slippers are like those of Goliath, and your mounts like those of Qārūn.[30] The receptacles you eat and drink from are like those of the Pharaohs, you mourn your dead like [they did] in the times before Islam, and you tread the paths of Satan. Where is the law (*sharīʿa*) of Muḥammad?"[31]

A poet once said

The shepherd safeguards his flock from the wolves
How so were the shepherds themselves the wolves?[32]

While another recounted

O ranks of the learned, O salt of the earth
What restores the salt when it has been tainted?[33]

A gnostic was asked, "Do you see that a person who finds solace in disobedience does not know God?" To which he replied, "I have no doubt that whoever finds this world preferable to the hereafter

---

27 Abū Nuʿaym narrated a similar tradition, *Ḥilya*, 2:360.

28 Abū Nuʿaym narrated a similar tradition, *Ḥilya*, 9:146.

29 ʿAbdallāh b. Ṭāhir b. al-Ḥusayn al-Wazīr was known for the extravagance of this clothing.

30 Qārūn is a figure exemplified in the Qurʾān for arrogance due to his wealth, Indeed, Qārūn was from the people of Moses, but he tyrannized them. *And We gave him of treasures whose keys would burden a band of strong men; thereupon his people said to him, Do not exult. Indeed, God does not like the exultant* [28:76].

31 Narrated by al-Salafī, *Muʿjam al-safr*, 804.

32 Abū Bakr al-Ṭarṭūshī, *Sarāj al-mulūk*, 1:211.

33 Ibn ʿArbashāh, *ʿAjāʾib al-maqdūr*, 485.

does not know God تعالى and what you ask is of much less consequence than this."[34]

Do not suppose however that abandoning wealth is sufficient for one to be considered among the ranks of the scholars of the hereafter; for high station and prestige are more injurious than wealth, for this reason Bishr [b. al-Ḥārith al-Ḥāfī] stated, "Saying [the phrase] 'he narrated this *ḥadīth* to us,' is among the doorways that lead to this world; so when you hear a man say, 'He narrated this *ḥadīth* to us,' in reality he is saying, 'Make space for me' [in the circle of scholars]."[35]

Bishr b. al-Ḥārith buried some ten satchels and reed containers of books, saying while he did so, "I yearn to narrate *ḥadīth*, if only the yearning to narrate *ḥadīth* would depart from me I would do it."[36] He and others also stated, "If you yearn to narrate *ḥadīth*, do not narrate *ḥadīth*, when you no longer yearn to narrate *ḥadīth* then do so."[37]

This is the case because the delight derived from the prestige of benefiting others and the lofty rank of advising the public [giving] spiritual direction are greater than all the delights of this world; whoever follows his desires in this is among the sons of this world; this is why [Sufyān] al-Thawrī said, "The temptation of narrating *ḥadīth* is more perilous than the temptation of kin, wealth, or sons; how can one not fear its perils when it was said to the most eminent of the messengers [of God] صلى الله عليه وسلم, *And if We had not strengthened you, you would have almost inclined to them a little* [17:74].[38]

Sahl b. ʿAbdallāh رحمه الله used to say, "Knowledge is altogether this worldly, whereas acting according to it pertains to the hereafter;[39] without sincerity, action is but dust blowing in the wind."

He said as well, "Except for the scholars, the people are dead. Apart from those who act, the scholars are intoxicated [with the world]. Apart from the sincere, those who act are deluded. The

34 Abū Nuʿaym narrated a similar tradition, *Ḥilya*, 6:279.

35 Abū Ṭālib al-Makkī, *Qūt al-qulūb*, 1:135.

36 Abū Ṭālib al-Makkī, *Qūt al-qulūb*, 1:156.

37 Abū Ṭālib al-Makkī, *Qūt al-qulūb*, 1:156; and al-Khaṭīb al-Baghdādī, *Sharaf aṣḥāb al-ḥadīth*, 230, as well.

38 Abū Ṭālib al-Makkī, *Qūt al-qulūb*, 1:156.

39 Al-Khaṭīb al-Baghdādī, *Iqtiḍāʾ al-ʿilm al-ʿamal*, 20.

sincere person remains apprehensive until his life is sealed in that sincerity."[40]

Abū Sulaymān al-Dārānī stated, "When a man seeks *ḥadīth*, or marries, or journeys in search of sustenance, he has inclined toward the world."[41] In this, he meant seeking narrative chains of high repute, or seeking those *ḥadīth* that are not essential to the path of the hereafter.

Jesus عَلَيْهِ السَّلَامُ said, "How can a person be counted among the people of knowledge while on his path to the hereafter he is turned toward the world; how can a person be counted among the people of knowledge if he seeks knowledge in order to apprise others of it, not in order to put it into practice."[42]

Ṣāliḥ b. Ḥasān al-Baṣrī stated, "I encountered worthy masters who constantly sought protection with God from the corrupt scholar of the *sunna*."[43]

Abū Hurayra رَضِيَ اللَّهُ عَنْهُ narrated that the Messenger of God صَلَّى اللَّهُ عَلَيْهِ وَسَلَّمَ said, "Whoever seeks the knowledge by which the countenance of God تَعَالَى is sought, but also seeks with it the affairs of the world, will not find even the fragrance of heaven on the day of resurrection."[44]

God تَعَالَى has described the reprehensible scholars as those who devour the world by means of [their] knowledge and He described the scholars of the hereafter as having reverence and as ascetics; He عَزَّ وَجَلَّ said, speaking of the reprehensible scholar, *And* [*mention, O Muḥammad*], *when God took a covenant from those who were given the scripture,* [*saying*], *"You must make it clear to the people and not conceal it." But they threw it away behind their backs and exchanged it for a small price* [3:187]. He تَعَالَى says, characterizing the scholars of the hereafter, *And indeed, among the people of the scripture are those who believe in God and what was revealed to you and what was revealed to them,* [*being*] *humbly submissive to God. They do not exchange the verses of God for a small price. Those will have their reward with their Lord* [3:199].

40 Abū Ṭālib al-Makkī, *Qūt al-qulūb*, 1:157 and there is something similar, al-Khaṭīb al-Baghdādī, *Iqtiḍāʾ al-ʿilm al-ʿamal*, 22.

41 Abū Ṭālib al-Makkī, *Qūt al-qulūb*, 1:135.

42 Al-Dārimī, *Sunan*, 380, within a longer *ḥadīth*.

43 Abū Ṭālib al-Makkī, *Qūt al-qulūb*, 1:141.

44 Abū Dāwūd, 3664; and Ibn Māja, 252.

A scholar from among the predecessors stated, "[On the day of resurrection] the scholars will be assembled with the ranks of the prophets, while the judges will be assembled with the rulers."[45] It has been said of the meaning of the term 'judges', "Any jurist whose goal is seeking worldly gain with his knowledge."

Abū l-Dardā' رَضِيَ ٱللَّهُ عَنْهُ narrated that the Prophet صَلَّى ٱللَّهُ عَلَيْهِ وَسَلَّمَ stated,

> "God عَزَّ وَجَلَّ sent inspiration to one of His prophets to proclaim, 'Say to those who study God's decrees for other than the religion, and who pursue knowledge for other than its application, who seek the world through the deeds intended for the hereafter; for the people who wear sheep's clothing while their hearts are like those of wolves, their tongues are sweeter than honey while their hearts are as bitter as the aloe plant; I alone do they deceive and ridicule! Verily I will bring upon them a tribulation the likes of which will leave even the most forbearing man in dismay.'"[46]

Al-Ḍaḥḥāk [b. Muzāḥim] narrated a *ḥadīth* through Ibn ʿAbbās رَضِيَ ٱللَّهُ عَنْهُمَا from the Messenger of God صَلَّى ٱللَّهُ عَلَيْهِ وَسَلَّمَ, "The scholars of this community are of two types of people. The first is the one upon whom God has bestowed knowledge and who disperses it among the people [for their benefit], he takes no recompense nor does he barter it away at any price; upon him the birds of the heavens, the fish of the waters, the animals roaming the land, and the noble recording angels all offer blessings; and on the day of resurrection he will come before God تَعَالَىٰ as a noble leader of his people until he joins the company of the prophets. Then there is a person upon whom God has given knowledge in this world, but who disperses it sparingly among God's servants; he takes recompense for it and barters it for a price; such a person on the day of resurrection will be bridled with reins of fire and it will be proclaimed over the heads of all creation, 'This is So-and-so the son of So-and-so, God bestowed knowledge on him in the world and he withheld it from the servants

45 Abū Ṭālib al-Makkī, *Qūt al-qulūb*, 1:157.

46 Narrated by al-Tirmidhī, 2404; al-Khaṭīb al-Baghdādī, *al-Faqīh wa-l-mutafaqqah*, 1068; Ibn ʿAbd al-Barr, *Jāmiʿ bayān al-ʿilm wa-faḍlih*, 1139.

of God, took recompense for it and bartered it for a price! He will be punished until his debt toward the people is repaid.'"[47]

More egregious than this is the story that was narrated, "A man in the service of Moses عَلَيْهِ ٱلسَّلَامُ began to say, 'Moses, God's chosen one, narrated to me . . . ,' and 'Moses, God's "confidant" narrated to me . . . ,' and 'Moses, God's conversant, narrated to me . . . ,' until he became wealthy and his possessions multiplied. Moses عَلَيْهِ ٱلسَّلَامُ, missed him one day and began to ask about him, yet he found not a trace. Then one day a man approached him leading a pig with a black rope around its neck, [seeing this] Moses asked him, 'Are you familiar with So-and-so?' To which the man responded, 'Yes, he is this pig.' [Raising his voice] Moses called out, 'O my Lord, I beseech you to return him to his former state that I may ask him what has afflicted him.' Whereupon God عَزَّوَجَلَّ revealed to Moses, saying, 'Had you entreated me as Adam entreated me [to forgive him and Eve] and the prophets after him, I would not respond to your call. But I will inform you why I have treated him thus. It is because he sought worldly gain through religion.'"[48]

More egregious yet is the narration transmitted, on the one hand, from Muʿādh b. Jabal رَضِيَ ٱللَّهُ عَنْهُ; or—by way of another narration, from the Prophet, that the Messenger of God صَلَّى ٱللَّهُ عَلَيْهِ وَسَلَّمَ stated, "Among the temptations for the scholar is that speech becomes more beloved to him than attentively listening. Speech allows for eloquent expression and superfluous embellishment, and leaves the speaker susceptible to error; whereas in thoughtful silence there is integrity and knowledge. Some scholars hoard their knowledge; they love not that it be found with other scholars. Such a scholar is destined for the first level of the fire. Other scholars take their knowledge as though they were the ruler; so that, should anyone contradict him in any aspect of his knowledge or take his standing [as a scholar] lightly he becomes incensed. Such people are destined for the second level of the fire. Still other scholars deem their knowledge and erudition suitable only for the noble and affluent; they do not regard the people of need worthy of it. These are destined for the

47 Narrated by al-Ṭabarānī, *al-Muʿjam al-awsaṭ*, 7183.

48 Abū Ṭālib al-Makkī, *Qūt al-qulūb*, 1:144; Narrated by Ibn ʿAsākir, *Tārīkh Dimashq*, 61:152.

third level of the fire. Some scholars make themselves legal advisers and proceed to issue faulty rulings; God تَعَالَىٰ loathes those who feign roles they are not suited for. These scholars are destined for the fourth level of the fire. Then other scholars employ the terminology of the Jews and Christians in their discourse, in order to enhance their knowledge. These are destined for the fifth level of the fire. Then there are the scholars who take their knowledge as a trait of chivalry, prestige, and standing among the people. Such people are destined for the sixth level of the fire. Some scholars are overcome with arrogance and vanity, so when they admonish others, they make stringent demands, but when they are admonished, they respond with disdain. These are in the seventh level of the fire.

Hold fast to silence! For by it you will overcome Satan. Beware, lest you laugh when there is nothing to be amused about, and do not set off without a destination in mind."[49]

According to another tradition, "Verily a servant may be praised from the East to the West, while with God he equals not even the weight of a gnat's wing."[50]

It was narrated that [one day] as Ḥasan [al-Baṣrī] left his study circle he was approached by a man from Khurasan carrying a leather satchel wherein there were five thousand dirhams and ten garments of the finest Khurasani linen and he said, "O Abū Saʿīd here is money for provisions and this is clothing." To which Ḥasan replied, "May God forgive you! Keep your money and your clothing;

---

49 Abū Ṭālib al-Makkī, *Qūt al-qulūb*, 1:144. "We have reported a severe narration concerning the stations of the malicious scholars, and we seek refuge with God from these people. We ask Him not to test us with any such station. We have reported this narration from one path as coming from the Prophet, and we have reported it as coming from Muʿādh b. Jabal رَضِيَ ٱللَّهُ عَنْهُ. I state that the *mawqūf* narration is more favorable to me. They narrated it to us from Mundhir b. ʿAlī, from Abū Nuʿaym al-Shāmī, from Muḥammad b. Ziyād, from Muʿādh b. Jabal, who also said that the Messenger of God صَلَّى ٱللَّهُ عَلَيْهِ وَسَلَّمَ had said it. However, I attribute it to Muʿādh." Thus he (Abū Ṭālib) mentioned it here with this wording. The origin is in Ibn al-Mubārak, *Zuhd*, 48. See also Ibn ʿAbd al-Barr, *Jāmiʿ bayān al-ʿilm wa-faḍlih*, 910, 911.

50 Abū Ṭālib al-Makkī, *Qūt al-qulūb*, 1:144; al-Bukhārī, 4729; Muslim, 6785, "A man of great weight and stature will be brought forward on the day of resurrection, while with God he equals not even the weight of a gnat's wing, and he recited, *so their deeds have become worthless; and We will not assign to them on the day of resurrection any importance* [18:105]."

we have no need of it. Indeed anyone who holds a study circle like this one of mine and accepts from people the likes of these, on the day of resurrection [he] will encounter God تَعَالَىٰ bereft of even the slightest portion [of God's good blessings].[51]

It has been narrated either directly from Jābir [b. ʿAbdallāh al-Anṣārī] رَضِيَٱللَّهُعَنْهُ or from the Messenger of God صَلَّىٱللَّهُعَلَيْهِوَسَلَّمَ, that he stated, "Sit only in the company of a scholar that calls you from five [things] to five [things]; from doubt to certainty, from pretense to sincerity, from desires to detachment, from arrogance to humility, and from enmity to counsel in good faith."[52]

God تَعَالَىٰ says, *So he came out before his people in his adornment. Those who desired the worldly life said, "Oh, would that we had like what was given to Qarun. Indeed, he is one of great fortune." But those who had been given knowledge said, "Woe to you! The reward of God is better for he who believes and does righteousness. And none are granted it except the patient* [28:79–80]. In these verses He تَعَالَىٰ qualified the people of knowledge as those who prefer the abode of the hereafter over the worldly domain.

The scholar [of the abode] of the hereafter has [certain] traits: his deeds do not contradict his speech, rather he enjoins upon others nothing that he himself is not the first to accomplish.

God تَعَالَىٰ has said, "*Do you order righteousness of the people and forget yourselves*?" [2:44].

And He تَعَالَىٰ has said, *It is most hateful to God that you should say that which you do not do* [61:3].

He تَعَالَىٰ has said as well in the story of Shuʿayb, *And I do not intend to differ from you in that which I have forbidden you* [11:88].

And He تَعَالَىٰ says, *And fear God. And God teaches you* [2:282]. And He تَعَالَىٰ says, *And fear God and know that God is severe in penalty* [2:196]. And, *fear God and listen* [5:108].

God تَعَالَىٰ said, addressing Jesus عَلَيْهِٱلسَّلَامُ, "O son of Mary, admonish yourself [first]. Then, if you have taken heed of it, admonish others; otherwise feel shame before me [and desist from admonishing others]."[53]

---

51 Abū Ṭālib al-Makkī, *Qūt al-qulūb*, 1:144.

52 Abū Nuʿaym, *Ḥilya*, 7:72; Abū Ṭālib al-Makkī, *Qūt al-qulūb*, 1:144.

53 Narrated by Aḥmad b. Ḥanbal, *Kitāb al-zuhd*, 300; and Abū Nuʿaym, *Ḥilya*, 2:382.

The Messenger ﷺ [speaking of the Night Journey], said, "On the night of my journey I passed by a people whose lips were being shredded with shears made of fire. I asked them who they were and they responded, 'We used to enjoin others to good and not do it ourselves; and forbid evil while doing it ourselves.'"[54]

He ﷺ stated, "The destruction of my community will be the corrupt scholar and the ignorant servant; the most malicious of the malicious are the reprehensible scholars, and the best of the best are the best of the scholars."[55]

Al-Awzāʿī رحمه الله stated, "The graveyards complained due to the stench of the corpses of disbelievers [interred in them]; God said, addressing them by way of inspiration: 'The stench of the entrails of the corrupt scholar is worse than that of which you are complaining.'"[56]

Fuḍayl b. ʿIyāḍ رحمه الله reported, "It has reached me that the judgment on the day of resurrection will begin with the corrupt scholars [even] before the idolaters."[57]

Abū l-Dardāʾ رضي الله عنه declared, "Woe be it once to one who knows not; woe be it sevenfold for one who knows but acts not [upon their knowledge]."[58]

[Abū ʿAmr ʿĀmir b. Sharāḥīl] al-Shaʿbī said, "On the day of resurrection a congregation of the people of heaven will look down upon a congregation of the people of the fire and ask them, 'What brought you to enter the fire, when it was by the grace of your teachings and guidance that God brought us into heaven?' Then they will respond, 'We used to enjoin the good and not do it [ourselves].'"[59]

---

54 Narrated by Aḥmad b. Ḥanbal, *Musnad*, 3:120. In another edition it is worded as: "We commanded good but did not do it, and we forbade evil but did it."

55 Cited by Ibn ʿAbd al-Barr, *Jāmiʿ bayān al-ʿilm wa-faḍlih*, 1162, from a *ḥadīth* of Ibn Wahb as attributed to the Prophet, the second line of the above narration was narrated by al-Dārimī, *Sunan*, 382; al-Zabīdī cites as examples of the first part of this *ḥadīth* that which is in *Qūt al-qulūb*, 1:140: "We narrated from ʿUmar and others, 'How numerous are the corrupt scholars and the ignorant servants, be wary of the corrupt scholar and the ignorant servant.'" See al-Zabīdī, *Itḥāf*, 1:369.

56 Ibn ʿAbd al-Barr, *Jāmiʿ bayān al-ʿilm wa-faḍlih*, 1163.

57 Ibn ʿAbd al-Barr, *Jāmiʿ bayān al-ʿilm wa-faḍlih*, 1164.

58 Ibn ʿAbd al-Barr, *Jāmiʿ bayān al-ʿilm wa-faḍlih*, 1212; and Abū Nuʿaym, *Ḥilya*, 1:211.

59 Ibn al-Mubārak, *Zuhd*, 64.

Ḥātim al-Aṣamm رَحِمَهُ ٱللَّهُ stated, "There is no one on the day of resurrection in a greater state of loss than a man who imparted knowledge to people who acted upon it, while he himself did not do so; they will be successful because of him while he will perish."[60]

Mālik b. Dīnār used to remark, "The admonition of a scholar who does not act on his knowledge, rolls off hearts like raindrops off a smooth stone."[61]

On this theme they also composed verses of poetry,

O you who admonish the people; suspicious you have become
When you fault them for matters you yourself come to them with[62]

You have taken to zealously advising them with admonitions
Yet by my life it is you who commit the gravest of transgressions

You fault the world and the people yearning for it
While you yearn for it more than they [yearn] for it[63]

Another [poet][64] once said,

Prohibit not behavior the likes of which you commit
Great shame upon you should such you yourself commit

Ibrāhīm b. Adham رَحِمَهُ ٱللَّهُ related, "I came upon a stone upon which was inscribed, "Turn me over and take heed." So I turned it over and found inscribed upon it, 'You do not act on what you know, how can you seek knowledge of that which you do not know?'"[65]

Ibn al-Sammāk رَحِمَهُ ٱللَّهُ said, "How many are there that remind others of God, while forgetting God themselves? How many instill the fear of God in others, acting with insolence toward Him? How many who bring others to intimacy with God are distant from Him? How many who invite [others] to God are fleeing from Him?

---

60 Ibn ʿAsākir cited a similar narration, *Tārīkh Dimashq*, 51:137–138.

61 Al-Khaṭīb al-Baghdādī, *Iqtiḍāʾ al-ʿilm al-ʿamal*, 97.

62 The first verse is from Abū l-ʿAtāhiya, *Dīwān*, 425.

63 A reference for the last two verses has not been found.

64 This line is ascribed to Abū l-Aswad al-Duʾalī and can be found in his *Dīwān*, 425. See also Ibn Ḥijja al-Ḥamawī, *Khizānat al-adab*, 8:564.

65 Abū Nuʿaym narrates a similar saying in *Ḥilya*, 3:358; see al-Zabīdī, *Itḥāf* as well, 1:372.

How many a reciter of the Qurʾān is divested of [the meanings of] God's verses?"[66]

Ibrāhīm b. Adham رَحِمَهُ ٱللَّهُ said, "We expressed ourselves eloquently in our speech [in Arabic] and made no grammatical errors; in our deeds we mis-spoke and were inarticulate."[67]

Al-Awzāʿī رَحِمَهُ ٱللَّهُ stated, "When eloquence in one's use of the Arabic language arrives, humility departs."[68]

[Abū ʿAbdallāh] Makḥūl related on the authority of ʿAbd al-Raḥmān b. Ghanim, who said, "Ten Companions of the Messenger of God صَلَّى ٱللَّهُ عَلَيْهِ وَسَلَّمَ informed me, 'We were occupied studying knowledge in the Quba Mosque when the Messenger of God صَلَّى ٱللَّهُ عَلَيْهِ وَسَلَّمَ came to us and said, "Learn what you will, God will never give you recompense until you act [on what you have learned]."[69]

[It is related that] Jesus stated, "The parable of someone who acquires knowledge but does not act according to it is like a woman who has had an illicit affair and becomes pregnant and when this becomes apparent she is exposed to public disgrace. Such is a person who does not act on his knowledge, God will expose them to disgrace on the day of resurrection before the entirety of all the witnesses there."[70]

Muʿādh [b. Jabal] رَضِيَ ٱللَّهُ عَنْهُ said, "Take heed of the inadvertent errors of the scholar, for he is held in high esteem by people who will take after him in his error."

ʿUmar رَضِيَ ٱللَّهُ عَنْهُ stated, "Should the scholar inadvertently err an entire people fall into error with him."[71] He said as well, "The destruction of an age is brought on by three things; one of them is the error of the scholar."[72]

Ibn Masʿūd رَضِيَ ٱللَّهُ عَنْهُ said, "A time will come to people in which the sweetness in their hearts [that is the fruit of faith] will become

---

66 Abū Nuʿaym, *Ḥilya*, 3:451.

67 Al-Khaṭīb al-Baghdādī narrates a similar narration, *Iqtiḍāʾ al-ʿilm al-ʿamal*, 151.

68 Abū Ṭālib al-Makkī, *Qūt al-qulūb*, 1:166.

69 Abū Nuʿaym, *Ḥilya*, 1:236; al-Khaṭīb al-Baghdādī, *Iqtiḍāʾ al-ʿilm al-ʿamal*, 8; al-Dārimī narrated this in his *Sunan* from Muʿādh b. Jabal رَضِيَ ٱللَّهُ عَنْهُ.

70 Al-Zabīdī ascribes this to Abū Ṭālib al-Makkī, *Qūt al-qulūb*.

71 Ibn al-Mubārak has cited a similar saying and ascribed it to Jesus in *Kitāb al-zuhd*, 1474.

72 Ibn ʿAbd al-Barr, *Jāmiʿ bayān al-ʿilm wa-faḍlih*, 1867.

bitter [lit., salty]; at that time knowledge will benefit neither the scholar nor his pupil. The hearts of their scholars will be similar to salt flats, the rain drops from the heavens will drop upon it but there is no sweetness to be found. This occurs when the hearts of the scholars bend toward the love of the world and prefer it over the hereafter; that is the time in which God تَعَالَىٰ divests them of the founts of wisdom [that had resided therein] and He extinguishes the lamps of guidance from their hearts. When you encounter a scholar [of those times] he will inform you on his tongue that he is in awe of God, yet impiety is clear in his comportment. How fertile are the tongues in those days and how barren are the hearts! By God—the One, there is no god but He—that is only because the teachers will teach for other than the sake of God; and the students will study for other than the sake of God [as well].[73]

It is written in the Gospel, "Do not seek knowledge of that which you do not know until you have acted on that which you already know."[74]

[The Companion] Ḥudhayfa رَضِيَ ٱللَّهُ عَنْهُ declared, "You exist in a time when whoever abandoned a tenth of that which he had acquired of knowledge will perish. A time is coming in which whoever acts on [even] a tenth of that which he has acquired of knowledge will be saved.[75] This will be because of the great number of dissolute [among the scholarly classes.]"

Know that the scholar is similar to the judge, and the Messenger of God صَلَّى ٱللَّهُ عَلَيْهِ وَسَلَّمَ stated, "There are three kinds of judges; a judge who passes judgment according to the truth and he is knowledgeable [of the law], such will be in paradise; a judge who passes judgment with injustice, knowingly or not, he will be in hell; and a judge who bases his judgments on criteria other than God's decrees, he will be in hell as well."[76]

Kaʿab [al-Aḥbār] رَضِيَ ٱللَّهُ عَنْهُ related, "At the end of time the scholars will teach people restraint from worldly pursuits while not restraining themselves; they will arouse the fear [of God and the hereafter]

---

73 See al-Zabīdī, *Itḥāf*, 1:374.

74 Abū Ṭālib al-Makkī, *Qūt al-qulūb*, 1:138.

75 Abū Ṭālib al-Makkī, *Qūt al-qulūb*, 1:138; narrated as attributed to the Prophet in al-Tirmidhī, 2267.

76 Al-Tirmidhī, 1322; Abū Dāwūd, 3573; Ibn Māja, 2315.

in the people but they will not fear, they will dissuade others from frequenting the rich and powerful while they will frequent them; they will prefer this world over the hereafter, they earn their provision with their [eloquent] use of language, they patronize the wealthy rather than the poor, they are as jealous over [their] knowledge as women are over their men; they will become incensed with one of their companions should they frequent another [scholar's circle]."[77] Those are the despotic [scholars], the enemies of the All-Merciful!

It was narrated that the Prophet صَلَّى ٱللَّهُ عَلَيْهِ وَسَلَّمَ stated, "It may well be that Satan will overtake you with knowledge." It was asked, 'O Messenger of God, how could that be?' He responded, 'He says [to you] seek knowledge, but do not act until you have attained knowledge'; [if a person takes his advice] he will not cease speaking of knowledge, all the while deferring to act until he dies having never acted [on his knowledge]."[78]

Sarī l-Saqaṭī related, "A man who had previously sought the attainment of outward knowledge ardently went into seclusion to devote himself to worship, so I asked him about that."

He said, "I saw in a dream someone saying to me, 'How long will you continue to squander knowledge [with no benefit to yourself], may God squander you!'"

I said [in my own defense] "I am preserving it."

To which he responded, "Action is the means of preserving knowledge."

Whereupon I abandoned the quest and devoted myself to acting [on my knowledge].[79]

Ibn Masʿūd رَضِيَ ٱللَّهُ عَنْهُ stated, "Knowledge is not defined by an abundance of narrations [of *ḥadīth*]; [rather] knowledge is awe [of God in one's heart]."[80]

Ḥasan [al-Baṣrī] said, "Gain whatever knowledge you want, I swear by God, you will have no recompense from God until you act

77 Abū Ṭālib al-Makkī, *Qūt al-qulūb*, 1:140.

78 Al-Khaṭīb al-Baghdādī cited a similar narration in *Jāmiʿ li akhlāq al-rāwī wa-ādāb al-sāmiʿ*, 1:132; see al-Zabīdī, *Itḥāf*, 1:376.

79 Abū Ṭālib al-Makkī, *Qūt al-qulūb*, 1:133.

80 Narrated by Aḥmad b. Ḥanbal, *Kitāb al-zuhd*, 867.

on it; the foolhardy are devoted to transmitting reports, while the scholars are devoted to watchful care [of their states]."[81]

Mālik b. Anas رضي الله عنه stated, "Seeking knowledge is a worthy pursuit, its transmission is worthy when accompanied with sound intention; yet take heed of your custom and surroundings from the time morning finds you until nightfall, and prefer nothing to it."[82]

Ibn Masʿūd رضي الله عنه related, "The Qurʾān was sent down so that [people] act on it, thus you took its study as an action. But there will come a people who will straighten it like a lance, they will not be the preeminent among you. The scholar that does not apply his knowledge is like an ailing patient who prescribes medication or a starving man who expounds upon delectable food that neither of them finds. This is alluded to in God's words, *And for you is destruction from that which you describe* [21:18].[83]

It was narrated from reports, "Among that which I fear most for my community is the error of the scholar and the disputation of the hypocrites over the Qurʾān."[84]

Among the traits of a scholar of the hereafter is his concern with knowledge that will be beneficial in the hereafter; pursuing compliance [with God's decrees]; and avoid those fields of study whose benefit is minimal, and wherein there is an excess of disputation and idle talk.

The example of a person who turns his attention from the knowledge of [proper] conduct and occupies himself with disputation is similar to a man afflicted with multiple ailments who has encountered by chance a physician well versed in his art; time [for his treatment] however is short and it is feared that the opportunity may be lost. Yet he engrosses himself in inquiring into the specific properties of the various remedies and medicines and marvels at the practice

81 This report has been transmitted as attributed to the Prophet, as originating from a companion, and as originating from a follower. Abū Ṭālib al-Makkī, *Qūt al-qulūb*, 1:135; al-Zabīdī, *Itḥāf*, 1:377.

82 The major transmitters report it from Mālik, 37. See also *Qūt al-qulūb*, 1:135, and *Ḥilya*, 6:319.

83 Abū Ṭālib al-Makkī, *Qūt al-qulūb*, 1:135; al-Ājirī reported something similar in *Akhlāq ḥamlat al-qurʾān*, 31, from al-Fuḍayl b. ʿIyāḍ.

84 Narrated by al-Ṭabarānī, *al-Muʿjam al-kabīr*, 20:138.

of medicine and he neglects the important matter about which he is personally concerned [i.e., his health]; that is pure foolhardiness.

It has been narrated that a man approached the Messenger of God صَلَّىٱللَّهُعَلَيْهِوَسَلَّمَ and said, "Teach me the little known facets of knowledge."

So he صَلَّىٱللَّهُعَلَيْهِوَسَلَّمَ asked him, 'What have you done with the most essential facets of knowledge?'

The man asked, 'What are the most essential facets of knowledge?'

He صَلَّىٱللَّهُعَلَيْهِوَسَلَّمَ asked the man, 'Have you come to know the Lord most exalted?'

He said, 'Yes.'

He صَلَّىٱللَّهُعَلَيْهِوَسَلَّمَ then asked him, 'What have you done concerning the rights due to Him?'

He retorted, 'As God has willed it.'

The Messenger of God صَلَّىٱللَّهُعَلَيْهِوَسَلَّمَ asked him, 'Have you come to know about death?'

He responded, 'Yes.'

He صَلَّىٱللَّهُعَلَيْهِوَسَلَّمَ then asked, 'What have you prepared for it?'

He responded, 'As God has willed it.'

[At this] he صَلَّىٱللَّهُعَلَيْهِوَسَلَّمَ said, 'Go and gain a mastery over these matters, then come and we will instruct you in the little known facets of knowledge.'"[85]

[Ḥātim al-Aṣamm]

It is most appropriate that learning be of the nature that has been related from Ḥātim al-Aṣamm, who was the student of Shaqīq al-Balkhī عَلَيْهِٱلسَّلَامُ, when Shaqīq [his teacher] asked him, "How long have you kept my company?" To which Ḥātim responded, 'Thirty-three years.' Whereupon Shaqīq asked him, 'What have you learned from me during this period of time?' He told him, '**Eight** matters.' [Amazed by this] Shaqīq remarked, 'Verily we are God's alone and to Him we return. My entire life has gone by with you and you have learned but eight matters?' Ḥātim responded, 'O my teacher, I learned only these, and it is not my wont to lie.' So he said, 'Tell

85 Abū Nuʿaym, *Ḥilya*, 1:24; Ibn ʿAbd al-Barr, *Jāmiʿ bayān al-ʿilm wa-faḍlih*, 1222; see al-Zabīdī, *Itḥāf*, 1:379.

me these eight matters, so I can hear them.' Ḥātim spoke saying:

"The **First**: I observed humankind and saw that everyone had an object of love and that he remained with his beloved until the graveside; upon reaching his grave he abandoned him. I made my worthy actions my beloved, when I enter my grave my beloved will be with me. "Well done, O Ḥātim!" Shaqīq declared, "What is the **second**?"

He responded, "I considered God's تَعَالَىٰ words, *But as for he who feared the position of his Lord and prevented the soul from* [*unlawful*] *inclination, then indeed, paradise will be* [*his*] *refuge* [79:40–41]. I knew His words سُبْحَانَهُ to be the truth, so I began striving with my soul, restraining it from pursuing its passions until it eventually settled into obedience to God تَعَالَىٰ [and surrendered].

The **Third**: "I observed humankind, and I saw that everyone who has something valuable and dear to them elevates it and guards it. Then I considered God's تَعَالَىٰ words, *Whatever you have will end, but what God has is lasting* [16:96], whereupon, whenever something dear to me and valuable came to me, I gave it back to God that it might remain in trust with Him."

The **Fourth**: "I observed humankind, and saw every one of them depending on wealth, social stature, nobility, and kith and kin. I considered them carefully and found them all to be of no value, then I regarded God's words, *the most noble of you in the sight of God is the most righteous of you* [49:13]; whereupon I undertook to attain piety (*taqwā*), that I might become noble in God's view."

The **Fifth**: "I observed humankind and I saw some people blaming others and some slandering others, all this derived from envy [regarding money, fame, and knowledge]. Then I considered God's عَزَّوَجَلَّ words, *It is We who have apportioned among them their livelihood in the life of this world* [43:32]. So I abandoned envy and avoided frequenting the crowds [of people]. And then, knowing that our provision in this world is God's province سُبْحَانَهُ, I forsook enmity against them."

The **Sixth**: "I observed humankind, some of them treating each other unjustly, some of them fighting with others; I took recourse to God's عَزَّوَجَلَّ words, *Indeed, Satan is an enemy to you; so take him as an enemy* [35:6]. So I took him as my sole enemy, and strove to take every precaution against him; God تَعَالَىٰ bore witness that he is my enemy, and I abandoned enmity for all creation but him."

The **Seventh**: "I observed humankind and saw each of them striving earnestly for a crust of bread [in this world], humiliating themselves and falling into illicit practices; then I considered carefully His تَعَالَىٰ words, *And there is no creature on earth but that upon God is its provision* [11:6] and I knew that I was one of the creatures of the earth for whom God had guaranteed its provision, so I occupied myself with what I owed Him and I abandoned what He owed me."

The **Eighth**: "I observed humankind and I saw them all placing their trust in created beings; this one on his land and property, this one on his business, this one on his craft and trade, and this one on his physical well-being. Every created being placed his trust and relied on another created being like himself; so I turned my attention to His تَعَالَىٰ statement, *And whoever relies upon God—then He is sufficient for him* [65:3] so I put my trust entirely in God عَزَّوَجَلَّ and He is sufficient for me."

Whereupon Shaqīq replied, "O Ḥātim, May God تَعَالَىٰ grant you success. I have considered the Torah, the Gospels, the Psalms, and the Qurʾān, and I found that all good and every benefit of religion revolves around these **eight** precepts; whoever avails themselves of them has indeed availed themselves of the essentials of the four books."[86]

Only the scholars of the hereafter devote themselves to the deep understanding and perfection of this branch of knowledge. As for the scholars of this world, they occupy themselves with whatever gives them ready access to wealth and status; they pay little attention to the likes of these realms of knowledge that God sent all the prophets عَلَيْهِمُ السَّلَامُ [to humankind] with.

Al-Ḍaḥḥāk b. Muzāḥim stated, "I encountered them (the Companions) and all they taught one another was scrupulousness (*waraʿ*); whereas today all they teach one another is theology."[87]

Among the traits of a scholar of the hereafter is that he inclines not toward extravagance in his food and beverages, nor elegance in

86 Abū Nuʿaym narrates a shorter version, *Ḥilya*, 8:79; in *Letter to a Disciple*, al-Ghazālī cites a much longer and detailed version this story, for an English translation see *al-Ghazālī: Letter to a Disciple*, trans. Mayer.

87 Abū Ṭālib al-Makkī, *Qūt al-qulūb*, 1:96.

his clothing, nor opulence in his furnishings or residence. Rather he prefers moderation in all that; in this he is similar to the predecessors رَحِمَهُمُ ٱللَّهُ and he inclines toward simple sufficiency with the minimum in everything. Whenever his inclination in the direction of penury increases, his proximity to God increases, and his rank among the scholars of the hereafter becomes elevated.

An apt testimony to this is the story related by Abū ʿAbdallāh al-Khawwāṣ, who was among the companions of Ḥātim al-Aṣamm. He relates, "I entered [the city of] Rayy [in southern Khurasan] with Ḥātim; with us were three hundred twenty men who all intended to make the pilgrimage and were all dressed in course woolen garments, they had neither leather packs nor food with them. On arrival we entered the residence of a merchant who lived an ascetic life and loved the poor and indigent. He hosted us that night and in the morning he said to Ḥātim, 'Have you any need of me? For I was intending to pay a visit to one of our jurists who has fallen ill.'

Ḥātim said, 'There is great worth in paying a visit to the infirm, and consideration for a jurist is itself worship, I will come with you.'

The infirm [scholar] was Muḥammad b. Muqātil, the judge of Rayy. When we came to the door of the house we found that it was resplendently beautiful, which left Ḥātim pondering and he said, "Is this what the door of a scholar looks like?"

Then they were granted permission and they entered, whereupon they beheld a vast well-appointed residence, expansive and immaculately kept, in which there were wall hangings, utensils [of all sorts] and curtains. Ḥātim continued to ponder; then they entered the reception hall in which [Muḥammad b. Muqātil] was present, reclining upon bedding that had been laid out, at his head was a young boy in whose hand was a fan to ward off flies.

The visitor sat at his head and asked him about the state of his health, all the while Ḥātim was still standing; Ibn Muqātil beckoned him to be seated, but he responded, 'I will not be seated.'

So he said to him, 'You must have a request?'

So Ḥātim said, 'Yes.'

And he asked, 'What is it?'

He said, 'I have a question to ask of you.'

'Ask me.' Said Ibn Muqātil. Ḥātim asked him to sit upright and after he sat upright:

Ḥātim asked, "From where did you acquire this knowledge of yours?"

"From trustworthy sources who transmitted it to me," he replied.

[Then] "from whom," he asked.

"From the Companions of the Messenger of God صَلَّى ٱللَّهُ عَلَيْهِ وَسَلَّمَ," he said.

Ḥātim asked, "And the Companions of the Messenger of God صَلَّى ٱللَّهُ عَلَيْهِ وَسَلَّمَ from whom?"

"From the Messenger of God صَلَّى ٱللَّهُ عَلَيْهِ وَسَلَّمَ," he answered.

"And the Messenger of God صَلَّى ٱللَّهُ عَلَيْهِ وَسَلَّمَ from whom?" Ḥātim continued.

"From Gabriel عَلَيْهِ ٱلسَّلَامُ from God سُبْحَانَهُ," Ibn Muqātil replied.

Whereupon Ḥātim asked, "Then, in that which Gabriel عَلَيْهِ ٱلسَّلَامُ conveyed from God تَعَالَىٰ to the Messenger of God صَلَّى ٱللَّهُ عَلَيْهِ وَسَلَّمَ, and the Messenger of God صَلَّى ٱللَّهُ عَلَيْهِ وَسَلَّمَ conveyed to his Companions, and his Companions to the trustworthy transmitters, and from these trustworthy transmitters to yourself; have you heard, 'Whoever is a prince in his dwelling place and his means are far-reaching will have a greater abode with God عَزَّ وَجَلَّ [in the hereafter]?"

He responded, "No."

So he asked, "What have you heard?"

To which he replied, "Whoever disengages himself from this world while thirsting for the hereafter, loves the needy and accomplishes good works toward attaining the hereafter will have a place of honor with God."

So Ḥātim asked, "Whom do you take as your example, then the Prophet صَلَّى ٱللَّهُ عَلَيْهِ وَسَلَّمَ and his Companions رَحِمَهُمُ ٱللَّهُ and the upright [of this community] or Pharaoh and Nimrod, the first to have built with mortar and baked brick?"

"O malicious scholars! When the uneducated multitudes who fight like dogs over the world and thirst for its goods see the likes of you, they proclaim, 'The [venerable] scholar lives thus! I am certainly no worse than he.'

Whereupon Ḥātim left his presence and Ibn Muqātil's illness grew worse.'"

"The news of what had come to pass between Ḥātim and Ibn Muqātil reached the people of Rayy and they said to Ḥātim, 'Surely al-Ṭanāfisī [who resides] in Qazwin lives more extravagantly than he [Ibn Muqātil].'

So Ḥātim took to the road and sought him out; he entered and said, "May God have mercy on you, I am a non-Arab (*ʿajamī*), I ask that you instruct me on the fundamentals of my religion and the key to my prayers; how should I perform my ablutions for the prayer?"

He responded, 'Yes, willingly. O young man! Bring a vessel of water'; and it was brought. Al-Ṭanāfisī took a seat and performed his ablutions, washing each required part of the body three times, then he said, 'This is how you make your ablutions.'

Ḥātim said, "Stay where you are, so that I can perform my ablutions in front of you to be sure of what I seek."

So al-Ṭanāfisī stood up and Ḥātim seated himself and performed the ablutions, then he washed his forearms four times each, whereupon al-Ṭanāfisī said, 'O you there, you have been wasteful.'

Ḥātim asked him in what way and he told him he had washed his forearms four times each.

To which Ḥātim cried out, "O praise to God the Almighty, in a handful of water I have been wasteful and you in all this have not been wasteful!"

Here al-Ṭanāfisī understood that his intent had been just this and not instruction. He went into his house and did not emerge among the people for forty days.

So when Ḥātim entered Baghdad, the people of the city gathered around him and said, "O Abū l-Raḥmān; you are a non-Arab who speaks Arabic poorly [not following the rules of grammar], yet not a person addresses you in discourse without you silencing them!"

He responded, "I have three character traits by which I overwhelm anyone who engages me in an argument; I delight when my opponent hits upon the truth, I feel remorse when he errs, and I am careful not to accuse my opponent of being ignorant."

This news reached Aḥmad b. Ḥanbal رَحِمَهُ ٱللَّٰهُ who said, "God be praised! How astute a person this is! Arise, let us visit him now!"

As soon as he came into his presence he said to him, "O Abū ʿAbd al-Raḥmān, what preserves our well-being in the world?"

He responded, "O Abū ʿAbdallāh, there is no well-being in the world until you have four character traits; (1) forgive the common folk their ignorance, (2) defend them from your own ignorance, (3) spend generously of whatever you have among them, (4) lose all hope of acquiring their possessions; if you have become thus, well-being will be yours."

Then he departed for Medina. The people of Medina gathered to welcome him and he asked them, "O people, which city is this?"

They replied, 'This is the city of the Messenger of God صَلَّى ٱللَّهُ عَلَيْهِ وَسَلَّمَ.'

He asked, "Where is the palace of the Messenger of God صَلَّى ٱللَّهُ عَلَيْهِ وَسَلَّمَ that I may perform my prayers in it?"

They told him, 'He had no palace, indeed he had a modest house level with the ground.'

He asked, "Where are the palaces of the Companions رَضِيَ ٱللَّهُ عَنْهُمْ"

They replied, 'They had no palaces, they only had modest houses level with the ground.'

To which Ḥātim exclaimed, "O people, so this is the city of Pharaoh!"

Whereupon they took hold of him and took him to the local ruler and said this non-Arab says that this is the city of Pharaoh. The governor asked why [he said that] and Ḥātim responded, saying, "Do not be hasty in judging me! I am a non-Arab and a stranger here; I entered this region and asked the people here, "Whose city is this?"

They told me, 'The city of the Messenger of God صَلَّى ٱللَّهُ عَلَيْهِ وَسَلَّمَ.'

So I asked, "Where is his palace?". . . And he continued with the story, then he said, God تَعَالَىٰ says, *There has certainly been for you in the Messenger of God an excellent pattern* [33:21]. Then he [turned to the people] and exclaimed, "Whose example have you been following, the Messenger of God صَلَّى ٱللَّهُ عَلَيْهِ وَسَلَّمَ or Pharaoh who was the first person to build with mortar and baked brick?" Hearing this, they released him and let him go on his way."[88]

This is the story of Ḥātim al-Aṣamm رَحِمَهُ ٱللَّهُ. Other examples of their threadbare attire and their forsaking adornment that testifies to the simplicity of the lives of the predecessors will come in its proper place.

---

88 Abū Nuʿaym, *Ḥilya*, 8:80.

The reality in this matter is that self-adornment is permissible, not forbidden; but excess involvement with it provokes fondness for it until it is difficult to relinquish; in most cases continuous concern with adornment is only possible when one pursues it constantly by means that necessitate that acts of disobedience are committed, such as flattery, excessive attention to people, pretentiousness before them, and other similar matters that are prohibited. It is prudent to avoid that because whoever delves deeply into the world finds no well-being therein; if well-being came from delving deeply into it, the Prophet صَلَّى ٱللَّٰهُ عَلَيْهِ وَسَلَّمَ would not have gone to such lengths to forsake the world, to the extent that he removed a robe embroidered with patterns,[89] and removed a gold ring during the Friday sermon,[90] and other examples that will follow.

[Letter to Imām Mālik b. Anas رَحِمَهُ ٱللَّٰهُ]

It was said that Yaḥyā b. Yazīd al-Nawfalī wrote [a letter] to Mālik b. Anas رَحِمَهُ ٱللَّٰهُ:

> *In the Name of God the Merciful the Compassionate*
> May the Blessings of God be upon His Messenger
> Muḥammad among the Foremost and the Very Last
> From Yaḥyā b. Yazīd b. ʿAbd al-Malik to Mālik b. Anas
> To the point:
>
> It has reached me that you wear fine clothing, and partake of refined foods, sit upon carpets and have positioned a gatekeeper at your door. [It has reached me as well] that you have established yourself in a gathering of knowledge in which a raised dais has been built for you and people travel long distances to sit in your company and have taken you as their leader and are pleased with your opinions. Fear

89 Al-Bukhārī, 373; Muslim, 556, and the quote cited here is his, "The Prophet صَلَّى ٱللَّٰهُ عَلَيْهِ وَسَلَّمَ prayed in a robe that had embroidered patterns upon it, and said, "These patterns have distracted me, take this [robe] to Abū Jahm and bring me a simple garment made of wool."

90 Al-Bukhārī, 5867; Muslim, 2091: "The Messenger of God صَلَّى ٱللَّٰهُ عَلَيْهِ وَسَلَّمَ used to wear a ring made of gold; [one day] he discarded it saying, 'I will never wear it again.' And the people discarded their rings as well."

God, O Mālik! Remain steadfast in humility!
I have written to you with sincere counsel from myself, a missive that only God تَعَالَىٰ has looked upon.

May the peace of God be with you.

Mālik wrote back in reply:

In the Name of God the Merciful the Compassionate

May the Blessings of God be upon Muḥammad, his family, his Companions, and Peace

From Mālik b. Anas to Yaḥyā b. Yazīd,

May the peace of God be upon you.

To the point:

Your missive has reached me; and it has been received by me in the spirit of the sincere counsel, compassion, and respect with which it was sent. May God grant you piety, and recompense you with beneficence for this counsel. I seek attainment of my goal from God; there is no strength or might save with God, He is the Exalted, the Mighty.

As for that which you have mentioned in your missive, that I partake of refined food and wear fine clothing, and have a gatekeeper, and seat myself upon a raised dais; [you are correct] we do those things and we seek forgiveness from God تَعَالَىٰ. God تَعَالَىٰ has said, *Say,* "*Who has forbidden the adornment of God which He has produced for His servants and the good* [*lawful*] *things of provision?* [7:32]. I am fully aware that foregoing such things is better than involvement in them. Do not leave us out of your correspondence as we will not leave you out of ours.

Greetings of peace to you.

Regard carefully the equanimity of Mālik when he admits that forsaking such matters is better than being occupied with them, and how he judges them in fact to be within the realm of the permissible, and in both points of view he spoke the truth.

A person of Mālik's status, whose soul permits itself the equanimity and the contrition seen in the face of such counsel, has the self-control to stand firm at the limits of the permissible, and not be driven to pretension and flattery, or to transgress by committing reprehensible acts. Anyone else would not be capable of such comportment.

So inclination toward the indulgence of things within the realm of the permissible is an immense hazard [to the spiritual life], and far removed from the traits of fear and apprehension; for the unique trait of those who know God is apprehension, and the unique trait of apprehension is to be distanced from any hint of risk.

Among the traits of a scholar of the hereafter is that he constrains himself from frequenting the rulers; in fact he never enters their presence as long as he has a means to flee from them; in fact it is far more suitable to avoid at all costs mixing with them, even though they may come to him. For indeed the world is sweet and verdant, its reins are in the hands of the rulers. Those keeping their company are seldom exempt from attempting to curry [the ruler's] favor and incline their hearts toward [the rulers]; despite their being unjust tyrants, it is the obligation of every religious person to be critical of [them] and straighten their circumstances by making evident to everyone their tyranny and dissolute behavior.

One entering their presence is either attracted to their luxurious lifestyle, thus diminishing in his own eyes those graces God has granted him; or he desists from criticizing them and falls to flattering them; or he endeavors at great length to address them in a manner that pleases them and reflects their circumstances positively, which is evident confusion [of mind]; or he desires and strives to attain their worldly goods, and that is detestable.

In the *Kitāb al-Ḥalāl wa-l-Ḥarām* [Book 14, *The Lawful and the Unlawful*] I discuss what may lawfully be accepted from the treasury of the rulers and what cannot be lawfully accepted from largesse, tributes, and other such things.

On the whole, frequenting them is a key to malevolence; the path of the scholars of the hereafter is one of caution.

The Messenger of God ﷺ stated, "Whoever takes up the nomadic life will become brusque and harsh in his attitudes; whoever takes up the hunter's life will fall into ignorance; and whoever frequents rulers will fall into trial and tribulation."[91]

The Prophet ﷺ remarked as well, "There will be over you rulers, some among them you will know and criticize; whoever criticizes them will be absolved of wrongdoing, and whoever is averse to them will be protected; but anyone who is content with them and obeys them, God will distance him from His mercy." He was asked, 'Shall we not go to battle against them?' To which he ﷺ responded, "No, as long as they maintain the prayers.'"[92]

Sufyān stated, "There is chasm in hell in which only the Qurʾān reciters who frequent rulers will reside."[93]

Ḥudhayfa [b. al-Yamān] رضي الله عنه warned, "Beware of the stations of trial and tribulation": He was asked what they were and he responded, "The gates of the princes, one of you enters the presence of the ruler and acknowledges him deceitfully, and says about him that which he utterly lacks."[94]

The Prophet ﷺ said, "The scholars are deputies of God's messengers over servants of God, as long as they do not associate with the rulers; if they fall into this they have betrayed the messengers of God, so beware of them and shun them." This was narrated by Anas.[95]

Al-Aʿmash was told, "You have revived knowledge because of the multitudes that have taken it from you." He responded, "Do not be hasty! A third died before attaining understanding, another third remain at the gates of the rulers and are the most malicious of humankind, and of the remaining third only a small portion will prosper."[96]

---

91 Abū Dāwūd, 2859.

92 Muslim, 1854.

93 Ibn ʿAbd al-Barr, *Jāmiʿ bayān al-ʿilm wa-faḍlih*, 1097.

94 ʿAbd al-Razzāq, *al-Muṣannaf*, 11:316; Abū Nuʿaym, *Ḥilya*, 1:277.

95 Narrated from Anas by al-ʿUqaylī (in his *al-Ḍuʿafāʾ*) as cited in Ibn ʿAbd al-Barr, *Jāmiʿ bayān al-ʿilm wa-faḍlih*, 1113; and al-Daylamī, *Musnad al-firdaws*, 4210; and al-Munāwī said, quoting al-Suyūṭī, "Ibn Jawzī's attribution of this *ḥadīth* as 'fabricated' is a forbidden thing to do, there are other *ḥadīth* that testify to this meaning; so in accordance with the dictates of the study of *ḥadīth*, I judge this *ḥadīth* to be well attested to." Al-Munāwī, *Fayḍ al-qadīr*, 4:383. Al-Zabīdī, *Itḥāf*, 1:388.

96 Ibn ʿAbd al-Barr, *Jāmiʿ bayān al-ʿilm wa-faḍlih*, 1115.

For this reason Saʿīd b. al-Musayyab رَحِمَهُ ٱللَّهُ stated, "When you see a scholar associating with the princes beware of him, for he is a thief."[97]

Al-Awzāʿī said as well, "No one is more detestable to God تَعَالَىٰ than a scholar who frequents the agents of the ruler."[98]

The Messenger of God صَلَّىٱللَّهُعَلَيْهِوَسَلَّمَ stated, "The worst of the scholars are those who visit the rulers, and the best of the rulers are those who visit the scholars."[99]

Makḥūl al-Dimashqī رَحِمَهُ ٱللَّهُ related, "Anyone who learns the Qurʾān and gains an understanding of the religion, then keeps the company of the ruler, humbling himself before him, and desiring the wealth he possesses, has waded into the fire as deeply as the number of steps he has taken to get there."[100]

Saḥnūn stated, "Nothing is more loathsome for a scholar than for someone to come to his circle; and not find him, then asks him, [only] to be told, "He is with the prince."[101]

He also related that I used to hear it said, "When you see a scholar enamored of the world, distrust his sincerity in your religion." [I heard this] until I experienced that myself. After being in the presence of this ruler I never failed to call myself to account so that I might gain insight into what had occurred inwardly. You all know with what insolence, severity, and aversion to his predilections I confront him; and still I only wished I could be saved from

---

97 The narration ascribed here to Saʿīd b. al-Musayyab has been attributed to the Prophet from Abū Hurayra as, "When you see a scholar frequently in the company of the ruler, know that he is a thief." Narrated by al-Daylamī, *Musnad al-firdaws*, 1077, from al-Zabīdī, *Itḥāf*, 1:389.

98 Evidence for this is the narration of Abū Hurayra as attributed to the Prophet. Ibn Māja reports it with the wording: "The most detestable of God's creation is the scholar who frequents the agents of the ruler," from al-Zabīdī, *Itḥāf*, 1:389. This has been mentioned by al-Daylamī, *Musnad al-firdaws*, 822, and by al-Rāfiʿī, *al-Tadwīn fī akhbār qazwīn*, 3:450.

99 Ibn Māja, 256; in Abū Nuʿaym, *Ḥilya*, 3:243, citing a statement by Salama b. Dīnār.

100 This quote has been narrated from a *ḥadīth* of Muʿādh as attributed to the Prophet صَلَّىٱللَّهُعَلَيْهِوَسَلَّمَ, related by Abū l-Shaykh in *al-Thawāb* and by al-Ḥākim, *Tārīkh*, as "Should a man read the Qurʾān and gain understanding of the religion then go to the gate of the ruler, humbling himself to him and yearning for that which he possesses, he has waded into the fire of hell in accord with the steps he has taken," from al-Zabīdī, *Itḥāf*, 1:390.

101 Ibn ʿAbd al-Barr, *Jāmiʿ bayān al-ʿilm wa-faḍlih*, 1117.

even entering his presence; and given that, I never accepted from him a thing, not even a drink of water." Then he stated, "The scholars of our age are worse than the scholars of the children of Israel, they provide the ruler with legal proofs for the dispensations that accord with his own penchants; if the scholars had provided him with what he was responsible for and what [leads to] his eventual welfare and success, he would have found their company burdensome and shunned them, and this would be deliverance for them with their Lord."[102]

Ḥasan [al-Baṣrī] said, "Among those who preceded there was a man who came early to Islam and was a Companion of the Messenger of God ﷺ—ʿAbdallāh b. al-Mubārak [the narrator of this tradition] said here that, 'Ḥasan intended Saʿd b. Abū Waqqāṣ رضي الله عنه,' whose custom it was not to frequent rulers and in fact to shun them; so his sons asked of him, "Those who are not like you in companionship and precedence in Islam approach those rulers, if only you approached them [how honored you would be]."

To which he responded, "O my sons, should I approach a corpse encircled by people!? I swear by God, even if I were capable of that I would not join them." They said, 'O father, then we will perish frail and emaciated.'

He replied, "O my sons, it is more beloved to me that I die a frail believer than die a corpulent hypocrite."[103]

Ḥasan added, "He overcame them, I swear by God, for he knew that earth consumes flesh and fat, not faith in God."[104] This statement indicates that being in the presence of rulers gives no security from hypocrisy and it is in opposition to faith.

---

102 Al-Qāḍī ʿIyāḍ, *Tartīb al-madārik*, 1:357.

103 He رضي الله عنه continued in this state of forbearance and modest lifestyle until he encountered his Lord, alone in his palace located in al-ʿAqīq, in 55 H., he was carried by bearers and buried in Baqīʿ; he was the last to die of the ten who were promised paradise, and an example for those afflicted with trial and tribulation, and living proof of someone who found their refuge in the solitary life and avoiding the afflictions of social turmoil. Al-Zabīdī, *Itḥāf*, 1:391.

104 Ibn Abī l-Dunyā, *al-ʿUzla wa-l-infirād*, 202. It is related by al-Balādhurī, *Ansāb al-ashrāf*, 12:389. It is reported from Iyās b. Qatāda who was a follower.

Abū Dharr said to Salama, "O Salama, frequent not the gates of the rulers, you will not gain anything from their worldly goods but they will take something greater from your religion."[105]

All of this is a great trial and temptation for the scholars, and a harsh expedient for Satan to use against them, in particular for someone who is eloquent and sweet tongued; for Satan never ceases to suggest to him, "In your good counsel to them and your visits to them you constrain them from committing injustice and bring them to enact the precepts of the law"; until the scholar comes to imagine that associating with them is an aspect of religious practice; then when he comes into their presence, in no time he is exceedingly courteous in his speech and flatters them, then falls into praise and adulation; sincere religion perishes in comportment like this.

It has been said, "When scholars used to seek knowledge, they acted; and when they acted, they were devoted [to God], and when they were thus devoted [to God], they disappeared from the public eye, whereupon they were sought after [by the people], and when they were sought after, they fled."[106]

ʿUmar b. ʿAbd al-ʿAzīz wrote to Ḥasan [al-Baṣrī] رَحِمَهُ ٱللَّهُ, 'Now then, point out to me a folk from whom I can seek assistance concerning the affairs of God's commandments.'

Ḥasan wrote back, 'As for the [truly] religious people, they want nothing to do with you; as for the worldly, you want nothing to do with them; so seek out those of noble lineage, for they are protective of their nobility, lest they sully it with a betrayal.'[107]

---

105 Narrated by Ibn Abū Shayba, *al-Muṣannaf*, 38887.

106 Abū Nuʿaym, *Ḥilya*, 5:234; from Yazīd b. Maysira رَحِمَهُ ٱللَّهُ. In Abū Ṭālib al-Makkī, *Qūt al-qulūb*, this saying is attributed to Sufyān al-Thawrī. Al-Zabīdī's commentary on this passage helps clarify the metaphoric nature of this narration. He writes, "The learned, as they acquire knowledge, devote themselves to practice, and as they devote themselves to practice they become occupied with God تَعَالَىٰ, which is the result of sincere devotion [to God], and as they become occupied with God, they lose their human attributes and gain the attributes of the angels, when they lose their human attributes, and arrive to this stage, God causes love of them to descend upon the hearts of the inhabitants of the heavens and the earth and they become sought after, and as they become sought after, they flee from humankind seeking security from them and wellbeing of their own hearts." Al-Zabīdī, *Itḥāf*, 1:391.

107 Abū Ṭālib al-Makkī, *Qūt al-qulūb*, 1:134.

This narration is about ʿUmar b. ʿAbd al-ʿAzīz رَضِيَ ٱللَّهُ عَنْهُ, who was the most ascetic person of his age; if [according to Ḥasan] a condition of being a [truly] religious person meant avoiding him, in what manner can [one] justify seeking out others, among the rulers, and frequenting them?

The scholars among the predecessors, such as Ḥasan, al-Thawrī, Ibn al-Mubārak, Fuḍayl, Ibrāhīm b. Adham, and Yūsuf b. Asbāṭ relented and [agreed] not to criticize the worldly scholars from among the learned of Mecca, Shām [greater Syria] and other regions in their discourse, either because they are inclined to worldly well-being, or [because] they frequent the rulers.

Among the traits of a scholar of the hereafter is that he does not hasten to issue rulings; in fact he constrains himself and shuns its perils as long as he can find a means to evade it. If one were questioned on a matter he had knowledge of based on the text of the Book of God, of the text of a *ḥadīth*, or consensus, or clear analogy, he would offer an opinion. However if he were questioned about a matter upon which he had doubts, he would say, "I do not know." If he were asked about an opinion that he had arrived at after considerable thought and effort, he would warily defend his own position while proffering the opinion of another, if the other opinion were competent.

This is being judicious, for the danger of exercising independent judgment is great.

A report relates, "There are three branches of knowledge: the manifest text of the book, the established *sunna*, and 'I do not know.'"[108]

Al-Shaʿbī stated, "Half of knowledge is [being able to say] 'I do not know.'"[109]

The recompense of one who remains silent for the sake of God's good grace when he has no knowledge [of something], is no less than one who engages in discourse; this is because acknowledging one's ignorance is more difficult for the soul to bear, this was also the custom of the Companions and the predecessors رَحِمَهُمُ ٱللَّهُ. When Ibn ʿUmar was asked for a ruling he replied, "Go to such and such

108 This is ascribed to Ibn ʿUmar رَضِيَ ٱللَّهُ عَنْهُمَا, narrated by al-Ṭabarānī, *al-Muʿjam al-awsaṭ*, 1005; also in Ibn ʿAbd al-Barr, *Jāmiʿ bayān al-ʿilm wa-faḍlih*, 1387.

109 Al-Dārimī, *Sunan*, 186.

commander who has taken on the obligations of the people and place it around his neck."[110]

Ibn Masʿūd رضي الله عنه said, "Anyone who delivers rulings for every legal inquiry people ask of him is certainly crazy."[111]

He said as well, "The scholar's shield is 'I do not know,' [for] if he errs in its use, his vital organs will be struck."[112]

Ibrāhīm b. Adham رحمه الله stated, "There is nothing more difficult for Satan to bear than a scholar who speaks when knowledge dictates, and is silent when knowledge dictates. He declares, 'Look at this one, his silence is harder for me to bear than his discourse!'"[113]

Some early scholars depicted the *abdāl*[114] as saying, "They eat only out of necessity; and speak only out of necessity."[115] Meaning, they speak not until questioned, and when questioned, if they find one who suffices them [in responding], they remain silent. If they are obliged, they respond; however, they consider initiating discourse before being questioned a hidden yearning to speak [and be heard].

ʿAlī and ʿAbdallāh [b. Masʿūd] رضي الله عنهما passed a man who was engaged in discourse with some people; they said, "This one is saying, 'Know me well.'"[116]

Someone said, "a scholar is the one who, when questioned on a matter [of religion], feels as though he were having a molar removed."[117]

Ibn ʿUmar used to say, "You want to make of us a bridge by which you cross over to the abode of hell?"[118]

---

110 Abū Ṭālib al-Makkī, *Qūt al-qulūb*, 1:131.

111 Al-Dārimī, *Sunan*, 176.

112 Cited by al-Ṣanʿānī, *al-Amālī fī āthār al-ṣaḥāba*, 162; this saying has been cited by other predecessors as well.

113 Abū Nuʿaym has narrated the likes in *Ḥilya*, 8:26.

114 *Abdāl* (sing. *badal*) means "substitutes," a group of people variously numbered at four, seven, forty, or seventy; they form an essential part of Sufi cosmological hierarchy. These friends of God are divinely chosen to communicate blessing and mediate miracles in post-prophetic ages. Renard, *Historical Dictionary*, 229.

115 Abū Ṭālib al-Makkī, *Qūt al-qulūb*, 1:154. The one giving this depiction is Fazāra al-Shāmī as indicated elsewhere.

116 Abū Ṭālib al-Makkī, *Qūt al-qulūb*, 1:155.

117 Abū Ṭālib al-Makkī, *Qūt al-qulūb*, 1:155, and *al-Jāmiʿ li-akhlāq al-rāwī wa ādāb al-sāmiʿ*, 1459, has something similar.

118 Abū Ṭālib al-Makkī, *Qūt al-qulūb*, 1:155, clarifies what Ibn ʿUmar meant: "Because you will say, Ibn ʿUmar gave us a legal opinion on this."

Abū Ḥafṣ al-Nīsābūrī said, "The scholar is the one who, when asked a question, dreads that he will be asked [about it] on the day of judgment, 'From where did you answer?'"[119]

When questioned on a matter, Ibrāhīm al-Taymī used to weep and say, "Could you find none other than myself, until you were obliged to come to me?"[120]

It was the wont of Abū l-ʿĀlīya al-Riyāḥī, Ibrāhīm [al-Nakhaʿī], Ibrāhīm b. Adham, and [Sufyān] al-Thawrī to only engage in discourse with two or three individuals or a small gathering of up to ten, if the number increased they would depart.[121]

The Messenger of God ﷺ stated, "I do not know if Ezra [ʿUzayr][122] was a prophet or not, I do not know if Tubbaʿ[123] is cursed or not, and I do not know if Dhū l-Qarnayn[124] was a prophet or not."[125]

When the Messenger of God was questioned about the most worthy and most evil places on the earth he responded, "I do not know," and even when Gabriel questioned him about them he responded, "I do not know." Then God عَزَّوَجَلَّ taught him that the most worthy place was the mosque and the most evil were the market places.[126]

When Ibn ʿUmar رَضِيَٱللَّهُعَنْهُمَا was asked about ten issues, he responded on one issue and kept silent on the other nine.[127] Whereas, Ibn ʿAbbās رَضِيَٱللَّهُعَنْهُمَا, when asked about ten matters, responded to nine and remained silent about the one remaining.[128]

Among the [early] jurists the ones who said, "I do not know" were more numerous than those who declared, "I know"; among [the

---

119 Abū Ṭālib al-Makkī, *Qūt al-qulūb*, 1:155.

120 Abū Ṭālib al-Makkī, *Qūt al-qulūb*, 1:155.

121 Abū Ṭālib al-Makkī, *Qūt al-qulūb*, 1:155.

122 Referred to in the Qurʾān 9:30, *And the Jews say, "Ezra is the son of God"*; his story is in 2:259.

123 Tubbaʿ is referred to in the Qurʾān: *Are they, then, better than the people of Tubbaʿ and those before them? We destroyed them, [for] indeed, they were criminals* [44:37]; *And the companions of the thicket and the people of Tubbaʿ* [50:14].

124 Dhū l-Qarnayn, lit., 'the two-horned one' is referred to in Qurʾān 18:83–98.

125 Abū Dāwūd, 4674, and the last phrase is in from al-Ḥākim al-Nīsābūrī, *al-Mustadrak*, 2:14.

126 Al-Ṭabarānī, *al-Muʿjam al-awsaṭ*, 7136.

127 Abū Ṭālib al-Makkī, *Qūt al-qulūb*, 1:131.

128 Abū Ṭālib al-Makkī, *Qūt al-qulūb*, 1:131.

former] were Sufyān al-Thawrī, Mālik b. Anas, Aḥmad b. Ḥanbal, al-Fuḍayl b. ʿIyāḍ, and Bishr b. al-Ḥārith."[129]

ʿAbd al-Raḥmān b. Abī Laylā related, "In this mosque [in Medina] I encountered one hundred twenty Companions of the Messenger of God ﷺ; every one of them, if asked about a *ḥadīth*, or a ruling, preferred that his brothers would suffice him in responding."[130] According to another version, he said, "If one of them was presented with a question, he would refer it to another, and he would turn it over to another until it returned to the first person asked."

It has been narrated that a roasted [sheep's] head was bestowed on one of the People of the Bench[131] who was in the utmost need; he bestowed it in turn on another who bestowed it on another, it circulated thus among them until it returned to the first one.[132]

Regard carefully how the affairs of the scholars of today have become the opposite of this; that which was shunned is sought and that which was sought is shunned.

The evidence for the preference to avoid giving rulings is what has been reported as traceable back to him ﷺ; he stated, "Only three people should issue rulings, the ruler, or one commanded to do so [by the ruler] or one who is posturing."[133]

---

129 Abū Ṭālib al-Makkī, *Qūt al-qulūb*, 1:131.

130 Abū Ṭālib al-Makkī, *Qūt al-qulūb*, 1:131; Ibn ʿAsākir, *Tārīkh Dimashq*, 36:87.

131 The People of the Bench were a group of early Muslims known as *ahl* (or *aṣḥāb*, "companions") *al-ṣuffa*, who lived in poverty in a portico attached to the Prophet's mosque in Medina. They thus modeled simplicity of life and utter dedication to the Prophet ﷺ. Some traditional sources have seen in the Arabic word for bench (*ṣuffa*) a possible etymological origin of the term *ṣūfī*. Renard, *Historical Dictionary of Sufism*, 52.

132 Imām al-Ghazālī cites this occurrence here as an example of the matter of passing the request for a ruling from one to another until it comes back to one originally asked. Al-Zabīdī, *Itḥāf* 1:398.

133 Abū Ṭālib al-Makkī, *Qūt al-qulūb*, 1:131, who said, "We have reported it as traceable to..."; Aḥmad b. Ḥanbal, *al-Musnad*, 6:22, reports something similar; al-Ṭabarī, *al-Muʿjam al-kabir*, 18:76, who begins the narration with, "No one should give a public address except the commander..." There are many other reports to support this.

Some of the early scholars related, "The Companions avoided four things: leadership, taking charge of property entrusted to someone, last wills and testaments, and dispensing rulings."[134]

One of them said, "The swiftest among them to give a ruling was the least of them in knowledge; while the one who was most reticent to do that was the most scrupulous."[135]

The Companions and the Followers رَضِيَ اللَّهُ عَنْهُمْ occupied themselves with five matters: reciting the Qurʾān, spending time in the mosque [in prayer], remembering God, and commanding good and forbidding evil. That was because they heard his صَلَّى اللَّهُ عَلَيْهِ وَسَلَّمَ statement, "Every word uttered by a son of Adam will be against him, not in his favor, except three [things he said], enjoining worthy conduct, forbidding that which is contemptible, and remembering God تَعَالَى."[136]

And God says, *No good is there in much of their private conversation, except for those who enjoin charity or that which is right or conciliation between people. And whoever does that seeking means to the approval of God—then We are going to give him a great reward* [4:114].

One of the early scholars saw one of the people of opinion of Kufa in a dream. The one who had the dream asked him, "What have you discovered about your views on rulings and opinion?" At this, he grimaced and turned away from him, and said, "We found it all for nothing, with no laudable end."[137]

[ʿUthmān b. ʿĀṣim] Abū Ḥaṣīn said, "One of them issues a ruling on a matter which, if it had been asked of ʿUmar b. al-Khaṭṭāb, he would have called together the People of Badr [in consultation]."[138]

Reticence to speak on the part of the early scholars was their custom except in the case of urgent necessity. In a report it states, "If you see a man who is silent and an ascetic, approach him, for he [will] bestow wisdom."[139]

---

134 Abū Ṭālib al-Makkī, *Qūt al-qulūb*, 1:132.

135 Abū Ṭālib al-Makkī, *Qūt al-qulūb*, 1:132; Ibn ʿAbd al-Barr, *Jāmiʿ bayān al-ʿilm wa-faḍlih*, 1525.

136 Al-Tirmidhī, 2412; Ibn Māja, 3974.

137 Abū Ṭālib al-Makkī, *Qūt al-qulūb*, 1:132.

138 Al-Bayhaqī, *al-Madkhal*, 803; and Ibn ʿAsākir, *Tārīkh Dimashq*, 38:410.

139 Ibn Māja, 4101.

It was said, "A scholar is either a scholar of the [common] folk, who issues rulings—they are the companions of the pillars of the mosques; or [he is] a scholar of the elect, who is knowledgeable of oneness and of the acts of the hearts—they are the companions of the lodges and live in seclusion."[140]

It was once stated, "Aḥmad b. Ḥanbal is like the Tigris River, everyone comes and dips their cup into it and draws water; Bishr b. al-Ḥārith is like a covered well of sweet water, people only approach it one at a time."[141]

They used to say, "So-and-so is a scholar, so-and-so is a theologian, so-and-so talks more, and so-and-so is more knowledgeable."[142]

Abū Sulaymān [al-Dārānī] said, "Realization is closer to silence than it is to discourse."[143]

A scholar of old related, "When knowledge increases, discourse decreases."[144]

Salmān [al-Fārisī] wrote to Abū l-Dardāʾ رضي الله عنهما whom the Messenger of God صلى الله عليه وسلم made his brother in the Pact of Brotherhood of Medina;[145] "O my brother, it has reached me that you have established yourself as a physician prescribing medicine to the ailing and unwell; regard this issue carefully, if you are truly a physician, then speak, for your discourse will surely be a remedy; but if you were only putting on the appearances of a physician—O God—O God—do not be the cause of a Muslim's death!" From that time on, Abū l-Dardāʾ was hesitant to respond when asked [for a ruling].[146]

When Anas b. Mālik رضي الله عنه was asked a question, he would say, "Ask my master Ḥasan [al-Baṣrī]."[147]

[Likewise] Ibn ʿAbbās رضي الله عنهما, when questioned, would respond, "Ask Jābir b. Zayd."[148]

---

140 Abū Ṭālib al-Makkī, *Qūt al-qulūb*, 1:132.

141 Abū Ṭālib al-Makkī, *Qūt al-qulūb*, 1:132.

142 Abū Ṭālib al-Makkī, *Qūt al-qulūb*, 1:132. Al-Ghazālī intended to show the difference between knowledge and discourse.

143 Abū Ṭālib al-Makkī, *Qūt al-qulūb*, 1:132.

144 Abū Ṭālib al-Makkī, *Qūt al-qulūb*, 1:132.

145 Al-Bukhārī, 1968.

146 Abū Ṭālib al-Makkī, *Qūt al-qulūb*, 1:147.

147 Narrated by Ibn Abī Shayba, *al-Muṣannaf*, 36745.

148 Abū Ṭālib al-Makkī, *Qūt al-qulūb*, 1:147.

And Ibn ʿUmar رَضِيَ ٱللَّهُ عَنْهُمَا would say, "Ask Saʿīd b. al-Musayyab."[149]

It has been related that a Companion narrated twenty *ḥadīth* in the presence of Ḥasan [al-Baṣrī] and was then questioned about the explanation of each; so he said, "I can only possess what I have narrated [to you]." So Ḥasan began to explain each *ḥadīth*, one by one, while those present marveled at his comprehensive memory and his detailed explanations, until the Companion took up a handful of pebbles and cast them at those present, saying, "You question me about matters of understanding, and this erudite scholar is among you?!"[150]

Among the traits of a scholar of the hereafter is that the greater part of his devotion to knowledge is to the knowledge of inward reality, contemplation of the heart, and realization of the path and journey to the hereafter;[151] and sincere hope lies in its unveiling through striving [in God's cause] and meditation. For striving leads to unveiling of the subtleties of the sciences of hearts, and through them founts of wisdom flow forth from the heart. As for texts and formal education, these do not suffice in that. Rather the wisdom that surpasses all reckoning and conception reveals itself through [spiritual] striving, and meditation. The practice of outward and inward actions, sitting with God تَعَالَىٰ in solitary retreat with presence of heart and pure reflection while severing one's ties to all but God تَعَالَىٰ; that is the key to inspiration and the fountain of unveiling. How many have long been striving to acquire knowledge but are not capable of going beyond the literal sense of the words he has heard? And how many have limited their education to the essentials, are steadfast in practice and contemplation of the heart, such that God has opened to them the subtleties of wisdom that would confound the intellects of [even] those bestowed with perception.

149 Narrated by Ibn Saʿd, *Ṭabaqāt al-kabīr*, 7:140; Abū Ṭālib al-Makkī, *Qūt al-qulūb*, 1:148.

150 Abū Ṭālib al-Makkī, *Qūt al-qulūb*, 1:147.

151 This occurs through the mediation of a perfected guide or skilled gnostic, in whose assembly one gains the benefit of that (mediation). See al-Zabīdī, *Itḥāf*, 1:402.

This explains the saying of the Messenger of God ﷺ, "Whoever implements his acquired knowledge, God will make an heir to knowledge not known to him."[152]

In one of the previous scriptures, it states, "O Children of Israel, do not say: knowledge is in heaven, who will come down with it? Or, that it is in the depths of the earth, who will bring it up? Or, it is beyond the seas, who will cross over and bring it? Knowledge is secured in your hearts. Learn, in My presence, the demeanor of the spiritual adepts and mold [yourselves] for My sake in the moral character of the veracious. I will make that knowledge manifest in your hearts so that it covers you and fills you to overflowing."[153]

Sahl b. ʿAbdallāh al-Tustarī used to say, "The scholars, servants, and ascetics all leave this world and their hearts are locked; only the hearts of the veracious and the martyrs are unlocked. Then he recited, *And with Him are the keys of the unseen; none knows them except Him. And He knows what is on the land and in the sea. Not a leaf falls but that He knows it. And no grain is there within the darknesses of the earth and no moist or dry* [*thing*] *but that it is* [*written*] *in a clear record* [6:59].[154]

If the discernment of the heart—of one who has a heart—by its inner light did not rule over outward knowledge, the Messenger of God ﷺ would not have said, "Ask your heart for a ruling, even if they give you a ruling, even if they give you a ruling, even if they give you a ruling."[155]

He ﷺ stated, in that which he related from his Lord, "My servant continues to draw near to me with supererogatory acts [of worship] until I love him. When I love him, I am his hearing with which he hears, and his sight with which he sees, and his hand with which he strikes, and his foot with which he walks. If he were to

152 Narrated by Abū Nuʿaym, *Ḥilya*, 10:14.

153 Abū Ṭālib al-Makkī, *Qūt al-qulūb*, 1:137.

154 Abū Ṭālib al-Makkī, *Qūt al-qulūb*, 1:152.

155 Aḥmad b. Ḥanbal, *Musnad*, 4:228. This is specified for someone who has a heart and listens carefully to it. He witnesses what is established by its evidence while he is free of its desires and commitment. This is the case because understanding is not merely a verbal description. See al-Zabīdī, *Itḥāf*, 1:403.

ask [something] of Me, I would surely give it to him; and were he to seek refuge with Me, I would surely grant him refuge."[156]

Many subtle meanings of the secrets of the Qurʾān arise within the hearts of those who have committed themselves to remembrance and contemplation, [meanings] that the commentaries are devoid of and the worthy commentators have never encountered. And should that be unveiled to the introspective disciple, and then shown to the commentators[157] they would recognize its merit, know that it was from exhortations of untainted hearts and from the delicate grace of God تَعَالَىٰ through the lofty aspirations directed toward Him. Such is the case with the sciences of unveiling and the secrets of the sciences of [proper] conduct, and the subtleties of the promptings of the hearts. Verily, every one of these sciences is an unfathomable ocean into which every seeker plunges to the capacity of what has been provided for him, and in accordance with the worthy acts he has been destined to achieve.

[Imām ʿAlī رَضِيَ ٱللَّهُ عَنْهُ on Scholars of the Hereafter]

ʿAlī رَضِيَ ٱللَّهُ عَنْهُ characterized these scholars in a lengthy *ḥadīth*, saying,

> "Hearts are vessels, the best of them contain the most. People are of three kinds: those learned in the affairs of their Lord, those who seek knowledge along the path of salvation, and the common [folk] that follow after every braying fool, and incline in the direction of every breeze, they do not seek to be illuminated by the light of knowledge, nor take shelter in a well-established refuge. Knowledge is superior to wealth; knowledge will guard you, whereas you must guard wealth. Knowledge increases as it is dispensed, whereas wealth decreases as it is spent. Love of knowledge is a religion by which one lives; it vouchsafes obedience throughout one's life and worthy words after one's death. Knowledge passes judgment, whereas wealth is subject

156 Al-Bukhārī, 6502.

157 They are the righteous commentators who are protected from attachments to desire. See al-Zabīdī, *Itḥāf*, 1:404.

> to judgment. The usefulness of wealth diminishes as it dwindles. Those hoarding wealth perish, even while still alive; whereas scholars remain as long as time goes on.

Then ʿAlī رَضِيَ اللَّهُ عَنْهُ sighed deeply and said,

> "Ah! Herein [and he pointed to his chest][158] is abundant knowledge, if I could but find a bearer for it. Instead all I find is an unreliable seeker who uses the tools of religion in pursuit of worldly gain, who talks endlessly about the blessings God bestows upon His saints, and makes a show of his proofs to people. Or I find a person who blindly follows the people of Truth, yet at the first inkling of any ambiguity doubt is sown in his heart and he has no insight. Neither of these two types [are guardians of the religion];[159] neither this one nor that one. Neither the person who is accustomed to pleasure and easily swayed to satisfy his cravings, nor one who is seduced by accumulating and hoarding wealth; a captive of his own passions; they resemble grazing cattle more than anything.
>
> O God, this is how knowledge perishes, when those who bear it perish. The earth, however, will never be empty of one who upholds God's proofs—whether apparent and revealed, or in fear and duress—so that the clear proofs of God and their elucidation might not come to naught. But how many are they in number and where are they? They are few in number, of immense worth. The prominent [ones] are no longer to be found [in our day], but their likenesses exist in the hearts of humankind. Through them God safeguards His proofs until He safely consigns them to the hearts of those like them, and sows them in the hearts of those resembling them. Through them, the knowledge of the essential realities takes hold and they directly experience the spirit of certitude. They take their comfort in what

158 The addition in brackets is from al-Zabīdī, *Itḥāf*, 1:405, and makes the phrase more comprehensible.

159 The addition in brackets is from Abū Ṭālib al-Makkī, *Qūt al-qulūb*, 1:134; in al-Zabīdī, *Itḥāf*, 1:405.

> those accustomed to comfort shun, and are accustomed to what the heedless find repugnant. They keep the company of this world with their physical bodies, while their souls are conjoined to the loftiest abode. These are the saints of God عَزَّوَجَلَّ among his creation; His trustees and agents on His earth and those who call to His religion."

Then ʿAlī رَضِيَٱللَّهُعَنْهُ wept and said, "What I would give for a glimpse of them."[160]

This portion, cited at the end of the text, is his characterization of the scholars of the hereafter, it is the knowledge whose benefit derives most from steadfast action and devotion to [spiritual] striving.

[Scholars of the Hereafter and Certitude]

Among the traits of a scholar of the hereafter is that he is steadfast in giving everything to strengthen his certitude. For certitude is the foundational principle of religion. The Messenger of God صَلَّىٱللَّهُعَلَيْهِوَسَلَّمَ stated, "Certitude is faith in its entirety."[161]

It is essential to learn the knowledge of certitude, by which I mean its beginning stages, whereupon the heart will open to its pathways; for this reason the Prophet صَلَّىٱللَّهُعَلَيْهِوَسَلَّمَ said, "Learn the knowledge of certitude."[162] In other words, keep the company of those endowed with certitude and hear the knowledge of certitude from them, be steadfast in following their example, that you may strengthen your certitude as theirs became strong. A modicum of certitude is superior to an abundance of acts.

[The Prophet] صَلَّىٱللَّهُعَلَيْهِوَسَلَّمَ, when asked about an individual of worthy certitude but many sins, and another, steadfast in his worship, but with little certitude replied, "Every human being has sins, but when someone is naturally disposed to intelligence and is disposed toward certitude, his sins do him no harm; for whenever he

---

160 Narrated by Abū Nuʿaym, *Ḥilya*, 1:79–80; Abū Ṭālib al-Makkī cites this tradition twice in *Qūt al-qulūb*, in its entirety at 1:134, then with some commentary at 1:143. See al-Zabīdī, *Itḥāf* as well for detailed account of this tradition, 1:405–406. And al-Khaṭīb al-Baghdādī, *Tārīkh Baghdād*, 6:376.

161 Narrated by Abū Nuʿaym, *Ḥilya*, 5:34; and al-Bayhaqī, *Shuʿab al-īmān*, 9265.

162 Narrated by Abū Nuʿaym, *Ḥilya*, 6:95; and Ibn Abī l-Dunyā, *al-Yaqīn*, 7.

sins, he repents, asks forgiveness, and feels contrition. Thus his sins are atoned for, leaving him ample grace that will gain him entrance to paradise."[163]

For this reason he ﷺ said, "The very least [of the blessings God] bestowed on you are certitude and persevering patience, for the one who has been given his share of these two, it does not matter if he neglects his nightly vigils or daytime [voluntary] fasting."[164]

In his advice to his son, Luqmān said, "O my dear son, knowledge without certitude is not possible, a person only acts in accord with his certitude; one who acts diminishes not in his efforts until his certitude diminishes."[165]

Yaḥyā b. Muʿādh said, "Verily, in unity there is light, and in idolatry there is fire; the light of unity burns away the sins of the people of unity more completely than the fire of idolatry burns away any worthy deeds of the idolaters."[166] He meant by the light of unity, certitude.

God تَعَالَىٰ alludes to those of resolute certitude in several places in the Qurʾān, emphasizing that certitude is the binding link between well-being [in this world] and salvation [in the hereafter].[167]

If you were to ask: "What does certitude signify, and what makes it strong or weak? First and foremost, before one undertakes the pursuit and learning of a matter it is absolutely necessary to com-

---

163 Narrated by al-Ḥākim al-Tirmidhī, *Nawādir al-uṣūl*, 242; Abū Ṭālib al-Makkī, *Qūt al-qulūb*, 1:135; also see al-Zabīdī, *Itḥāf*, 1:409; Ibn Ḥajar al-ʿAsqalanī, *al-Maṭālib al-ʿāliyya*, 7:266, 269.

164 Abū Ṭālib al-Makkī says in *Qūt al-qulūb*, 1:194, "It is reported from him ﷺ that patience is the perfection of action and reward. He mentioned it in a narration reported by Shahr Ḥūshab al-Ashʿarī, from Abū Umāma al-Bāhilī, from the Prophet ﷺ. He said also it is a statement of ʿAlī in *al-Asrār al-marfūʿa*." This is derived from the verse of God تَعَالَىٰ, *And mankind have not been given of knowledge except a little* [17:85]. As for persevering patience in action, this is also little, as God تَعَالَىٰ says, *except for those who believe and do righteous deeds—and few are they* [38:24].

165 Abū Ṭālib al-Makkī, *Qūt al-qulūb*, 1:135; also see al-Zabīdī, *Itḥāf*, 1:410.

166 Abū Ṭālib al-Makkī, *Qūt al-qulūb*, 1:136; also see al-Zabīdī, *Itḥāf*, 1:410.

167 For example: *We have shown clearly the signs to a people who are certain [in faith]* [2:118]; *And we made from among them leaders, guiding by our command when they were patient and [when] they were certain of Our signs* [32:24]; *This [Qurʾān] is enlightenment for mankind, and a guidance and a mercy for a people who are certain [in faith]* [45:20]; *And on earth are signs for the certain [in faith]* [51:20].

prehend its meaning; for indeed when the formal guise of a matter is not understood, it is impossible to pursue it."

Know then, that certitude is an expression applied in common by two groups of scholars who employ it for different meanings.

With regard to the proponents of speculation and the theologians, they use it to express an absence of doubt;[168] since the soul's inclination to assess the veracity of a thing has four stations.

The first station comprises an equal assessment of a matter's veracity or falsehood; this is referred to as doubt. [This is] similar to a case in which someone asks you whether or not God تعالى will chastise a particular individual who is unknown to you; your soul does not incline to a judgment on him in the affirmative or the negative; the possibility of each assessments is equal; this is termed doubt.

The second station involves your soul inclining toward one of two assessments while holding the possibility of the other [being the case], but because it is just a possibility, it does not refute the first opinion. [This is] similar to being asked about the piety and rectitude of a specific individual that you are familiar with and whether or not he will be chastised by God if he were to die in this state. Here your soul inclines toward his not being chastised more than it inclines that he will be; this is becaues of the evident signs of [his] piety. Yet in spite of this, you admit the possibility of there being something hidden in his inner soul and innermost being that could merit chastisement. In this case, the possibility is proportionate to that inclination, but this does not negate its being the most likely scenario; this station is termed supposition.

The third station comprises the soul's inclination to the affirmation of a thing in such a way that it is convinced and no other option comes to mind; and if it does so the soul would reject it. This however is not founded upon verifiable realization, for should the person at this station carefully evaluate and listen to the discursive arguments that give rise to doubt and present other options that could be the case, his soul assents to their being possibilities; this is termed conviction that approaches certitude. This is the conviction of the common people in all the matters of the law, as they have

168 Doubt is its opposite. This is according to the school of linguistics. Al-Zabīdī, *Itḥāf*, 1:410.

become implanted within them from solely hearing [from the scholars]. [This happens to] the point that every partisan group trusts the veracity of its own school and the sagacity of its founder and those who follow his school. If anyone goes before them and contends [that there is a] possibility of error on the part of his founder, he would be wholly averse to accepting it.[169]

The fourth station [in their opinion] comprises verifiable realization attained by way of demonstrative argumentation in which there is no doubt whatsoever, nor is doubt even conceivable therein; when the existence of any doubt and or its possibility are negated, this knowledge is called certitude in their terms.

An example of this is, if [one] asked an intelligent individual, "Is there anything in existence that is pre-eternal?" Now, it is not possible to assess the veracity of this intuitively, for pre-eternity [as a concept] is imperceptible, unlike the sun or the moon; for the veracity of the existence of these two [comes from] the senses. Nor is the knowledge of the existence of a beginningless, pre-eternal thing necessary in the way that the knowledge that two are more than one is; or even similar to the knowledge that the occurrence of an event without any prior cause is impossible; for this too is necessary. It is therefore not unjustified for the natural impulse of the intellect to be reticent to affirm the veracity of the existence of pre-eternity based on an extemporary and intuitive manner.

Then, there are those people who hear of [pre-eternity] and categorically affirm its veracity, and continue thus over time, based solely on the authority of hearing; that is conviction, and it is the state of all the common folk. There are other people that affirm its veracity based upon proof, in that it is said to them, If there were not in existence that which was pre-eternal, and given, that all extant beings are phenomena; then, if they were all phenomena, they are phenomena without an [original] cause, or there is among them a phenomenon without an [original] cause, and that is impossible; and that which occasions the impossible is impossible. The intellect subsequently affirms the veracity of the existence of something pre-eternal necessarily. This is because of the three categories, which are: all existent beings are pre-eternal, or all are phenomena,

169 See al-Ghazālī, *al-Iqtiṣād fī l-iʿtiqād*, 228, for an in-depth exposition of this point.

or some are pre-eternal and some are phenomena; if all existence were pre-eternal our objective has been achieved—since it affirms the pre-eternity of the entirety [of existence]; if the entirety were phenomena, then this is impossible, as it results in the existence of phenomena without a cause; this then affirms the veracity of either, the third category or the first category.

All knowledge assimilated in this manner is termed by those scholars [of speculation] knowledge of certitude: [regardless of] whether it was acquired by speculation as we have mentioned, or by way of sense perception, or by means of the natural disposition of the intellect, such as knowledge of the impossibility of a phenomena without a cause; or by way of unanimous narration from reliable sources,[170] like the knowledge that Mecca exists [even though you have not been there]; or by way of direct observation, such as the knowledge that cooked scammony[171] is a purgative; or by evidence as we mentioned earlier.

The condition for employing this term, for them, is the non-existence of doubt in their terminology; every knowledge in which there is no doubt whatsoever is called certitude. Given this meaning for the term, certitude cannot be qualified with the attribute of weakness, as there are no variant degrees in the negation of doubt.

The second terminology [involving the knowledge of certitude] is the term employed by the jurists, the people of the Sufi path, and the majority of scholars. It is not at all involved with considerations of probability or doubt; on the contrary, it involves the manner in which this knowledge overwhelms and prevails over the heart, until it could be said, So-and-so is weak in his certitude of death, even though he does not doubt its eventuality; or it could be said, So-and-so is strong in his certitude of his sustenance being provided him [from God], despite his acknowledging that it may not be provided him.

So, however the soul may incline toward affirming the veracity of a matter, and it has overwhelmed his heart, and dominated it

---

170 *Tawātur* refers to a report from a large enough number of narrators to make an agreement to lie inconceivable.

171 Scammony: An eastern Mediterranean plant (*Convolvulus scammonia*) having large roots that yield a resin formerly used as a cathartic. Al-Zabīdī, *Itḥāf*, 1:413.

to the point it becomes the judging and determining factor in the soul in assessing possibility and refutation, that is termed certitude.

There is no doubt that humankind all share the conviction of the eventuality of death and entertain not the slightest doubt regarding its imminence; yet among them are those that pay it no heed, nor do they make preparations for it, as though they were not certain of its eventuality at all; whereas [there are others] among them whose hearts have been overcome by it to the point that the entirety of their concerns are immersed in preparation for it, leaving no room for any other pursuits. A state such as this is expressed as strength of certitude. One of the scholars said, "I have not seen certitude devoid of all doubt, more similar to doubt devoid of all certitude than I have seen in [people's attitudes toward] death."[172]

In accordance with this terminology, it is possible to qualify certitude with the attributes of weakness and strength.

We intended by our statement, "The distinguishing trait of scholars of the hereafter is resolute dedication to strengthening their certitude," the combining of two meanings: on the one hand the negation of all doubt; on the other, the governance of certainty over the soul such that it is the dominant factor for judgment and determination.

When you have understood this you know what we intended in our statement, "Verily, certitude is devisable into three categories: weakness and strength, decrease and increase, and hidden and apparent."

As for the attribution of strength and weakness, according to the second use of the term [as employed by the jurists, the people of the Sufi path, and the majority of scholars], in the sense of overwhelming and dominating the heart; the degrees of certitude between strength and weakness have no end. The disparity between the people in their preparations for death according to the disparity of their certitude indicates this meaning.

As for the variation of hidden and apparent, there is no dispute therein either, for it pertains to that which prompts possibility[173]

---

172 Abū Nuʿaym narrated this from Salama b. Dīnār, *Ḥilya*, 3:232.

173 This is the second stage of the first use of the term certitude. Al-Zabīdī, *Itḥāf*, 1:415.

which in turn cannot be disputed—I mean in the second use of the term, or in that which negates doubt therein also for which there is no means of disputing it. For you surely discern a disparity between your affirmation of the existence of Mecca and the existence of Fadak, for example, and between your affirmation of the existence of Moses and the existence of Yūsha [Joshua][174] عَلَيْهِمَاالسَّلَامُ, although you have no doubt about either matter at all, as the knowledge of both is based upon *tawātur*. Yet one of them is more distinct and definite in your heart than the second because the reason behind one of them is stronger based on the greater number of reliable sources. In a similar manner, the speculative thinker achieves this result through known speculation based on evidence, for the clarity [of a theory] derived through one proof is not dissimilar to the clarity of one derived through multiple proofs, though they may be equal in dispelling doubt. The theologian who acquired his knowledge from books and oral transmissions would most likely deny this and not call his own soul to account over the disparate states it encounters.

[Increase and Decrease of Certitude]

As for decrease and increase, this is due to the numerous associated aspects of certitude; just as it is said, "So-and-so is more knowledgeable than so-and-so," meaning, that which he knows is more vast. In like manner a scholar may be sound in his certitude in all aspects of the dictates of the law, or he may be sound only in his certitude of a part of them.

Should you ask: I have understood the meaning [and stations] of certitude, its qualities of strength and weakness, its decrease and increase, and its being apparent and hidden, meaning the negation of doubt on the one hand, or overwhelming the heart, on the other; so what are the associated elements of certitude and its currents, and in what is certitude to be striven for? For as long as I do not know wherein certitude is to be sought, I will be incapable of seeking it."

Know that the totality of that which the prophets and messengers عَلَيْهِمُالسَّلَامُ have brought, from the first to the last are the currents

174 Yūsha is not mentioned specifically in the Qurʾān but it is held that he was the youth who accompanied Moses on his journey to find Khiḍr in Qurʾān 18:59.

that derive from certitude. For the word 'certitude' [itself] alludes to a specific realization and is associated with known objects by which laws are obtained. One could never hope to enumerate them all, yet I will allude here to some of the most essential of them.

Among them is unity, which is that one perceives all things coming from the Cause of all causes and lends no credence to means, perceiving means as subservient entities having no autonomy of determination, one who asserts the veracity of this is a person of faith. Then, if he has negated any possibility of doubt from his heart filled with faith, then one becomes a person of certitude, according to one of the two meanings of the term. Then, if his heart is completely overwhelmed with faith, there ceases to be in him any anger toward the means, or any contentment with them and gratitude for them. In his heart, the means sit like a pen and the hand [in the way] that a benefactor's right of disposal [is] by way of his signature. No one is grateful toward the pen, nor toward the hand [that signed the document], nor is one angry toward them, instead they are seen as subservient entities and means. Such a person is a person of certitude in accordance with the second meaning of the term, and this is the loftier of the two, and it is the fruit of the first certitude, its spirit and consequence.

To the degree that one realizes that the sun, the moon, the stars, the minerals, plants and animals, and every created being are obedient to His command, as the pen is to the hand of the writer and that the pre-eternal [divine] power is the origin of all existence, his heart will be overwhelmed with the dominance of reliance [upon God], contentment [with Him], and surrender [to His will], and [he will] become a 'person of certitude,' exempt of all anger, malice, jealousy, and malevolent character. This is one of the doorways of certitude.

Among them is trust in God's سُبْحَانَهُ guarantee of sustenance in His تَعَالَىٰ saying, *And there is no creature on earth but that upon God is its provision . . .* [11:6], and certitude that it will come to him, and that the measure destined for him will reach him, to the point that this overwhelms this heart. All the while he is gainfully employed, aggravated neither by covetousness, greed, nor by a feeling of loss over that which has passed him by. Certitude such as this results in a broad array of acts of obedience and praiseworthy inner character traits.

Among them is that the heart is overwhelmed [knowing] that whoever does an atom's weight of good will see it, and whoever does an atom's weight of evil will see it. This is certitude in divine recompense and retribution, to the point that one perceives the association between obedience and reward like the association between bread and satisfaction from hunger, and the association between disobedience and chastisement like the association between poison and vipers and death. In the manner that one ardently strives to attain bread to satisfy hunger and then preserves whatever was found, be it small or large, likewise one ardently strives to perform acts of obedience—all of them—great and small. And in the manner that one strives to avoid the smallest amount of poison or a great amount, likewise one strives to avoid acts of disobedience, be they few or many, minor or egregious.

The first meaning of certitude is often found among the generality of believers, whereas the second meaning is a trait specific to those brought nigh to God سُبْحَانَهُ.

The fruit of this type of certitude is sincere meditation on action and inaction, on [guarding against] random thoughts, on the utmost piety, and being on guard against all malicious deeds; the more this certitude overwhelms [the heart], the more intense [one's] caution [against evil] will be and the more dominant [one's] preparations [for good] will be.

Resulting from this is the certitude that God تَعَالَىٰ is ever observant of you in every state, He witnesses the inner notions of your conscience, your hidden inclinations and your thinking. Every person of faith is certain of this, according to the first meaning, which is negation of doubt. As for the second meaning, which is the goal, it is precious and a trait particular to the veracious. Its fruit is that [even] in seclusion the person is steadfast in correct conduct, in every state and activity, like one sitting before a great king who is watching him. In this circumstance he remains seated with averted gaze, his deportment is correct, [he is] resolute and on his guard against any gesture that might contradict the demeanor of acceptable conduct, and all the while his inner thoughts reflect his outward circumstances.[175] When he realizes with certainty that God تعالى is as observant of his innermost thoughts as humankind is of his outward appearance, then he will strive to the utmost to augment, purify, and enhance his inward state to the Eye of God تعالى that never sleeps; this will outstrip his striving to enhance his outward aspect for everyone else's sake.

This station of certitude makes one an heir to reticence, fear [of God], contrition, humility, self-surrender, humility, and an array of praiseworthy character traits. And these traits engender diverse acts of obedience that reflect noble character.

Certitude in each of these categories is similar to a tree, and these noble traits in the heart are like limbs branching out from it. The efforts and acts of obedience engendered by these traits are like the various fruits and flowers stemming from the branches. Certitude is therefore the origin and the foundation; its currents and categories surpass that which we have enumerated here. Mention of them will come in the [fourth] *Rubᶜ al-munjiyat* [Quarter of Deliverance], for the moment this degree should be sufficient to comprehend the meaning of the term.

Among the traits of a scholar of the hereafter is that he has a mournful countenance, is contrite, and casts down his gaze, and is reticent in his speech. His demeanor reflects [his] apprehension [of God], as does his clothing,[176] his bearing, his action and repose, his manner of discourse and his silence. No one regards him without being reminded of God تعالى . His very appearance is proof of his earnest comportment. [As is said], "The worthy steed is discernable by its traits."[177] Likewise the scholars of the hereafter are discernable by their traits:[178] tranquility, humble demeanor, and humility.

---

175 That is, his outward actions equal his inner actions concerning sincerity and humility to the master because there is no distinction between the one and the other. See al-Zabīdī, *Itḥāf*, 1:418.

176 This is the case because there is no fashionable clothing, no conspicuous wealth, and no embroidered clothing. None of this is part of the clothing of the scholars of the hereafter. See al-Zabīdī, *Itḥāf*, 1:418.

177 This is a parable that alludes to the outward traits of something being indicative of its inward traits. This parable uses the term *al-firār/al-furār/al-farār*, which means inspecting the teeth of an animal or examining its traits toward evaluating its value.

178 In reference to the verse, *You will know them by their [characteristic] sign* [2:273].

It has been said, "The finest garment God تَعَالَى confers on a servant is humble submission in tranquility; this is the raiment of the prophets, and the outward traits of the righteous, the veracious, and the true scholars."

As for vain discourse and affected speech, losing oneself in laughter, and vehemence in demeanor and speech, all of these are signs of wantonness, a [false] sense of security, and heedlessness of the horrific extent of God's تَعَالَى chastisement and the severity of His wrath. This is the norm among the sons of the world, those who neglect God, not of those knowledgeable of Him.

This is the case because among the scholars there are three categories, as Sahl al-Tustarī رَضِيَ ٱللَّهُ عَنْهُ used to say, "There is the one who knows of God's commands but not of the 'Days of God,'[179] they issue rulings concerning the lawful and the unlawful, [but] this knowledge does not engender apprehension. [Then there is] the one who knows of God but not of God's command or the 'Days of God,' they are the generality among the believers; and [then] there is the one who knows of God, the 'Days of God,' and the command of God, they are the veracious ones";[180] the traits of apprehension and reverence prevail over them.

He intended, by the 'Days of God,' His enigmatic censure and His inward grace that He sent forth in the centuries past and on those present.[181] The fear and reverence of anyone whose knowledge encompasses that is great.

ʿUmar رَضِيَ ٱللَّهُ عَنْهُ stated, "Acquire knowledge, and learn for the sake of knowledge, tranquility, dignified bearing, and clemency; humble yourselves before those from whom you learn, so that those who learn from you might humble themselves before you. Do not be

---

179 Al-Zabīdī cites the Qurʾānic verse in which God تَعَالَى addresses Moses عَلَيْهِ ٱلسَّلَامُ, *And We certainly sent Moses with Our signs, [saying], "Bring out your people from darknesses into the light and remind them of the days of God"* [14:5]; al-Zabīdī, *Itḥāf*, 1:419.

180 Abū Ṭālib al-Makkī, *Qūt al-qulūb*, 1:140; also see al-Zabīdī, *Itḥāf*, 1:420; also see Renard, *Knowledge*, 148.

181 This phrase is included in Abū Ṭālib al-Makkī, *Qūt al-qulūb*, 1:140; also see al-Zabīdī, *Itḥāf*, 1:420.

overbearing scholars, lest your knowledge be imparted [to others] by your ignorance."[182]

It was related, "God has not given a servant knowledge without, at the same time, granting him clemency, humility, and worthy character with affability."[183] This is what constitutes beneficial knowledge.

About this meaning it was related, "Whoever God bestows knowledge, asceticism, humility, and worthy character upon is the *imām* of the pious."[184]

It was related in a report, "Verily the best of my community are a people who laugh out loud at the magnanimity of God's compassion, and weep in secret out of fear of His chastisement; their physical bodies are on the earth, and their hearts are in the celestial realm; their souls abide in the world, and their intellects are fixed upon the hereafter; they walk with tranquility, and seek the means of drawing near [to God]."[185]

Ḥasan [al-Baṣrī] used to say, "Clemency is the minister of knowledge, affability its father, and humility its raiment."[186]

Bishr b. al-Ḥārith [al-Ḥāfī] said, "Whoever seeks high rank by means of knowledge is seeking proximity to God تَعَالَىٰ by that which He hates; such a person is indeed despised in the celestial realms and on earth."[187]

It was reported from the stories of the Israelites that one of the wise among them compiled 360 volumes on wisdom, such that he became known as the "Sage." Whereupon God تَعَالَىٰ revealed to their prophet, "Say to so-and-so, 'You have filled the earth with hypocrisy, and you have not brought Me anything other than that. I will not accept any of your hypocrisy.'" The man felt remorse and abandoned this, mingled with the commoners, wandered in the marketplaces, and took charge of the affairs of the Children of

182 Abū Ṭālib al-Makkī, *Qūt al-qulūb*, 1:140; also see al-Zabīdī, *Itḥāf*, 1:420; narrated by al-Daynūrī, *al-Majālisa wa-jawāhir al-ʿilm*, 1197.

183 Abū Ṭālib al-Makkī, *Qūt al-qulūb*, 1:141; also see al-Zabīdī, *Itḥāf*, 1:419.

184 Abū Ṭālib al-Makkī, *Qūt al-qulūb*, 1:141; al-Zabīdī said, "This is as related in *Qūt al-qulūb* and [al-Ghazālī] followed him in citing it, yet al-ʿIrāqī does not mention it and I have not found it in other than *Qūt al-qulūb*." al-Zabīdī, *Itḥāf*, 1:419.

185 Narrated by al-Ḥākim al-Nīsābūrī, *al-Mustadrak*, 3:17; and al-Bayhaqī, *Shuʿab al-īmān*, 749.

186 Abū Ṭālib al-Makkī, *Qūt al-qulūb*, 1:141; also see al-Zabīdī, *Itḥāf*, 1:421.

187 Abū Ṭālib al-Makkī, *Qūt al-qulūb*, 1:141; also see al-Zabīdī, *Itḥāf*, 1:421.

Israel, and so he became humble in himself. Whereupon God تَعَالَىٰ revealed to their prophet, "Tell that person, 'Now you have achieved My good pleasure.'"[188]

Al-Awzāʿī رَضِيَ ٱللَّٰهُ عَنْهُ handed down a tradition that Bilāl b. Saʿd used to say, "One of you said, 'I seek protection from God from the likes of him' when he saw a royal guard, while you look at the worldly scholars acting pretentiously before the people; [these scholars] anticipate rank and station [from the rulers] and yet you express no aversion toward them. In fact they deserve to be loathed more than that guard."[189]

[Most Worthy Acts]

It was narrated that, "Someone asked, 'O Messenger of God صَلَّى ٱللَّٰهُ عَلَيْهِ وَسَلَّمَ, which pious acts are most worthy?'

He replied, 'Avoiding forbidden things while your mouth is ever moist with the remembrance of God تَعَالَىٰ.'

Then it was asked, 'Which companion is the best?'

He صَلَّى ٱللَّٰهُ عَلَيْهِ وَسَلَّمَ responded, 'A companion who, when you remember God, supports you; and should you forget he reminds you.'

Then it was asked, 'Which companion is the worst?'

He said صَلَّى ٱللَّٰهُ عَلَيْهِ وَسَلَّمَ, 'A companion, who, if you forget does not remind you; and when you remember God does not support you.'

Then it was asked, 'Who is the most knowledgeable person?'

He صَلَّى ٱللَّٰهُ عَلَيْهِ وَسَلَّمَ replied, 'The one most steadfast in apprehension of God.'

Then they asked, 'Tell us who are the best among us, so we can keep their company.'

He answered, 'Those are the people, who, when seen, God تَعَالَىٰ is remembered.'

Then they said, 'Who are the worst people?'

He said, 'O God forgiveness!'

They asked, 'Tell us, O Messenger of God!'

---

188 Abū Ṭālib al-Makkī, *Qūt al-qulūb*, 1:141; originally narrated by Abū Nuʿaym, *Ḥilya*, 5:237; also see al-Zabīdī, *Itḥāf*, 1:421.

189 Abū Ṭālib al-Makkī, *Qūt al-qulūb*, 1:141; also see al-Zabīdī, *Itḥāf*, 1:421–422.

He said, 'The scholars, when they have become corrupted.'"[190]

The Messenger of God صَلَّى ٱللَّهُ عَلَيْهِ وَسَلَّمَ stated, "On the day of resurrection the people who reflected most on this world will be the most secure [from God's wrath]. The people who will laugh most in the hereafter are those who wept most in [this] world. Those who will know the greatest joy in the hereafter are those whose grief was most enduring in this world."[191]

ʿAlī رَضِيَ ٱللَّهُ عَنْهُ addressed the people in his sermon saying, "My obligation is a pledge, and I am answerable for it. The crops of a people will not wither from piety, the roots of a tree will not thirst due to good guidance. The most ignorant person is the one who does not know his own worth; the most loathsome of God's تَعَالَىٰ creatures is a man who collects knowledge, and makes forays with it into the dark depths of tribulation. Those like him among the people and those of base character call him a scholar, yet he did not undertake the pursuit of knowledge for even an entire day. He departs early in the morning and amasses quantities of that of which a little is better than a great deal. Then, after slaking his thirst on brackish water, and accruing that which is of no use, he seats himself among the people issuing rulings in order to clarify what has confused others. Then, when a substantive issue descends on him, he prepares a long-winded opinion based on his own perspective. In [the process of] dispelling ambiguities he resembles a spider's web, he has no idea whether he has hit or missed the mark. He carries on in ignorance, haphazardly striking out in the dark. He makes no excuses for himself for that which he knows not and escapes unscathed. Nor does he gain a firm hold with his molars onto sound knowledge and actually benefit from it. Blood weeps over him [for lost justice], his judgments render forbidden women permissible. By God, such a person is incapable of giving back what has come to him, nor is he suited for the obligation laid upon him. These are the ones destined to wail and weep all the days of their lives in this world."[192]

---

190 Abū Ṭālib al-Makkī, *Qūt al-qulūb*, 1:142.

191 Abū Ṭālib al-Makkī, *Qūt al-qulūb*, 1:152; also see al-Zabīdī, *Itḥāf*, 1:422; there is a similar narration from Abū Nuʿaym, *Ḥilya*, 2:93.

192 Narrated by Wakīʿ, *Akhbār al-quḍāt*, 1:32; Ibn Qutayba, *ʿUyūn al-akhbār*, 1:60; Ibn ʿAsākir, *Tārīkh Dimashq*, 42:504, all with similar versions; also in Abū Ṭālib al-Makkī, *Qūt al-qulūb*, 1:142; also see al-Zabīdī, *Itḥāf*, 1:422–423.

ʿAlī said as well, "When you hear of knowledge, keep it close, and do not associate it with levity and empty discourse, lest hearts reject and discard it."[193]

One of the predecessors said, "When a scholar laughs out loud, he spits out a bit of knowledge."[194]

It has been related, "When a teacher combines in himself three traits, namely patience, humility, and worthy character, the blessing upon the one who learns from him is complete; and when the one who learns [from him] combines in himself three traits, namely, intellect, correct conduct, and good understanding, then the blessing upon the teacher is complete."[195]

In summary, the scholars of the hereafter persist in upholding the character traits set out in the Qurʾān because they learned the Qurʾān in order to act on its teachings, not for rank and station.

Ibn ʿUmar رَضِيَ ٱللَّهُ عَنْهُمَا stated, "We lived during a period when one of us was brought to the faith before the Qurʾān. A particular *sūra* would be revealed, whereupon one would learn its lawful and unlawful aspects, and its injunctions and prohibitions, and its limits. I have seen, as well, men who were brought to the Qurʾān before faith, whereupon one of them recites what is between its opening chapter and its conclusion, and does not know what it enjoins or what it prohibits, and limits. He casts it away as though he were casting away spoiled dates."[196]

Another report, similar in meaning, states, "We Companions of the Messenger of God صَلَّى ٱللَّهُ عَلَيْهِ وَسَلَّمَ were brought to the faith before the Qurʾān. After you, there will come a people to whom the Qurʾān will be given before the faith. They will articulate its letters properly, but fall short of its injunctions; they will say, 'We have recited [the Qurʾān], who recites better than we do? We have acquired knowledge, who is more knowledgeable than we are?' That is the extent

193 Narrated by al-Bayhaqī, *al-Madkhal*, 388.

194 Cited by al-Dārimī, *Sunan*, 603; Abū Nuʿaym, *Ḥilya*, 3:133; from ʿAlī b. Ḥusayn رَحِمَهُ ٱللَّهُ. Ibn ʿAbd al-Barr, *Jāmiʿ bayān al-ʿilm wa faḍlih*, 940.

195 Abū Ṭālib al-Makkī, *Qūt al-qulūb*, 1:145.

196 Narrated by al-Ḥākim al-Nīsābūrī, *al-Mustadrak*, 1:35; al-Bayhaqī, *al-Sunan al-kubrā*, 3:120.

of their share of the Qurʾān." According to another version, "They are the most iniquitous of this community."[197]

It was said, "Five character traits mark the scholars of the hereafter, [these are] understood from five verses of the Book of God عَزَّوَجَلَّ: apprehension, reverence, humility, noble character, and asceticism, which is a preference for the hereafter over this world.

As for apprehension, it is from His تَعَالَىٰ saying, *From among His servants, only those who fear God are those who have knowledge* [35:28].

As for reverence, it is from His تَعَالَىٰ saying, [*being*] *humbly submissive to God. They do not exchange the verses of God for a small price* [3:199].

As for humility, it is from His تَعَالَىٰ saying, *And lower your wing to those who follow you of the believers.* [26:215].

As for noble character, it is from His تَعَالَىٰ saying, *So by mercy from God,* [*O Muḥammad*], *you were lenient with them* [3:159].

As for asceticism it is from His تَعَالَىٰ saying, *But those who had been given knowledge said, "Woe to you! The reward of God is better for he who believes and does righteousness"* [28:80].[198]

After reciting His تَعَالَىٰ words, *So whoever God wants to guide, He expands his breast to* [*contain*] *Islam* [6:125]. Someone asked, "O Messenger of God, what is this 'expansion'?" He replied, "When the light descends into the heart, it expands its center so that it becomes spacious." Someone asked, "And is there some indication of that?" The Prophet صَلَّى ٱللَّهُ عَلَيْهِ وَسَلَّمَ replied, "Yes, [it means] to become disenchanted with the abode of delusion, turn to the eternal abode, and prepare for death before its descent."[199]

Among the traits of a scholar of the hereafter is that he primarily pursues knowledge as it pertains to action and that which corrupts [acts] and perplexes hearts, [that which] arouses temptation and incites evil. For the basis of all religion is preserving oneself from evil.

For this reason the poet said,

Evil have I known though not for evil's sake but to avoid

---

197 Abū Ṭālib al-Makkī, *Qūt al-qulūb*, 1:145; Ibn Māja, 61; al-Bayhaqī, *al-Sunan al-kubrā*, 3:120.

198 Abū Ṭālib al-Makkī, *Qūt al-qulūb*, 1:146.

199 Narrated by al-Ḥākim al-Nīsābūrī, *al-Mustadrak*, 4:311; and al-Bayhaqī, *Shuʿab al-īmān*, 10068; Abū Ṭālib al-Makkī, *Qūt al-qulūb*, 1:148.

Its toils; and he who knows it not will surely be ensnared thereby

This is the case because works as accomplishments are within reach of everyone, the furthest reaching—even more—the loftiest, is constancy in the remembrance of God تَعَالَىٰ, on the level of the heart and upon the tongue. The essence of the matter, however, is the realization of that which corrupts and distracts. In this the ramifications are manifold, divided into lengthy domains of discourse. For all of this there is the utmost need, and it has become a general necessity in the journey on the path of the hereafter.

[Worldly Scholars]

As for the worldly scholars, they pursue the study of erudite branches of knowledge related to issuing judgments and judicial decisions, they tire themselves conceiving hypothetical cases that, will never arise though time ends; and should they arise, they occur to others, not to them. And if one of these cases occurs, there would be plenty [of people] capable of responding to it. [They do all this] while they forsake that which is incumbent upon them, and ignore their circumstances again and again, night and day, in their inner thoughts and temptations, and their actions.

How far from well-being is one who sells the concerns incumbent upon himself in exchange for the concerns of others that occur only rarely, and [who] favors high esteem and proximity among humankind over proximity to God تَعَالَىٰ, and [who] covets being called by the reprobates among the sons of the world, a man of stature and a realized scholar, well-versed in the intricacies of erudition!?

His recompense from God تَعَالَىٰ is that he reaps no benefit in this world from the people's acceptance of him; in fact, the calamities of time only serve to sully his comfort and well-being. Then on the day of resurrection he will arrive impoverished and grieving when he beholds the profit of those resolute in action and the triumph of those brought nigh; surely *that is* clear loss.

Ḥasan al-Baṣrī رَضِيَ ٱللَّهُ عَنْهُ bore the closest resemblance of anyone to the discourse of the prophets عَلَيْهِمُ ٱلسَّلَامُ, and was the nearest to the Companions رَضِيَ ٱللَّهُ عَنْهُمْ in his bearing, the merit of his status is unanimous. The greater part of his discourse dealt with those inner prompting of the heart and the corruption of action, the temptations of souls, and the obscure characteristics concealed among the base passions of the soul.

So someone asked him, "O Abū Saʿīd [i.e., Ḥasan], you speak [about this knowledge] with words we have not heard from anyone but you; from whom did you learn this?" He replied, "From Ḥudhayfa b. al-Yamān."[200]

Ḥudhayfa was asked, "We see you speaking [about this knowledge] with words we have not heard from anyone but you among the Companions, from whom did you acquire this?" He said, "God's Messenger صَلَّى ٱللَّهُ عَلَيْهِ وَسَلَّمَ addressed me specifically. The people would ask him about [the means of attaining] the good, but I made it my habit to ask about evil out of fear of falling into it, I knew that the good would not pass me by."[201]

He [Ḥudhayfa] once said, "I knew that whoever had no knowledge of evil, had no knowledge of good." And in another version, "People used to say, 'O Messenger of God, what is incumbent upon one who does this or that?' They would ask him about worthy actions, whereas I would ask, 'O Messenger of God, what does this or that action corrupt?' When he saw me asking about the perils that put actions in danger, he addressed me in particular with this knowledge."

Ḥudhayfa رَضِيَ ٱللَّهُ عَنْهُ was specifically endowed with knowledge of the hypocrites [among the early community] and was singled out by an understanding of the knowledge of hypocrisy, its causes, and the subtleties of tribulations. ʿUmar and ʿUthmān and the prominent among the Companions رَضِيَ ٱللَّهُ عَنْهُمْ made it a habit to question him about tribulations, their general and particular aspects.

He [Ḥudhayfa] was asked as well about the hypocrites and thereby provided information about the number of them remaining, but he did not mention their names.[202]

ʿUmar asked him about himself, whether he knew of any trace of hypocrisy in him, and Ḥudhayfa absolved him of that.[203]

200 Abū Ṭālib al-Makkī, *Qūt al-qulūb*, 1:150.

201 Al-Bukhārī, 3606; Muslim, 1847.

202 Abū Ṭālib al-Makkī, *Qūt al-qulūb*, 1:150; also see al-Zabīdī, *Itḥāf*, 1:429.

203 Narrated by Wakīʿ, *al-Zuhd*, 477; and Ibn ʿAsākir, *Tārīkh Dimashq*, 12:276; *Qūt al-qulūb*, 1:150; also see al-Zabīdī, *Itḥāf*, 1:430.

When ʿUmar was called to attend a funeral to perform the prayer over the deceased, he would look around, and if Ḥudhayfa was present, he would pray over the deceased; and if not, he left.

He [Ḥudhayfa] was known as the master of the secret.[204]

The scholars of the hereafter are known for [paying] meticulous attention to the stations of the heart and its states, for it is the heart that is hastening to God's تَعَالَىٰ proximity.

[Today] this domain of knowledge is little known and its traces are lost; if a scholar turns his attention to some aspect of it he is regarded with suspicion and ostracized [from the circles of learning]. It is said of him, "This is but the exaggerated speech of those who admonish the commonality, where is the proof?" For them proof lies in the subtleties of disputations.

The poet[205] was correct when he stated,

The paths are multiple, and the paths of the truth are unique,
Those journeying on the path of the truth do so one by one.

They are not known nor their intentions well apprised,
They tread the path resolutely; their goal in mind.

While people remain heedless of that which they seek,
The majority of them are oblivious to the path of truth.

In summary, the majority of humankind only incline toward the easiest things and that which accords best with their natural dispositions; verily the truth is bitter, being resolute in it is arduous, comprehending it is demanding, its path—in particular the realization of the properties of the heart and cleansing it of blameworthy traits—is not well traveled; for all that is an unending source of agony for the spirit. A person on this path is similar to someone drinking medicine in hope of being cured, he bears its bitterness, or someone fasting his entire life, who endures hardship so that he may break his fast at the moment of passing from this world. When will yearning for a path such as this abound?

---

204 Al-Bukhārī, 3743.

205 Al-Khaṭīb al-Baghdādī, *Tārīkh Baghdād*, 5:231, also see al-Zabīdī, *Itḥāf*, 1:430.

[Remembrance and Admonition]

For this reason it was related, "In Basra there were 120 people who spoke about remembrance and admonition [to the multitudes], whereas there were only three who spoke about the knowledge of certitude, the states of the heart, and the attributes [and stations] of the inner self. They were Sahl al-Tustarī, al-Ṣubīḥī, and ʿAbd al-Raḥīm [b. Yaḥyā l-Aswad]." Uncountable multitudes participated in the sessions of those [who spoke about remembrance and admonition], while to these [three] minimal numbers, seldom exceeding ten attended. For things precious and of great value are suited only for the elect, that which is dispensed upon the common [folk] is of easy access.

Among the traits of a scholar of the hereafter is that, in his pursuit of knowledge, he relies on his insight and on his perception of his heart's purity, not on bound volumes and texts, nor on following the example of what he only hears from others. For the true exemplar is the Law Giver صَلَّى ٱللَّهُ عَلَيْهِ وَسَلَّمَ and what he ordained and spoke of. The Companions رَضِيَ ٱللَّهُ عَنْهُمْ are taken as examples, such that their actions testify to their having heard from the Messenger of God صَلَّى ٱللَّهُ عَلَيْهِ وَسَلَّمَ.

Then when one takes as their exemplar the Law Giver [i.e., the Prophet Muḥammad] عَلَيْهِ ٱلصَّلَاةُ وَٱلسَّلَامُ, in that they accommodate his words and acts with willing acceptance, it befits them to seek ardently to comprehend the subtleties of his inner secrets. For verily the one who follows his example does such and such because the Law Giver [i.e., the Prophet Muḥammad] صَلَّى ٱللَّهُ عَلَيْهِ وَسَلَّمَ did so. There is no doubt that his actions comprised a secret; therefore it is incumbent upon one following him to diligently seek knowledge of the secret inner facets of his acts and his words. Anyone who thinks it sufficient to memorize what was said is a vessel of knowledge, not a person of knowledge. For this reason it has been stated, "So-and-so is among the vessels of knowledge," although he was not referred to as a scholar, since his interest was in memorization rather than learning the wisdom and secrets therein.

Anyone from whose heart the veil has been lifted and illuminated by the light of [God's] guidance becomes worthy of being emulated, and taken as an example themselves; such a person ought not to follow the example of another. For this reason Ibn ʿAbbās رَضِيَ ٱللَّهُ عَنْهُمَا said, "Knowledge can be taken from any given person, or declined, except from the Messenger of God صَلَّى ٱللَّهُ عَلَيْهِ وَسَلَّمَ."[206] [An example of this is] [Ibn ʿAbbās], who studied jurisprudence under Zayd b. Thābit and Qurʾānic recitation under Ubayy b. Kaʿb, then he came to differ with them both on matters of jurisprudence and recitation.

One of the predecessors related, "Whatever came to us from the Messenger of God صَلَّى ٱللَّهُ عَلَيْهِ وَسَلَّمَ we accept wholeheartedly, whatever came to us from the Companions رَضِيَ ٱللَّهُ عَنْهُمْ [some matters] we take from them and [some] we decline, whatever came to us from the Followers; well, they are people and we are people."[207]

The specific merit of the Companions is that they witnessed the evident signs of the states of the Messenger of God صَلَّى ٱللَّهُ عَلَيْهِ وَسَلَّمَ, and because of the firm hold of their hearts of matters comprehended by these evident signs that allowed them to perceive matters in their correct context without need of going into variants of narrative or interpretation; for the light of prophecy had flooded down upon them and guarded them, for the most part, from error.

If reliance on orally transmitted knowledge from others in imitation was frowned on, then reliance on books and composed treatises was disapproved of even more. For books and compositions were an innovation; there was nothing of them at all during the time of the Companions and the first Followers. They only appeared after 120 Hijra [738 CE], which is after the passing away of all the Companions, and most of the Followers رَضِيَ ٱللَّهُ عَنْهُمْ, after the passing away of Saʿīd b. al-Musayyib, and Ḥasan (al-Baṣrī), and the foremost Followers. In fact the earliest generations were averse to writing down prophetic traditions and writing books, lest they distract the people from memorization, recitation of the Qurʾān, and from reflection and contemplation. They would say, "Keep it in memory as we have memorized it."[208]

---

206 Narrated by al-Ṭabarānī, *al-Muʿjam al-kabīr*, 11:269, in a *ḥadīth* attributed to the Prophet.

207 Narrated by al-Bayhaqī, *al-Madkhal*, 22, from Abū Ḥanīfa رَحِمَهُ ٱللَّهُ.

208 Abū Nuʿaym, *Ḥilya*, 3:363, citing from al-Zuhrī who said, "We used to dislike writing but the sultan forced us to use it, then we disliked to prevent people from using it." It is reported that he was the first to record knowledge.

For this reason, Abū Bakr al-Ṣiddīq and a faction of the Companions رضي الله عنهم were averse to gathering the Qurʾān into a single volume; they said, "How can we do something that the Messenger of God صلى الله عليه وسلم did not do?" They were afraid the people would rely on written copies of the Qurʾān. So they said, "Let's leave the Qurʾān [as it is] so that they learn it from each other through audition and recitation, so that it will be their custom and concern." Finally, ʿUmar and the remaining Companions insisted on writing down the Qurʾān, on the one hand out of fear of negligence and indolence on the part of the people, and on the other hand, to take care to preserve it in the event that conflicts arose and there was no original text to refer to, [especially] in the case of a word or a reading of verses with levels of meaning. Therein, Abū Bakr's رضي الله عنه heart became opened to that, and he collected the Qurʾān into one bound volume.[209]

Aḥmad b. Ḥanbal was critical of Mālik writing *al-Muwaṭṭaʾ*, and said, "He innovated something that the Companions رضي الله عنهم had not done."[210]

It has been said, "The first book written in Islam was the book on the traditions by Ibn Jurayj, and on exegetical texts by Mujāhid, ʿAṭāʾ [b. Abī Rabāḥ], and the companions of Ibn ʿAbbās رضي الله عنهم in Mecca; then the book of Maʿmar b. Rāshid al-Sanʿānī in Yemen, in which he collected diverse *ḥadīth* and arranged them thematically with chapter headings; then the book *al-Muwaṭṭaʾ* by Mālik b. Anas in Medina, then the *Jāmiʿ* of Sufyān al-Thawrī."[211]

Then in the fourth century [AH/tenth century CE] the innovation of writing treatises on theology appeared; and immersion into disputation and the obsession with critiquing the statements of others increased; then, the general population began to incline toward it, and toward stories and admonition by public advisors. From that time onward, the knowledge of certitude began to fade, and the domain [concerning the] knowledge of hearts, and scrutiny

209 Abū Ṭālib al-Makkī, *Qūt al-qulūb*, 1:159; also see al-Zabīdī, *Itḥāf*, 1:433–434.

210 Perhaps this criticism was in the beginning of his career, for later on he collected *ḥadīth* in his *Musnad*. That was when he saw that the people were in need of it. See al-Zabīdī, *Itḥāf*, 1:434.

211 Abū Ṭālib al-Makkī, *Qūt al-qulūb*, 1:159; Ibn Ḥajar al-ʿAsqalānī, *Fatḥ al-bārī*, 6; also see al-Zabīdī, *Itḥāf*, 1:433–434.

into the qualities of the soul, and the wiles of Satan became a little known science, and all but a few turned their backs on it. At this point, those trained in dialectics and theology were called learned scholars, and the storyteller with his embellished rhetorical style and his rhyming prose, [was called] a scholar; all this [happened] because their audiences were made up of common [people] who possessed no means of differentiating between what comprises the reality of knowledge and what does not. This was because they had no access to the lives and knowledge of the Companions رَحِمَهُمُ ٱللَّٰهُ, which would have enabled them to discern between those others and them [Companions]. So the appellation of 'scholar' continued, and the title was inherited from one generation to another, and the knowledge of the hereafter was rolled up like a scroll, and the ability to discern the disparity between knowledge and discourse disappeared, except among a select few. When they were asked, "Is so-and-so more knowledgeable than so-and-so?" it would be said, "So-and-so has more knowledge, and so-and-so talks more." The elect among the scholars understood the difference between knowledge and the ability to engage in discourse.

In this manner in the passing centuries the religion grew weak; so how might one appraise this era of yours? Things have come to a point that anyone who expresses an adverse opinion toward the present state of affairs is called insane!?

The best people can do is to occupy themselves with their own souls and remain silent.

[Invented Matters]

Among the traits of a scholar of the hereafter is that he diligently guards against falling into invented matters, though the public may be in accord with them. He is not deceived by the general agreement of the people about issues that were invented after the Companions رَحِمَهُمُ ٱللَّٰهُ, and he is resolute in his inquiries into the inner states of the Companions, their lives and conduct, and in what domains were their greatest concerns. Was it in the study and writing of books, disputation, issuing judicial decrees, governance and assuming responsibility for pious endowments, wills, and the wealth of orphans, frequenting the rulers, and exercising polite etiquette in their company? Or was it fear and remorse, thoughtful reflection, and striving, watchfulness over the inner and outer states, avoiding all sin, the minute and the major, a resolute striving to comprehend the hidden desires of the soul, and machinations of Satan, and more, which is entailed in the sciences of the inner state?

Know for certain, that the most knowledgeable person of a given time, and those who are closest to the truth are those who most closely resemble the Companions [in character] and who are nearer to realizing the path of the predecessors; for from them the religion has been inherited. For this reason, when someone said to ʿAlī رَضِيَ ٱللَّهُ عَنْهُ, "You have differed with so-and-so [on such-and-such a point]." He responded, "The best of us is the one among us who follows this religion."[212]

There is consequently little need to worry about disagreeing with the people of one's time if one is in conformance with the people of the time of the Messenger of God صَلَّى ٱللَّهُ عَلَيْهِ وَسَلَّمَ; for people reflect a point of view as it accords with their own context due to their natural inclination toward it, in no manner do they permit themselves to admit that that point of view could be the cause that prevents them from entering heaven. Then, [beyond this] they claim that it is the only path leading to heaven.

That is why Ḥasan [al-Baṣrī] used to say, "Two innovations that have originated in Islam are a man with spurious views who supposes that heaven is for those who hold a view similar to his, and a person who lives an opulent lifestyle, worships the world, who is enraged [at times] and content [at others] with it, and who strives for nothing else. May they both be condemned to the fire! For surely a man comes to this world—[and finds himself] between a profligate man of wealth who summons [him] to this world and a master of desire who summons [him] to his desire—but God preserves him from them. He then yearns for the path of righteous predecessors, inquires of their deeds and demeanor and takes them as his exemplars. Such a person will encounter a worthy reward. May you all be like this."[213]

---

212 Abū Ṭālib al-Makkī, *Qūt al-qulūb*, 1:161; also see al-Zabīdī, *Itḥāf*, 1:436.

213 Abū Ṭālib al-Makkī, *Qūt al-qulūb*, 1:161; also see al-Zabīdī, *Itḥāf*, 1:436.

It was related from Ibn Masʿūd رَضِيَ ٱللَّٰهُ عَنْهُ in a report stemming from him and also traced back to the Prophet, "There are two realities only: speech and guidance. The best speech is the word of God, and the best guidance is the guidance of the Messenger of God صَلَّى ٱللَّٰهُ عَلَيْهِ وَسَلَّمَ. Beware of invented matters, for the most evil of matters are the invented ones; for every invented matter is an innovation, and every innovation is reason for error. Indeed, the time will not be long before your hearts become hardened. Verily, everything that is yet to come is near. Indeed, the only thing distant is that which will not come."[214]

And in a sermon the Messenger of God صَلَّى ٱللَّٰهُ عَلَيْهِ وَسَلَّمَ stated, "Give glad tidings to those whose preoccupation with their own faults distracts them from the faults of the people, who are generous with the possessions they have acquired licitly, who associate with the people of understanding and wisdom, and who eschew the reprobates and disobedient. Give glad tidings to those who humble themselves, and are of noble demeanor and inward rectitude; and who hold their own evil at a distance from the people. Give glad tidings to those who act upon their knowledge, and who give generously from the overabundance of their wealth, who are reticent in their speech, and for whom the *sunna* offers sufficiency and breadth, and who do not go beyond it to innovation."[215]

Ibn Masʿūd رَضِيَ ٱللَّٰهُ عَنْهُ used to say, "At the end of time, being well guided will be superior to having an abundance of worthy works."[216]

He said as well, "You reside in a time in which the best among you makes haste in accomplishing an abundance of affairs; after you will come another time, in which the best among them will be the one who proceeds prudently and acts haltingly due to the abundance of matters that raise doubts."[217]

In this, he surely spoke the truth! Whoever does not proceed prudently in this time and follows the multitudes in the circum-

214 Ibn Māja, 46; Abū Ṭālib al-Makkī, *Qūt al-qulūb*, 1:161; also see al-Zabīdī, *Itḥāf*, 1:436–437.

215 Abū Nuʿaym, *Ḥilya*, 3:202; Abū Ṭālib al-Makkī, *Qūt al-qulūb*, 1:161; also see al-Zabīdī, *Itḥāf*, 1:437; al-Bayhaqī, *Shuʿab al-īmān*, 10079.

216 Narrated by al-Bukhārī, *al-Adab al-mufrad*, 789; Abū Ṭālib al-Makkī, *Qūt al-qulūb*, 1:161; also see al-Zabīdī, *Itḥāf*, 1:437.

217 Abū Ṭālib al-Makkī, *Qūt al-qulūb*, 1:161; also see al-Zabīdī, *Itḥāf*, 1:438–439.

stances in which they abide, and plunges into that which they have plunged, will perish as they have perished.

Ḥudhayfa رَضِيَ ٱللَّهُ عَنْهُ said something even more astonishing than this, "What you today consider to be your worthy acts were looked upon as reprehensible in a former time; and what you consider your reprehensible acts today will be seen as worthy in a time to come. However, you will remain steadfast in well-being [with God], as long as you realize the truth, and the truly knowledgeable person in your midst should not be regarded with contempt."[218]

He surely spoke the truth; for indeed the majority of what are considered worthy deeds in these times were looked upon as reprehensible in the times of the Companions رَضِيَ ٱللَّهُ عَنْهُمْ; for example, among the foremost worthy deeds of our times is the decoration and embellishment of mosques and spending enormous sums on the intricate details worked into their construction, then covering their floors with fine carpets. Whereas, formerly, spreading reed mats in the mosque was considered an innovation; and it was said, "It was a novelty introduced by al-Ḥajjāj [b. Yūsuf al-Thaqafī]."[219] The earliest generations rarely placed anything between themselves and the earth.[220]

Likewise, [among the most outstanding scholarly pursuits of our times] is immersion in the intricacies of dialectics and disputation; imagining that therein lies the greatest means of gaining proximity to God, whereas in fact it is among the reprehensible pursuits.

Another novel practice of our time is chanting the Qurʾān and the call to prayer [in a melodious fashion].[221]

---

218 Abū Ṭālib al-Makkī, *Qūt al-qulūb*, 1:161; also see al-Zabīdī, *Itḥāf*, 1:439; Ibn ʿĀsākir, *Tārīkh Dimashq*, 40:91.

219 This is similar to what has been reported about Qatāda making prostration. While prostrating, a piece of reed entered his eye. He said, "May God curse al-Ḥajjāj for innovating the use of these mats that harm the people while praying." See Abū Ṭālib al-Makkī, *Qūt al-qulūb*, 1:171.

220 They loved to make prostration on the ground out of humility to God تَعَالَىٰ, reverence, and humbleness. See al-Zabīdī, *Itḥāf*, 1:439.

221 "Until one cannot understand the recitation itself, and grammatical errors arise and the words are no longer unintelligible; by lengthening the short vowels, and shortening the long vowels, and applying nasalization to clear syllables and vocalizing clearly the nasalizations." Al-Zabīdī, *Itḥāf*, 1:440.

Another novel practice is over concern with neatness and anxiety over one's ritual purity, envisaging far-fetched scenarios about the ritual purity of one's clothing, while showing few scruples for whether one's food is lawful and unlawful, and such examples go on and on.[222]

Verily, Ibn Masʿūd رَضِيَ ٱللَّهُ عَنْهُ spoke the truth when said, "Today you are in a time in which desire is subordinate to knowledge. But a time will come upon you in which knowledge will be subordinate to desire."[223]

Aḥmad Ibn Ḥanbal said, "They abandoned knowledge and dedicated themselves to issues that only rarely occur. How little there is of understanding among them. God is our only support!"[224]

Mālik b. Anas said, "In the past, people never used to ask about these matters the way they do today. Nor were the scholars used to saying, unlawful and lawful; rather, I found them using the terms, discouraged and recommended."[225]

He means here that they were in the habit of regarding the subtleties of what constituted a discouraged act and an encouraged act; as far as the unlawful was concerned, its shameless nature was evident.

Hishām b. ʿUrwa used to say, "Do not ask them today about what novel practices they have instigated, for they have already prepared a response for that question; inquire of them instead about the *sunna*, for they know nothing of it."[226]

Abū Sulaymān al-Dārānī used to say, "It is not incumbent on anyone who has been inspired to accomplish a worthy act to carry it out until he hears of it in a tradition; whereupon he should praise God تَعَالَىٰ if it accords with his motivation."[227]

He said this because the points of view that have recently been invented have impacted what is heard and become attached to hearts; to the point that it may confound the purity of the heart, whereupon

222 See Abū Ṭālib al-Makkī, *Qūt al-qulūb*, 1:163.

223 Abū Ṭālib al-Makkī, *Qūt al-qulūb*, 1:167.

224 Abū Ṭālib al-Makkī, *Qūt al-qulūb*, 1:167; also see al-Zabīdī, *Itḥāf*, 1:442; also narrated by al-Khaṭīb al-Baghdādī, *al-Kifāya*, 388.

225 Abū Ṭālib al-Makkī, *Qūt al-qulūb*, 1:167; also see al-Zabīdī, *Itḥāf*, 1:442.

226 Abū Ṭālib al-Makkī, *Qūt al-qulūb*, 1:167; also see al-Zabīdī, *Itḥāf*, 1:442.

227 It is reported by Ibn Abī Ḥātim, *Tafsīr*, 17451, and by Abū Ṭālib al-Makkī, *Qūt al-qulūb*, 1:167; also see al-Zabīdī, *Itḥāf*, 1:442.

one might imagine falsehood to be the truth; therein caution should be taken by recourse to the testimony of the traditions.

For just such a reason, when Marwān b. al-Ḥakam introduced the pulpit[228] at the place of prayer for the prayer of the feast-day (*ʿīd*), Abū Saʿīd al-Khudrī رَضِيَ اللَّهُ عَنْهُ stood before him and said, "O Marwān, what is this innovation?" He replied, "It is not innovation. It is something better than you know. The people have increased in number, and I wanted the voice [of the *imām*] to reach them all. Whereupon Abū Saʿīd responded, "By God, you will never come forth with a thing better than that which I know! By God, I will not perform the prayer behind you today."[229]

He disapproved of that because it had been the custom of the Messenger of God صَلَّى اللَّهُ عَلَيْهِ وَسَلَّمَ, when delivering the feast day and prayer for rain sermon to lean upon a bow or a staff, not upon the pulpit.[230]

A well-known *ḥadīth* reports, "Whoever introduces something into our religion that had not previously been a part of it, is to be abandoned."[231]

Another report states, "Whoever deceives my community, upon him will be the curse of God, His angels, and the entirety of mankind." Someone asked, "O Messenger of God صَلَّى اللَّهُ عَلَيْهِ وَسَلَّمَ, what does 'deceiving your community' mean?" He responded, "Devising a novel practice and forcing it upon the people."[232]

The Messenger of God صَلَّى اللَّهُ عَلَيْهِ وَسَلَّمَ stated, "God عَزَّ وَجَلَّ has an angel who, each day, proclaims, 'Whoever contradicts the *sunna* of the Messenger of God صَلَّى اللَّهُ عَلَيْهِ وَسَلَّمَ will not be accorded his intercession.'"[233]

The similarity of one who transgresses against the religion by innovating a practice that contradicts the *sunna*, in relationship to

---

228 The pulpit, or *minbar*, is a staircase usually situated to the right of the prayer niche (*miḥrāb*) or *qibla* of a mosque; it may be very rudimentary and mobile or heavily decorated and built of stone and immobile. It is used to elevate the *imām* over the congregation in order that he be seen and his sermon heard by all attendees of the Friday congregational prayer and the feast-day prayers.

229 Abū Ṭālib al-Makkī, *Qūt al-qulūb*, 1:168; also see al-Zabīdī, *Itḥāf*, 1:443.

230 Narrated by al-Ṭabarānī, *al-Muʿjam al-kabīr*, 2:24; the origin of leaning [upon something] during sermons is from Abū Dāwūd, 1096, and Ibn Māja, 1107.

231 Al-Bukhārī, 2697; Muslim, 1718.

232 Abū Ṭālib al-Makkī, *Qūt al-qulūb*.

233 Abū Ṭālib al-Makkī, *Qūt al-qulūb*, 1:174; also see al-Zabīdī, *Itḥāf*, 1:443–444.

someone who commits a sin is similar to someone who disobeys the king, and attempts to overthrow his kingdom, in relation to someone who failed to carry out a specific command; that is forgivable, whereas attempting to overthrow the kingdom is not.

One of the scholars said, "Remaining silent on matters about which the righteous predecessors spoke is indolence; while discussing matters on which they were silent is affectation."[234]

Another said, "The truth is weighty; whoever exceeds its bounds, transgresses, whoever falls short of it is weak, and whoever upholds it will be granted sufficiency."[235]

And the Prophet صَلَّى ٱللَّهُ عَلَيْهِ وَسَلَّمَ stated, "Keep to the middle way, the one to which the most eminent take recourse and to which those following them will be elevated."

Ibn ʿAbbās رَضِيَ ٱللَّهُ عَنْهُمَا said, "Error has its own sweetness to the hearts of those in error."[236]

God تَعَالَىٰ says, [*And leave those*] *who take their religion as amusement and diversion* [6:70]; and the Most High says, *Then is one to whom the evil of his deed has been made attractive so he considers it good* [*like one rightly guided*]*?* [35:8].

It can be understood from these verses that every novel practice in the religion [that was] instigated after the Companions رَضِيَ ٱللَّهُ عَنْهُمْ that exceeded the bounds of necessity and demand, is a game and a pastime.

A story is told about Iblīs—God curse him!—that when he sent forth his minions in the time of the Companions رَضِيَ ٱللَّهُ عَنْهُمْ they returned to him tired and grieving. He asked them, "What is the matter?" They responded, "We have never seen the likes of these people; in no manner could we harm them and they have worn us out! So he replied, "You have no means of assailing them, for they have been Companions of their Prophet and they witnessed their Lord's revelation. Yet, a people will come after them, from whom you will achieve your needs."

When the Followers arrived, [Satan] sent forth his minions, whereupon they returned to him dejected and crestfallen, and they

234 Abū Ṭālib al-Makkī, *Qūt al-qulūb*, 1:175; also see al-Zabīdī, *Itḥāf*, 1:444.

235 Abū Ṭālib al-Makkī, *Qūt al-qulūb*, 1:175; also see al-Zabīdī, *Itḥāf*, 1:443–444.

236 Abū Ṭālib al-Makkī, *Qūt al-qulūb*, 1:175; also see al-Zabīdī, *Itḥāf*, 1:444.

reported, "We have never seen a more amazing people; we afflict them with sins again and again, then at the end of the day, they begin seeking forgiveness, whereupon God exchanges their sins for worthy deeds!" Whereupon he said, "You have no means of assailing them, due to the soundness of their [belief in] unity and their rectitude in following the *sunna* of their Prophet. But after them will come a people from whom you will know great joy and satisfaction, they will be your playthings, and you will lead them around by the nose-rope of their desires as you will; if they seek forgiveness, they will not be forgiven, nor will they repent, lest God exchange their sins for worthy deeds."

[The one relating the story then] said, "Then, after the first century there came a people among whom desires abounded. They found innovation attractive and they made it permissible and took it as their path in the religion; they did not seek forgiveness from God from it, they did not repent of it; whereupon the enemies overwhelmed them and led them wherever they willed."[237]

Then should you ask: "From where did the person relating this know what Iblīs had said, when he [certainly] has not seen Iblīs or spoken to him about that?"

Know that the secrets of the spiritual realms are unveiled to the masters of hearts at times by inspiration, which dawns on them by means of an insight (*wurūd*) from where they know not, and at times by a true vision, at times in a waking state by means of the unveiling of ideas through the witnessing of images, as is the case in the sleeping state, and this is the loftiest degree of inspiration, and it is among the degrees of preeminent prophecy; in the same manner that a true vision is one of the forty-six parts of prophecy.

Therefore, beware, lest your portion of knowledge be denial of everything that exceeds the confines of your own limits. Therein have perished the pedantic scholars who believed they had encompassed [in their knowledge] the entirety of intellectual knowledge.

Ignorance is superior to an intellect that calls to the denial of these matters where the words of God's saints are concerned.[238] For

237 Abū Ṭālib al-Makkī, *Qūt al-qulūb*, 1:175; also see al-Zabīdī, *Itḥāf*, 1:444–445.

238 This is the case because the noblest statements of ignorant people are a concession and referral to that which they do not know. It is the lowest of conditions for

whoever denies such things for God's saints, of necessity is compelled to deny them for the prophets, such a person would be entirely beyond the pale of religion.

One of the gnostics said, "The *abdāl* are dispersed over all parts of the earth and seek to be hidden from the eyes of the multitude, for they cannot bear to look upon the scholars of this age. This is because the *abdāl* regard these scholars as utterly ignorant of God; yet they themselves, and the ignorant multitudes surrounding them, consider them scholars."[239]

Sahl al-Tustarī used to say, "One of the most egregious of sins is being ignorant of one's ignorance, respecting the commoners, and listening to the discourse of the heedless."[240]

One ought not to lend an ear to the discourse of any scholar engrossed in the pursuit of the world, instead he should be taken to task for every word he utters; for every person is engrossed in that which they love, and prepared to defend that which is not in accord with his beloved. That is why God تَعَالَىٰ says, *and do not obey one whose heart We have made heedless of Our remembrance and who follows his desire and whose affair is ever* [*in*] *neglect* [18:28].

The disobedient among the commoners are better off than those who are utterly ignorant of the path of the religion, those who hold the opinion that they are of the scholars; because the disobedient sinner admits his own shortcomings, seeks forgiveness and repents. Whereas the utterly ignorant individual supposes that he is a scholar, and that he is pursuing the sciences that are the means to the world by way of traveling the path of the religion; so he neither repents nor seeks forgiveness, instead he persists, steadfast until death.

Because this state of affairs has so overwhelmed the majority of the people, all except those that God تَعَالَىٰ has saved, hope in their reform is all but lost, and the surest means of achieving well-being for a man cautious of his religion is to opt for seclusion and solitude from the multitude. The elucidation of which is coming in *Kitāb al-ʿuzla* [Book 16, *The Proprieties of Retreat*] God willing.

---

people seeking knowledge. Thus this is the view to that claim that certain types of ignorance are better than knowledge. See al-Zabīdī, *Itḥāf*, 1:446.

239 Abū Ṭālib al-Makkī, *Qūt al-qulūb*, 1:176; also see al-Zabīdī, *Itḥāf*, 1:446–447.

240 Abū Ṭālib al-Makkī, *Qūt al-qulūb*, 1:176; also see al-Zabīdī, *Itḥāf*, 1:447.

For this reason Yūsuf b. Asbāṭ wrote to Ḥudhayfa al-Marʿashī, "How do you regard a man who can no longer find anyone that is not a sinner with whom to remember God تَعَالَىٰ ; and whose shared moments of remembrance are [for that reason] an act of disobedience?"[241] He wrote this because he could find no one suited for it.

Indeed, in this he spoke the truth! For a person who mingles with people is never free of gossip or hearing gossip, or of keeping silent in the face of reprehensible actions; the best of his circumstances when mingling with the people is imparting knowledge to others or pursuing it for himself.

However, if this poor soul ponders his circumstances carefully, he would realize that the benefit accrued in imparting knowledge to others under these conditions is never untainted from the failings of pretentious behavior, the accumulation of wealth and leadership; and he would realize that the benefits of his own pursuit of knowledge only serve as a tool to seek worldly gain and as a means that leads to evil. Any knowledge he acquires is his bondsman in achieving that end, a prop and helper that facilitates all the necessary measures to reach his goal. His case is similar to one who sells a sword to a highwayman; knowledge is like a sword, its use in achieving the good is like using a sword on the battlefield, however, this does not permit its sale to one who clearly intends to use it for highway robbery.

These are among the twelve traits of the scholars of the hereafter; each of which comprises a diverse range of the worthy manners of the predecessors.

Therefore, be one of two people: either one distinguished by these traits, or one who admits their own shortcomings where these traits are concerned, yet acknowledges their worth. Take heed however, that you do not become a third, and confound your soul by considering the religion a means of attaining worldly gain, and you [do not] compare the demeanor of reprobates with that of the well guided scholars of rectitude, and [then] out of your ignorance and denial, you enter the ranks of those doomed to destruction and despair.

---

241 Abū Ṭālib al-Makkī, *Qūt al-qulūb*, 1:176.

We seek protection with God from the pretexts of Satan, from which the multitudes have already perished; and we ask God تَعَالَى to place us among those who have not been led astray by the life of [this] world, and who have not been deceived by the Deceiver.

7

On the Intellect and Its Noble Nature: Its Real Nature and Categories

An Elucidation of the Noble Nature of the Intellect

KNOW THAT THIS[1] [ELUCIDATION] is not a difficult case to make, especially given that the noble nature of knowledge was made evident prior to the intellect. The intellect is the source of knowledge, its point of origin and its foundation; knowledge springs forth from it like fruit from a tree, light from the sun, and vision from the eye. How could that which is the means of well-being in this world and the hereafter not be of noble nature?[2]

1 This final chapter deals with the concept of ʿ*aql*, here translated as intellect, but also by some as rational faculty, intelligence, mind, reason, reflective thought, faculty, or discursive reason.

2 As for worldly well-being: its loftiest station is to become through it God's vicegerent on His earth; as for in the hereafter, it is to attain the harvest of the hereafter that is spoken of in God's تعالى saying, *Whoever desires the harvest of the hereafter—We give him increase in its harvest* [42:20]; and the fruit of the harvest of the hereafter are in detail seven in number; abiding [life] without end, capability (*qudra*) without frailty, knowledge without ignorance, self-sufficiency without neediness, security without fear, repose without exertion, eminence without disdain." Al-Zabīdī, *Itḥāf*, 1:449.

How could it be doubted when even the dumb animals, with their limited ability of discrimination are subdued before the intellect, until even the largest of the beasts in body size and the most savage of them and the most aggressive, upon seeing the likeness of a human being cowers and is filled with awe, because of his awareness of the human being's mastery over him, and his unique ability to devise schemes and strategies.

For that reason the Messenger of God صَلَّى ٱللَّهُ عَلَيْهِ وَسَلَّمَ said, "An elder among his people is like a prophet among his community."[3]

That is not due to his vast wealth, nor his imposing persona, nor the size of his tribe; rather it is due to his experience, which is the fruit of his intellect.

For this reason we see that even while the Turks, the Kurds, the Bedouin Arabs, and all humans may resemble beasts of burden in many respects, they all instinctively treat their elders with reverence and respect.

For that reason as well, when many of the bitter enemies of the Messenger of God صَلَّى ٱللَّهُ عَلَيْهِ وَسَلَّمَ were plotting his murder and their eyes fell upon him, they were dazed by his generous countenance and were in awe of him. The glow that shone from the prestige of his countenance due to the light of prophecy became visible to them, even though [what they saw] was the inner intellect that resided deep inside him.

The noble nature of the intellect is self-evident; our intention here, is to cite that which the reports (*akhbār*) and Qurʾānic verses relate concerning its noble nature.

God تَعَالَىٰ has called it light (*nūr*) in His تَعَالَىٰ words, *God is the light of the heavens and the earth. The example of His light is like a niche within which is a lamp, the lamp is within glass, the glass as if it were a pearly [white] star lit from [the oil of] a blessed olive tree, neither of the east nor of the west, whose oil would almost glow even if untouched by fire. Light upon light. God guides to His light whom He wills. And God presents examples for the people, and God is Knowing of all things* [24:35].

---

3 Narrated by al-Rāfiʿī by means of al-Khalīl al-Ḥāfiẓ in his *Mashyakha*, with its chain of narrators making it attributed to the Prophet as is also found in al-Rāfiʿī, *al-Tadwīn fī akhbār Qazwīn*, 3:95; also see al-Zabīdī, *Itḥāf*, 1:449.

God also calls the knowledge resulting from it [the intellect] spirit and life in His تَعَالَىٰ words, *And thus We have revealed to you an inspiration of Our command* [42:52]; and also, *And is one who was dead and We gave him life and made for him light by which to walk among the people like one who is in darkness, never to emerge therefrom?* [6:122].

And when He تَعَالَىٰ mentions light and darkness He intends in it knowledge and ignorance, as in His تَعَالَىٰ saying, *He brings them out from darkness into the light* [2:257].

The Messenger of God صَلَّىٰ ٱللَّهُ عَلَيْهِ وَسَلَّمَ said, "O people, comprehend your Lord and counsel one another to engage the intellect [in their affairs], through this you will grasp what you have been commanded to do and what you have been forbidden to do. And know that it will render you worthy of distinction in your Lord's presence. Know well, that the possessor of intellect—though unappealing to the eye, held in low esteem, of modest rank and threadbare—is anyone who conforms to God's edicts. Whereas the ignorant is one who disobeys God's تَعَالَىٰ edicts, though they may be appealing to regard, held in high esteem, of lofty rank, well attired, and eloquent in speech. Monkeys and swine possess more intellect in God's تَعَالَىٰ sight than someone who has disobeyed Him. Do not be deluded by worldly people's praise of you, for they are the ones in utter loss."[4]

The Messenger of God صَلَّىٰ ٱللَّهُ عَلَيْهِ وَسَلَّمَ also said, "The first thing that God created was the intellect. Then He said to it, 'Advance,' and it advanced, and He said to it, 'Go back,' and it went back, and He said to it, 'By My majesty and might, I have not created any creation nor anything dearer to me than you. By you do I take and by you do I give; by you I dispense my recompense and by you I chastise.'"[5]

Should you ask, "So this intellect, if it is an accident [of a contingent nature], then how was it created before physical entities or substances? And if it were of a substance, then how could a substance be self-subsisting, without being attributed [to any contingent entity]?

4 See al-Zabīdī, *Itḥāf*, 1:452.

5 Narrated by al-Ṭabarānī, *al-Muʿjam al-kabīr*, 8:283; Abū Nuʿaym, *Ḥilya*, 7:318; al-Bayhaqī, *Shuʿab al-īmān*, 4312; also see al-Zabīdī, *Itḥāf*, 1:452–455, for a detailed rendering of this *ḥadīth*.

Know that this is a matter of the domain of the science of unveiling, its discussion in the domain of the knowledge of conduct is inappropriate and our objective here is the sciences of conduct.

Anas b. Mālik رَضِيَ اللَّهُ عَنْهُ said, "In the presence of the Prophet صَلَّى اللَّهُ عَلَيْهِ وَسَلَّمَ a crowd of people praised a certain man to the utmost degree; whereupon the Messenger of God صَلَّى اللَّهُ عَلَيْهِ وَسَلَّمَ asked them, 'How is he with regard to his intellect?' They then responded, 'We apprise you of his resolve in worshiping God and carrying out all manner of worthy deeds, and you ask us about his intellect?' So the Messenger of God صَلَّى اللَّهُ عَلَيْهِ وَسَلَّمَ responded, 'The fool causes more harm through his foolhardiness than that caused by the inequity of the wicked man. Know that the servants of God will be raised up tomorrow in degrees of proximity to their Lord, in accordance with their intellects.'"[6]

It was related on the authority of 'Umar رَضِيَ اللَّهُ عَنْهُ that the Messenger of God صَلَّى اللَّهُ عَلَيْهِ وَسَلَّمَ said, "No one acquires anything [in this world] like the excellence of intellect that leads him who possesses it to worthy guidance and turns him from base behavior; nor does the faith of the servants of God reach its fruition, or his religion its integrity, until his intellect has become complete."[7]

The Messenger of God صَلَّى اللَّهُ عَلَيْهِ وَسَلَّمَ said, "Indeed a person gains through worthy character the degree of one who fasts and spends the night in prayer. A person's worthy character, however, is not complete until his intellect is made whole, whereupon his faith becomes whole, and he obeys his Lord and disobeys the enemy, Iblīs."[8]

It was also related on the authority of Abū Saʿīd al-Khudrī رَضِيَ اللَّهُ عَنْهُ that the Messenger of God صَلَّى اللَّهُ عَلَيْهِ وَسَلَّمَ said, "There is a firm support for all things, and the firm support of the person of faith is his intellect and his acts of worship are in proportion to his intellect. Have you not heard the words of the reprobates [in hell]: *And they will say, "If only we had been listening or reasoning, we would not be among the companions of the blaze"* [67:10].[9]

---

6 This *ḥadīth* was narrated by al-Ḥakīm al-Tirmidhī, *Nawādir al-uṣūl*, 242.

7 Similar narrations have been cited by al-Ṭabarānī, *al-Muʿjam al-ṣaghīr*, 1:241; and al-Bayhaqī, *Shuʿab al-īmān*, 4338.

8 The first sentence is from Abū Dāwūd, 4798; its completion is from the *ḥadīth* cited by Dāwūd b. al-Muḥabbar, *al-ʿAql*; see al-Zabīdī, *Itḥāf*, 1:456.

9 Among the *ḥadīth* cited by Dāwūd al-Muḥabbar, *al-ʿAql*; see al-Zabīdī, *Itḥāf*, 1:456.

It is related that ʿUmar رَضِيَ ٱللَّهُ عَنْهُ asked Tamīm al-Dārī, "What comprises the quality of leadership among your people?" He responded, "Intellect." ʿUmar said, "You have spoken truthfully. I asked the Messenger of God صَلَّى ٱللَّهُ عَلَيْهِ وَسَلَّمَ as I have asked you and he responded as you have responded then he صَلَّى ٱللَّهُ عَلَيْهِ وَسَلَّمَ said, 'I asked Gabriel عَلَيْهِ ٱلسَّلَامُ, 'What constitutes the quality of leadership?' He said, 'Intellect.'"[10]

Al-Barāʾ [b. ʿĀzib b. al-Ḥārith] related that one day a great number of questions were asked of the Messenger of God صَلَّى ٱللَّهُ عَلَيْهِ وَسَلَّمَ, whereupon he said, "O People! For each and every thing there is a faithful steed, and a man's faithful steed is his intellect; the most surely guided and experienced of you to the journey's end is the one among you who is most endowed with intellect."[11]

Abū Hurayra رَضِيَ ٱللَّهُ عَنْهُ related, "When the Messenger of God صَلَّى ٱللَّهُ عَلَيْهِ وَسَلَّمَ returned from the Battle of Uḥud he heard the people saying, "So-and-so was more valiant than so-and-so, and so-and-so suffered more than anyone else," and the likes of this, whereupon he صَلَّى ٱللَّهُ عَلَيْهِ وَسَلَّمَ said, "As for all this, you have no knowledge of any of it." They responded, 'How could that be, O Messenger of God?' He صَلَّى ٱللَّهُ عَلَيْهِ وَسَلَّمَ said to them, "They fought in proportion to that which God allotted them of intellect. The support they rendered and their intentions were to the extent of their intellects. That which befell them [on the field] befell them according to an array of degrees and on the day of resurrection those stations will be allotted them in accordance with their intentions and their intellects."[12]

On the authority of al-Barāʾ [b. ʿĀzib b. al-Ḥārith] as well, it is related that the Messenger of God صَلَّى ٱللَّهُ عَلَيْهِ وَسَلَّمَ said, "The angels have been diligent and expended great effort in obedience to God سُبْحَانَهُ according to the intellect; those of firm faith among the sons of Adam have been diligent according to their intellects, and the most

10 Among the *ḥadīth* cited by Dāwūd b. al-Muḥabbar, *al-ʿAql*; for variants see al-Zabīdī, *Itḥāf*, 1:457.

11 Among the *ḥadīth* cited by Dāwūd b. al-Muḥabbar, *al-ʿAql*; for variants see al-Zabīdī, *Itḥāf*, 1:456.

12 Among the *ḥadīth* cited by Dāwūd b. al-Muḥabbar, *al-ʿAql*; for variants see al-Zabīdī, *Itḥāf*, 1:457.

accomplished among them in obedience to God عَزَّوَجَلَّ is the most unique among them in intellect."[13]

ʿĀʾisha رَضِيَٱللَّهُعَنْهَا reported that she said, "O Messenger of God! By what criterion is mankind distinquished in this world?" He responded, "By the intellect." I asked, "And in the hereafter?" He answered, "By the intellect." I asked, "Will they not be recompensed according to the worth of their actions?" Then he صَلَّىٱللَّهُعَلَيْهِوَسَلَّمَ said, "O ʿĀʾisha, did they attain anything but that which God had given them of the intellect? Their works were according to that which they were given of the intellect, and according to their works they will be recompensed."[14]

Ibn ʿAbbās رَضِيَٱللَّهُعَنْهُمَا said, "The Messenger of God صَلَّىٱللَّهُعَلَيْهِوَسَلَّمَ said, 'There is a tool for each and every thing, and the tool of one firm in faith is the intellect. For each and every thing there is a faithful steed, and a man's faithful steed is the intellect. For each and every thing there a firm support, the firm support of the religion is the intellect. Every people has a goal they seek, and the goal of God's servants is the intellect. Everyone has one who invites [others] to it, [and it is] the intellect. For every merchant there is merchandise, and the merchandise of the diligent on the path of God is the intellect. Every household has its keeper, and keeper of the homes of the veracious is the intellect. For every ruined and dilapidated place there is one who comes to rebuild it, the restoration of the hereafter [takes place] through the intellect. For each and every man there is a posterity to which he is related and by which his memory is perpetuated, the posterity of the veracious that are related to Him and remembered by Him is the intellect. For each and every journey there is a pavilion and the pavilion of the believers is the intellect."

The Messenger of God صَلَّىٱللَّهُعَلَيْهِوَسَلَّمَ said, "The most beloved to God عَزَّوَجَلَّ of the believers is the one who stands upright in obedience to God عَزَّوَجَلَّ and gives good counsel to His servants, whose intellect is whole in itself, who counsels himself and regards [the

13 Among the *ḥadīth* cited by Dāwūd b. al-Muḥabbar, *al-ʿAql*; for variants see al-Zabīdī, *Itḥāf*, 1:457.

14 Among the *ḥadīth* cited by Dāwūd b. al-Muḥabbar, *al-ʿAql*; for variants see al-Zabīdī, *Itḥāf*, 1:457.

world] with insight; he acts upon its precepts all the days of his life, and prospers and engenders well-being."[15]

The Messenger of God ﷺ stated that, "Those of you most gifted with intellect are the foremost among you in fear of God and the best among you in fulfilling what He commanded and abandoning what He prohibited, even though they may be the least among you in supererogatory worship."[16]

An Elucidation of the Real Nature of the Intellect and its Categories

KNOW THAT PEOPLE HAVE differed among themselves on both the definition and true nature of the intellect; the majority has ignored the fact that this term has been applied to a broad array of divergent meanings. This is the reason for their divergent opinions.

The truth that lifts the veil on this matter is that the word 'intellect' is a term that is used interchangeably in relation to four [different] meanings. In the same manner that the word 'eye' (*ʿayn*) for example, has numerous meanings, the same is true in similar cases. Therefore, it is inappropriate, to ask for a single definition for all its varied categories; on the contrary, it is befitting that each category be dealt with singly, in order to unveil [the unique connotation of] each.

The first [meaning of *ʿaql*]: It is the attribute that differentiates human beings from all other animals and affords them the ability to apprehend the speculative sciences and to organize the subtle rational disciplines. Al-Ḥārith b. Asad al-Muḥāsibī intended this as his definition of 'the intellect.' He said, "It is an innate inclination whereby the speculative sciences are grasped and understood. It is like a light cast into the heart that prepares it thereby to comprehend the existent entities."[17]

15 Among the *ḥadīth* cited by Dāwūd b. al-Muḥabbar, *al-ʿAql*; for variants see al-Zabīdī, *Itḥāf*, 1:458.

16 Among the *ḥadīth* cited by Dāwūd b. al-Muḥabbar, *al-ʿAql*; for variants see al-Zabīdī, *Itḥāf*, 1:458; Ibn Ḥajar also cites it in *al-Maṭālib al-ʿāliyya*.

17 In another citation when asked about the intellect, al-Muḥāsibī stated that, "It is light of natural disposition that increases with experience and becomes stronger with knowledge and long standing patience." Ibn al-Subkī in his biographical entry on al-Muḥāsibī, *Ṭabaqāt al-shāfiʿīya*; see al-Zabīdī, *Itḥāf*, 1:459–160.

Anyone who refutes this point of view [of al-Muḥāsibī] and relegates the intellect to the domain of necessary sciences, and nothing more has been unjust; for a person who is negligent of the sciences and a sleeping person both possess 'intellect,' according to this assessment of the term. [They both have] an innate inclination, despite the fact that they lack [knowledge] in the sciences. It is as if the attribute of 'living' is an inclination that predisposes the body to self-motivated movement and response to sense perception. Similarly the intellect is a natural inclination that prepares certain animals for the speculative sciences.

If it were feasible, then, to equate human beings and donkeys in their innate inclinations and sense perception, and if it were said that, "The only distinction between them is that God تَعَالَىٰ, according to the dictate of predilection, creates in human beings sciences that He has not created in the donkey and the other animals"; it would be feasible to equate the inanimate beings and the donkey in the attribute of 'life' and say, "The only distinction between them is that God تَعَالَىٰ creates in the donkey movements that are unique to the donkey, according to the dictate of predilection." For, if the donkey were considered inanimate and lifeless, it must necessarily be concluded that every movement observed on his part, and in the order observed, derived from God سُبْحَانَهُ. As it would likewise be concluded, necessarily, that, "The only trait that differentiates the donkey from an inanimate object in movement is a characteristic natural inclination expressed by the term 'life'"; in like fashion the distinction between human beings and animals in the comprehending of the speculative sciences is by means of the innate inclination expressed by the term 'intellect.'[18]

It is like the innate quality present in a mirror that differentiates it from other corporeal bodies and gives it the ability to reflect images and colors in a manner unique to each, namely its polish or sheen. In the same manner the eye is distinguished from the forehead by its characteristics and attributes which endow it with sense perception. Hence the relationship of the innate inclination to the sciences is similar to the relationship of the eye to sense percep-

18 Thus ends the defense of al-Muḥāsibī's definition of the intellect. See al-Zabīdī, *Itḥāf*, 1:460.

tion; and the relationship of the Qurʾān and the law to this innate inclination in guiding it to the unveiling of the sciences related to it is like sunlight to eyesight. This is how this natural inclination ought to be understood.

The second [meaning of *ʿaql*]: It is the science that comes or types of knowledge that come into being in the disposition of a child; it discerns the possibility of possible occurrences and the impossibility of the impossible. It is like the knowledge that two is more than one, and that one person cannot be in two places at the same time. This is the definition intended by a certain theologian when he defined 'the intellect' by saying, "It is a facet of the necessary sciences, like the knowledge of the possiblility of possible occurrences, and the impossibility of the impossible."

This meaning is sound in itself, for these sciences do indeed exist; and referring to it as 'the intellect' is apparent; the error however, lies in refuting [the intellect's quality as] an innate inclination and saying, "Nothing other than these sciences exist."

The third [meaning of *ʿaql*]: It is the sciences derived through the observation of events and circumstances as they arise. For a person who has become worldly through a variety of experiences and disciplined by the many paths he has journeyed upon is generally said to be a person of intellect. Whereas a person to whom these qualities are not ascribed is said to be a person devoid of intellect, stupid, and ignorant. This is another category of knowledge that is referred to as 'the intellect.'

The fourth [meaning of *ʿaql*] applies when the faculty of that innate inclination results in the capacity to discern the consequences of one's actions. For example, [it is] the ability to control and overcome the desires that motivate one to seek immediate gratification. One who has attained this capacity is called a 'possessor of intellect,' when his decision to undertake or restrain himself regarding a matter is in accordance with a careful consideration of the consequences, not [according to] the dictates of a desire for immediate gratification. This is also among the distinguishing traits of humankind and ways whereby they are differentiated from all the other animals.

[As to these four definitions of the term *ʿaql*, here it is incumbent to point out to the reader that]

The first [of these categories] is the foundation of the other three, the root, and fountain-head.

The second is the branch closest to the first.

The third is the offshoot that branches off from both the first and second; since the empirical sciences are derived from the faculties of the innate inclination of the intellect and the necessary sciences.

The fourth is the final fruit and its ultimate goal.

The first two derive from innate predisposition and the final two are acquired through applied effort.

In addressing this, ʿAlī [may God enoble his face] said,[19]

I saw the intellect as two, distinct one unto another
One a disposition, one acquired through hearing

[Knowledge acquired through] hearing affords no benefit
If there is no innate disposition to it

Just as the sun renders no benefit
When the light of the eye is precluded

The first category, [that of an innate inclination], is intended in the words of the Messenger of God ﷺ, "God created nothing more honored by Him than the intellect."[20] The final, [the fruit of the intellect], was intended in the words of the Messenger of God ﷺ when he said, "When the people draw nigh to God by righteousness and worthy acts, you must draw nigh by means of your intellect."[21] This is the meaning intended in the words the Messenger of God ﷺ spoke to Abū l-Dardāʾ رضي الله عنه, "Increase in intellect, you will increase in proximity to your Lord." To which he responded, 'May my father and mother be your ransom! How could such be for me?' The Messenger of God ﷺ said, "Eschew God's تعالى forbidden things, accomplish God's تعالى obligatory acts, you will be one who possesses intellect; undertake worthy endeavors, your share of esteem and honor will increase in this world,

19 From the ʿAlī b. Abī Ṭālib, *Anwār al-ʿuqūl li-waṣī l-rasūl*, 161.

20 Narrated by al-Ṭabarānī, *al-Muʿjam al-kabīr*, 8:283; Abū Nuʿaym, *Ḥilya*, 7:318; and al-Bayhaqī, *Shuʿab al-īmān*, 4312.

21 Narrated by Abū Nuʿaym, *Ḥilya*, 1:18.

and in the next you will attain a station of proximity and nobility from your Lord."[22]

Saʿīd b. al-Musayyib related that ʿUmar, Ubayy b. Kaʿb, and Abū Hurayra رَضِيَ اللَّهُ عَنْهُمْ entered into the presence of the Messenger of God صَلَّى اللَّهُ عَلَيْهِ وَسَلَّمَ and asked, "O Messenger of God صَلَّى اللَّهُ عَلَيْهِ وَسَلَّمَ who is the most knowledgeable among the people?" He صَلَّى اللَّهُ عَلَيْهِ وَسَلَّمَ responded, "The possessor of intellect." They then asked, "Who is most devout in their practices?" To which he صَلَّى اللَّهُ عَلَيْهِ وَسَلَّمَ replied, "The possessor of intellect." They then asked, "Who is the most worthy among the people?" He again replied, "The possessor of intellect." Whereupon they asked, "Is the possessor of intellect [among us], a person who is established in upright character, whose eloquence is evident, who is open-handed and generous, and of high repute among his peers?" To which he صَلَّى اللَّهُ عَلَيْهِ وَسَلَّمَ responded, *And gold ornament. But all that is not but the enjoyment of worldly life. And the hereafter with your Lord is for the righteous* [43:35]; verily, one possessed of intellect is the one who is pious, though in this world they may be regarded with little esteem and humble."[23]

The Messenger of God صَلَّى اللَّهُ عَلَيْهِ وَسَلَّمَ said, in another *ḥadīth*, "The possessor of intellect is one who has faith in God, affirms [the message] of His messengers, and is conscientious in obedience to Him."[24]

[From this] it seems that the linguistic origin of the term applies to that innate inclination, and likewise its actual function. It was only applied to the sciences in that it is its fruit, in the same manner a thing is known by its fruit. It is said, "Knowledge is 'reverence' [in the heart]; and the scholar is the one who reveres God تَعَالَىٰ." For reverence is the fruit of knowledge, thus it applies figuratively to meanings other than innate inclination. Our goal however is not in-depth research into the linguistic implications of the term.[25]

The goal [is to affirm] that these four categories do indeed exist and that the term *ʿaql* applies to them all. There is no differ-

---

22 Narrated by al-Ḥakīm al-Tirmidhī, *Nawādir al-uṣūl*, 242.

23 Among the *ḥadīth* cited by Dāwūd al-Muḥabbar, *al-ʿAql*; for variants see al-Zabīdī, *Itḥāf*, 1:462.

24 Among the *ḥadīth* cited by Dāwūd al-Muḥabbar, *al-ʿAql*; for variants see al-Zabīdī, *Itḥāf*, 1:462.

25 With this, al-Ghazālī is indicating that he opposes the linguists concerning the classification they use for the term; see al-Zabīdī, *Itḥāf*, 1:463.

ence of opinion as to the existence of any of them except the first category [namely, that it is an innate inclination that differentiates human beings from all other animals and affords them the ability to apprehend the speculative sciences]. However the sound opinion is that it does exist, moreover, it is in fact the origin of the use of the term, and these other sciences are inherently integral aspects of that innate inclination, and are only manifest when in the course of events, causes arise that bring them forth into existence; it is thus as though these sciences do not derive from occurrences of external origins; on the contrary, it is as if they were latently existent in it, then became manifest.

An example of this is ground water; it becomes manifest when shafts are dug underground, then it collects [in basins and cisterns] and is discernable by the senses; it is not the case that it arises by bringing something new to it. The same is true in the case of the oil in the almond, and rose water in the rose.

This is why God تَعَالَىٰ says, *And* [*mention*] *when your Lord took from the children of Adam—from their loins—their descendants and made them testify of themselves,* [*saying to them*], "*Am I not your Lord?" They said,* "*Yes, we have testified*" [7:172]. The intent in this verse was the attestation of their souls, not the attestation of the tongue [alone]; for in the matter of the attestation of the tongue—once tongues and individuals were created—people were separated into those who attest [to God's truth] and those who deny it.[26]

For this reason He تَعَالَىٰ says, *And if you asked them who created them, they would surely say,* "*God*" [43:87]. Meaning, if you were to reflect upon their circumstances, their souls and innermost beings would attest [to the verse] [*Adhere to*] *the fiṭra of God upon which He has created* [*all*] *people* [30:30], meaning: all the children of Adam were endowed with the innate disposition of faith in God عَزَّوَجَلَّ,

26 "Among them are those who remain steadfast to their original covenant from the first moment, and among them there are those who reaffirm their covenant later, by the grace of God تَعَالَىٰ, then there are those who never attested at all. So the covenant is attested to in Qurʾānic verse, but not as a verbal covenant; that which the author has cited here is an allusion to the fruit of the intellect, as the realization of God and the utmost degree that a person can reach in that; therefore the most highly esteemed fruit of the intellect is the realization of God سُبْحَانَهُ worthy obedience, and restraint from disobedience." Al-Zabīdī, *Itḥāf*, 1:463.

moreover [they have] the ability to realize the inherent nature of things as they are.[27] By this I mean that the realization of things is as if it is contained in the souls in order to bring the propensity of them near to full comprehension.

Then [just] as faith has been embedded into the soul as an innate disposition humankind has been divided into two categories: those who have turned their backs on it and forgotten, they are the disbelievers; and those who reflect on their conscience and remember, like someone who had carried [on his person] a written attestation and forgot it carelessly, then remembered it. This why God تَعَالَىٰ says, *that they might remember* [2:221]; and God تَعَالَىٰ also says, *And that those of understanding would be reminded* [38:29]; and He تَعَالَىٰ says, *And remember the favor of God upon you and His covenant with which He bound you* [5:7]; and God تَعَالَىٰ says as well, *And We have certainly made the Qurʾān easy for remembrance, so is there any who will remember?* [54:17, 54:22, 54:32, 54:40].

Calling this manner [of knowing] 'remembrance' is not far-fetched, for remembrance is of two sorts.

One of them is that one remembers a picture that had been present in his heart, yet vanished after having been present.

The other is that one remembers a picture that was an integral aspect in the heart by innate disposition.

The realities discussed here should be apparent to anyone who regards them with the light of insight, but [they are] opaque and burdensome, however, for one who takes only from the readily available transmitted reports and initiated customs, rather than through unveiling and direct perception. This is why you see such men stumbling over Qurʾānic verses similar to these cited here, haphazardly flailing away in an effort to elucidate the import of 'remember' and the 'attestation of the soul,' and giving the impression that there are numerous ambiguities in the reports and Qurʾānic verses, until this overcomes him and he regards them in disdain, and believes that therein are incoherencies.

---

27 Al-Ghazālī did not say, "even more so with the capability to realize God تَعَالَىٰ." For he meant by faith the necessary realization of God, which is the realization of each person that he is acted upon and that he is given the ability to do what he does and move among various conditions. It is not an independently acquired realization. See al-Zabīdī, *Itḥāf*, 1:463.

An example of such a person is that of a blind man who enters a house and stumbles over the well-arranged utensils therein, then says, "What is the matter here with these utensils! Why haven't they been put up in their places, out of the way?" Whereupon he is told that, "They are in their proper places; the real defect is in your eyesight."

Defective insight follows the same course, however it is more devastating and of greater detriment, for the soul is like a mounted soldier and the physical body the trusty steed; blindness on the part of the soldier is a greater detriment than blindness on the part of the horse.

Comparing inward insight and outward eyesight God تَعَالَىٰ says, *The heart did not lie* [*about*] *what it saw* [53:11].

God تَعَالَىٰ also says, *And thus did We show Abraham the realm of the heavens and the earth that he would be among the certain* [*in faith*] [6:75].

God تَعَالَىٰ refers to its opposite as blindness, when He تَعَالَىٰ says, *For indeed, it is not eyes that are blinded, but blinded are the hearts which are within the breasts* [22:46].

God تَعَالَىٰ also says, *And whoever is blind in this* [*life*] *will be blind in the hereafter and more astray in way* [17:72].

All these are matters that have been made evident to the prophets, some by means of visual perception, and some by insight, are all called perception.

To summarize, whoever's inner insight has not become piercing will grasp nothing through it of the religion but its husk and mere semblance, not its kernel and realities.

These then, are the categories to which the term 'intellect' applies.

An Elucidation on People's Disparities in the Intellect

PEOPLE HAVE LONG DIFFERED on the disparities of the intellect [and the manner in which it differs among people]. There is no sense in occupying oneself by citing the discussions of those whose attainments [in this domain] are minimal; on the contrary it is more suitable and of greater import to hasten directly to a clear exposition of the truth in the matter.

The evident truth therein is that it be said: These disparities touch all four categories [of the intellect], with the exception of the second, which is that of necessary knowledge of the possibility of possible occurrences and the impossibility of impossible circumstances, for certainly one who knows that two is greater than one, realizes, as well, the impossibility of a single body simultaneously occupying two places, and the impossibility of a single entity being both created and pre-eternal, and so on with other comparable examples. And anyone who comprehends such examples, comprehends them as verifiable, devoid of any doubt. Where the other three categories are concerned, disparity becomes an issue.

The fourth category concerns the mastery of the capacity [of the intellect] to restrain the desires. There is no concealing the disparity between people therein; furthermore there is no concealing the disparate states of a given individual therein.

At times this disparity is due to disparate desire; for one possessed of intellect may be capable of avoiding certain desires and not others. The issue, however, is not limited to this consideration alone. A youth, for example, may be incapable of abstaining from illicit sexual relations, yet when he grows older and his intellect matures and he is able to do so. By contrast, the strength of one's desire for ostentatious show and public rank only increases with age, it does not weaken.

The reason for this is the disparity in the knowledge that discerns the inherent danger of that desire. For this reason a physician is capable of restraining himself from certain harmful foods, while one equal to him in intellect may not be capable of that, if he is not a physician, though he may in fact believe that on the whole such food is harmful. Because the knowledge of the physician, however, is more exhaustive, his fear is greater. In this manner, fear becomes a soldier in the service of the intellect, and an instrument in restraining the desires and overcoming them. For this reason the scholar is more capable of disavowing disobedience than the ignorant person is; this is because of his knowledge of the harm inherent in disobedience. By this I [am] referring to the true scholar, not those of the flowing head coverings who dote and rave and prate.

Even though the disparity [discussed above] was the result of desire, it does not imply disparity of the intellect, though it may have resulted from the base of knowledge; we continue to apply the term 'intellect to this category of knowledge,' for by it the innate inclination of the intellect is strengthened, disparity therein thus relates to the name applied to it.

The disparity may derive solely from the innate inclination of the intellect itself [in a given individual]; should it become stronger its capacity to restrain desire without a doubt would be more effectual.

As for the third category: It concerns empirical sciences. No one refutes the disparity of people therein, for they differ from one another in the measure of the correct conclusions [they] draw and in the alacrity of [their] comprehension, the cause for which is either a disparity in the innate inclination, or a disparity of personal experience.

As for the first category, it is the foundational principle [of all the categories]—I mean the innate inclination. There is no disputing disparity therein, for it is like a light that rises within the soul, bringing forth its dawn. Its first rays begin to illuminate the soul at the age of discernment, whereupon it does not cease to develop and increase gradually, step by step, until it reaches its fruition as one approaches the age of forty.

An example of this is the light of dawn. Its initial stages are faint and indistinct, difficult to discern; then it gradually begins to increase until it reaches its fruition with the rising of the orb of the sun itself.

The disparity of the light of insight is similar to that of the light of eyesight itself; the difference between a person with impaired vision and [one who is] keen-sighted is readily discernable. Moreover, God's عَزَّوَجَلَّ habit or custom courses throughout His creation in a process of a gradually ongoing creation. For example, until the innate inclination of desire does not appear in a boy all at once upon his reaching puberty; on the contrary, it appears little by little in progressive degrees. Thus, it is with all the faculties and characteristic traits.

Anyone who refutes the disparity of the people in this innate inclination is someone who has been divested of the fetters of the intellect.

Whoever imagines [for example] that the intellect of the Prophet ﷺ is comparable to the intellect of the inhabitants of the rural regions or the coarse Bedouin is himself more contemptible than anyone among these rural types.[28] How might anyone refute the disparity in this innate inclination, when, if it were not for this, the people themselves would not differ from one another in [their] comprehension of the sciences, and they would not be grouped into the simple-minded, who are only capable of understanding after long and tedious explanation by a teacher; and into the bright who comprehend with the slightest hint or allusion; and into the accomplished scholar from whose soul flows forth the realities of affairs without need of teaching. As God تَعَالَىٰ says *. . . whose oil would almost glow even if untouched by fire. Light upon light. . .* [24:35].

Such is the case of the prophets عَلَيْهِمُ ٱلسَّلَامُ to whom enigmatic matters are made evident without studying or hearing oral reports. This is expressed by the term 'inspiration'. The Prophet ﷺ spoke of this when he said, "Verily the holy spirit breathed into my innermost heart, 'Love whomever you will, for verily you will part from them; live as long as you will, verily you will die; do whatever you wish, verily you will be recompensed accordingly.'"[29]

This unique manner of bestowing knowledge from the angels to the prophets differs from explicit revelation that invokes hearing a distinct voice through the auditory sense of the ear, or witnessing an angel by means of actual eyesight; for this reason this sort

---

28 Abū Nuʿaym, *Ḥilya*, 4:26, narrates that Wahb b. Munabbih said, "I read seventy-one books, and in all of them found that God had bestowed upon no one from the beginning of the world until its end, an intellect that could compare to the intellect of Muḥammad ﷺ, except like a grain of sand among all the grains of sand in the world; and verily Muḥammad is the most incomparable of people in intellect and the most outstanding among them in discernment." Al-Zabīdī, *Itḥāf*, 1:467.

29 The beginning of this *ḥadīth* was narrated by ʿAbd al-Razzāq, *al-Muṣannaf*, 11:125, and Abū Nuʿaym, *Ḥilya*, 10:26; the remainder of the *ḥadīth* is in *Ḥilya*, 3:202, and al-Bayhaqī, *Shuʿab al-īmān*, 10058.

of revelation is referred to in the tradition as, 'breathing into the innermost heart.'

The stations of revelation are manifold, delving therein is inappropriate in a discussion of the knowledge of conduct, it is more appropriate to [discuss it in] the domain of the knowledge of unveiling.

Do not suppose, however, that realization of the degrees of revelation demands the rank of one receiving revelation, for it is not far-fetched for a physician, who is himself unwell to be familiar with the degrees of health, or for a reprobate to know the degrees of justice, though he may be devoid of any of them, for knowledge is one thing and the existence of what is known is another. Not everyone who knows of prophecy or sainthood is a prophet or a saint, nor is everyone who has knowledge of piety, scrupulous discernment, and their subtle nuances, pious or scrupulous.

Humankind are divided into those who attain mindfulness from within themselves and comprehend, and into those who only understand through exhortation and instruction, and those for whom neither exhortation nor instruction render any benefit. [This is] similar to the division of the earth into places where water accumulates and becomes abundant until it flows forth from the earth in free flowing springs, and places where one must dig into the earth so that the water may come forth in irrigation canals, and places where excavation is of no benefit [because] the land is without water. All this is based upon the disparity in the substances of the earth and their qualities. The disparity between the souls [of humankind] and the innate inclination of the intellect is similar to this.

A tradition narrated on the authority of ʿAbdallāh b. Salām رَضِيَ ٱللَّهُ عَنْهُ attests to the disparity of the intellect itself [among people]. He questioned the Messenger of God صَلَّى ٱللَّهُ عَلَيْهِ وَسَلَّمَ—in a long *ḥadīth* at the end of which there is a description of the immensity of the throne, in which the angels asked, "O our Lord! Have you created anything of greater magnitude than the throne?" God تَعَالَىٰ replied, "Yes, the intellect." Whereupon they inquired, "How vast is its magnitude?" God تَعَالَىٰ replied, "How far from the mark [you are]! Knowledge of it is beyond comprehension! Have you knowledge of the number of grains of sand [in creation]?" They responded, "No." God عَزَّ وَجَلَّ

responded, "I have created the categories of the intellect as diverse as the number of grains of sand. Among humanity there are those who have been given a grain, and among them are those who have been given two, among them are those who have been given three or four [grains], and among them are those who have been given a goodly share, and among them are those who have been given a camel's load, and among them are those who have been given more than that."[30]

If you should ask, "Why do certain people among the Sufis disparage and blame 'the intellect' and knowledge derived from the intellect?"

Know that the reason for this is that the people [of our times] have altered the meanings of the terms 'the intellect' and 'knowledge derived from the intellect' to refer to dialectics and disputation based upon the refutation of contradictions and established scholarly criteria; all of this constitutes the domain of theology. It was consequently impossible for the Sufis to convince these people [that]—"Indeed, you have erred in applying these terms in this way"—[they knew] that these meanings would never be erased from their hearts, given their habitual use in the people's routine discussions, and given that their meanings had become deeply rooted in [people's] hearts. As a result the Sufis were critical of the [manner of the use of the] terms 'intellect' and 'knowledge derived from the intellect,' [all the while] they employed the same terms in their discourse within their own domain [Sufism].

How could the light of inner insight by which God تَعَالَىٰ and the truth of the prophets become known, be conceived of disparagingly or with blame, when God تَعَالَىٰ has praised it so highly?[31]

If it (*ʿaql*) were regarded with blame, what would be worthy of praise after that?

If the law is praiseworthy in itself, by what means can the veracity of the law be ascertained?

---

30 This was narrated summarily by al-Ḥakīm al-Tirmidhī, *Nawādir al-uṣūl*, 242, Ibn al-Muḥabbar narrated it in its entirety in *al-ʿAql*, see al-Zabīdī, *Itḥāf*, 1:469.

31 *And these examples We present to the people, but none will understand them except those of knowledge* [29:43].

For if the veracity of the law were ascertained by means of the inherently flawed and blameworthy intellect, then it cannot be trusted, then the law would be flawed and blameworthy as well.[32]

No heed is paid to [the statement of] one who says, "Verily, the law is comprehended through the eye of certitude and the light of firm faith, not through the intellect." For we intend by the term 'intellect' that which he intends by the terms 'eye of certitude' and 'light of firm faith'; namely the inherent inward quality by which humankind is differentiated from the animals, and through which they comprehend the true nature of reality.[33]

The great majority of these confused statements have arisen from the ignorance of certain groups of people who sought to know realities through words and terms, whereupon they wandered about as a result of the confusion that constitutes the technical terminologies of the people, terminologies that are but derived from words and terms themselves.

This should suffice in the elucidation of the intellect. God knows
best where rectitude lies. *The Book of Knowledge* is complete.
Being the first book of the Quarter of Worship from
the books of *The Revival of the Religious Sciences*
Praise be to God, Lord of the worlds. May
God send blessings of peace upon the
best of His creation, our master
Muḥammad, and the
entirety of
his family

It is followed by [Book 2] *Kitāb qawāʿid al-ʿaqāʾid*
[*The Principles of the Creed*]

32 "For if that upon which the veracity of something is dependent is untenable, that upon which it depended is untenable as well." See al-Zabīdī, *Itḥāf*, 1:469.

33 "Their words, 'Verily, it [the Law] is comprehended by the eye of certitude and the light of firm faith' are correct; their words, 'not by the intellect'" are incorrect. This was their error refuted by Imām al-Ghazālī, see al-Zabīdī, *Itḥāf*, 1:470.

Bibliography

Works in Western Languages

Asad, Muhammad. *The Message of the Qurʾān*. Gibraltar: Dar al-Andalus, 1980.

Renard, John. *Historical Dictionary of Sufism*. Lanham, MD: Scarecrow Press, 2005.

———. *Knowledge of God in Classical Sufism*. Mahwah, NJ: Paulist Press, 2004.

Works in Arabic

al-ʿAbbās b. al-Aḥnāf, b. al-Aswad al-Yamāmī. *Dīwān al-ʿAbbās b. al-Aḥnāf*. Edited by ʿĀtika al-Khazrājī. Cairo: Maṭbaʿat Dār al-Kutub al-Miṣriyya, 1954.

ʿAbd al-Qādir b. ʿUmar al-Baghdādī. *Khizānat al-adab wa-lubb lubāb lisān al-ʿArab ʿalā shawāhid sharḥ al-Kāfiya*. Beirut: Dār Ṣādir, 1968[?].

ʿAbd al-Razzāq b. Hammām al-Ṣanʿānī. *al-Muṣannaf*. Edited by Ḥabīb al-Raḥmān al-ʿAẓamī. Beirut: Maktab al-Islāmī, 1983.

Abū l-Aswad al-Duʾalī. *Dīwān*. Edited by Muḥammad Ḥasan al-Yāsīn. Beirut: Dār wa-Maktabat al-Hilāl, 1998.

Abū l-ʿAtāhiya, Ismāʿīl b. al-Qāsim b. Sūwayd. *Abū l-ʿAtāhiya ashʿārʾahu wa-akhbārahu*. Edited by Shukhrī Fayṣal. Damascus: Dār al-Mallāḥ, 1964.

Abū Dāwūd, Sulaymān b. al-Ashaʿth al-Sijistānī. *Sunan Abū Dāwūd*. Edited by ʿIzzat ʿAbīd al-Daʿās and ʿĀdil al-Sayyid. Beirut: Dār Ibn Ḥazm, 1997.

Abū Nuʿaym al-Iṣbahānī, Aḥmad b. ʿAbdallāh. *Ḥilyat al-awliyāʾ*. Cairo: Maṭbaʿāt al-Saʿāda wa-l-Khānijī, 1357 AH.

———. *Tārīkh Iṣbahān*. Edited by Sayyid Kusrawī Ḥasan. Beirut: Dār al-Kutub al-ʿIlmiyya, 1990.

Abū Ṭāhir al-Salafī, Aḥmad b. Muḥammad. *Muʿjam al-safr*. Edited by

ʿAbdallāh ʿUmar al-Barūdī. Beirut: Dār al-Fikr, 1993.

Abū Ṭālib al-Makkī, Muḥammad b. ʿAlī. *Qūt al-qulūb*. Cairo: al-Maṭbaʿat al-Maymaniyya, 1310 AH.

Abū Yaʿlā, Aḥmad b. ʿAlī. *Musnad Abū Yaʿlā al-Mawṣūlī*. Edited by Ḥusayn Salīm Asad al-Dārānī. Damascus: Dār al-Maʾmūn li-l-Turāth and Dār al-Thaqafa al-ʿArabiyya, 1989.

Aḥmad b. Ḥanbal. *Musnad al-Imām Aḥmad b. Ḥanbal*. Edited by Shuʿayb al-Arnāʾūṭ. Beirut: Muʾassasat al-Risāla, 1995.

———. *al-Zuhd*. Edited by Muḥammad ʿAbd al-Salam Shāhīn. Beirut: Dār al-Kutub al-ʿIlmiyya, 1999.

al-Ājirī, Muḥammad b. al-Ḥusayn. *Akhlāq ḥamlat al-Qurʾān*. Edited by Fawāz Aḥmad Zamarlī. Beirut: Dār al-Kitāb al-ʿArabī, 1987.

al-ʿAjlūnī, Ismāʿīl b. Muḥammad. *Kashf al-khafāʾ*. Beirut: Dār Iḥyāʾ al-Turāth al-ʿArabī, 1351 AH.

ʿAlī b. Abī Ṭālib. *Anwār al-ʿuqūl li-waṣī l-rasūl*. Edited by ʿAbd al-Majīd Hamū. Beirut: Dār Ṣādir, 2010.

al-Balādhurī, Aḥmad b. Yaḥyā. *Ansāb al-ashrāf*. Edited by Suhayb Zakkār and Riyāḍ Zarkalī. Beirut: Dār al-Fikr, 1996.

al-Bayhaqī, Aḥmad b. al-Ḥusayn. *al-Madkhal ilā l-sunan al-kubrā*. Edited by Muḥammad Ḍiyāʾ al-Raḥmān al-ʿĀẓamī. Riyadh: Dār Aḍwāʾ al-Salaf, 1420 AH.

———. *Manāqib al-Shāfiʿī*. Edited by Aḥmad Ṣaqr. Cairo: Maktabat Dār al-Turāth, 1971.

———. *Shuʿab al-īmān*. Edited by Muḥammad al-Saʿīd b. Bayūnī Zaghlūl. Beirut: Dār al-Kutub al-ʿIlmiyyya, 2000.

al-Bukhārī, Muḥammad b. Ismāʿīl. *al-Adab al-mufrad*. Edited by Muḥammad Fūʾād ʿAbd al-Bāqī. Cairo: al-Maktab al-Salafiyya, 1997.

———. *Ṣaḥīḥ al-Bukhārī*. Istanbul: n.p. [reprint of Beirut: Dār Ṭūq al-Najāt, 1422].

al-Damīrī, Muḥammad b. Mūsā. *Ḥayāt al-ḥayawān al-kubrā*. Edited by Ibrāhīm Sāliḥ. Damascus: Dār al-Bashāʾir, 2005.

al-Dārimī, ʿAbdallāh b. ʿAbd al-Raḥmān. *Musnad al-Dārimī* [*Sunan*]. Edited by Ḥusayn Salīm Asad al-Dārānī. Riyadh: Dār al-Mughnī, 2000.

al-Daylamī, Shīrawayh b. Shahdār. *al-Firdaws bi-maʾthūr al-khiṭṭāb = Musnad al-firdaws*. Edited by Saʿīd b. Basyūnī Zaghlūl. Beirut: Dār al-Kutub al-ʿIlmiyya, 1986.

al-Daynūrī, Aḥmad b. Marwān. *al-Majālasa wa-jawāhir al-ʿilm*. Beirut: Dār Ibn Ḥazm, 2002.

al-Dhahabī, Muḥammad b. Aḥmad. *Siyar aʿlām al-nubalāʾ*. Edited by

Shuʿayb al-Arnāʾūṭ, et al. Beirut: Muʾassasat al-Risāla, 1996.

al-Ḍiyāʾ al-Dīn al-Maqdisī, Muḥammad b. ʿAbd al-Wāḥid. *al-Aḥādīth al-mukhtāra*. Edited by ʿAbd al-Malik ʿAbdallāh b. Dahīsh. Beirut: Dār Khiḍr, 2001.

al-Ghazālī, Abū Ḥāmid Muḥammad b. Muḥammad. *Faḍāʾiḥ al-Bāṭiniyya* ed Muḥammad ʿAlī l-Quṭb (Beirut and Sidon: al-Maktaba al-ʿAṣriyya, 2001).

———. *al-Iqtiṣād fī l-iʿtiqād*. Edited by Anas Muḥammad ʿAdnān al-Sharfāwī. Jedda: Dār al-Minhāj, 2008.

———. *Khulāṣat al-mukhtaṣar wa-naqāwat al-muʿtaṣar*. Edited by Amjād Rashīd Muḥammad ʿAlī. Jedda: Dār al-Minhāj, 2007.

———. "Kīmiyāʾ al-saʿāda" in *Majmuʿāt rasāʾil al-Imām al-Ghazālī*. Vol. 5. Edited by Aḥmad Shams al-Dīn. Beirut: Dār al-Kutub al-ʿIlmiyya, 1997.

———. *Maqṣad al-asnā*. Edited by Maḥmūd Bījū. Damascus: Maṭbʿat al-Ṣabāḥ, 1999.

———. *Mishkāt al-anwār*. Edited by ʿAbd al-ʿAzīz al-Sayrawān. Damascus: Dār al-Īmān, 1990.

———. *Mīzān al-ʿamal*. Edited by Sulaymān Dunyā. Cairo: Dār al-Maʿārif, 1964.

———. *al-Munqidh min al-ḍalāl*. Edited by Maḥmūd Bījū. Damascus: Maṭbʿat al-Ṣabāḥ, 1992.

Translations:

The Book of Knowledge. Translated by Nabih Amin Faris. Lahore: Sh. Muḥammad Ashraf, 1962.

"The Book of Knowledge,' Being a Translation, with Introduction and Notes of al-Ghazzālī's Book of the 'Iḥyāʾ, Kitāb al-ʿIlm." Translated by William Alexander McCall. PhD thesis, Hartford Seminary, 1940.

Faḍāʾiḥ al-Bāṭiniyya wa-Faḍāʾil al-Mustaẓhiriyya [The infamies of the Bātinites and the virtues of the Mustaẓhirites]. Partially translated by Richard J. McCarthy in *Al-Ghazali: Deliverance from Error*, 151–244. Louisville, KY: Fons Vitae, n.d.

al-Ghazālī: Letter to a Disciple. Translated by Tobias Mayer. Cambridge: Islamic Texts Society, 2005.

al-Ghazālī's Moderation in Belief. Translated by Aladdin M. Yaqub. Chicago: University of Chicago Press, 2013.

al-Ḥabashī, Muḥammad b. ʿAbd al-Raḥmān Jamāl al-Dīn. *Nashr ṭayy al-taʿrīf fī faḍli ḥamlati al-ʿilm al-sharīf wa-l-radd ʿalā mā fīhim min al-sakhīf*. Jedda: Dār al-Minhaj, 1997.

al-Ḥākim al-Nīsābūrī, Muḥammad b. ʿAbdallāh. *al-Madkhal ilā l-ṣaḥīḥ*.

Edited by Rabīʿa Hādī l-Madkhalī. Beirut: Muʾassasat al-Risāla, 1404 AH.

———. *al-Mustadrak ʿalā al-Ṣaḥiḥayn*. Hyderabad: Dāʾirat al-Maʿārif al-Niẓāmiyya, 1335 AH [repr. Beirut: Dār al-Maʿrifa, n.d.].

al-Ḥakīm al-Tirmidhī, Muḥammad b. ʿAlī. *Nawādir al-uṣūl*. Beirut: Dār Ṣādir, n.d. [reprint Cairo, 1293 edition].

al-Haythamī, Nūr al-Dīn. *Bughiyat al-bāḥith ʿan zawāʾid Musnad al-Ḥārith b. Abī Usāma*. Edited by Ḥusayn Aḥmad Ṣāliḥ al-Bākrī. Medina: Markaz Khidma al-Sunna wa-l-Sīra al-Nabawīy, 1992.

Ibn ʿAbd al-Barr, Yūsuf b. ʿAbdallāh. *al-Intiqāʾ fī faḍāʾil al-thalāthat al-aʾimmat al-fuqahāʾ*. Edited by ʿAbd al-Fattāḥ Abū Ghudda. Beirut: Dār al-Bashāʾir al-Islāmiyya, 1997.

———. *Jāmiʿ bayān al-ʿilm wa-faḍlih*. Edited by Abū al-Ashbāl al-Zuhayrī. Riyadh: Dār Ibn al-Jawzī, 1994.

———. *al-Tamhīd*. Casablanca: Wizārat al-Awqāf, 1967.

Ibn ʿAbd Rabbihi, Aḥmad b. Muḥammad al-Andalūsī. *al-ʿIqd al-farīd*. Edited by Aḥmad al-Amīn, Aḥmad al-Zayn, and Ibrāhīm al-Ibārī. Cairo: Lajnat al-Taʾlif wa-Tarjama wa-Nashr, 1940.

Ibn Abī ʿĀṣim, Aḥmad b. ʿAmr. *al-Sunna*. Beirut: Dār Ibn Ḥazm, 2004.

Ibn Abī l-Dunyā, ʿAbdallāh b. Muḥammad al-Qurashī. *Dhamm al-dunyā*. Edited by Muḥammad ʿAbd al-Qādir Aḥmad ʿAṭā. Beirut: Muʾassasat al-Kutub al-Thaqafiyya, 1993.

———. *al-ʿUzla wa-l-infirād*. Edited by Mashūr b. Ḥasan Āl Salmān. Riyadh: Dār al-Waṭan, 1997.

———. *al-Yaqīn*. Edited by Yāsīn Muḥammad al-Sawās. Beirut: Dār al-Bashāʾir al-Islāmiyya, 2004.

Ibn Abī Ḥātim, ʿAbd al-Raḥmān b. Muḥammad b. Idrīs. *Ādāb al-Shāfiʿī wa-manāqibihi*. Edited by ʿAbd al-Ghanī ʿAbd al-Khāliq. Cairo: Maktabat al-Khānijī, 2001.

———. *Tafsīr al-qurʾān al-ʿaẓīm*. Edited by Asad Muḥammad al-Ṭayyib. Riyadh: Maktabat Nizār Muṣṭafā al-Bāz, 1997.

Ibn Abī Shayba, ʿAbdallāh b. Muḥammad. *Muṣannaf*. Edited by Muḥammad ʿAwāmma. Jedda: Dār al-Minhāj, 2006.

Ibn ʿAdī al-Jurjānī, ʿAbdallāh. *al-Kāmil fī ḍuʿafāʾ al-rijāl*. Edited by Suhayl Zakkār and Yaḥyā Mukhtār Ghazāwī. Beirut: Dār al-Fikr, 1988.

Ibn ʿArbashāh, Aḥmad b. Muḥammad. *ʿAjāʾib al-maqdūr fī akhbār taymūr*. Edited by Aḥmad Fāyaz al-Ḥamṣī. Beirut: Muʾassasat al-Risāla, 1986.

Ibn ʿAsākir, ʿAlī b. al-Ḥasan. *Tārīkh Dimashq*. Edited by Muḥibb al-Dīn ʿUmar b. Gharāma al-ʿUmrāwī. Beirut: Dār al-Fikr, 1995.

Ibn Baṭṭa, Ubaydallāh b. Muḥammad al-Abkarī. *al-Ibāna ʿan sharīʿāt al-*

firqa al-nājiyya. Edited by Sayyid ʿImrān. Cairo: Dār al-Ḥadīth, 2006.

Ibn Farḥūn, Ibrāhīm b. ʿAlī. *al-Dībāj al-madhhab*. Edited by ʿAlī ʿUmar. Cairo: Maktabat al-Thaqāfa al-Dīniyya, 2003.

———. *Fatḥ al-bārī bi-sharḥ Ṣaḥīḥ al-Bukhārī*. Edited by Muḥammad Fuʾād ʿAbd al-Bāqī. Damascus: Maktabat al-Ghazālī, 1996.

———. *Lisān al-mīzān*. Edited by ʿAbd al-Fatāḥ Abū Ghudda. Beirut: Dār al-Bashāʾir al-Islāmiyya, 2002.

———. *al-Maṭālib al-ʿāliyya*. Edited by Ayman Abū Yamānī and Ashrāf ʿAlī. Cairo: Muʾassasat Qurṭūba and Riyadh: al-Maktabat al-Makkiyya, 1997.

Ibn Ḥibbān = Muḥammad b. Ḥibbān al-Bustī. *Rawḍat al-ʿuqalāʾ*. Edited by ʿAbd al-ʿAlīm Muḥammad al-Darwīsh. Damascus: al-Hayʾa al-ʿĀmma al-Sūriyya lil-Kitāb, 2009.

Ibn Ḥijja al-Ḥamawī, Taqī l-Dīn Abū Bakr b. ʿAlī. *Khizānat al-adab wa-ghāyat al-arab*. Būlāq: al-Maṭbaʿat al-Āmira, 1874.

Ibn al-Jawzī, Jamāl al-Dīn ʿAbd al-Raḥmān b. ʿAlī b. Muḥammad. *al-Mawḍūʿāt*. Edited by ʿAbd al-Raḥmān Muḥammad ʿUthmān. Medina: al-Maktabat al-Safafīya, 1966.

Ibn Khallikān, Aḥmad b. Muḥammad. *Wafayāt al-aʿyān*. Edited by Iḥsān ʿAbbās. Beirut: Dār Ṣādir, 1968.

Ibn Māja, Muḥammad b. Yazīd. *Sunan Ibn Māja*. Edited by Muḥammad Fuʾād ʿAbd al-Bāqī. Cairo: Dār Iḥyāʾ al-Kutub al-ʿArabiyya, 1954.

Ibn al-Mubārak, ʿAbdallāh. *Dīwān al-Imām*. Edited by Mujāhid Muṣṭafā Bahjat. Mansoura: Dār al-Wafāʾ, 1992.

———. *Zuhd wa-l-raqāʾiq*. Edited by Ḥabīb al-Raḥmān al-ʿAẓamī. Beirut: Dār al-Kutub al-ʿIlmiyya, n.d.

Ibn Nabāta al-Miṣrī, Jamāl al-Dīn. *Dīwān*. Cairo: Dār Iḥyāʾ al-Turāth al-ʿArabī, n.d.

Ibn Qayyim al-Jawziyya, Muḥammad b. Abī Bakr. *Miftāḥ dār al-saʿāda*. Edited by Bashīr Muḥammad ʿAyūn. Damascus: Maktabat Dār al-Bayān, 1998.

Ibn Qutayba al-Dīnawayrī, ʿAbdallāh b. Muslim. *ʿUyūn al-akhbār*. Cairo: Dār al-Kutub al-Miṣriyya, 1930.

Ibn Saʿd = Muḥammad b. Saʿd al-Baṣrī. *Ṭabaqāt al-kabīr*. Edited by ʿAlī Muḥammad ʿUmar. Cairo: Maktabat al-Khanjī, 2001.

Ibn al-Ṣalāḥ, ʿUthmān b. ʿAbd al-Raḥmān. *Fatāwa*. Edited by ʿAbd al-Muʿṭī Amīn Qalaʿjī. Beirut: Dār al-Marʿīfa, 1986.

Ibn al-Ṭuyūrī, al-Mubārak b. ʿAbd al-Jabbār. *al-Ṭuyūriyyāt*. Edited by Dasmān Muʿālī and ʿAbbās al-Ḥasan. Riyadh: Dār Aḍwāʾ al-Salaf, 2004.

Ibn Waḍāḥ = Muḥammad b. Waḍāḥ al-Qurṭubī. *al-Bidaʿ wa-nahī ʿanha*. Edited by Muḥammad Aḥmad Dahmān. Cairo: Dār al-Ṣafā, 1990.

al-Jāḥiẓ, ʿAmr b. Baḥr. *al-Bayān wa-l-tibyīn*. Edited by ʿAbd al-Salam Hārūn. Cairo: Maktabat al-Khānijī, 1998.

al-Khaṭīb al-Baghdādī, Aḥmad b. ʿAlī. *al-Faqīh wa-l-mutafaqqih*. Edited by ʿĀdil Yūsuf al-ʿAzāzī. Riyadh: Dār Ibn al-Jawzī, 1421 AH.

———. *Iqtiḍāʾ al-ʿilm al-ʿamal*. Edited by Muḥammad Nāṣir al-Dīn al-Albānī. Beirut: al-Maktab al-Islāmī, 1984.

———. *al-Jāmiʿ li-akhlāq al-rāwī wa-ādāb al-sāmiʿ*. Edited by Muḥammad ʿAjjāj al-Khaṭīb. Beirut: Muʾassasat al-Risāla, 1991.

———. *al-Kifāya fī ʿilm al-riwāya*. Edited by Zakariyya ʿUmayrāt. Beirut: Dār al-Kutub al-ʿIlmiyya, 2006.

———. *Sharaf aṣḥāb al-ḥadīth*. Edited by Muḥammad Saʿīd Khaṭīb Ughlī. Ankara: Jāmiʿat Anqara, Kulliyya al-Ilāhiyyāt, n.d.

———. *Tārīkh Baghdād*. Edited by Muṣṭafā ʿAbd al-Qādir ʿAṭā. Beirut: Dār al-Kutub al-ʿIlmiyya, 1997.

Mālik b. Anas. *al-Muwaṭṭaʾ*. Edited by Muḥammad Fuʾād ʿAbd al-Bāqī. Cairo: Dār Iḥyāʾ al-Kutub al-ʿArabiyya, n.d.

al-Munāwī, Muḥammad ʿAbd al-Raʾūf b. ʿAlī. *al-Taysīr bi-sharḥ al-jāmiʿ al-ṣaghīr*. Būlāq: N.p., 1286.

al-Mundharī, ʿAbd al-ʿAẓīm b. ʿAbd al-Qawī. *al-Targhīb wa-l-tarhīb*. Edited by Muḥyī l-Dīn Mistū, Samīr al-ʿAṭṭār, and Yūsuf Badawī. Damascus: Dār Ibn Kathīr, 1999.

Muslim b. al-Ḥajjāj al-Qushayrī al-Nīsābūrī. *Ṣaḥīḥ Muslim*. Edited by Muḥammad Fuʾād ʿAbd al-Bāqī. Cairo: Dār Iḥyāʾ al-Kutub al-ʿArabiyya, 1954.

al-Nawawī, Yaḥyā b. Sharaf. *al-Majmūʿ sharḥ al-madhhab*. Edited by Maḥmūd Maṭrajī. Beirut: Dār al-Fikr, 1996.

———. *al-Minhāj fī sharḥ ṣaḥīḥ Muslim*. Damascus: Maktabat al-Ghazālī, 1349 AH.

al-Nisāʾī, Abū ʿAbd al-Raḥmān Aḥmad b. Shuʿayb. *al-Mujtabā = Sunan al-ṣughrā*. Edited by Markaz al-Buḥūth wa-Taqnīya. Cairo: Dār al-Taʾṣīl, 2012.

———. *Sunan al-Nasāʾī*. Cairo: al-Maṭbaʿat al-Maymaniyya, 1312 AH.

al-Qāḍī ʿIyāḍ b. Mūsā l-Yaḥṣabī. *Tartīb al-madārik*. Edited by Muḥammad Sālim Hāshim. Beirut: Dār al-Kutub al-ʿIlmiyya, 1998.

Quḍāʿī, Muḥammad b. Salāma. *Musnad al-shihāb*. Edited by Ḥamdī ʿAbd al-Majīd al-Salafī. Beirut: Muʾassasat al-Risāla, 1985.

al-Rāfiʿī, ʿAbd al-Karīm b. Muḥammad. *al-Tadwīn fī akhbār Qazwīn*. Edited by ʿAzīzallāh al-ʿAṭāriddī. Riyadh: Dār al-Bāz, 1987.

al-Rāghib al-Iṣfahānī, al-Ḥusayn b. Muḥammad. *al-Dharīʿa ilā makārim al-sharīʿa*. Edited by Abū Yazīd Abū Zayd al-ʿAjamī. Cairo: Dār al-Salam, 2007.

al-Ramhurmuzī, al-Ḥasan b. ʿAbd al-Raḥmān. *al-Muḥaddith al-fāṣil bayna al-rāwī wa-l-wāʿī*. Edited by Muḥammad ʿAjjāj al-Khaṭīb. Beirut: Dār al-Fikr, 1984.

al-Sakhawī, Muḥammad b. ʿAbd al-Raḥmān. *al-Maqāṣid al-ḥasana fī bayān kathīr min aḥādīth al-mushtahira ʿalā l-ālsina*. Edited by ʿAbdallāh al-Ghumārī and ʿAbd al-Wahhāb ʿAbd al-Laṭīf. Cairo: Maktabat al-Khānijī, 1991.

al-Ṣanʿānī, ʿAbd al-Razzāq b. Hammām. *al-Amālī fī āthār al-ṣaḥāba*. Edited by Majdī al-Sayyid Ibrāhīm. Cairo: Maktabat al-Qurʾān, n.d.

al-Shāfiʿī, Muḥammad b. Idrīs. *Dīwān*. Edited by Yūsuf ʿAlī Badawī. Damascus: Maktabat Dār al-Fajr, 2000.

al-Shaʿrānī, ʿAbd al-Wahhāb b. Aḥmad. *Ṭabaqāt al-kubrā*. Edited by Aḥmad Saʿd ʿAlī. Cairo: Muṣṭafā l-Bābī l-Ḥalabī, 1954.

al-Subkī, ʿAbd al-Wahhāb b. ʿAlī. *Ṭabaqāt al-shāfiʿīya al-kubrā*. Edited by Maḥmūd Muḥammad al-Ṭanāḥī and ʿAbd al-Fattāḥ al-Ḥilū. Cairo: Dār Iḥyāʾ al-Kutub al-ʿArabiyya, 1396.

al-Sulamī, Abū ʿAbd al-Raḥmān. *al-Arbaʿīn fī l-taṣawwuf*. Hyderabad: Majlis Dāʾirat al-Maʿārif al-ʿUthmānīya, 1981.

al-Suyūṭī, ʿAbd al-Raḥmān b. Abī Bakr. *al-Ālaʾlī l-maṣnūʿa fī al-aḥādith al-mawḍūʿa*. Beirut: Dār al-Maʿrīfa, 1983.

———. *al-Durr al-manthur fī l-tafsīrī bi-maʾthur*. Beirut: Dār al-Fikr, 2002.

al-Ṭabarānī, Sulaymān b. Aḥmad. *al-Muʿjam al-awsaṭ*. Edited by Maḥmūd al-Ṭaḥḥān. Riyadh [?]: Maktabat al-Maʿārif, 1985.

———. *al-Muʿjam al-kabīr*. Edited by Ḥamdī ʿAbd al-Majīd al-Salafī. Beirut: Dār Iḥyāʾ al-Turāth al-ʿArabī, n.d.

———. *al-Muʿjam al-ṣaghīr*. Beirut: Dār al-Kutub al-ʿIlmiyya, 1983 [repr.].

———. *Musnad al-Shāmiyīn*. Edited by Ḥamdī ʿAbd al-Majīd al-Salafī. Beirut: Muʾassasat al-Risāla, 1989.

al-Ṭarṭūshī, Muḥammad b. al-Walīd Abū Bakr. *Sarāj al-mulūk*. Edited by Muḥammad Fatḥī Abū Bakr. Cairo: al-Dār al-Miṣriyya al-Lubnāniyya, 2006.

al-Tirmidhī, Muḥammad b. ʿĪsā. *Sunan al-Tirmidhī* (*al-Jāmiʿ al-ṣaḥīḥ*). Edited by Aḥmad Shākir, Muḥammad Fuʾād ʿAbd al-Bāqī, and Ibrāhīm ʿAṭwa. Beirut: Dār Iḥyāʾ al-Turāth al-ʿArabī, n.d. [reprint of Cairo, 1938 edition].

al-ʿUkbarī, ʿAbdallāh b. al-Ḥusayn. *al-Tibyān fī sharḥ al-dīwān = Sharḥ Dīwān al-Mutanabbī*. Edited by Muṣṭafā al-Saqā, Ibrāhīm al-Ībārī, and

ʿAbd al-Ḥafīẓ Shalabī. Cairo: Maktabat wa-Maṭbaʿāt Muṣṭafā l-Bābī l-Ḥalabī, 1971.

al-ʿUqaylī, Muḥammad b. ʿAmr. *al-Ḍuʿafāʾ*. Edited by Ḥamdī ʿAbd al-Majīd al-Salafī. Riyadh: Dār al-Ṣamīʿī, 2000.

al-Yūsī, al-Ḥassan. *Zahr al-akam fī l-amthāl wa-l-ḥikam*. Edited by Muḥammad al-Ḥijjī and Muḥammad al-Akhḍar. Casablanca: Dār al-Thaqāfa, 1981.

al-Zabīdī, Muḥammad Murtaḍā, *Itḥāf al-sadā al-muttaqīn bi-sharḥ Iḥyāʾ ʿulūm al-dīn*. [Cairo]: al-Maṭbaʿ al-Maymūniyya, 1311/1894.

al-Zamakhsharī, Maḥmūd b. ʿUmar. *Rabīʿ al-abrār*. Edited by Salīm al-Nuʿaymī. Tehran: Dār al-Dhakhāʾir, 1990.

Wakīʿ b. al-Jarrāḥ al-Rūʾāsī. *al-Zuhd*. Edited by ʿAbd al-Raḥmān ʿAbd al-Jabbār al-Fariwāʾī. Riyadh: Dār al-Ṣumaʿī, 1994.

Wakīʿ, Muḥammad b. Khalaf. *Akhbār al-quḍāt wa-tawārikhahum = Ṭabaqāt al-quḍāt*. Edited by ʿAbd al-ʿAzīz Muṣṭafā l-Marāghī. Beirut: ʿĀlam al-Kutub, n.d.

Qurʾānic Verses Cited

2:44, 169, 183
2:89, 174
2:118, 215
2:121, 150
2:129, 17
2:146, 17, 174
2:196, 183
2:221, 259
2:257, 249
2:269, 104
2:273, 224
2:282, 183
2:283, 17
3:7, 114
3:18, 3
3:159, 229
3:163, 152
3:187, 17, 179
3:199, 179, 229
4:5, 167
4:83, 4
4:114, 208
4:145, 174
5:7, 259
5:108, 183
6:59, 211
6:70, 242
6:75, 260
6:79, 93
6:91, 93
6:122, 249
6:125, 229
7:7, 4
7:26, 4
7:32, 198
7:52, 4
7:172, 258
7:175–176, 174
7:179, 87
8:22, 11
9:28, 138
9:122, 14, 17, 87
11:6, 192, 221
11:29, 161
11:88, 183
11:108, 24
12:21, 68
13:43, 4
14:5, 224
16:43, 14, 145
16:96, 191
16:125, 17
17:14, 50
17:72, 260
17:74, 178
17:85, 157, 215
18:28, 244
18:59, 220
18:67–68, 145
18:70, 145
18:105, 182
20:24, 102
21:7, 14, 145
21:18, 189
21:84, 68
22:46, 260
23:12, 41
24:35, 248, 263
26:215, 229
26:224–225, 97
27:40, 4
28:31, 102
28:76, 177
28:79–80, 183
28:80, 4, 229
29:43, 4, 265
29:49, 4
29:64, 50
29:68, 133
29:69, 58
30:30, 258
32:24, 215
33:4, 143
33:21, 196
33:72, 28
35:6, 192
35:8, 242

Index

jinn, 114, 132
Job, 68
journey, xlvii, 3, 34, 42, 47, 153, 154, 155, 156, 157, 161, 184, 210, 230, 251, 252
judges/judgeship, xlvii, 46, 61, 76, 89, 180, 187, 198
judgment, day of, 36, 114, 135, 162
judiciary, 54, 116, 117
Junayd, 55, 98
jurisprudence, xlix, lii, 1, 5, 30, 31, 34, 35, 40, 41, 42, 44, 45, 47, 48, 54, 59, 62, 63, 67, 69, 76, 78, 86, 89, 90, 110, 111, 113, 114, 118, 121, 146, 147, 154, 156, 158, 163, 165, 234
  branches of, 63
  practice of, 43
  principles of, 41, 110, 131
  schools of, 90, 109, 113, 114, 132, 135
  sciences of, 162
jurists, 5, 7, 31, 40, 41, 42, 44, 45, 46, 47, 53, 54, 58, 59, 60, 61, 62, 63, 64, 86, 89, 113, 116, 117, 120, 121, 125, 129, 142, 150, 180, 193, 207, 218, 219
justice, 148, 158
  people of, 91
Kaʿab [al-Aḥbār], 188
Kaʿba, 93, 154
al-Khawwāṣ, Abū ʿAbdallāh, 193
al-Khiḍr, 145
kings/princes, 10, 25, 27, 53, 117, 118, 153, 176, 200, 201, 222, 242
kinship, 132
knowledge, 22, 142, 231, 245
  and wealth, 9, 212
  and works, 61, 151
  characteristics of, 12
  disparity in, 261
  dissemination of, 161, 162
  esoteric, 31, 48, 101
  exoteric, 47
  fields of, 165
  ʿilm al-ẓāhir, 47
  importance of, 11
  inward, viii, 55
  kalām, 31, 56, 57, 91, 111, 112, 124
  levels of, 25
  light of, 126, 139, 177, 212
  nature of, 247
  of hypocrites, 231
  of [practical] conduct, li, 48, 52, 189
  of Qurʾān, 41
  of [spiritual] unveiling, li, 48
  of the hereafter, xlvii, 1, 30, 50, 53, 59, 63, 67, 68, 69, 71, 74, 89, 95, 236
  of this world, 146
  outward, li, 27, 55, 188, 211
  perils of, 69, 135
  preservation of, 188
  seeking of, 15, 16, 22, 30, 37, 153, 159, 189, 227
  virtues of, 1, 3, 23, 24, 25
  ʿilm, 14, 37
language, xlvii, 28, 38, 40, 41, 64, 110, 152, 165, 186, 188
lawful, 23, 34, 44, 46, 224, 228, 240
  ḥalāl, 16, 44
laws, 80, 90, 102, 116, 162, 175, 221, 255
  principles of, 142
  sharīʿa, 177
  terms of, 101
leadership, 251
legal opinions, 43, 88, 89, 90, 113, 117, 122, 206
legerdemain, 39
logic, 57
love, 7, 11, 12, 13, 52, 65, 73, 97, 98, 106, 128, 176, 203, 244
  for God, 98, 211
  from God, 211
  objects of, 191
  of authority, 136
  of esteem/prestige, 163, 164
  of the world, 187
  of wealth, 134
Luqmān, 13, 215

About the translator

DR. KENNETH HONERKAMP is a professor in the Department of Religion at the University of Georgia at Athens, where he teaches world religion, Islamic studies, and Arabic. He is a graduate of the Qarawiyyine University of Morocco (1981), the University of Georgia at Athens (1995), and the University of Aix-en-Provence, France where he earned his PhD (2000) for his critical edition and analysis of the *Major Collection of the Letters of Spiritual Guidance* (*Rasāʾil al-kubra*) of Ibn ʿAbbād of Ronda (d. 792/1390). Prior to this he spent ten years studying Islamic law in various traditional institutions in Pakistan. While there, he was exposed to the pedagogic methodologies employed in the *madrasa*s of the then Northwest Frontier Province. He spent twenty years in Morocco where he gained extensive knowledge of Moroccan Sufi orders and spent time in the manuscript libraries of Rabat, Fes, and Marrakesh. His interests lie in the areas of teacher/disciple relationships, Islamic education, and Sufism. He has published numerous articles on Sufism and the lives and teaching methods of well-known Moroccan Sufi masters such as Ibn ʿAbbād (d. 792/1390), Ḥasan al-Yūsī (ca. 1631–91), and Mulay Abū Yazāʿ Yallanūr (d. 572/1177). He has published over ten previously unedited treatises by Abū ʿAbd al-Raḥmān al-Sulamī of Khurasan (d. 412/1021) in the *Collected Works of Sulami* project published by the University of Tehran. In his edition of *Three Early Sufi Texts*, published by Fons Vitae, he has translated two of Sulamī's texts; *Darajāt al-ṣādiqīn* and *Kitāb bayān tadhallul al-fuqarāʾ* into English. His critical edition and study of the *Rasāʾil al-kubrā* of Ibn ʿAbbād of Ronda was published by Dar al-Mashriq (Lebanon, 2005). More recently, he has edited a collection of the teachings of Imām al-Shādhilī from the Tunisian period of the Shādhilī order and the versified *Ḥikm* of Ibn ʿAṭā Allāh by Ibn ʿAbbād entitled *Budhiyat al-murīd*; he continues work on the critical editions of the collected sermons of Ibn ʿAbbād of Ronda.

This publication was made possible through the generosity of international donors and through the support of a grant from the John Templeton Foundation. The opinions expressed in this publication are those of its authors and do not necessarily reflect the views of the John Templeton Foundation.